KENNEL DESIGN
The Essential Guide
to Creating Your Perfect Kennels
DAVID KEY

Kennel Design - The Essential Guide to Creating Your Perfect Kennels
by David Key

ISBN: 0-9538002-2-9 | 978-0-9538002-2-3

Published March 2008 by David Key

Publisher: David Key

Kay & David Key
Kennel & Cattery Design
PO Box 146, Chipping Norton
Oxfordshire OX7 6WA, UK
+44 (0)1608 646454
www.kenneldesign.com
www.catterydesign.com

Printed and bound by:

Cambridge University Press
University Printing House
Shaftesbury Road
Cambridge CB2 2BS
United Kingdom

Photographs:

Book kennels photographs Kay & David Key
Jacket and book stock images by Istockphoto
Contributing photographers where shown

KENNEL DESIGN

The Essential Guide
to Creating your Perfect Kennels
DAVID KEY

DEDICATION

This book is dedicated to:
the experts involved in increasing
our understanding of dog welfare
and
to the pioneering people already providing
caring and high quality accommodation for dogs
and
especially to those thinking about setting up kennels.
We hope this book inspires you!

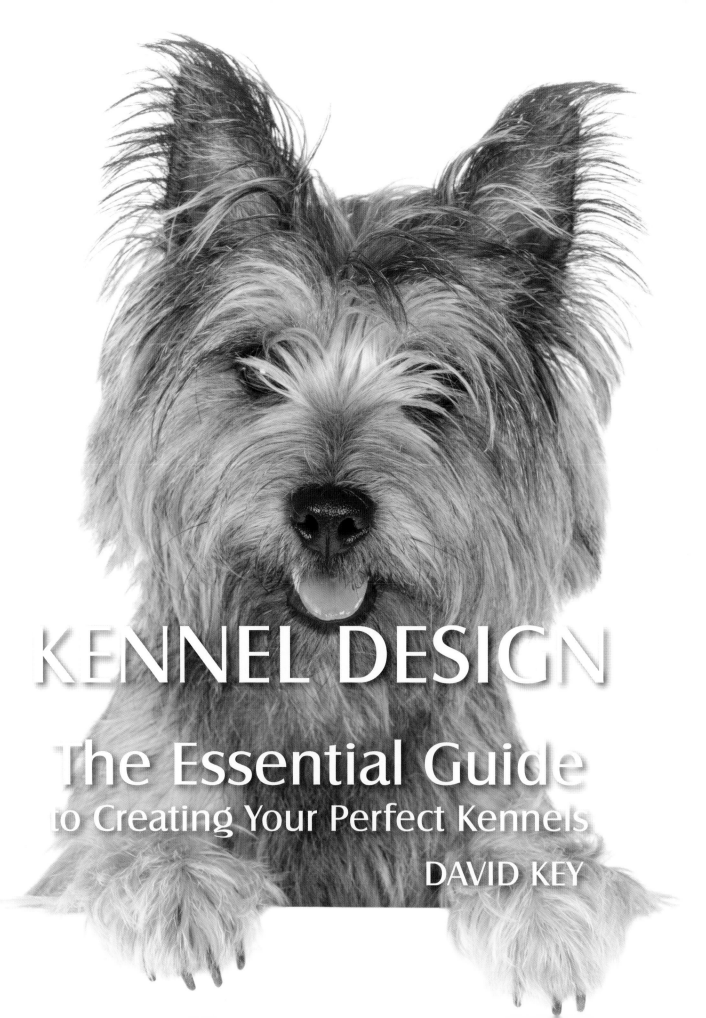

KENNEL DESIGN

The Essential Guide
to Creating Your Perfect Kennels

DAVID KEY

CONTENTS

CONTENTS

CONTENTS

CONTENTS

Foreword by Clarissa Baldwin OBE

Chief Executive of Dogs Trust

At Dogs Trust we are changing the way kennels look and feel forever.

This is why I am so delighted to introduce you to a book that will inspire and encourage you, and show you the many benefits that good kennel design has for you and the dogs in your care.

We have proved beyond doubt that a modern, inviting kennel facility has many more advantages than you may at first imagine.

There are enormous benefits to the dogs of course, but also to the visitors. Our facilities make them feel welcome, inspiring them to return for future visits and to tell their friends about us!

Our new purpose-built state-of-the-art rehoming centres are light, bright and designed to be as dogfriendly as possible.

For example at our West London Rehoming Centre at Harefield (which you can read about on page 274), we have some of the best rehoming facilities to be seen anywhere in the world.

A Dog is for Life, Not Just for Christmas

It was 30 years ago that our Trustees asked me, as Head of Public Relations, to devise a slogan that would prevent the impulse buying of dogs as presents. Out of the dozen or so suggestions offered, they seemed to like one in particular, and "A dog is for life, not just for Christmas" was born.

Over the years, it has been hi-jacked by a number of different people. I've seen "God is for life, not just for Christmas", "Brussels sprouts are for life...", "A no claims bonus is for life..." and even one involving a product sold by a chain of adult shops that I won't explain here. It has been spotted in various different languages and I must say that both "Un cane e per la vita, non solo per Natale" and "Un perro es para la vida, no justa para Navidad" do have a certain ring to them.

It's such a simple message but perhaps that's the secret of its success.

I'm looking forward to the day when it's no longer necessary to use the slogan. But I fear that the day when everybody understands the full responsibilities of dog ownership is still some way off.

So Dogs Trust will keep pushing the slogan to get the message across that our four-legged friends are not disposable objects. Rather they are the most wonderful companions, bringing great joy to our lives and giving us unconditional loyalty. In return, all we have to do is to take our responsibilities seriously and treat them with the love and attention that they deserve – through good times and bad. That seems like a fair deal to me.

If you want to help spread the word, go to www.dogstrust.org.uk/information/ourpublications and order your free "A dog is for life, not just for Christmas" car sticker.

Dogs Trust is dedicated to rescuing abandoned dogs, finding them new, loving homes as quickly as possible. At any one time Dogs Trust looks after more than 1,400 dogs of all shapes, sizes, ages and temperaments. We run 17 rehoming centres in the UK that care for over 15,000 dogs every year. In every one of them you'll find dogs that are looking for a 'forever' home.

We continue to modernise our older sites, so all of our Rehoming Centres offer the best facilities for the dogs. Each development builds on experience gained in previous projects, creating an even happier environment for dogs.

Continued...

FOREWORD

Change the Way Kennels Look & Feel

Some years ago, we commissioned market research to find out the public's view of animal rescue facilities. The results were not encouraging. Interviewees were afraid to visit rehoming centres, describing them as dark, dingy places – the phrase 'death camps' was used on more than one occasion. That research has always been in our minds when designing our centres and we've tried our utmost to ensure that visiting a Dogs Trust property is a happy experience.

The same negative feelings are generated by many kennels - no wonder people are reacting so positively to new facilities!

If the public do not visit us, we simply won't be able to find homes for our dogs and if our dogs aren't happy, then the visiting public will not adopt them. So, each new centre design aims to do everything possible to keep our canine guests happy and healthy.

And finally, as well as happy customers and happy dogs, we want happy staff! Some of our longer-serving staff will remember having to take tea breaks in dilapidated garden sheds and queuing to use a portaloo for their 'comfort' breaks. I'm pleased to report that their dedication is now rewarded with more acceptable amentities.

I'm desperately proud of the Dogs Trust facilities you'll see in this book. But I know that we've yet to build the completely perfect centre – no-one has. But each time we build, we get a bit closer to the ideal.

Whatever type of dog facility you're looking to build, I am certain this book will help you create a first class kennels facility for your customers, both two and four legged.

For further information please:

■ Phone our Helpline on
  0207 837 0006
  (8:30am - 5:30pm, Mon to Fri)

■ Visit our website at
  www.dogstrust.org.uk

■ Write to us at Dogs Trust
  17 Wakley Street
  London EC1V 7RQ
  Reg Charity 227523

Clarissa Baldwin OBE is the Chief Executive of Dogs Trust (formerly the National Canine Defence League), a post she has held for 18 years. prior to this post she was head of Public Relations at the NCDL, joining the charity in 1974. Before joining the charity, Clarissa worked in a public relations consultancy.

ACKNOWLEDGEMENTS

Clarissa Baldwin OBE and Matthew Taylor of Dogs Trust

I would like to express my heartfelt gratitude to **Clarissa Baldwin OBE**, Chief Executive of Dogs Trust for her positive support, encouragement and enthusiastic involvement with this book which includes writing the Foreword, and her willingness to help us demonstrate how kennels can be calmer, more enjoyable and inviting places for both dogs and people, with case studies and photographs. My personal thanks to **Matthew Taylor**, Head of Property at Dogs Trust for his support and generosity of time. Having known Matt for over 10 years, his thoughtful, gentle character is matched only by a professional dedication that myself and many others in the animal welfare world greatly appreciate.

Gwen Bailey

My special thanks to dog behaviour expert **Gwen Bailey** for her invaluable contribution on improving dog welfare in kennels. Having known and worked with Gwen for nearly 20 years, I know how dedicated she is to helping advance our understanding of dog welfare, especially in increasing the successful rehoming of rescue dogs, and their welfare in the kennels environment.

Gwen Bailey
Gwen Bailey has a BSc(Hons) degree in Zoology
Trustee for Battersea Dogs and Cats Home
Founder of Puppy School, a network of UK puppy trainers
www.puppyschool.co.uk
www.dogbehaviour.com

Gwen has successfully solved behaviour problems in thousands of rehomed dogs, helping to prevent dogs with behavioural problems being passed from home to home, and improving rehoming success rates.

Gwen worked for a leading UK national animal welfare charity from 1988-2002 and pioneered the use of dog behaviour knowledge in the rehoming of unwanted animals and improvement of welfare in kennels. The first person to be appointed by a national animal welfare charity as an Animal Behaviourist, she eventually headed a team of behaviourists.

Gwen lectures at national and international conferences, runs training courses for staff at animal charities around the world and has written many books and education leaflets. Gwen is now working on preventing behaviour problems among puppies and to encourage friendly, well-behaved dogs for the future.

Contributing Organisations

- **RESCUE:** Battersea Dogs and Cats Home, Blue Cross Bromsgrove, Dogs Trust Bridgend, Dogs Trust Highway Farm, Dublin SPCA, Mayhew Animal Home, San Francisco SPCA. **POLICE:** Nottinghamshire Police

- **BOARDING:** The Canine Country Club, Gentian Hill Boarding Kennels, Lucies Farm Luxury Dog Resort, Park Kennels, West Lodge Boarding Kennels

- **SPONSORS:** Dogs Trust, Agora Management Limited, Pedigree Pens Limited, Kennel Sales, PetAdmin

Proofreading

My ever grateful thanks to **Diana Stimson** and **Martin Brice** for their invaluable contribution to proofreading.

Design, Layout, Editing

Although this book has my name on it, this is very much a joint effort with Kay for publishing this book to a format that is professional, easy to read, and turned what can be a technical, dry subject matter into an engaging and appealing book. This dedication can only come through a love of animals and a desire to help the many fantastic people we deal with around the world who want to create exceptional kennels.

DAVID KEY

David Key is a **Consultant in Kennel and Cattery Design** and has advised hundreds of potential and existing kennel and kennel owners worldwide – from ideas, improvements and planning through to designs, building and technical details.

For over 20 years David has also been responsible for **The Blue Cross Animal Welfare Charity** animal and staff buildings and property at their dog and cat adoption, companion animal and equine rescue and rehoming centres. During this time David founded an **Animal Welfare Charity Design Forum**, with the aim of sharing information between leading national animal welfare charities in the UK to prevent costly design, materials or building mistakes.

David has been professionally involved with animals for over 30 years. His experience spans companion animals, wildlife and wild animals and he has provided guidance and advice to animal welfare organisations, rescues, boarding, veterinary clinics and animal hospitals, quarantine, architects, police forces, customs and excise, breeding and multi-pet owners. David's interest started by helping out with a friend's show kennels while still at school, and occasionally working with the local RSPCA Inspector. This progressed to working at local boarding kennels and cattery for over 10 years and later at a zoological gardens. This unusual combination of animal work and practical skills developed into an interest in buildings, particularly relating to animal accommodation.

In 2000, David and Kay created the ***Kennel and Cattery Design*** business to help promote the kennel and cattery design books, help people find resources and suppliers , and provide an international service for people looking for information on how to build and start up kennels or a cattery. Kay runs the business on a day-to-day basis and David provides consultancy and technical building advice, as well as continuing to look at design issues, construction methods and materials that help to improve animal welfare accommodation. David and Kay live in Oxfordshire, UK with their much-loved rescue dogs and cats.

When not writing books, looking after Blue Cross property and advising on kennel and cattery design, David manages to squeeze in some time for cross-country skiing and mountaineering in Norway, Greenland and Canada.

Kennel Design

David's original book *Essential Kennel Design* was first published in 2000 in answer to requests from charities, sanctuaries, authorities and potential/existing kennel owners for more information on materials, designs, building-related issues, cost planning and general information on detail that was lacking in many of the books available on kennel building-related issues. In addition, the Kennel Design website was developed to make the information widely available:

www.kenneldesign.com & www.boardingkennels.org

Cattery Design

David's Cattery Design book was published in 2007, with the aim of providing much needed inspiration and guidance to give owners accurate information, and allow them to construct to the best possible standards within budget. The standards of many existing catteries are even more shocking than kennels, and the lack of previously available guidance on building and construction may partly explain this.

www.catterydesign.com & www.boardingcatteries.org

AIM OF THIS BOOK AND ACCOMPANYING WEBSITE

We believe it is essential to give *as much information as possible* to potential and existing kennel owners. Our mission is to raise the expectations, standard and design of kennels by providing owners with advice on options and choices.

With this book and the accompanying website www.kenneldesign.com we give you the inspiration, information and support you need to build the best standard of kennels you can, to match your requirements as well as the dogs' needs and create a building that is easy to maintain. To do this, you will need to understand how well designed kennels help reduce stress and provide a healthy and happy environment in which dogs can be accommodated.

We often find that people want to provide more than one type of kennels, especially if they already have a customer base. Breeders, groomers, veterinarians and quarantine kennels consider offering a boarding facility to increase income, just as people who want to create boarding kennels may want to help dogs further by providing rescue accommodation, and some rescue centres think about offering boarding as a way of raising funds to help more dogs. There will be additional considerations for multiple kennels, especially when dealing with dogs of unknown health history.

Whatever the function for which your kennels will be used, it is important that you spend your build money wisely, and we want to help ensure that you have the information to do so.

We encourage you to think deeply about the style and quality
of business you want to create,
because quality and caring kennels are greatly in demand

It is not enough just to describe how to construct kennels, because to make the right choices you need to understand exactly what makes good design, and how this is healthier for dogs. Happy dogs will make your kennels successful, and we want you and your clients to be proud of, and delighted with your kennels.

What is in This Book

Who Was This Book Written For?

This book will give insight to everyone involved with dogs, (welfare organisations, boarding, breeding, charities, rescue centres, quarantine, multi-dog and working dog owners, designers, authorities, architects and surveyors, veterinary surgeons, colleges and universities) to provide an awareness of the changes in design, and options available. This book will provide you with an encouraging, easy-to-read guide with hundreds of photographs, an overview of systems and designs, and show you how dog accommodation can be improved with dog welfare knowledge and robust finishing details.

International Flavour

The international flavour of this book is useful to potential and existing kennel owners. It provides ideas from different countries, highlights different philosophies and guidelines, and will reach a far greater number of people wanting help and advice to create or upgrade kennels – yet it also shows that dogs have the same needs, no matter where they live.

It is interesting to see the similarities between the United Kingdom, America and Canada in terms of statistics and trends. Today, with dogs being the second most popular pet, dog owners spending more on their pets and having higher demands/expectations – there is now, more than ever, a need to provide enough accommodation to meet this demand.

The most important concept when creating kennels:

Awareness of dog welfare is an integral part of helping us create kennel buildings and management skills that are as dog-friendly as possible. The combination of understanding what dogs need, and knowing what the construction choices are, means you can create the perfect kennels for your situation and budget.

What this book contains:

- ### Large, full-colour photographs
  To provide you with inspiration and ideas, this book is lavishly packed with colour photographs, many of which are full page or double-page spreads so that you can see lots of detail – just like looking through a window.

- ### The surprising extent to which kennel styles affect dog welfare
  Understanding just how much accommodation standards affect dogs. How to improve the quality of life for a confined dog, and what is appropriate therapy for dogs housed in less than ideal conditions

- ### Case studies
  British, American and Irish organisations show how unique each organisation is (which is often what makes it successful), and to illustrate important points by showing how they are put into practice in real life. As you will see, there is always something that could have been improved on, and always plenty to be pleased with.

- ### Design, material and equipment options
  Descriptions, advantages and disadvantages of different layout/design styles and kennel types, materials and equipment all combine to help you make an informed choice for your own situation

- ### Best practice and avoiding mistakes
  Advice on best practice for planning/zoning and building kennels. Common mistakes and how to avoid them. What you must do, and what not to do. What dogs require, and legislation governing kennels

Other Ways We Can Help You

Our contact details are:

Kay & David Key
Kennel & Kennels Design, PO Box 146, Chipping Norton, Oxfordshire OX7 6WA, UK
Phone: +44 (0)1608 646454
Email: kaykey@kenneldesign.com
Websites: www.kenneldesign.com
              www.boardingkennels.org
              www.catterydesign.com

www.kenneldesign.com

How our kennel design website can help you:

- Kennels business plan

- Kennels property audit

- Directory of suppliers, products, manufacturers, services - making it easy to find suggested items in this book

- Kennel designs (plans/blueprints)

- Books

- Help and advice

- Latest information

- Support, encouragement and inspiration

If you enjoy the case studies in this book, you might like to contact us about your story. We can publish this on our websites and provide links to your website to help generate new visitors for you.

Just go to www.kenneldesign.com

www.boardingkennels.org

If you already have, or are considering starting boarding kennels, we have a website with special search facilities to help generate new business for you, new kennels get up to 90% of bookings through it.

Just go to www.boardingkennels.org

CARE AND MANAGEMENT

The most important factor for a successful kennels facility is its care and management

---

It would probably be worth putting that statement on every page. However, it is obvious that a well-designed building can only improve matters. Whether for dog wellbeing, staff morale, easier cleaning and maintenance, or all of these improvements, this book will help you understand the building options available, to get the best result for you.

Everyone has an opinion about what makes good kennels.
If you could include every dog welfare suggestion in this book within your kennels, it would be wonderful! With building and property prices, site constraints and a finite budget, you must find the right balance to build to the best standard you can.

Always remember that it is an option for you to <u>build half</u> of your ultimate design at the standard you want.
It will cost less initially, be faster to build, and will generate income earlier so you will have funds to build the second half at a later date.

As you will see, you can create kennels that match as many of your ideals as possible on a small scale, stand head and shoulders above the 'standard/commonly used' type of kennels and have your clients do your marketing for you.

The Commercial Kennels
A boarding facility of just six kennels can provide a good income if a high quality and caring service is provided, together with good accommodation and services. Higher fees (for boarding this is possibly at least double those of standard kennels) will reflect the level of personal care, cost of building, socialisation and understanding that is offered in a way that a large facility would be unable to match. Once your income is established, you will then be able to increase the number of dogs you can accommodate, or you may prefer not to lose the personal touch, and increase profit in other ways.

The Rescue Kennels/Shelter
A rescue centre has many options to improve dog welfare and increase the adoption success rate. There are many ways buildings can assist you, such as creating separate areas for socialisation, getting to know potential owners and understanding how to make the accommodation more dog-friendly - which makes for a more pleasing environment for both potential adopters and staff. Consideration given to making the facility a welcoming and enjoyable place to be will increase the amount of time visitors spend there, and therefore increase the likelihood of more adoptions, return visits, volunteering, etc. For organisations coping with a very tight budget, there are ways you can improve the kennels without significant cost, by using environmental enrichment and dog therapy.

How to Create Your Perfect Kennels - Design Development Chart
On the next page you will find a chart that lists the sort of things you will need to think about to create a complete design for your kennels or dog hotel. Whether you fill the chart in as you go along or read through the book first before completing it, this chart will form the basis of your kennel design, and ensure you think about the essential requirements of your building/s to get the ideal result for your situation. To get to your ideal kennel building, the design process is complex, and involves many more elements than you may be expecting.

CREATE YOUR PERFECT KENNELS

ITEM:	MY DECISION:
Kennels function/s:	
New build/conversion/upgrade:	
Kennels only:	
Site located/purchased	
Feasibility of planning/zoning permission: • Spoken to Planning Officer • Spoken to Animal Welfare Officer • Spoken to Traffic and Highways Officer	
Local legislation/guidelines to comply with: • Licence/permit and animal welfare • Environment • Building	
Kennels aspect:	
Kennels style: • U, L, single, double, square/rectangular • Indoor, Semi-Outdoor	
Location of ancillary buildings/items: • Reception, Isolation, Admissions • Car Parking • Laundry, Toilet/s • Storage, Refuse	
Total number of kennels:	
Kennels image:	
Size of kennels:	
Height of kennels:	
Type of kennels: • Full-height, walk-in • Holding kennels/admissions • Whelping • Socialisation/rehoming • External exercise area/socialisation room or playroom	
Corridor/walkway widths:	
Corridor/walkway internal/external:	
Corridor/walkway covered:	

USE THIS CHECKLIST TO HELP YOU CREATE YOUR PERFECT KENNEL DESIGN. (YOUR FINAL DESIGN INVOLVES MAKING DECISIONS ON ALL THESE ELEMENTS)

ITEM:	MY DECISION:
Project manager:	
Building method:	
External construction materials:	
Internal construction materials:	
Thermal insulation:	
Floor finishes:	
Wall finishes:	
Metalwork: (Size of mesh and metalwork treatment)	
Dividing wall/panel/barrier construction:	
Lighting:	
Heating:	
Cooling:	
Ventilation:	
Condensation:	
Fixed furniture: • Benches, play platform	
Moveable furniture: • Bedding, Seating, Viewing platforms	
Environment enrichment methods:	
Utilities: • Heating, electricity, water	
Drainage method:	
Sewage disposal:	
Water disposal:	
Kitchen units and equipment:	
Laundry machinery:	
Cleaning/disinfection policy:	
Cleaning/disinfection methods:	
Website name/s purchased:	
Secure fencing for your own dogs: (especially if this is a new property or near a busy road)	
Landscaping:	

TODAY'S DEMANDS

TODAY'S PET
OWNERS WANT
MUCH MORE FOR
THEIR DOGS

WHY QUALITY KENNEL DESIGN IS ESSENTIAL

There are still far too many sub-standard kennels in existence.

The aim of this book is both to help people build new, quality accommodation for dogs, and to improve or replace the sub-standard. In recent years there has been a significant improvement in the quality of animal accommodation in good boarding or breeding establishments, charities and sanctuaries. Knowing which new products are available, and all the options, will help you define your requirements. This is all aimed at helping you get everything you want right at the start, and preventing you from being disappointed with the finished result when you start to use it in real life.

The increase in standards can also be partly attributed to:

- ### Professionalism
  A new generation of people wishing to create a better standard of kennels, often with qualifications or experience in animal care, or who already have experience of running a business or working with dogs. For example, those using redundancy money to achieve their dream of opening kennels, to work from home with no commuting and to be secure will be very appealing – after all, the job of looking after other people's dogs cannot be outsourced to Asia!

- ### Lifestyle
  More people wanting to change their lifestyle, wishing to improve both their personal lifestyle and provide quality accommodation, wishing to do something worthwhile with their lives, to love what they do and to 'make a difference'. This is often in conjunction with seeing what local kennels have to offer and thinking "*I can do better*"

- ### Financial
  A greater capital investment than ever before is now required, which seems to be acting as a filter, leaving mainly the people who really do want to run kennels for the love of it and, most importantly, to do it well

- ### Awareness and expectation
  A visual awareness of standards and increased customer expectations caused by greater television, press and internet coverage of upscale/upmarket facilities, and increases in the amount of money owners spend on their dogs

- ### Knowledge
  A better understanding and knowledge of the housing requirements for dogs. This book will make that information readily accessible to all

- ### Construction
  The choice of building materials and designs available

- ### Legislation Many older kennels are struggling to have their boarding licence renewed to comply with up-to-date regulations. These kennels will either need to invest in new buildings for the future, sell the business or close down

- ### Client demand
  To run kennels, especially a new business, it is better to keep 10-20 kennels in use constantly, than to have the associated running/construction costs of a larger facility, which will take time and staff to fill, or have empty kennels

- ### Caring kennels reduce stress to increase success
  With smaller, quality businesses you also have the benefit of better kennel management, happier dogs and staff, better income or greater rehoming rates, repeat business, a better public image, strong business development, a trusted, personal and caring service that looks better to customers and feels more personal and inviting to them

Although a well-run establishment with quality, caring, enthusiastic staff can overcome many design faults by providing a high level of care to the dogs and their owners, – buildings constructed to a high standard can **only** be beneficial and improve the efficient running of the property

Well-designed kennels with high quality appeal sets you apart, reinforces your image and standards, and the 'wow' factor will become your signature.

Animal welfare organisations have helped to remove the notion that kennels need to provide only a secure environment with little emphasis on the animals' needs and requirements. The advances in products, materials, equipment and design for animal buildings have been immense in the past decade, and it is often the welfare charities that lead the way (they need to have robust, healthy buildings for animals and people and often build or upgrade new centres in many locations).

Dog welfare/behaviour knowledge clearly describes the needs and requirements of dogs, so we should use this information to our advantage, and create much healthier and more stimulating environments – whether it is boarding for two weeks, a temporary stay while a new home is found, or permanently in a home environment.

Hopefully, by the end of this book you will see how quality design and specification are extremely important to all aspects of your business, and will be able to assess the features to make your kennels building work efficiently.

Making it a Success

Success comes from dog welfare and public perception, a sense of pride and satisfaction, and providing a healthy, pleasing working environment for staff that will also allow more time to focus attention on the dogs.

The **only disadvantage** to building quality kennels is the initial capital cost. However, our clients have shown that this cost can be recouped quickly, as the fees/rehoming rates increase.

In the long term of course, robust, quality, correctly designed and specified kennel buildings can **reduce expenditure** and **become an investment** for the owner's future.

THE DEMAND FOR QUALITY AND CARING KENNELS

Today, there is a high and increasing demand for good quality kennels or dog hotels with a caring service that provides the owner with a variety of choices.

We are delighted to find that the majority of people coming to us for advice now are extremely caring, professional and dedicated people determined to set up the best kennels they can. The amount of passion, research, work, commitment, investment and dedication required will quickly become obvious – and if it is not for you, it will soon become apparent.

Having purchased this book, it is obvious you are already quite committed to the idea of running kennels. So, if you find out that the more you understand and learn, the more determined and passionate it makes you – then you are probably doing it for the right reasons and we will do our utmost to help you achieve your dream of building or upgrading your kennels.

It is *wonderful* to see someone go from thinking about the whole lifestyle and career change as an idea, to planning exactly what they want and getting it built, while avoiding costly mistakes that are usually made with building kennels – and finally opening them.

Running your own business doing something you love CHANGES YOUR LIFE.

This will become apparent when you start reading the case studies in this book (starting with the next few pages) and also illustrates how this not only changes your life, but the lives of your clients and their dogs.

If creating kennels is your dream, then naturally you will want to provide the best accommodation and care, earn a good living, have fun and really enjoy what you do – providing a safe, healthy environment for dogs.

It is a roller coaster journey, but having all the right information to hand will make things SO much easier.

Understanding the Pet Market

Anyone seriously considering opening kennels will need to know what the 'market' is for the type of organisation they want to run. The attitude people have towards pets evolves, and you need to be aware of this as it will affect the success and requirements of your kennels. **This will affect you whatever type of kennels establishment you are thinking of.** The rising number of people living single, busy lives now means we are treating our pets as child substitutes. Young, affluent single people now treat their dogs to all the comforts of home, buying gourmet foods, accessories, and presents.

Around 40% of UK and USA dog-owning households will have 2 or more dogs

---

Today's lifestyle has more people living alone, or couples going out to work, more people working from home and wanting urban living, and so the self-sufficient, free-living, independent cat is coming into its own. Dog ownership is decreasing, yet the amount of care and money owners are willing to spend on goods and services is increasing. Owners are looking for more choices, better options - things with 'wow' factor to treat their dogs.

You will need to keep in touch with new advances, products, news and the multitude of health, veterinary, behavioural and care queries that dog owners may throw at you. Signing up to email newsletters or magazines is an easy way to achieve this.

Internet/Web

With the easy accessibility of the internet, more pet owners are able to seek out the kind of kennels that 'match' what they want or expect for their dog, rather than just choosing the nearest. In better quality boarding establishments for example, dog owners are travelling far further than the traditional catchment area of 20-30 miles. It is also becoming more common to go on holiday and take your pets with you to a boarding establishment nearby - allowing owners time with their dogs, and private time as well.

If you are going to invest in building or upgrading kennels, it is essential you understand the market. There is no longer a need to charge 'what everyone else is charging' when you are providing a far better facility and service, and are able to cast your business net much farther afield by using the internet - and, most importantly, you will need to recoup your investment.

Pets are Good for You

Just thinking about and caring for another living being helps nurture feelings of empathy and understanding, and makes us feel less alone. Pets provide joy, love, comfort, friendship, understanding of life, are 'part of the family'; they even help to keep us healthy and teach us commitment and responsibility.

Several international studies have shown that pets are good for people.
Pets help to lower blood pressure, heart rate, cholesterol and triglyceride, reduce stress and anxiety, offer instant relaxation, help to prevent heart disease, provide greater psychological stability, lower health care costs and help to fight depression, headaches, insomnia, indigestion, help us recover faster from illness and lower the frequency of allergies and even help with Alzheimers and living in a retirement home.
So, as well as loving and caring for your pet, owning one can improve your mental and physical health.

Pets can help educate **children** about life. In this hi-technology age it is even more important to have a foundation for learning about nature, nurture and unconditional love that humans may be unable to provide. Pets can increase the attention span of children with learning difficulties. The benefits of pets to the **elderly** are enormous, including providing a link to the outside world.

CASE STUDY:
THE PERSONAL TOUCH

Organisation: Gentian Hill Boarding Kennels
Location: UK, Devon
Kennels Type: Semi-outdoor
Kennels Function: Boarding
Number of Kennels: 12 originally, extending to 16
Unit Size Sleep: 5ft x 5ft/1.5m x 1.5m and 6ft x 6ft
Unit Size Exercise: 7ft 10" x 5ft–9ft/2.4m x 2m–2.9m
Date Built: 2004

www.gentianhillboardingkennels.co.uk

INSPIRING A NEW GENERATION OF OWNERS, THIS PIONEERING KENNELS SET A HIGHER STANDARD IN DOG BOARDING BY CREATING A CARING, PERSONAL, AND HOMELY BUSINESS ACHIEVING A NEW AND UNPRECEDENTED CLIENT DEMAND

GENTIAN HILL BOARDING KENNELS

Jane Cole lived in a beautiful location with her children and dogs, enjoyed her house, horses, and parrots. Having built an extension to her home, the next dream she wanted to make happen was to turn her hobby into a permanent lifestyle.

Jane will be a familiar figure to many who have visited our websites because she was the first person to build using our kennel blueprints. Having chosen the 12 kennels plans, she started her journey into self-building kennels.

Many of our customers have spoken to her, and she has been an inspiration to a lot of people - particularly regarding the need (and market) for a better quality of kennels building.

In fact, Jane's progress was watched by many on our website from around the world, as she gave us updates and feedback on the impact her kennels were having in the less affluent, but stunning countryside of the South-West of the UK.

> *"If anyone's in any doubt about the need for good kennels, they needn't be!"*

"Business is booming! The phone doesn't stop all day and the follow-up paperwork is time-consuming as we are solidly booked up until September, half full for Oct/Nov and almost December, so I can be a little more choosy about clients I take now! I've got to the point where some policies need to be made about opening and phone-answering times. I wasn't prepared for just how busy we would be. I am looking at taking someone on to help. We are also working hard on the new reception building at the moment. We are walking the dogs three times a day now, but for shorter periods than when they were just walked twice - but they love getting out more."

Jane had done it - she had taken the kennels world by storm. A lot of effort had gone into getting herself known on the web, radio and by word of mouth, especially by local veterinarians and dog owners. Customers often asked her *"Why aren't all kennels like this?"*

Just two months after opening Jane told us: *"We were fully booked for Christmas and having to turn people away!"*. Given that Christmas is a peak season for kennels, where virtually every business probably turns away 2-3 times the customers they normally take, this was perhaps to be expected - but a good sign so early on. Although a very busy time of year to start such a learning curve - it was still a real boost to morale, especially when money is disappearing quickly during the build, and begins to trickle back in as the customer base is built up over time.

Just six months after opening, the news from Jane was even more positive, and she told us *"If anyone's in any doubt about the need for good kennels, they needn't be! I've been so busy it's been unbelievable as I'm snowed under with bookings and continually turning people away. It's been full, full, full since Christmas and it's getting busier and busier.*

"It's going really, really well and I'm getting 90% of my bookings from www.boardingkennels.org. I've already got bookings for Christmas and next year, from customers who want to be guaranteed their dogs will get in.

THE CARE DOG OWNERS HAVE BEEN LONGING FOR

Jane's only problems have been how to deal with people who just don't turn up, especially when she turned so many people away - it is very frustrating and is a lot of money to 'lose' - dealing with all the paperwork, and the only other problem is some dogs chewing her beautiful bedding.

One year after opening Jane was averaging 24 dogs a day (50% of customers had two or more dogs), and could have filled another 16 kennels for single dogs!

THE DEMAND INCREASES

Receiving 15-30 messages on the phone each day, Jane referred clients she couldn't accommodate on to other new boarding kennels designed by Kennel & Cattery Design, to ensure clients were referred to someone she knew, and where the standard of accommodation would be just as high. Jane said: *"My customers all love the kennels and think it's a beautiful place. There are lots of changes from when you were last here, we've put in lots of flowers and beautiful plants and are now busy building a separate reception. I can't wait for you to see it in its full glory.*

"The Environmental Health Officer licensed us for 3 dogs for each giant kennel - and I need more giant kennels! We're already at the point when we're considering whether to build another kennel block, but at the moment I'm happy to stay as we are. I now have my groomer here for 5 days a week and she is getting 6 dogs in a day." Jane had customers with a variety of reasons for boarding their dogs. One customer had a hip replacement, then contracted MRSA so her stay was for 8 weeks. Jane sent digital photos to reassure and comfort her that her 'baby' was well and happy.

Another customer enjoyed a 6-week cruise and Jane emailed her photos too, and was delighted when a large local animal rescue home started recommending her. The Police were considering Gentian Hill for a contract for the police dogs and the handlers were so keen for their dogs to come here they have offered to pay any shortfall from the budget themselves.

EARLY EXPANSION

"I've had people contact me from your website who are interested in building from your Blueprints and in the PetAdmin booking software. I tell them we would have struggled to have been such a huge success that we are today without you. Within such a short time we have already had to expand due to such high demand. We added another 6 giant kennels to give us more flexibility - and customers all want the larger kennels! We are told regularly that our customers refuse to board anywhere else... quite often booking their holidays around my diary. Every customer that has found us online through the website has booked with us so the percentage has increased. They love the website and tell me how informative it is, we have people come to us from hundreds of miles away, and even people returning home from abroad."

Jane says *"We strongly support other kennels following the same build and design as ours who have also sought your help and advice with their own builds. We still get lots of calls from the UK and abroad for help in setting up new businesses."* Jane loves the fact that her pioneering kennels inspire both dog owners and future kennel owners to seek higher standards of boarding and welfare for their dogs. As well as waking up to such a beautiful location, Jane's greatest satisfaction is doing something she loves every single day.

PROPERTY, LAND AND BUILDING COSTS

A combination of the following factors is leading to better accommodation for dogs:

- High property/land prices and increasing building costs (off-putting to those not serious about running kennels). In business terms, these are called 'barriers to entry'

- Increases in dog welfare understanding and legislation/standards

- Increases in the quality and availability of product/materials

- Increases in expectations and awareness from the public (TV, press, internet, etc.)

- Attraction to professional people prepared to invest in a lifestyle/career change

Property and Land Costs

If you already own suitable land on which to build your kennels, you are very lucky.

Property prices have increased dramatically in the past decade and it is now much more expensive to buy land, or property with land. There are rural grants available for up to 50% of the building cost and farmers are being encouraged to diversify into other markets. Farmers should be aware of the many differences between the livestock they have been used to, and dealing with companion animals (pets) and their owners. As we shall see later, there are continual improvements in the understanding of dog welfare and animal accommodation standards.

From our experience with many people wanting to build or upgrade their kennels or dog hotel, the increase in property prices seems to filter out those not prepared to invest in their animal accommodation, leaving those more determined and committed.

Higher land/property and building costs now demand greater investment than ever before, and you will need to earn a higher income to help pay for them. At the same time, dog owners are spending more on their pets and desire more choices and better services. This is one of the many reasons why we so strongly recommend creating a high quality facility - you need to attract the customers who are interested in better care and services for their pets, and who want the choice.

It makes sense that you **only invest in a long-term prospect that you really care about**.

Increasing the Value of your Property

There is no doubt that placing a quality business on a property increases the value of that property. Despite the increased costs of rural properties, many on main roads will be less attractive to most home buyers but of inherent value to the potential kennels or small business owner, as it increases the ease of access to customers and also increases the awareness of 'passing trade' about your business. Free advertising!

Keeping Your Privacy and Keeping Your Own Dogs Safe

You need to ensure you have a private, secluded area away from the business and visitors. This allows you to separate your private life from your business - especially important when both are on the same property. Separate areas also allow your own dogs their freedom, without the stress and disturbance of seeing other dogs on their territory - nor should you allow your dogs to disrupt the kennelled dogs.

Visitor Hours

Establishing visitor hours for your own benefit and the dogs' security and stress levels is essential. Dogs will soon become familiar with your routine, and therefore more likely to accept it and settle down during quiet times. Constant interruptions will be frustrating for you (which dogs and owners will pick up immediately and react to) and a constant stream of strangers will be disrupting for the dogs.

Building Costs

The average inflation rate for construction is approximately 5%–7% per year. This doesn't sound like much until you realise that even in a short period such as three years, the building cost has increased by 15%–21%.

Equivalent to building a house.

It cannot be assumed that building for dogs will be less expensive to build than a house (for traditional masonry construction). The wear and tear kennels undergo means you will be spending _more_ on the specialist finishes, particularly walls and flooring.

For traditionally constructed buildings, you will often find the specification is very similar to that of a domestic house. The foundations, internal and external brick and block work, insulating and roofing materials, etc are the same. This means similar purchase and installation costs. If you think about it, you are actually building more small rooms, all needing heating, lighting and decorating, which will be more time-consuming, laborious and expensive than dealing with fewer large rooms.

These cost implications are mentioned purely to prepare you if you are not familiar with building and property costs

KENNELS ONLY, OR CATTERY TOO?

There are two options: to have kennels only, or kennels and cattery. However, it is obvious that cat-only facilities are a better choice for cats, and animal welfare organisations recommend cat-only facilities for boarding.

Obviously, it is better for cats to be in a cat-only facility (or at the very least a considerable distance away from the dogs) **An owner who has only a cat will always prefer to use a cat-only boarding facility.** They will prefer the peace, tranquillity and calm atmosphere. For many single people, couples, the elderly, and for those particularly keen on ensuring their cats' welfare is of prime importance – a cat-only facility is the only option.

Kennels only

We are now seeing a definite move towards specialist cat-only or dog-only facilities, and businesses of a smaller, manageable nature with more emphasis on a purpose-built building reflecting design ideas from homes and hotels such as space, light, personal service, care and quality. As you will see in the remainder of this chapter, there are several reasons for this change of emphasis and why the fewer-but-larger kennels in a dog-only facility is proving to be so successful.

People naturally gravitate towards either dogs or cats, even if they like both species.

The danger is that cats will always come second when you also have dogs on site, purely because there is more urgency to walk dogs and clean kennels

---

Kennels and Cattery

It is currently very common in the USA to have both a dog and cat facility on the same site, housing a large number of animals, whereas in the UK there is a much greater number of cat-only facilities. For owners who have both a cat and a dog, it is far more convenient for them to have one multi-purpose facility that caters for both, and there will probably always be a place for this type of operation. When owners are going on holiday it is always a rush, and particularly so if they have children. It is fair to say that convenience is part of the equation and it may not make sense to them to have to use two separate boarding establishments. A dual-purpose facility can work equally as well.

If you do take the kennels and cattery option, careful consideration needs to be given to the initial design and layout to provide a private, quiet and secluded area for the cats, which is far enough away from the kennels. Although better for noise levels, this can have a **disadvantage** for the cats, in that the kennels building is often some distance away from the main core centre of activity, and consequently it removes the opportunity for the cats to watch the daily activity associated with staff and visitors coming and going.

INCOME AND DECIDING ON THE NUMBER OF KENNELS

High quality, caring, lower number kennels or dog hotels specialising in larger rooms or suites are *much* easier to keep fully booked all year round.

A low number of high quality and caring kennels also:

- Costs less to build and set up

- Has less/no staff issues

- Easier to sell in the future

- More profitable as fees can be higher

- Allows you to develop the business at your own pace

- More satisfying as you can spend more time with each dog, and think creatively about their care

- More rewarding as you can develop relationships with your clients to provide a more personal service

However, by far the biggest factor in deciding how many kennels to have is your budget. Please remember that this can be broken into phases; you don't have to do it all at once.

Income is an important part of your business plan and you should work out your potential income as well as building and running costs. By carefully looking at the figures now, you can give yourself the best cash flow and profitability from the start.

Boarding management books suggest working out your '**worst case scenario**' on income, which is **averaged** as being a 'third-full' as a guideline (excluding multiple dog families), and working out your '**average income**' to work towards, that being 'half-full'. Historically, it's not usually suggested that you work out your '**maximum**' figure. However, we suggest you work to a higher rate if you are running a quality and caring service with up to 20 kennels – as you are more likely to be full than someone with 100 kennels to fill. In fact, we know from our clients that **85% <u>minimum</u> occupancy is easily achievable for quality boarding establishments providing a personal, caring service**.

Obviously higher fees cannot be charged without knowing the minimum, average and maximum prices in your area, or without providing that 'something extra' and investing in the business. These must be researched (our online Business Plan helps you assess your potential income). It is essential to know what other kennels charge in your area when working out the feasibility – and it is most important to visit these kennels to see **what level of service** they provide for their fees.

In our experience, a quality and caring higher standard kennels can charge <u>double</u> the fee of low to average standard kennels; (average daily fees are £7–£14 in the UK and $10–$30 in the USA). **This means that you can build half the number of quality kennels and your income will be the same as (or more than) building twice the number at a lower standard.**

A new factor to take into consideration is that, thanks to the internet, dog owners are now assessing kennels from much farther afield than the traditional 20-30 mile catchment area. If holidaying in the same country, dog owners now book kennels at their holiday destination so their pet is nearby. Adopters or sponsors may see a rescue dog on a website or webcam hundreds of miles away. Obviously this arrangement is not suitable for all dogs, but you should certainly take this into consideration in your marketing and fees.

Create Flexible Accommodation

What impact would 2 or 3 dogs from the same household have on your income and ability to accommodate them? As around 40% of dog owners have more than one dog, so you will need to provide ample flexibility for your business.

We suggest that at the very least you provide various sizes of kennel to suit different activity levels, requirements and numbers of dogs from the same households. **Ideally, every kennel should be able to accommodate at least 2 dogs**, and some larger options will be useful for 3 or more dogs sharing.

In some circumstances a multi-dog family will not get on as well as the owner suggests or would like, so it may be necessary to provide accommodation for quiet, nervous or bullied dogs separately from their housemates. You should also think about providing accommodation for special needs such as low bedding for elderly dogs, blind or deaf dogs, larger and more stimulating kennels for very active dogs, puppy-friendly kennels, etc.

By looking through the statistics for your business plan in the catchment area, the average number of dogs owned per household, and the number of households with dogs for various countries (even researching down to local town and village level), you will soon get a feel for the number of 'dog families' in your area.

> It is amazing how quickly people find out that a lovely, friendly new kennels has opened, and recommend it to their friends

A better income for high quality and caring commercial kennels

Playing around with figures such as your fees/rates will show you how you can have a smaller, quality, caring facility (which is of course exactly the style of business we are actively encouraging) and charge accordingly. Of course it is worthwhile working out what your 'maximum capacity' is – you will know what your ceiling income will be – although it is unlikely you will have every kennel allocated for every day of the year, at least you will know what your 'limits' are.

There will be seasonal swings (such as Christmas, Easter and summer holidays) when you could fill your kennels several times over – but equally there may be less busy times (February is notorious for being quiet). However, for a more personal, caring kennels, the bookings may well be continual! Playing the 'what if' scenario with your income can be extremely useful, and you will need to plan ahead to counter the 'no-show' clients who just forget to turn up or cancel. Have a good policy in place such as a 50% deposit with booking to reduce this problem as much as possible.

By matching your fees with the quality of the buildings and service you provide, you will find that you can make more money, or more adoptions when working with fewer dogs

The more time you spend with the dogs you are looking after, the happier and less stressed they will be and so will their owners, your future customers.

Thinking Laterally

You can make as much money by selling a designer collar or other dog items to your existing clients as you could boarding their dog for a weekend – and it requires no more kennels, just space for stock.

Happy Dogs

You know when your dogs are happy, playful, not quite themselves, or even miserable, don't you? Your clients will be just the same. If dog owners don't feel that their 'baby' was happy staying with you, or looked after well enough, it is highly unlikely that they will actually tell you – you just won't ever see them or their custom again.

Taking time to talk to owners about their dog, both before and after their stay, is important

---

It may be hard to believe, but a kennel owner who is dedicated to extremely high standards of service and care, low numbers of dogs, in a good location and marketed well, can earn the same income as a typical facility with ten times as many kennels. However, this will _only_ work for those truly committed and dedicated to creating happy dogs and extremely high standards. On the next few pages we have an example of an exceptional and highly successful boarding kennels with just 6 kennels, dedicated to providing an unique service that meets the demand from more discerning dog owners.

CASE STUDY:
PUTTING ON THE RITZ

Organisation: Lucies Farm Dog Resort
Location: UK, Worcestershire
Kennels Type: Semi-outdoor
Kennels Function: Boarding
Number of Kennels: 6
Kennel Sleep Area: 6ft 6" x 8ft/2m x 2.4m
Kennel Run Area: 6ft 6" x 8ft/2m x 2.4m
Year Built: 1996

www.dog-hotel.co.uk

AN EXCLUSIVE DOG RESORT SET IN A GLORIOUS LOCATION PROVIDES A WEALTH OF CHOICES FOR DOGS AND OWNERS. THE REGULARLY UPDATED PHOTO GALLERY SHOWS HOW MUCH TIME IS DEDICATED TO CARING AND WHAT FUN THE DOGS HAVE

LUCIES FARM LUXURY DOG RESORT

With only a few guests allowed at once, this exclusive resort has just 6 kennels. When you drive up to the wide, pretty painted timber gates and press the buzzer, you know you are about to enter a secluded and beautiful resort that caters for owners' wishes, and provides a great deal of space and places to just 'be a dog' and have fun.

Owners Craig and Marjorie Walsh understand completely how owners feel leaving their dogs when they have to go away on business. Having previously owned a company with offices in five countries meant lots of travel, sometimes away from the farm for months at a time. The guilt they felt leaving their dogs was only reduced by the knowledge they were in luxurious surroundings, being cared for by attentive staff. Their Ritz Canine Dog Spa offers hydrotherapy, acupuncture, and even a dog massage in the Zen Den or by the lake. Just look at the online gallery to see how much dogs enjoy this.

THE WOW FACTOR

The biggest wow factor (apart from the location and exclusivity) is the sheer variety and amount of fun the dogs have as can be seen in the enormous online photo gallery (12,000 photos at the time of writing) showing dogs having fun. It's very easy to see that dogs are allowed to be dogs, get wet or muddy, play hard and enjoy themselves thoroughly by exploring everything from streams to farmlife in the grounds. The photos a n d webcams show how much fun guests have every day, and how often they return.

The slideshow in the photo gallery shows dogs playing, running, searching and having fun in lots of places, including the lake (in and around), fetching tennis balls from the water, watching ducks and chickens as well as the farm animals. There is much more stimulation for dogs packed into this one place than can be encountered on a five mile stroll at home!

EXCLUSIVITY AND CHOICE

With plenty of play room, the resort is in 57 acres in glorious countryside and proudly calls its facilities 'the premier resort destination for man's best friend'. Set in the most stunning gardens, with surrounding acres full of ducks, chickens, pigs and alpacas in the fields, there are streams, ponds and a fountain to swim in.

Offering such a high degree of personal care and attention, Lucies Farm Luxury Dog Resort is truly in a class of its own, with 6 staff caring for the dogs staying in their 6 suites. There is underfloor heating, choice of music, a range cooker for special requests, air conditioning during the summer, and exciting grounds to explore. With the high staffing levels and small number of suites available, at just under £50 ($100) per day, owners are happy they can watch their dogs via a secure webcam from anywhere in the world, and request the personalised service they want them to have.

Marjorie's delicious home baked organic dog cookies from her published recipe book have special ingredients dogs adore including aniseed (catnip for dogs!), oatmeal, peanut butter and carob.

Cooking for Dogs
Tempting Recipes
for Your Best
Friend to Enjoy

Marjorie Walsh

What are you most pleased with?

All of it - it really works well for us. The best thing has to be the amount of time we can dedicate to every guest as we have so few suites - it's enormously fulfilling and we just love our lifestyle. We also love to see the look on our clients' faces when they see the complimentary 'doggie basket' we give them when they leave!

What would you do differently?

We would have included a dedicated reception area, and we would have built the kennels further away from neighbours. Living in a village location means having to be aware of the effect that even a single dog bark can have. Oh, and invent an indestructible dog bed for our more 'chewy' guests!

KENNEL DESIGN: THE ESSENTIAL GUIDE TO CREATING YOUR PERFECT KENNELS

LUCIES FARM LUXURY DOG RESORT

LUCIES FARM LUXURY DOG RESORT

LUCIES FARM LUXURY DOG RESORT

HOW KENNELS DESCRIBE THEMSELVES

Having looked at hundreds of kennel web sites worldwide, there seem to be three phrases used by kennel owners: 'luxury', 'five star' and even 'state-of-the-art'. These descriptions can commonly be found for very basic and even sub-standard buildings! Coupled with no, or few photographs, this is obviously confusing for clients, and is perhaps designed to.

Many older properties that haven't had any investment still describe themselves as luxury. We found that approximately 90% of web sites checked also referred to their businesses as 'luxury'. Considering the poor quality of many kennels, there is obviously a chasm between promise and reality.

However kennels are described, the buildings, presentation and staff speak for themselves

---

In this section we look at clarifying the difference between basic, sub-standard, luxury/five star and state of the art.

The Basics

The basic, minimum requirements for kennels are:

- Shelter and safety

- Privacy (somewhere to hide to feel safe) without risk-increasing 'open' or 'nose-to-nose' contact between kennels

- Provision of health and veterinary care when required

- Fresh water and food

- Fresh air, daylight and sunshine

- Somewhere to rest and sleep

- Separate area for toiletting

- Daily routine with familiar, knowledgeable people

- Warmth

- Companionship

- Toys

- Something that smells of home and the owner
  and the most important of all...

- Activities and walks away from the kennels

Luxury and Five Star

'Luxury' is a very subjective word. To satisfy yourself that your kennels building really is 'luxury' you will need to visit several other kennels to establish for yourself what this actually means to you.

Luxury to People

This might be described as a five star hotel, with TV, pretty views, expensive furnishings, good food and drink, landscaping, flowers and hanging baskets, a choice of where to go and things to do, and an escape from it all.

Luxury to Dogs

Somewhere safe and warm (underfloor heating, heated beds and fresh air and sunshine) plenty of attention, things to watch and do, a variety of different beds and places to sit or rest, plenty of space and freedom to move around, being able to move to different levels at will, soft music, calm surroundings, enjoying the company of and a relationship with calm and softly-spoken carers, exciting games involving something to catch or chase, plenty of wildlife or domestic birds/animals to watch and, of course, freshly prepared treats.

To provide a true 'luxury' service, you have to go beyond dog owner knowledge to a more professional understanding of dog behaviour and needs

---

A Holiday?

Thinking in human terms, boarding kennels often describe themselves as a holiday for the dogs, a hotel, or a retreat.

Whatever the size of the kennel, the dog is still **in a different environment and has been moved out of their familiar home** for a temporary stay elsewhere – **this is extremely stressful**. The dog is 'moving house' and doesn't know for how long. Didn't you say 'that's the last time I do that for a while' the last time you moved house? This is why you need to think carefully about dog welfare and how you can improve it at your kennels. **By offering lower numbers of kennels, or short-stay introductions** especially for dogs who have never been in kennels before, you can establish a relationship with the dogs, and they will know what to expect and already be acquainted with you for longer visits.

Let's remember, dogs don't have the luxury of being able to choose to come and stay with you. Use your ingenuity, think up a variety of ways to keep the dogs happy and it will also be great fun for you, provide enormous satisfaction and ensure your clients return again and again and recommend you to their friends.

Every dog is an individual character and will need to be cared for correctly and entertained.
Not doing so will result in boredom, inactivity, abnormal behaviour, stress and ultimately illness

---

Sub-standard and Outdated

There are still far too many of these sub-standard kennels in existence.

All buildings have a limited life, and there comes a time when further investment cannot be justified and a complete rebuild is the only course of action. At this point, owners either upgrade, close or sell up to avoid the investment costs. These photographs show you examples of buildings that are sub-standard and outdated. The most shocking thing about these kennels is that they are _still_ being licensed by the local authorities.

When you compare these photographs with anything else in the book, you will soon see how times are changing.

Old kennels typically have narrow corridors, poor quality materials, unhygienic conditions and suffer from extremes of heat and cold.

Above: these kennel owners were shocked when clients queried their marker-pen cartoons - shocked because clients thought it was graffiti!

Above: old, dark and dingy kennels, little natural daylight or ventilation

Above: unhygienic run

Left: dark, cramped indoor-only kennel with no outlook for the dogs, newspaper to soak up the urine as the floor is unsealed, unhygienic, with an overpowering smell. Count the 6"/15cm tiles and you will see the width is just 2ft/60cm - not much room for this border collie - not even the bed fits in without being put in at an angle.

State-of-the-Art

'State of the Art' describes something that is the highest level of development at a particular period, showing architectural flair, innovative or successful ideas which are ahead of their time. Architects are used to providing this quality for people, but few understand what makes kennels achieve this status. State-of-the-art kennels are **very** high specification design and finish facilities which are a combination of aesthetics and practicality, but also encompass staff and animal welfare considerations

For charities, an extremely valuable (and proven) result of investing in the highest specification you can afford, is that it gets the organisation talked about, gives more likelihood of 'repeat business' and therefore more likelihood of increasing your ability to rehome more dogs. For boarding and commercial kennels this quality can be produced on a more **personal** scale by dog hotels aiming at the luxury and caring dog owner market.

Building fewer kennels that are large, bright and airy is the perfect way to give your kennels or dog hotel the 'wow' factor.

Maddie's Adoption Center, San Francisco SPCA (see case study page 158)

Canine Country Club, Cornwall/Devon UK (see case study page 170)   *Park Kennels, Oxfordshire UK (see case study page 84)*

Dogs Trust Salisbury

2

PURCHASE AND PLANNING

DON'T WORRY.
THERE ARE SIMPLE
STEPS TO HELP
OBTAIN YOUR
PLANNING/ZONING
PERMISSION

WHAT YOU MUST COMPLY WITH

People usually have exactly the same queries about running/building kennels wherever they are in the world, so the information contained in this book is relevant to everyone setting up kennels.

Finding out about legislation is usually the quickest part of the journey, as all you need to do is contact your local authority. In every country, things always differ greatly between regions, nothing is ever applied 'country-wide'.
Even when there are actual country guidelines, some authorities are strict regarding compliance with them, yet others have not even adopted them. Some countries have legislation or guidelines, and others have none.

Getting Permission to Build Kennels

Whatever country you live in, the first thing you should do is to contact your local authority regarding Planning/Zoning Permission and Animal Welfare or Boarding legislation or guidelines, as most types of business require permission.

For Building Permission, you will need to find out about:

- Planning/Zoning Permission to build or replace kennels

- Legislation/Animal Welfare Laws that will affect you

- Obtaining a licence/permit if you are going to be boarding dogs, running a sanctuary or breeding

There are usually two types of permission, one is **outline** permission (where you may not yet own the property and would like to see if permission would be granted with an overall plan of what is proposed) and the other is **full** permission where more detailed information and plans are required. It is advisable to obtain the services of an expert, one who is familiar with the local authority and who knows the topography. This is normally in the form of a planning consultant, architect, surveyor or even a good building contractor.

How to find your local authority:

- Look it up on your authority tax bill

- Look it up in your local business pages or phone book

- Look it up on the internet

Who to Speak to

Planning/Zoning Permission

Contact your local authority's planning/zoning department for an application for building on or upgrading your property and discuss the possibility of opening kennels at your location. This will give you a good indication of how much ease or difficulty you may have with your application. They will take into consideration views from the traffic/highways department and the animal welfare or licensing officer.

In dealing with a planning application, local authorities can either:

- Approve it outright

- Approve it subject to conditions

- Refuse it

Supporting Statements:

Discuss the possibility of obtaining written statements from your existing contacts (such as your vet, dog club, dog rescues and animal warden/animal control officer) regarding the local need for good, quality kennels in your area. They may also provide interesting or helpful information (such as all the other kennels in your area are often fully booked, how they perceive the local standard, which kennels will be closing and what is the need for good kennels). If your contacts are willing to put their comments in writing, you can use these as 'supporting statements' to submit with your application and strengthen your case.

Licensing Application

Commercial kennels will require a licence in the UK and North America. Rescue kennels currently do not need a licence in the UK, but a permit will be required for North America. Speak to your local authority's licensing officer regarding your licence and application (this will be your environmental health/animal warden/animal control officer depending on your location) they may also be based at your local authority.

Environmental Issues

Speak to your local authority's environment officer/agency regarding the impact of the kennels on the environment and in particular about waste disposal, (your planning/zoning officer may also be able to help you with recommendations).

Your environmental health officer will probably be based at your local authority, but here are the main environment agency websites:

- UK: www.environment-agency.gov.uk
  Scotland: www.sepa.org.uk

- USA: www.epa.gov

- Canada: www.ec.gc.ca

- Europe: www.eea.eu.int

SITE LOCATION

One of the greatest difficulties is choosing the correct site for your requirements. These requirements will, of course, be subjective, but the important point to remember is they should take into account your needs in 10 years' time; not only the next two years.

One of the first decisions to be made is whether to build on a greenfield site or to purchase an existing kennels. Both options have factors for and against. To highlight the pros and cons of both options, some of the more salient points follow.

How Much Land is Required?

Generally, the *minimum* amount of land you need is one acre for boarding kennels. Obviously the amount of land depends on the scale of operation you intend to develop. You will need to incorporate car parking, reception, storage, laundry, kitchen, exercise areas/paddocks. Equally important is to have a private area and garden for your own use, and of course for your own dogs.

PURCHASE OF AN EXISTING BUSINESS

Choosing to purchase an existing business provides you with the **advantages** of a ready-made client base, an audited income, existing buildings and infrastructure. The **disadvantages** of buying an existing business are the payment for the 'goodwill' and possibly purchasing buildings that are past their useful working life. Goodwill is a negotiable sum and relates to the popularity of an established business, which is treated as a saleable asset. This varies from business to business and can be a substantial amount.

Some of the questions that you need to ask and satisfy yourself that this is the correct establishment to purchase are:

- **Location** – Is the location right for my needs?

- **Existing Licence** – Is the existing licence adequate? Does it have any spare capacity for any future expansion? **Future Licensing** – Will the licence be renewed without extra costs or conditions to bring the buildings up to the local authority and your own required standard?

- **Expansion** – Is the site suitable for expansion and development? Will the local planning authority allow any further expansion?

- **Car parking** – Is there sufficient for customers, staff, delivery vehicles, etc?

- **Existing Accommodation** – Are the existing animal accommodation and associated buildings suitable for your requirements?

- **Legislation** – Do the kennels comply with current local standards? To obtain an animal boarding licence the establishment needs to ensure that it complies with local guidelines. (In the UK it is the owner who holds the licence, not the business).

- **Infrastructure** – Is the infrastructure adequate for the current demands being imposed on it? (e.g. electricity, gas, water supply and drainage). Is there any spare capacity for expansion? All of these areas are the lifeblood of the premises; without them daily activities can be made extremely difficult. We will look at this in greater detail later in the book

- **Drainage** – Does the drainage system work correctly? Drainage is a major area of concern to kennel owners.

- **Complaints** – Have there been any complaints to, or any restrictions imposed by the local authority regarding noise, opening times, vehicular/foot traffic, pollution, etc?

- **Residential Accommodation** – Does the site have the right amount of residential accommodation? Is there suitable space available to construct accommodation if required? Will the local authority permit this?

- **Access** – Can the access be maintained all year? Does the land suffer from flooding, making part of the property unusable during the winter months?

- **Planning and Zoning** – Do all of the buildings have planning consent? For more information on this see the following section on Planning

Some of the most informative details can be obtained about an existing property by spending time watching the staff go about their daily routine. What might be a minor irritation to them in terms of building design and layout could prove to be unworkable for you. Generally, there are very few kennels available for sale that do not require additional works to bring them up to the required standard. This should be remembered when negotiating the purchase price and used in your favour.

BUYING A KENNELS BUSINESS

Peter Reed MNAEA, MICBA, Kennel Sales

DECIDE WHAT YOU WANT

When buying a property, doing your homework is extremely important. You are buying with your wallet, so buy for financial reasons, do not let your heart take over. **What is it that you want to buy and for what reasons?** How many facilities have you seen? Do friends own one? Visit 10 facilities around you, pay attention to the construction, style and condition. Having found a style that you like, try to find the price of the kennels 'as new' for comparisons to work with.

Consider the location: do you have connections, family, relatives and friends nearby? Are you happy with the location, giving consideration to both plus and negative points? **Good catchment areas are expanding and developing residential areas, with pleasant surroundings**. Avoid dying areas with noticeable decaying in the locality, flight paths, proposed by-passes, pylons, sewage treatment plants, railway lines, landfill sites and areas liable to flooding. **Check the type of land and drainage**, agricultural fields with crops, livestock or possible treatments that can give concerns for allergies, smells and noise.

Any competitors in the area need to be checked out including the quality of facilities, service and fees. They are your competition, and no matter how good or bad they are, you are hopefully aiming to be better! **The accounts are all-important -** it is upon these the business will be assessed by accountants and bank managers. **Having considered all these points (good and bad), what is the property worth to you?** Bear in mind there are possibly far more potential purchasers considering this property than you might imagine, and that one day you will also want to sell the property to someone going through the same thought process as you are. Find an independent financial adviser who will give independent advice, preferably with kennel-financing experience.

WE'RE HERE FOR THE LONG-TERM

A number of purchasers come to our office/kennels and cattery just to talk about the nature of the business. Intending purchasers have had work experience before buying their kennels. We talk with purchasers of kennels about setting up kennels, and also purchasers (who have been unable to find their ideal kennels) about starting one up from scratch. Customers (not always buying through ourselves) talk to us about the best ways of expanding, modernising or replacing their facilities.

We have even visited owners thinking about selling, shown them where they are going wrong (giving themselves more work than necessary), talked them out of selling by showing them how to run their facility more efficiently. They spread the word, and we shall get the property on our books one day!

Upon completion I say to most purchasers: we are still here if they want to talk about anything to do with kennels or a cattery, where to buy things, how to deal with certain circumstances, just phone us, and even if we can't help you, we probably know someone who can.

In February 2008 we celebrated 23 years of selling kennels and cattery businesses. We would like to sincerely thank our customers for their help, encouragement and many recommendations, **making us the largest specialist agency selling kennels and catteries**. So not only will you have the services of the largest specialist agency, on a 'No Sale, No Fee' basis - we pay all advertising costs (doing more advertising than any other), a non-restrictive contract and with a commission rate starting at 1%.

BUYING OR SELLING IN THE UK?

Interested? We hope you will be. If you are thinking of buying, selling or indeed already trying to sell your kennels business (privately or through another agency without success), why not give us a call? **We know discretion is important, we ourselves are boarding kennels and cattery owners**, so don't be shy, just give us a call, even in the evenings on:

**01277 356641 at Kennel Sales, Ladybird Kennels, Roman Road
Ingatestone, Essex, CM4 9AD, UK.**

www.kennelsforsale.co.uk

SELLING A KENNELS BUSINESS

PLAN AHEAD

When thinking about selling your facility, work to a time scale. About three years before you do anything dramatic, start work behind the scenes. Bring the accounts up to date, as it is upon these that potential purchasers will try to raise their mortgage. The accounts will be looked at by bank managers, accountants and financial advisers who may have no knowledge of the kennels business, despite giving advice based on the accounts.

When selling anything, first impressions count. Imagine yourself as a purchaser, can you see any faults, necessary repairs, rubbish to be cleared or tired paint work? None of these will stop a sale, but may give intending purchasers greater confidence, rather than focusing on what costs they will incur immediately after having bought the property.

Keep an eye on local similar residential properties. Your property, when valued, will start with a comparison to local residences. This will be added to the approximate value of your facilities, taking into consideration their construction, age and condition. This will be further added to by the business, based largely upon the trading accounts. Obtain any information on possible planning permissions to the property, or local developments that might affect it.

CHOOSING AN AGENT

Call in an agent with an understanding of the business and see what comparable properties they have sold recently. Some will continue offering properties on their register when already sold by a rival (giving the appearance of offering more properties and being bigger than they actually are) so check who sold the properties you are interested in. Often properties are offered by different agents and perhaps owners too, and when sold, some agents may still show the property on their register as 'sold' for some time.

When we are the selling agent, we confirm the property was sold by us, and when. The date is there for all to see, and for valuers to use as needing comparisons. We remove all properties sold through other agents from our register after contracts have exchanged.

Before making a decision, request agents send information of their services/charges before they visit.

- Are there fees for: visiting your property, registering it, advertising, or even for removing it if it doesn't sell?
- Check fees are based upon the eventual selling price, and not on an inflated asking price
- Will they explain their terms fully before you sign any contract? Ask for a copy of their contract before they visit. You then have time to consider the implications, or ask your solicitor to cast an eye over it, before you agree to whatever terms are offered

Check the difference between terms:

- **Sole Agency:** The vendors instruct one agent to act on their behalf, normally for a set length of time, and thereafter may continue until a sale is achieved
- **Joint Sole Agency:** The vendors instruct two agents to act together on their behalf, normally for a set time, and may continue until a sale is achieved
- **Multiple Agency:** The vendor instructs as many agents as they wish, all of whom will act independently and in competition with each other. The best (or sometimes the luckiest) agent that finds the successful purchaser is paid for their effort
- **Sole Selling Rights:** The vendor instructs one agent to act on their behalf. No matter who purchases the property, the agent is entitled to the fees (even if selling privately to a relative, the agent has the rights to claim their fees!)

A few days making the right decision is easier to live with than an expensive wrong decision. For further advice, speak to someone who recently purchased a property, asking where they obtained the best service.

While it may be easy to offer a property privately (through websites/adverts) an agent will also:

- Try to cut out the 'sight seeing'
- Have experience and knowledge to know what seems 'right' or 'wrong' in a transaction
- Check the financial background and mortgage capabilities of interested parties, thus cutting out time wasters and unnecessary solicitors' costs
- Liaises with other agents within a chain, reporting periodically on proceedings or problems
- Liaise with solicitors to try to make the sale as smooth and untroubled as possible

PURCHASE OF A BROWNFIELD OR GREENFIELD SITE

Brownfield Site

A brownfield site is a plot of land that has previously been developed, used or occupied by a permanent structure, and is a land type that is frequently becoming an option for many businesses. The planning requirements are exactly the same as for any other site, but the main consideration is to establish what the site's previous business use has been. Clearly the risks for the site (or part of it) to have some form of contamination is far greater. Before the site is purchased, establish the extent of any contamination, the type of contamination, and the costs for either removing it or sealing it in. Specialist advice should be obtained if there are concerns about the possibility of contamination issues.

Greenfield Site

A greenfield site is land with or without buildings. For the purpose of this book, it is regarded as land that has had no animal-related buildings attached to it. This option has many long-term advantages over the purchase of an existing business, particularly if you want to develop a larger complex, have clear ideas about what standard you want, or start smaller due to initial budget constraints. A greenfield site gives the option to construct modern, well-designed buildings, to your own requirements. It also allows development of the site from scratch, to ensure that the buildings are high standard and in the correct position. It removes any restrictions that may occur with existing premises. The proposed development can also be phased over a period of time, to take into account restrictions on time and finances.

What to check:

- Locating a suitable site that is close to an area of habitation; but not so close as to result in complaints to the local authority e.g. traffic generation, noise
- Satisfying the local authority in terms of planning/zoning
- To develop a successful business can take a considerable amount of time; the interim period be can financially difficult
- A time delay before any revenue starts to come in
- Does the surrounding area have enough capacity to sustain another commercial or welfare centre?
- Ensure you have enough income to cover the build time AND the first six months of opening ideally. This can be done by continuing employment for you or a partner, or allow sufficient amount in your loan to cover this period
- Use the building time productively to get organised with your marketing and image
- If you haven't worked professionally with dogs before, and you have the opportunity to work voluntarily for a rescue organisation, seize the opportunity as it will be time well spent
- If you have never run any business before, a slower start might be more beneficial to you as you can build your confidence and knowledge at your own pace

Additional Costs:

For greenfield sites, or if major upgrading works are proposed, there will be hidden costs. Some examples are:
- **Services Upgrade** – upgrading utility supplies can be extremely expensive
  All utility providers (e.g. water, gas, drainage and electricity) will charge for any works incurred. The level of works required, the required increase in the rate of supply, and the complexity of the works, dictate the cost
- **Road Access** – these can be either private or public
  Generally you can construct any private road on your land and to whatever specification is adequate for the works being carried out. However, for public roads (local authority owned) it is an entirely different prospect. There will be specifications set by the local authority and generally, this type of work will be carried out by the local authority

PLANNING/ZONING PERMISSION

As already mentioned, the first difficulty is locating a suitable site; the second major obstacle is obtaining permission for a new site, or to develop an existing business. Most types of business development require permission from the local authority. Clearly, if there has been any business use on the land, a precedent has been set, which can be highly beneficial to your case.

The local planning authority is interested in any new planning application for many reasons. The more usual ones likely to influence the authority's decision are:

- **Appearance and scale** – External appearance of the development, and the size and scale of the development

- **Neighbours** – Any authority will be concerned about how your application could affect your neighbours. Noise, loss of light to their property, loss of privacy, increased traffic and disturbance are all possible reasons for refusal

- **Topography** – How the buildings will sit on the land

- **Environment** – Minimising the impact on the environment

- **Traffic** – Not creating or perpetuating unacceptable traffic or transport conditions, reducing the need to travel (called 'sustainable development')

- **Risk** – Avoiding the development of land that is unstable, at risk of flooding, or likely to increase the risk of flooding elsewhere

- **Highways** – Providing a safe access to the highway. (There are set standards for access, these are known as 'visibility splays'. The splay required by the authority will depend on the location, the type of road, etc)

- **Car Parking** – Authorities will often set standards for the number of spaces required on developments

- **Archaeological Areas** – Areas of archaeological importance can influence any development

- **Trees** – These can restrict development. Before any development is undertaken it is worth checking to see if the trees have any preservation orders

- **Services/Utilities** – Any existing utility services within the boundary. It is not uncommon to find either on the site, or close to it, utility services such as gas, water, drainage, electricity or radio masts. For example, one site with a 250mm/10" mains gas pipe running across one corner has a restriction that no building can be constructed within 3m/10ft either side of it.

- **Rights of Way** – If a public right of way crosses your site, it could prevent the siting of a new building. It is possible to have this diverted – but it can be a lengthy process

- **Contaminated Land** – There are risks and costs involved with dealing with contaminated land

- **Wildlife** – Any old building/s that have not been used for a number of years (particularly in rural areas) might have become the home of endangered species such as bats, owls, etc. Many of these species are protected under wildlife or environmental legislation. (The authority might insist that a professional survey is carried out before granting planning permission if there is a suspicion that the property might house endangered species)
Other animals that will be of interest to local authority are certain reptiles, newts, etc

- **Party Walls** – Walls shared with your neighbours

Summary of Planning Route

1. **Location** of suitable greenfield site or existing business

2. **Establish any new development required**

3. **Basic design sketches to show to the Planning Officer**

4. **Pre-application meeting with Planning Officer** to go over the proposed scheme in greater detail, establish if planning consent is likely to be of concern to the officer (this is important – there is little point in submitting an application if it will never be granted planning permission). Some possible reasons for refusal have already been identified; further reasons may be that the development is in an area designated Green Belt, Conservation Area or is a Listed Building. If any of the above applies to your site, this could have major implications for your application. The Local Structure plan will show if any of these apply. It is also worth checking prior to purchase of the property

5. **Proposed scheme/design drawn up** to the required standard

6. **Application is submitted with payment**, signed declarations, scaled drawings of the proposed buildings, car parking, roads, etc, a scaled location plan (1:1,250) for most applications (if the site is extremely rural the authority might ask for a larger plan, say 1:2,500 for identification purposes, Design and Access Statements - DAS).
   It is normal for most authorities to ask for five copies of each drawing and plan. It is also useful to include a covering letter or supporting statement about the development. This allows the councillors a better insight at a personal level about your proposal

7. **Application is registered with the authority.** A receipt is sent to you and a reference number is allocated to your proposal. The acknowledgement letter will show when a decision should be made; this is normally between eight and 12 weeks after receipt)

8. **Application is advertised by the authority**

9. **Allow approximately four weeks then contact the authority** to see how your application is progressing.
   Generally, you need to know:
   - Any potential issues or problems (if there are problems, what needs to be done to overcome them)
   - Will the decision be taken by committee or by the planning officer?
   - When will the committee be considering your application?

10. **Continue to monitor the development.** Speak to any neighbours who might be affected by your proposal, (if the neighbours don't have any objections, ask them to write to the authority to support your proposal).

If there are concerns about your application, you must address these. Ignoring these concerns is likely to result in a refusal. **If it seems that the application is likely to fail**, you can either let it run then re-apply, withdraw the application (you will not be reimbursed any of your fees) or appeal against the authority's decision.
If there are no major issues and the application is successful, it will either be passed outright, or have conditions attached. If successful, the development will normally have a time limit of three years in which it must be completed.

If the application is unsuccessful, or you appeal, it is strongly recommended that you take the advice of a professional planning consultant.

Planning Tips

As already mentioned, planning can sometimes be a very complicated and protracted business. An application deemed suitable for the granting of planning permission at one location might not be granted permission at another, even though on paper they seem to have similar characteristics.

Kennel developments are always a concern to the authority, generally because of the potential noise issues. You can increase the likelihood of being granted permission by reducing the number of dogs, stress/noise-reducing design and materials, good management, and the emphasis on a more personal service where dog welfare is carefully considered - all result in noise-reduction, and reassurance to the authority and neighbours.

The following planning tips should be helpful to your situation:

■ Modest Development

The key to a successful application is to build it up slowly. If the plot or scheme is likely to be controversial, it is far better to establish the principle of development with a modest, smaller scheme. This is less likely to upset local residents. Once the business has established itself, it is far easier to apply for further development as the precedent has already been set, and it is harder for the local authority to refuse

■ Permitted Development

Certain types of development are exempt from planning permission. This allows smaller projects to proceed without having to go through the planning procedure. However, these 'permitted development' rules generally apply only to domestic situations, which do not involve any form of commercial business and are confined to curtilage of your property. This is something of a grey area and should be checked with the Planning Officer for verification.

■ Time Limits

Planning permissions are normally valid for only a set period of time from the date of permission has been granted (generally three years); although the authority may, in exceptional circumstances, substitute a period either longer or shorter. There is no guarantee that any new application submitted due to time-lapse will be granted permission. Planning policies are constantly changing. In some cases this might be to your advantage, and in others a disadvantage

■ Planning Fees

Each application for planning permission has to be accompanied by the relevant fee; the scale of fees being subject to regular increases.
Obviously, the larger the scale of the development, the greater the fee. The planning application will not be valid unless it is accompanied by the correct fee. There are a few, exceptional cases where no planning fee, or a reduced fee is payable, details can be obtained from the planning authority. Clearly, if the correct approach has been taken, sensible discussions have taken place with the planning authority and advice taken, hopefully any major obstacles will be avoided.

■ Wildlife and Country Legislation

Any old building/s that have not been used for a number of years, particularly in rural areas, might have become the home of endangered species such as bats, owls, etc. Many of these species are protected by legislation (e.g. the UK's Wildlife and Countryside Act 1981) and it is an offence to destroy, disturb or obstruct their access. Again, your local authority will be able to advise you (in the UK advice on any such issues should be taken from

English Nature www.english-nature.org.uk or Defra www.defra.gov.uk).

HOW DESIGN ISSUES CAN HELP YOUR APPLICATION

You can do a number of things to help your application in terms of design. These are:

- **Impact** – Consider the impact of any new buildings from a number of viewpoints and distances

- **Match existing buildings** – Impact can be reduced by relating the size, colour and materials to existing buildings. Use materials and colours that are common to the locality and blend in

- **Colour Tone** – Avoid bright intense colours – these can look very artificial and tend to fade more quickly than lighter toned colours

- **New buildings** – New buildings look best when forming part of a group, rather than standing alone. (Isolation buildings being an occasion when this rule will not apply)

- **Siting** – Try to site buildings in the folds of landform to provide shelter and screening

- **Hills** – Avoid locating buildings on the crest of hills

- **Slopes** – On sloping sites, align buildings parallel with the contours of the land

- **Proportion** – Large buildings can look out of proportion to older buildings; consider providing smaller buildings rather than one large unit

- **Roof pitch** – Try to match roof pitches to existing buildings where possible

- **Roofing materials** – Generally, roofing materials should be darker than the walls

Although extremely simple drawings for planning/zoning are still seen occasionally, the level of detail required by many local authorities for new developments has increased significantly over the past few years. Therefore, it is essential that you do as much fact-finding and homework as possible prior to submitting your application.

Check to see if there have been any previous planning applications on the site, or any development carried out in the vicinity – and speak to the owners and neighbours to see if they had any problems. Generally, once the application has been submitted all fees paid are not refundable, even if the applicant withdraws the application, or the authority rejects the application. It is important to keep in contact with the planning officer throughout the process to see if there have been any objections, and what the general feeling is about your application.

Before submitting a planning application for any animal-related development, contact the Planning Officer to discuss the project in advance

---

A pre-application meeting will allow the Planning Officer to pass comment before the application is submitted formally It must be remembered that the authority is not duty-bound to accept the opinion of the Planning Officer! At present, it is not unusual to find applications taking 8 – 14 weeks to be processed. Obviously the larger the development, the more detail and information the authority is likely to request.

Planning Conditions

If the application is successful, it is not unusual to find that the authority has imposed certain site-specific conditions.

The normal conditions for smaller scale developments will be:

- **Landscaping** – The authority might insist that a landscaping scheme is to be considered as part of the application

- **External Lighting** – For rural areas, most authorities do not want to see a large amount of artificial lighting and might restrict the use of floodlights, etc

- **Parking** – Providing and allowing sufficient parking on the premises for staff and clients, or ensuring that the vehicles can drive in, turn around on site and then drive out facing forwards (for safety reasons many authorities do not allow business operations to reverse out on to a road)

- **Road Signage** – If you wish to erect a business sign, this normally requires planning permission, and sometimes highways permission as well. This will depend on your location and the size of the sign board

Demolition

It may be necessary to demolish existing buildings on a newly acquired site. The reasons for this are to clear part of the site for future development, to remove or to make safe any structures in an unsafe condition.

The law regarding demolition is very specific and should not be taken lightly, with statutory requirements that must be adhered to. For any large-scale demolition, expert advice should be sought. Additional costs for demolition works need to be factored in.

In addition to the authority, the owner or their agent must also notify:

- Any utility companies (e.g. gas, electricity)

- The owner/occupiers of any building adjacent to the building concerned

ENFORCEMENT OF PLANNING CONTROL

Local planning authorities have powers to ensure that any unauthorised development that has been carried out - is rectified. Unauthorised development is not in itself an offence, the exception being protected/listed buildings. Once an unlawful development comes to the notice of the authority, it will decide what action is to be taken. This decision is taken upon the nature of the development, any local restrictions, and materials used, etc.

There are two ways an infringement can occur:

- A development that has been carried out without planning permission

- A development that has been granted permission, but has not complied with the specific conditions being imposed by the planning authority

SITE PURCHASE

Ensure that any site you intend to purchase will be granted planning permission, as this is most relevant to greenfield sites that do not have an established business use.

You do not have to own the land to submit
a planning application to develop it.

There have been a great many potential building plots advertised for sale, which on initial reading look very attractive and reasonably priced. However, many of these do not have any form of planning consent for development, and many **will never** be granted permission. Clearly without planning consent, the land has little financial value.

Before purchasing any plot it is worth checking the site's planning history. This will tell you what applications have been submitted or refused and quite often you will be able to obtain copies of old plans of any proposed development.

Meet the Planning Officer

It is always a good idea to try to meet the local planning officer to pass your ideas to them. Most will take the conservative and cautious approach when discussing projects informally. Any comments made by the planning officer do not have to be taken literally; planning is a very subjective issue.

Don't be disheartened if they do not enthuse about your project, their job is to assess every application objectively.

Flexibility

Be prepared to amend or alter your design slightly if this means that you will succeed with your application.

Delegated or Committee/Board Decision

There is a difference between a delegated decision and a committee/board decision. All chief planning officers have the power to grant a planning application under delegated powers. This means that there is no involvement of a full planning committee. This normally expedites the planning decision time.

The **disadvantage** is that if the application is recommended for refusal, you do not have any opportunity to try and convince them otherwise. It is vital to keep in contact with the authority and track your application.

Application Refusal

If your application is going to be refused, it is sensible to withdraw it. An application can be withdrawn at any time, up to the point of the decision notice. This, in theory, keeps the site plot 'clean' in planning terms. However, in reference to future applications, the authority will still mark the site. You will need to understand why your application was marked for refusal.

Clearly, there is little point in submitting another application for exactly the same scheme.

> If your application is going to be refused, it is sensible to withdraw it, find out the reasons for refusal, and address them on re-application.
>
> (This is another reason for monitoring the application throughout the planning route)

Planning Appeal:

If your application has been refused planning by committee; the entire process starts to become extremely protracted and complicated. At this stage, quite often there is little room for manoeuvre.

One option is to appeal against the authority's decision. This process is made by an independent inspector who will judge each case on its own merits, local policies, etc. However, this is a very risky business and will take at least six months. It is best avoided.

Planning Conditions:

Most planning applications will be subject to conditions. For smaller developments, these normally relate to material types, colour, fencing and landscaping.

It is often far too easy to forget about these conditions until two or three years after the granting of planning permission, only to be confronted with a letter from the authority stating that work needs to be completed in order to make the application lawful.

Four-year Rule

This is an odd piece of UK legislation, but one that could be in force in other countries. It is not something that should be relied upon as a way of securing a building or development of course, but is worth noting:

> *If something has been built without permission and no action has been taken against it for four years – then the authority cannot do anything about it.*

This could be useful, particularly If you are purchasing an existing business which does not have planning permission on any, or all, of the development. This does happen, particularly with rural properties, and is something that should be discovered on legal searches.

LANDSCAPING AND TREES NEAR BUILDINGS

Without question, a well landscaped site will improve the general appearance of that site beyond all recognition, will soften the overall look, can help with noise reduction (particularly by screening off private areas and non-animal work) and will enhance the property for your visitors/public.

Most planning applications will require some form of landscaping of the site; the extent required will vary according to the site, its location and the size of the development.

If you propose (or are required) to carry out landscaping operations, it is worthwhile discussing your requirements with a qualified landscape contractor or architect. Advice will be needed on the types of tree suitable for your location and how far they should be planted away from the buildings; this is particularly important.

Remember a mature oak or elm tree can grow to over 65ft/20m in height – imagine the effect on the buildings and foundations in 20 years' time.

Landscaping on a site should ideally be planned as part of the main construction, to allow for the most suitable species in relation to buildings, underground drainage pipes, service mains, etc. The proximity of neighbours' services, buildings, etc should also be taken into account.

A registered landscape contractor will advise on and design a suitable scheme for a site as part of his contract. It is also common practice for them to advise on any necessary replacements for trees/shrubs that have died, and to provide a **maintenance programme for the first year** following completion of the contract.

Tree Preservation Orders

In UK law, trees with a diameter of over 75mm/3" are regarded as permanent assets attached to the property/land; therefore, they cannot be felled, removed or topped without permission. This relates to 'timber-like' trees only, and not ornamental shrubs or bushes.

Owners of trees are responsible for ensuring that any tree on their property is in a safe and sound condition and does not obstruct public rights of way or highways.

If the land surrounding your property is designated a conservation area by the local authority, six weeks' notification is required before any work can be carried out on a tree. This period allows the authority the opportunity to make a decision whether a preservation order is required for the tree in question.

It is worth remembering that trees in the wrong place can prevent the development of a site.

COMMON, COSTLY ERRORS TO BE AVOIDED

Above all, have a clear idea of what you want to achieve.
Research the project thoroughly, and visit similar properties

Common, costly errors to be avoided are:

■ **Lack of forward planning**
Plan well ahead and try to foresee how your business will grow and expand. Allow for this, do not 'sterilise' a site by poor planning

■ **Single storey buildings constructed with insufficient foundations for adding a second storey**
This is particularly relevant if space is limited and the only way for expansion is to build upwards rather than outwards. (This generally relates only to traditional brick/block structures)

■ **Piecemeal building instead of a planned, integrated design**
This is where having a professional site survey carried out is extremely beneficial

■ **Inadequate car parking**

■ **Inadequate storage facility**

■ **Existing structures**
If converting a site, do not allow existing structures to stop the correct siting of new buildings/facilities

■ **Lack of quiet areas**

■ **Poor quality finishes**
e.g. floors/walls which need to be robust

■ **Poor location of various facilities** in relation to other units

■ **Not providing separate zones** for public and staff

MAKE YOUR MISTAKES ON PAPER -
NOT DURING THE BUILDING STAGE!

CASE STUDY:
LOCATION, LOCATION, LOCATION

Organisation: West Lodge Boarding Kennels
Location: UK, Cambridge
Kennels Type: Semi-outdoor
Kennels Function: Boarding
Number of Kennels: 64
Kennel Size Sleep: 4ft x 4ft/1.2m x 1.2m
Kennel Size Exercise: 4ft x 6ft/1.2m x 1.8m
Year Built: 1998

www.westlodgekennels.co.uk

THIS EXISTING BUSINESS IS IN A STUNNING SETTING WITH BEAUTIFUL MATURE GARDENS LOCATED JUST OUTSIDE AN AFFLUENT CITY. THERE IS ENORMOUS POTENTIAL TO UPGRADE TO A DOG HOTEL WITH THE CARE, COMMITMENT & VISION OF NEW OWNERS

WEST LODGE BOARDING KENNELS

Marc and Iris Wheeldon have taken their first step back after a whirlwind first year of taking on an existing kennels and cattery. With strong business backgrounds and experience of working with and showing dogs, and after a great deal of searching, they finally took the plunge when they came across this undeniably beautiful property.

"We visited many kennels for sale and were horrified with some of them" says Marc. *"We decided we would only buy kennels we would be happy for our own dogs to stay in. When we finally discovered this one with its beautiful setting, we just knew it was the one for us. Although we knew we wanted to upgrade the kennels eventually, the existing infrastructure would give us a good chance to think about our future plans while we learned how to run the business."* The year they took to think about what they wanted to do has paid off, having learnt what their clients want and the problems with the existing site, they know exactly where they would like to make improvements.

> *"Our customers are as excited about our plans as we are!"*

This was a very low-cost, high-impact way of showing clients what they wanted to do with the business, and they've had great support doing it. As shown in the photo below left, there is a window that looks through reception to the animal kitchen in the adjoining room. Their plan is to knock down the wall between the reception and kitchen to make it one very large and welcoming reception, to be able to sell more items such as food and toys. Currently the kitchen serves the three kennel buildings and cattery, and as the nearest building is 100ft/30m away this means a great deal of trekking across the grounds for staff, taking up a great deal of time, and in bad weather it is not at all pleasant.

WHERE TO START?

Marc and Iris wanted to focus on the older of the three kennel buildings and meet the criteria for being a dog hotel. This would increase their income to help them raise funds for refurbishing the remaining kennels. *"We knew we wanted to upgrade the kennels and that the location and setting was perfect for turning into a pet hotel - but we just weren't sure where to start."* says Marc. *"Already having the cattery and kennel design books, we had done our research thoroughly and wanted the best for our future development of the business, and to fully realise its enormous potential."*

They decided on an addition to the cattery using 'Pedigree Pens' and upgrading the first kennel building, as the logical and easiest way to start the upgrade to their new pet hotel.

THE CLIENTS

The client base was kept on paper cards, so there was no easy way to contact clients and introduce themselves as new owners. They are gradually adding customers to the PetAdmin system which they love, keeping the cards in case old clients pop in. One of the very first tasks was to update the reception area by repainting and adding new furniture.

Photographs by Marc Wheeldon

KENNEL DESIGN: THE ESSENTIAL GUIDE TO CREATING YOUR PERFECT KENNELS

THE FUTURE

As there was one kitchen shared between all three kennel buildings and the cattery, and at some distance away - creating functional areas for preparing food, water, cleaning and more storage was paramount. With new kitchens in place, it would be possible to turn the existing kitchen and reception into a much larger reception and retail area, naturally leading into the grooming room behind them.

Left: ideas for the new dog hotel
Below: kitchen left, reception right

Armed with all these ideas, Marc and Iris met their bank manager to discuss their plans for development. Before the meeting, Marc had bounced his ideas around with existing clients - who all gave him exceptionally positive feedback. Many were excited about their plans for the future, and wholeheartedly supported Marc and Iris' commitment to the care of their pets, now and in the future.

The bank manager gave them the go-ahead, starting with the cattery first. A design and 3Ds were drawn up by renowned manufacturer Pedigree Pens. UPVC units would allow fast installation (typically a week) rather than a longer construction period of a few months for a solid building. This would achieve many things: keep downtime to a minimum, provide light, bright and easy-to-clean pens, increase the cattery income, give dog owners an idea of the plans for the kennels, and be a good starting point for Marc and Iris to see how much more efficiently the pens could be cleaned and managed with the modern materials and integral kitchen. **It will take time to complete the project, but the benefits in satisfaction, efficiency and income will make all the work worthwhile, to realise the full potential of this beautiful site.**

Welcome to
West Lodge

Boarding Kennels at Abington

Mon - Sat   8.30am - 12.00pm
1.30pm - 5.30pm
Sunday   10.00am - 12.00pm
CLOSED BANK HOLIDAYS

Open

KEEP DOGS
ON LEADS
NO FOULING

KENNEL NOISE
AND DISTURBANCE
CAN BE REDUCED
BY KEEPING
NUMBERS LOW IN
EACH BUILDING.

THOUGHTFUL
KENNEL DESIGN
ALLOWS INDIVIDUAL
DOGS TO MAKE
CHOICES ABOUT
WHERE THEY
WANT TO BE
AT ANY GIVEN
MOMENT

ACOUSTIC MEASURES

Noise pollution is an ever-growing problem and its management is determined by several pieces of legislation, guidance and standards.

As noise is often one of the main determining factors when applying for planning permission for a new kennel development, it has to be taken seriously. A local authority has a duty to consider all aspects of the planning application to ensure that the development does not cause an unacceptable degree of disturbance to local communities.

Any local authority when studying a planning application for a new kennel development will consider many aspects. The main issues for consideration will be:

- Distance of applicant to nearest neighbour and predicted noise level at this location

- Location

- Topography

- Normal background noise levels

- Number of dogs to be housed

- Style and design of the kennels

- Sound insulation properties of the buildings

- Frequency and use of the kennels

- Is a noise problem likely to occur?

- Will the development affect the character of the land and surrounding area?

- What would the level of disturbance be? This could be noise, it could also be traffic generation

When considering an application for kennels, most local authorities in the UK (other countries have similar guidelines) will use one, or a combination, of the following guidelines to determine if your application will create any environmental issues for neighbouring properties;

- Planning Advice Note PAN56 'Planning and Noise'

- British Standard BS 8223:
  Sound Insulation and Noise Reduction for Buildings

- BS 4142:
  Method for Rating Industrial Noise Affecting Mixed Residential and Industrial Areas

- World Health Organisation (WHO):
  Guidelines for Community Noise

UNIT OF NOISE MEASUREMENT

The unit of measurement for sound is measured in decibels (dB)

The scale for this is logarithmic; this means that 90dB is ten times the intensity of 80dB and a hundred times the intensity of 70dB. An increase of 3dB doubles the sound intensity, so that 87dB is twice as noisy as 84dB.

To put this into some context, a normal office environment is approximately 50dB. The threshold for hearing is 0 dB, and 140 dB is the threshold of pain.

Units	Description
L_{A90}	**Background noise level** L_{A90} is the weighted noise level exceeded for 90% of the measurement period. (In BS 4142:1990, it is used to define background noise level.)
L_{Amax}	**Activity noise level** L_{Amax} is the maximum noise level recorded during the measurement period
L_{Aeq}	**Continuous noise level (activity)** L_{Aeq} is the equivalent continuous noise level averaged over the measurement period

Nature of Noise:

Sound is the transmission of vibrations at different frequencies; noise is defined as unwanted sound.

The ear is a pressure-sensitive mechanism, detecting small changes of pressure over a wide range of frequencies; the unit of measurement is known as the Hertz (Hz).

Humans are most sensitive to sounds at frequencies of 1000-5000Hz.

Dogs are most sensitive to sounds at frequencies from 500 Hz to 16,000Hz.

Reverberation Time:

Reverberation time is the time taken for the sound to decay to 60dB.

Kennels by their very nature have poor acoustic properties; hard smooth surfaces do not absorb noise, therefore, any noise generated tends to reverberate around the inside of the building. The longer the reverberation time, the more uncomfortable and echoing the building will be. For offices a comfortable working environment is considered to be 0.4-0.6 seconds, in sports halls and swimming pools this time can be as long as 4-6 seconds.

NOISE IMPACT ASSESSMENT

It is becoming increasingly common for local authorities to ask the applicant to carry out a noise impact assessment before any decision is taken for sites that are considered sensitive. This is undertaken by a specialist acoustic engineer and is dedicated to the applicant's site. The cost for this type of report will be circa £1,200/$2,400. Even with supporting evidence from a specialist it cannot be taken for granted that the application will be successful.

Many local authorities use a distance of 300 metres/1000ft as the yardstick when determining noise in sensitive areas and its possible effects on neighbouring properties.

Noise is one of the main reasons for complaint to local authorities relating to kennels; this has been particularly noticeable since the Environmental Protection Act 1995.

The law relating to noise is not unique to the UK. Future kennel owners in America, France and Australia have been looking at kennel design in the UK and associated problems, particularly in relation to noise. All had one thing in common; a restriction had been placed upon them by the local authority to reduce the noise levels from their kennels.

The World Health Organisation (WHO) guidelines state:

> *"During the daytime, few people are seriously annoyed by activities with L_{Aeq} levels below 55 dB. Sound pressure levels during the evening should be 5 dB lower."*

The WHO guidelines consider that to avoid sleep disturbance, indoor guidelines values for bedrooms are 30 dB (23.00 – 07.00) for continuous noise and 45 dB for single sound events. At night, sound pressure levels at the outside facades of dwellings should not exceed 45 dB L_{Aeq} and 60 dB L_{Amax}, so that people may sleep with bedroom windows open.

These values have been obtained by assuming that the noise from outside to inside with the windows partly open is 15 dB.

British Standard 8223 Sound Insulation and Noise Reduction for Buildings – Code of Practice (1999) states:

> *"For a reasonable standard in bedroom at night individual noise events should not normally exceed 45 dB L_{Amax}."*

This is taken as more than twice in any one-hour period.

One local authority gave a figure of L_{Aeq} 40 dB for daytime and L_{Aeq} 30 dB for night-time; these are _very_ low levels.

NOISE ABATEMENT NOTICE

When a local authority receives a call about a possible noise issue, they are duty-bound to investigate.

If the local authority is satisfied that a statutory nuisance exists, it will point this out to the owner and will seek to resolve the problem. Some local authorities go to extraordinary lengths to provide help and assistance to try to resolve problems and disputes.

If it is not possible to resolve this informally, an Abatement Notice will be served requiring the person responsible to stop the nuisance. In the UK this is issued under Section 80 of the Environmental Protection Act 1990 (EPA).

The EPA is split into eight categories, which include premises, smoke, smells, animals and noise.

The notice will normally state the required reduction in noise levels, the type of works necessary and what options are open to the owner. However, some authorities will simply issue the Notice without any clarification of the works required.

Once served, the owner must take steps to correct and improve the situation within the given timeframe, and also demonstrate that they have taken steps to provide a long-term solution. Failure to act can result in prosecution or even closure.

CASE STUDY:
PEACE AND QUIET WITH THE WOW FACTOR

Organisation:	Park Kennels
Location:	UK, Oxfordshire
Kennels Type:	Semi-outdoor
Kennels Function:	Boarding
Number of Kennels:	20
Sleep Area Size:	Approximately 2m x 2m/ 7ft x 7ft
Exercise Run Size:	Approximately 2m x 2.4m/7ft x 8ft
Year Built:	2006

www.parkkennels.co.uk

THIS KENNELS IS LIVING PROOF THAT A DOG FACILITY CAN BE AN ATTRACTIVE, CALM, RELAXED AND QUIET PLACE. IF YOU INCORPORATE ENOUGH GOOD DESIGN AND IDEAS YOU CAN ACHIEVE EVERYTHING YOU WANT IN A FIRST CLASS FACILITY

PARK KENNELS

When Jan and Rob Beaumont got in contact in 2005, they already had planning consent to convert a redundant farm building on their land. This large building measuring 24.4 m x 12.2/80ft x 40ft (shown below left) was formerly used as a poultry shed and had stood empty for some time.

The planning consent was fairly ambiguous in that it gave permission for 20 kennels with exercise runs. Although it is slightly unusual to gain planning consent without a fully specified design, it does occasionally happen. The main condition was that it had to remain timber clad to give some uniformity to two other similar buildings on the site, and no more openings should be cut into the walls.

From the outset they had a clear idea of the type of kennels they were aiming to build – they wanted to provide a 'first-class facility' with large 'room-like' kennels.

Initial feelings on first seeing the building were that this was going to be a challenge to provide a building with 'wow factor' that would be practical and fulfil all of the authority conditions. However, the photos below clearly show the level of work and achievement involved. After careful consideration it was decided it would be better from a planning point of view to keep the original sized building and construct the sleep and exercise runs within the existing footprint.

Rob and Jan had previously used a local building contractor. Given the level of work involved it was imperative to have a contractor they trusted and could work with. It was important the contractor understood the quality they wanted to achieve and would listen to the practical issues that arise with kennels. The high quality of the contractor has made all the difference; one with little interest or only wanted to complete the project as quickly as possible could have destroyed what has turned out to be a truly fantastic and successful project.

BEFORE

AFTER

KENNELS CAN BE CALM BEAUTIFUL PLACES

THE WORK INVOLVED

Although the local authority had originally insisted on retaining the existing timber cladding, it soon became clear that this was not a viable option. The condition of the timber was not of suitable quality to allow it to be removed and reused, so the building was re-clad using entirely new timber. In fact, by the end of the project there were only a few roof timbers that were original - all of the other elements were replaced. The building used solid concrete blockwork throughout for the external walls and dividing walls between the sleep and exercise runs. The floor was removed and replaced with a new fully-insulated floor, laid to falls (sloped) for drainage. Under the sleep area, electric underfloor heating mats were installed.

The blockwork was coated using a fibreglass-based system. This product has been used extensively in dairy farms and cattle parlours for many years and has proved to be an excellent finish for the kennels environment as well. The surface is applied to the blocks and can be coved around internal and external corners to give a seamless, hygienic, easy-to-clean surface that gives a professional appearance to the building. The floors to the sleep areas have a 300 x 300mm/12" x 12" fully vitrified tile giving an easy-to-clean hygienic surface. The main corridor uses industrial grade vinyl with heat-welded seams, providing a watertight system that is easy to clean. It also helps reduce noise and comes in a wide range of colours and patterns. A fully insulated roof with translucent panels provides lots of natural light and prevents extremes of temperature.

WELFARE ASPECTS

Three core ideas make this building different from many other double line kennels, giving it a relaxing, stress-free and quiet environment for the dogs:

- **Wide Central Corridor** – although this is a double line building, the corridor at 3m/10ft wide removes many of the concerns of similar buildings with much narrower corridor. This width, along with the height and high levels of natural light, also provide wellbeing and wow factor

- **Solid Partitions** – the use of all solid walls and dividing partitions full height to the ceiling provides the dogs with a secure, familiar room-like environment in which to relax

- **Glazed Doors** – The use of glass doors to the sleep area provides a more 'home-like' feel and one that the dogs are used to. Doors are offset from the kennel opposite, removing the eye-to-eye contact issues; and dogs are relaxed enough to sit by them and watch daily activities

WHAT CARING DOG OWNERS WANT

When clients phone after seeing the kennels on the internet, they ask "*Is it really as bright and spacious as it looks?*"! Jan hears lots of 'wow's, and mouths fall open in astonishment at how bright, light and large the kennels are - and especially how quiet. What is really heartwarming is the appreciation they see from clients who have used kennels and have had bad experiences. However, the interesting thing is that the majority of their clients have *never* used kennels before, having previously avoided holidays as it meant using typical kennels and their dog being unhappy.

A positive internet presence is one of the key factors for success as clients come from much farther afield, as well as local. Jan tells us "*We now get 40% of our business through www.boardingkennels.org and they are all the most lovely, caring customers. Most of our customers find us through the web and they are definitely the people I want to attract. They are exceptionally caring, at a time in their lives when they spend a great deal of time with their dog, they are their 'babies' and usually rescue dogs. Often they have never placed their dogs in kennels before, and they are all willing to travel to find somewhere that is going to provide the best care and accommodation at a high standard. Indeed, they feel relief, and are delighted enough to book several holidays!*"

With a strong business and marketing background, Jan researched the project very thoroughly. Conducting her own research she talked to people about their dogs and on what basis they chose kennels. For many, they wouldn't ask about the conditions their dog was staying in as long as there was a reasonably smart entrance and the fees were low. On investigating further she found out that husbands were often sent to take or pick up the dog, on a sort of 'if I don't see it it doesn't happen' basis, at least until a bad experience made them look into things further. The most shocking thing was finding out that people thought all kennels were the same and a 'necessary evil' for them to be able to go on holiday.

Changing this attitude has been one of the cornerstones for the success of Park Kennels. If people think all kennels are the same, and either avoid looking at them or avoid holidays because of this - it comes down to the same thing. Park Kennels proves a dog facility can be light, bright and astonishingly quiet, calm and relaxed. In fact, it is such a great success that we have a video as an example of what can be achieved at www.kenneldesign.com/videos and how different this is from what people expect kennels to be.

PARK KENNELS

WHAT CAN YOU DO?

The law recognises that some businesses have to make a noise in connection with their lawful operation. It is this caveat that allows business and trade premises to defend themselves against an abatement notice by demonstrating that they are employing 'Best Practicable Means' (BPM) to prevent or minimise noise nuisance. In taking abatement action the local authority will have to regard this defence.

Best Practicable Means (BPM):

- Having regard to the current state of technical knowledge

- The local condition and circumstances

- The financial implications

The means to be employed include the design, installation, maintenance and manner and periods of operation, the design, construction and maintenance of building and structures. Again, there are factors in all of the these that have to be taken into consideration for each individual case.

A defence at one property may not be so at another, carrying out a similar operation. The financial implications will be different for a multi-national food company when compared with a small, independent local business.

Best Practicable Means is to apply only so far as compatible with safety and safe working conditions.

In the case of kennels, BPM will take several avenues; these would include the welfare of dogs and how long they might have to be shut in, dogs sharing exercise runs, or if kennels/runs would have to be removed if facing neighbouring properties, etc.

Unfortunately there is no specific criteria relating to noise from kennels. The general guide used is to determine the pre-existing background noise levels of the site

The propagation of noise to adjoining properties is influenced by many factors, the greatest being the physical distance; the greater the distance the greater the spherical spread of the noise will be. Factors such as the ground conditions will also be taken into account.

Over long distances, it does become more difficult and complex to predict the levels of noise reduction.

A report carried out several years ago by an acoustic expert who had been commissioned to determine the noise levels at a neighbouring property at a distance of 240m/787ft from the kennels concluded that:

"No significant variation in noise level could be attributed directly to dog barking alone, even when the dogs were clearly audible".

MEASURES TO MITIGATE THE IMPACT OF NOISE

Noise has to be considered from two perspectives, although the end result is often the same. Noise is a major source of stress to the dogs in the kennels; it can be detrimental to the health of members of staff operating in the building and is also the biggest cause of complaint to the local authority.

Noise Within the Kennel Building:

Work carried out by the Universities Federation for Animal Welfare (UFAW) studied the nature of noise in kennels and how it can be reduced. They also investigated the problems and potentially damaging effects high noise levels have on dogs in relation to stress and disease.

It is recognised that dogs have far superior hearing than humans; in fact they can detect sounds only a quarter of the level the human ear can detect.

Clearly, most people soon realise and accept these high levels of noise, which are potentially harmful to humans, will undoubtedly have a detrimental effect on the dogs as well. Therefore action has to be taken to reduce these high levels; ideally this should be considered, and as much potential noise as possible 'designed out' rather than relying on remedial measures.

From studies using a basic hand-held noise meter, in larger, older kennels holding 15-20 dogs with mesh/bar doors and open ceilings, readings of around 100-108 dB were obtained; clearly this is unacceptable for both dogs and staff. To try to reduce the overall level we started (and are continuing) to carry out a programme of improvements and remedial works. This work has taken the form of installing acoustic roof and wall cladding; and in the worst cases total demolition of the building and replacement with better-designed kennels.

At one centre the recent installation of an acoustic ceiling resulted in a reduction of approximately 13dB from an average of 108dB to 95dB. Although this is still high and in the critical range, it has appreciably improved and reduced the overall noise intensity and the building has become 'tolerable'. With improved management systems, we hope to further reduce the levels.

The following chart gives you some indication of everyday noise levels:

NOISE LEVELS	SOUND LEVEL IN dB	SOUND SOURCE
Harmful range:	140 130	• Jet engine • Industrial riveting hammer
Critical range:	120 117 90	• Propeller aircraft • Generator • Heavy vehicle
Safe range:	70 60 50 30	• Private car • Ordinary conversation • Ordinary office • Quiet bedroom

PRACTICAL MEASURES TO MITIGATE NOISE LEVELS (INTERNALLY)

To mitigate noise levels inside buildings, the solutions will be:

- design solutions
- engineered solutions
- acoustic materials
- management solutions

In some cases it will be a combination of all three elements.

The Harmful Effects of Noise on Dogs and People

When constructing new kennels, the number of kennels, design and choice of materials used will have the most noticeable effect on how the dogs react in the kennel, to staff, visitors and other dogs. Traditionally, typical kennels were and still are extremely noisy places; they are not pleasant to visit and create enormous amounts of stress for the dogs.

The good news is that there are designs and materials that can make significant improvements in reducing noise and stress to all concerned. The only disadvantage is that these are initially more expensive.

Reducing noise is just one of the many reasons why we advocate the construction of fewer kennels that are more home-like, and stress-reducing.

The initial capital cost will be higher, but the long-term benefits will more than compensate

Designs that reduce noise levels automatically improve the quality of the building environment for all concerned - dogs and people, and makes life so much more pleasant. It's a win-win situation.

If you are still in doubt about the incredible difference kennel design can make to noise and stress levels, please view the following videos of charity and boarding kennels:
www.kenneldesign.com/videos

Design Solutions

■ **Choose a single-line design that is purpose-built**
Ideally you should look at the single line design to reduce dog stress and therefore noise as much as possible. Design is the critical area and, if finances allow, you should look at a new, purpose-built building rather than adapting an existing one

■ **Offset kennels**
If you must have a double-line design, offset the kennels as much as possible so dogs do not look onto each other

■ **Dogs should not face other dogs**
Do you have external exercise runs that face other exercise areas? This can be a major source of noise with dogs able to see each other, particularly if animals are constantly being moved around. If so, look at installing visual barriers such as fencing, landscaping, etc

■ **Glass not bars**
Look at using glazed doors instead of bars. You will find it quite astonishing just how much more relaxed the dogs are. Even without finding scientific data to support this, it is evident when you compare the two systems.
Think of the kennel compartment as a 'complete room' with full-height dividing walls running up to ceiling level

■ **Zone the building**
Try to break up the building into smaller compartments using solid walls and doors. Ideally, there should be no more than 10 kennels in any one section. Some organisations have brought this figure down to six kennels.

■ **Zone the sections**
Try to keep ancillary activities separate from the kennel work.
Install separation doors into the buildings to reduce the amount of disturbance to other areas. Ideally these should be solid, half hour fire-resistant doors; these are durable and will help protect the building and animals in the event of a fire. These doors should be fitted with an overhead closing device to ensure they function as fire doors; this will also help reduce the noise breakout as it is an automatic system and lessens the chances of doors being left open. Ensure the doors have vision panels for safety

■ **Solid partition walls**
Try to construct partitions/dividing walls between kennels out of solid concrete block; this will help reduce the transmission of noise between sections/buildings

■ **Home-like rooms**
Think of making the kennel more like a room by adding full height walls and a ceiling. Even a lightweight suspended ceiling will make the kennel feel more room-like, private and secure so dogs settle much more easily

■ **Avoid long straight corridors**
Long, linear corridors increase the amount of excitability of the dogs within the building due to them being aware of staff/visitors, but not able to see them. Long, straight corridors can also act as 'handrails' for noise. As noise travels less effectively round corners, anything that can break up the flow is advantageous. Think of adding a kitchen or separation door midway to achieve this

■ **Use acoustic materials**
Use acoustic ceiling tiles to help absorb noise. Vinyl flooring in corridors will also help - although smooth, it is not a 'hard' surface and therefore does not bounce noise around so much

Engineering Solutions

■ **Do not use metal partitions**

Look at the construction of the building.

Do you have metal divisions/partitions? These can generate HIGH levels of noise and increase the reverberation times. It is strongly advised to avoid metal divisions, but, if you must, the only way to help combat some of the high noise levels produced by this type of finish is to sandwich a layer of polystyrene/polyurethane between sheets

■ **Glazing thickness**

Use a minimum of 6mm/ ¼" thick glass, or double-glazed kennels

■ **Dog doors/hatches - avoid metal**

Use plastic type sliding hatches instead of single sheet metal.

■ **Add a ceiling to kennels**

Add a plasterboard ceiling with an overlay of insulation quilt. A secondary installation of an acoustic ceiling tile under the plasterboard would help reduce reverberant sound levels inside the building. The installation of an acoustic ceiling and wall baffles will bring significant improvements to the noise levels and reduce reverberation times (ensure that you specify a totally moisture resistant tile if you are installing a lightweight tile system).

Acoustic Materials

The installation of acoustic materials to the ceiling and any high-level areas will act as highly efficient sound absorbers, i.e. a reduction of sound within the room and a reduction in reverberation times.

Most of the proprietary ceiling tiles used in the kennel environment use similar materials and construction methods, i.e. a glass wool backing with a decorative microporous surface, laid in a suspended grid. The materials used also increase the insulation within the building. The tiles should have an overlay of insulation quilt.

The more common tiles used are the Hygiene range manufactured by Ecophon, or Parafon Fjord by Armstrong; both of these systems have excellent acoustic properties and are highly recommended for use in the kennel environment.

The tile should have the following properties:

■ A thickness of between 25-40mm (1" - 1½")

■ A moisture resistance of at least 90%

■ A decorative finish suitable for cleaning with a cloth. Products are available that will withstand cleaning by pressure washing, but these are expensive and are normally reserved for areas requiring high levels of hygiene such as food preparation rooms in commercial suppliers.

■ A product with a light coloured finish. The majority of tiles used are white, as this offers the highest level of light reflection. However, most of the larger manufacturers only offer tiles in a limited range of pastel colours.

Management Solutions

- Change metal feeding bowls for plastic; it is surprising how much noise is generated by dogs pushing bowls around the floor, or by staff dropping a metal bowl. If a dog will not eat from a metal bowl, but will accept food by hand - it may be that the dog is afraid of the bowl as it is so noisy. Try changing to ceramic, plastic or rubber-footed bowls

- Look at your management systems, minor changes here can help reduce noise (e.g. do visitors really need to see *all* of the dogs, can you provide staff and separate visitor zones?)

- Change metal mop buckets to plastic to help reduce noise

- Do you have noise-producing equipment in the kennel building (e.g. boilers, laundry equipment or ventilation fans?) Old equipment is not only less efficient than new, it also tends to be noisier

- Have strict opening and closing times. This provides quiet times for the dogs, and a routine for dogs and people

- Look at building higher quality, larger size, higher fee kennels with a reduction in the overall numbers

- Can you manage the dogs more effectively? For example in outside exercise paddocks, allow only certain areas of access at any one time to reduce negative excitement (barking and excitement due to frustration or stress)

- Improve your environmental and behavioural enrichment programme. A happy, relaxed, physically and mentally enriched dog is less likely to bark

Conclusion

The ONLY true way to reduce noise in kennels is
to construct purpose-built kennels that encompass
ALL of the design suggestions in this book

For older buildings that have been converted or are of a poor quality and standard, it might be cheaper and more cost effective in the long term to think about replacing these with new kennels. Again, this all needs to be part of your business philosophy and statement. Correct design and specification will go a long way to help resolving your problems.

Certainly if you have a serious noise complaint that is being investigated by the local authority, you will have to demonstrate ways in which the situation can be improved.

For certain locations there may be no alternative but to construct an indoor kennel design to manage the external noise in a controlled manner.

PRACTICAL MEASURES TO MITIGATE NOISE LEVELS (EXTERNALLY)

The majority of noise complaints for kennels relate to when the dogs are being fed, exercised, or are out in the external runs, or when dogs are being moved around the site. The owner will have a greater level of control over noise when the dogs are inside the building. Control is lessened when the dogs are brought out to the external runs.

There are many factors for how noise can affect neighbouring properties. Generally the location and the physical distance between the kennels and neighbouring properties have the greatest influence.

The following graph will give a good indication of how noise levels rapidly decrease once in the open. As previously stated, it is the character and duration of the noise that potential complainants can find so irritating.

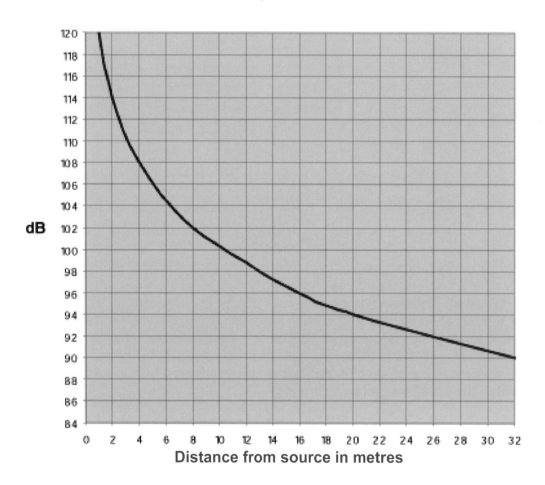

How Sound Levels Vary with Distance from Source

Distance from source in metres

Practical Solutions

■ **Neighbours**
Site kennels as far away from neighbours as possible

■ **Dogs should not face other dog runs**
Arrange exercise runs so that they do not face other runs or exercise/play areas

■ **Dogs should not face exercise paddocks/play areas**
One of the most commonly seen errors - you should NEVER site a play or exercise area where kennelled dogs can watch. It's extremely frustrating for confined dogs to watch other dogs playing or being walked. If in this situation, improve it by putting up a solid visual barrier - shrubs and landscaping can be extremely helpful in these situations

■ **Earth bunds**
Look at installing earth bunds (mounds) all around the kennels; on new constructions this can come from the site excavations. To be effective, the bunding requires to be at least 2.5m/8ft high, (tree shelterbelts are not suitable sound barriers). The bunding can then be landscaped to provide an aesthetic, visual barrier for your centre

■ **Geography**
If purchasing a new site, look at the surrounding geography. Is the site in a valley where strong prevailing winds could carry any noise onto potential neighbours? If so, can you position any non-kennel buildings in between? Although this will not stop the problem totally, it will help

■ **Solid walls**
Install solid partitions to help prevent dogs from seeing each other and racing up and down the exercise runs

■ **Reduce mesh in walkways/corridors**
If you have full height mesh safety corridors, look at replacing these by building a solid wall to 1m/3ft high with either mesh panels above or, better still acoustic louvres

■ **Install acoustic materials**
Install acoustic materials to the underside of the external exercise run roofing; this will help absorb some of the noise, and provide better shading with cooler exercise runs during the summer

■ **Manage and zone non-kennel areas**
Look at your site management techniques. Can you isolate any non-kennel works from other procedures?

■ **Minimise disturbance**
Try to minimise the amount of disturbance to the animals from non-kennel staff and visitors

■ **Landscaping**
Look at planting trees/shrubs around the site. Although having some physical effect on noise levels in themselves, they will have a far greater impact on reducing noise levels when used as visual barriers to prevent animals from seeing each other, or visitors walking around the site. Therefore landscaping can help to reduce noise levels substantially. Anything you can do to make dogs feel more at home helps them settle, just as in their home garden

■ **Acoustic Barriers**
A wide variety of acoustic barriers/fencing is available (often seen on motorways or commercial applications), and that either reflective or absorptive. On their own barriers won't totally resolve the noise issues, but they can help

CASE STUDY: A QUIET LIFE

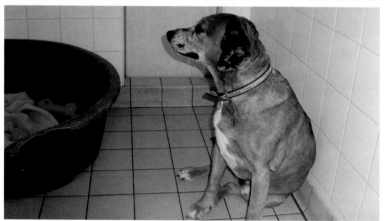

Organisation: Dogs Trust Bridgend
Location: UK, South Wales
Kennels Type: Indoor/Semi-outdoor
Kennels Function: Rescue and Rehoming
Number of Kennels: 44
Kennel Size Sleep: 1.8 x 2.0m/ 6ft x 6ft 6"
Kennel Size Exercise: 1.8 x 2.6m/ 6ft x 8ft 6"
Year Built: 2002

www.dogstrust.org.uk

THIS QUIET, RURAL LOCATION WAS THE ANSWER FOR A RESCUE CENTRE FOR IMPROVING DOG WELFARE AND REHOMING RATES. THIS PERFECT SETTING PROVIDES THE SPACE AND FREEDOM TO EXERCISE DOGS OFF-LEAD IN SECURE AREAS

DOGS TRUST BRIDGEND

TIME TO UPGRADE

The Dogs Trust has had a rehoming centre in Bridgend for over 30 years. The original premises were inadequate for any level of expansion, and the buildings were not of a standard that was conducive to a modern forward-thinking charity. However, the main area of concern was the lack of any off-lead exercise facility on the site. So, in 1998 the charity decided that it had outgrown its old premises and started looking for a new location.

Once a decision had been made to relocate, the next aim was to find suitable premises. Ideally, Dogs Trust wanted a site in the same vicinity as the old centre.

Matthew Taylor, Head of Property for Dogs Trust was tasked with this project – this was far easier said than done. Finding suitable premises can be a long and time-consuming business. Matthew commented that, at one stage, they began to wonder if it would even be possible to find suitable premises. The process involved physically driving around the area, knocking on doors, looking at maps, writing to existing kennels and smallholdings - in fact, any method he could think of to locate a suitable property. Luckily, it was the centre manager, Beverley Price, who finally located the current six acre site, just two miles from the original one.

PLANNING ISSUES

The site was purchased subject to gaining planning consent. An application was submitted, which showed a circular design of kennels with open mesh fronts.

Once submitted, this scheme brought a whole raft of concerns from neighbours with the local newspaper running scaremongering stories such as '80 dogs running free in the countryside'. Clearly this was totally unfounded - they had taken the term 'running free' to mean uncontrolled, whereas it just means exercising individual dogs off the lead in a secure area! However, it set alarm bells ringing for the charity.

The planning application was refused. Dogs Trust began an appeal against the decision, while at the same time doing some soul searching. The charity decided to look at alternative designs that would enable them to remove some of the local residents' concerns about the potential noise issues.

Wisely, Dogs Trust continued with their appeal for the first scheme, and running in parallel to it they submitted a second and far more radical scheme.
Thankfully, the second scheme was granted full planning consent and allowed it to overcome the neighbours' concerns about potential noise issues.

Centre Manager Beverley Price with Jet

WHAT ARE YOU MOST PLEASED WITH?

Beverley summed this question up simply by saying, 'less stressed dogs'. The well designed and constructed kennels, with space to allow dogs the opportunity for off-lead exercise and being able to run together in secure fenced paddocks. She is adamant that by providing a relaxing environment for the dogs it has enabled the centre to rehome more dogs and reduce the levels of stress.

It was clear to see that Beverley takes great pride in the centre and the work it does. The enthusiasm and continual quest to look for better systems, and ways of improving the quality of life for the dogs in her care was noticeable - and was reflected throughout the centre and all staff.

WHAT WOULD YOU DO DIFFERENTLY?

The only area for improvement given the opportunity to build again would be more storage areas for things like mops and brooms and a laundry for each building.

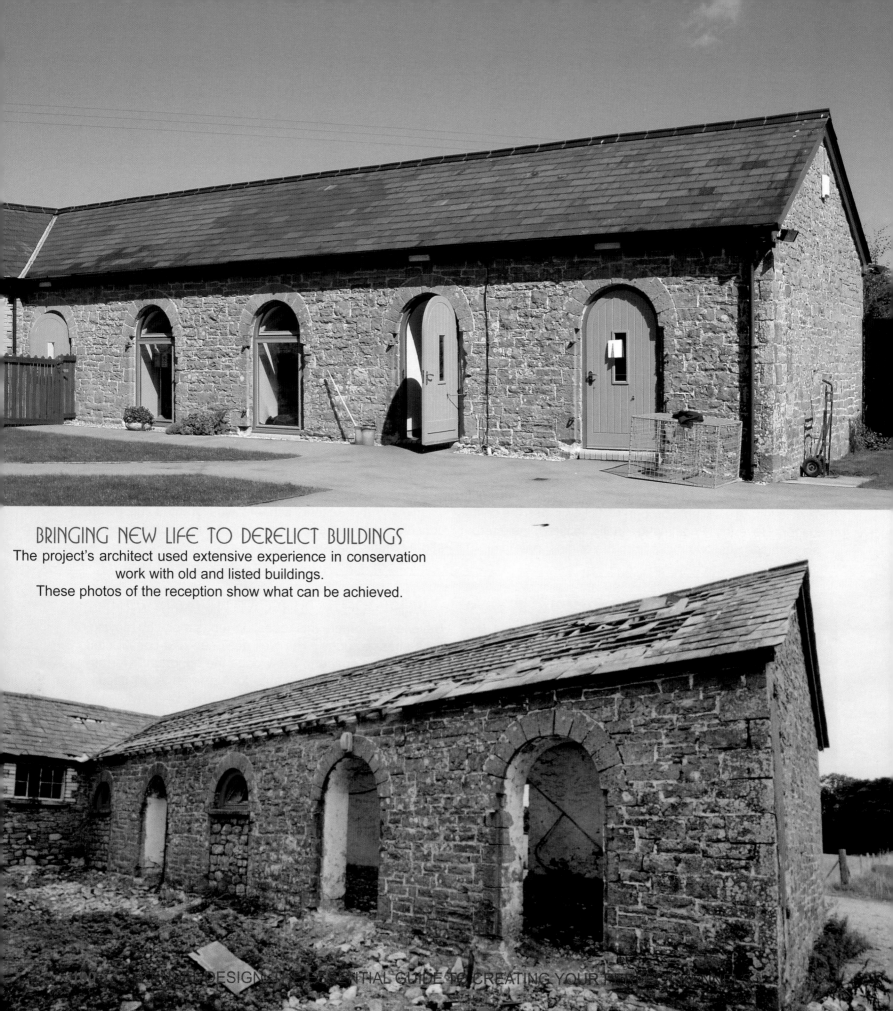

BRINGING NEW LIFE TO DERELICT BUILDINGS

The project's architect used extensive experience in conservation work with old and listed buildings.

These photos of the reception show what can be achieved.

PLANNING GRANTED

In the early days, the granting of planning permission caused great resentment towards the charity from some of the local residents. Even though they had obtained legal consent to construct the centre, Matthew admitted he had many sleepless nights. He was concerned about potential noise issues, further complaints, and any ill-feeling that the charity had secured planning consent against the local residents wishes.

CONSTRUCTION BEGINS

Construction commenced in 2001 with completion in June 2002. Once the construction phase was complete, there was still the task of involving the local residents and inviting them along to the official opening to show what the charity had achieved. This move proved to be a great success and has ensured that the centre has flourished and has been a positive asset to the locality.

KENNEL DESIGN

The design of the kennels is fairly traditional in that it is single line (the dogs do not face each other) with each sleep area having an attached exercise run, to which the dogs gain access via a sliding hatch. However, the difference here is that the exercise runs have glass on the outside, and the sleep areas have bars on the inside - a reversal of the traditional layout. Staff access corridors to the internal section, and public access via the exercise run corridor.

THE WINNING DESIGN

This winning design overcame the noise issues because it incorporated double-glazed units in UPVC for the external runs *instead of* open bars or mesh. The use of glass does reduce the level of negative excitement for the dogs and they settle far better, particularly in a rehoming centre that attracts a large number of visitors.

The main rehoming building has a total of 20 kennels. The second building (not open to the public) is three buildings in one - it holds the newly admitted dogs, puppies and isolation area.

Customers arrive and ask: "Have you got any dogs here? We can't hear any barking!"

RENOVATING BUILDINGS

In addition to the two new kennel buildings, new infrastructure, exercise paddocks and landscaping, the charity completely renovated the range of existing stone buildings on the site. These include reception, offices and the veterinary suite. These are very much the focal point and provide a very pleasant entrance into the centre.

As shown in the photographs opposite, the new reception is now a beautiful building, inviting to both staff and visitors.

SITE ISSUES

The site has large variations in ground levels, which does create additional issues with access and the type and scale of building that could economically be constructed. Simple things (like moving heavy supplies around the site) do become more problematic on a sloping site than on a level one, and the construction costs are higher.

GOOD DESIGN WORKS

When we asked Beverley what difference moving to a new purpose-built centre has made to the rescue dogs, she had no hesitation in saying: *"The overall design of the kennels, the beautiful and relaxing environment has made it so much easier to rehome dogs, equally important is the fact that the dogs are so much more relaxed."*

The centre provides an enjoyable experience for the dogs in their care as well as visitors at the centre. Beverley is still amazed when customers arrive and ask *"Have you got any dogs here? We can't hear any barking!"*.

WORKING WITH THE COMMUNITY

The Bridgend centre was the first Dogs Trust site to have a purpose-built veterinary suite. This has allowed the centre to develop a neutering programme - which has proved to be very successful, with a noticeable reduction in the number of unwanted puppies in the area. An extremely successful project.

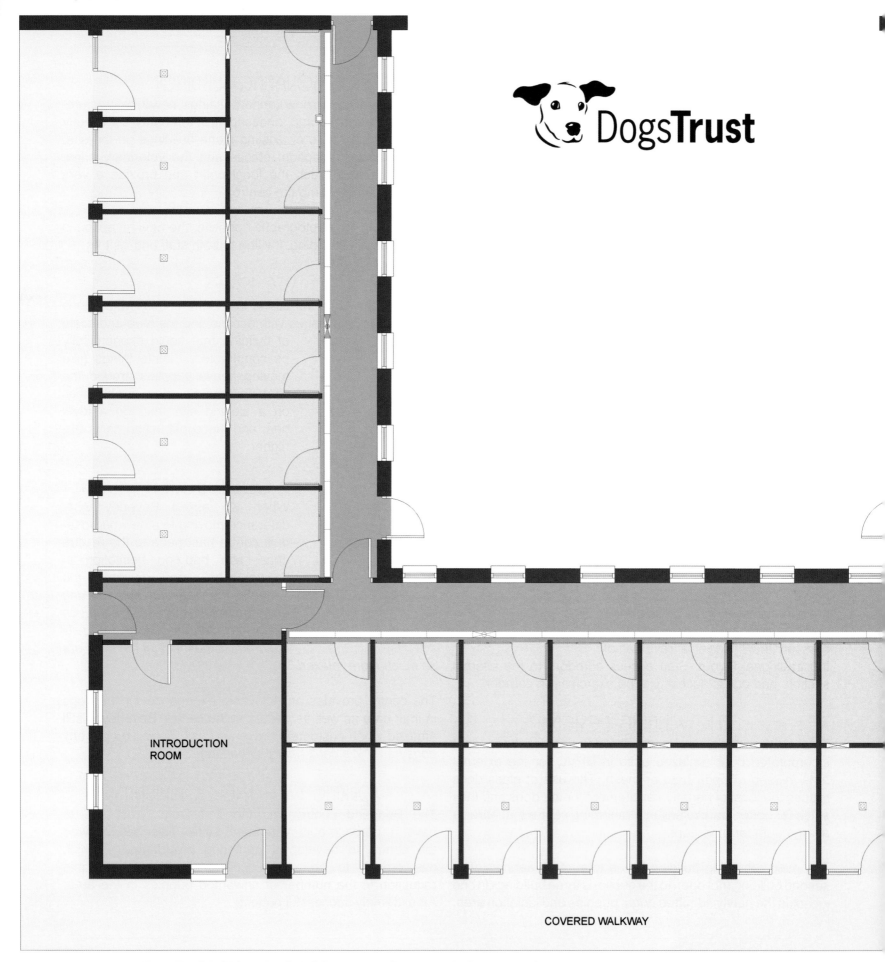

INTRODUCTION
ROOM

COVERED WALKWAY

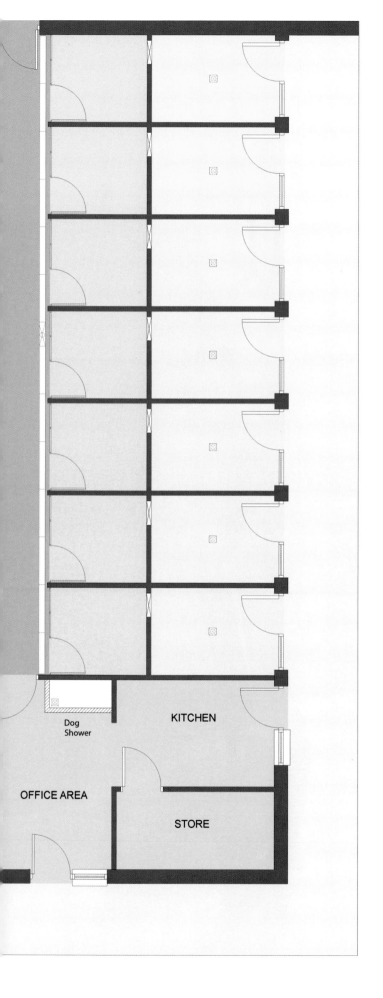

Dog
Shower

KITCHEN

OFFICE AREA

STORE

REHOMING

We are looking for the perfect home. Can you help? Some of us may bark a lot, but only because we want you to notice us.

Local Authority Planning Guidance Regarding Noise Issues

South Holland District Council in the UK produced the following guidance, and kindly granted us permission to publish it.

Supplementary Planning Guidance (1999) – Location of Premises For The Boarding And Breeding Of Dogs And Other Animals has been produced to provide more detailed information and guidance when considering planning applications.

It is also a useful guide to anyone considering a business that involves dogs.

Location of Premises for the Boarding and Breeding of Dogs and Other Animals

NOISE ISSUES

Supplementary Planning Guidance
Adopted December 1999

CONTENTS

1.   Introduction

1.1   Purpose

This Supplementary Planning Guidance (SPG) deals with the issue of noise impact from animal boarding and breeding premises and the locational matters that arise. Its purpose is to provide a standard publicised procedure for assessing such planning proposals. This enables:

- A consistent approach to be taken to the assessment of comparable applications

- A balance to be achieved between allowing such development and protecting the reasonable amenities of residual and other uses in the District

It also provides a means of assessing the suitability of new proposals for noise-sensitive uses (for example, new housing) in the vicinity of boarding and breeding premises.

1.2   So when will the SPG apply?

It will be a material consideration when determining planning applications for the development of new premises or for the extension of existing ones. (The SPG is not retrospective so it does not apply to developments that are permitted prior to its adoption). But when is it necessary to apply for planning permission to build or use premises for the boarding, breeding or keeping of animals? This is established by reference to the Town and Country Planning Acts, related Statutory Instruments and the particulars of the proposal.

The Council's advice by the way of practice is as follows:

- For a case involving less than 7 adult dogs – may possibly represent a change of use. Discuss your proposal with your local authority. In determining whether a planning application will be required, regard will be given to the circumstances of the case. This includes the key consideration of location, also the type of property, and the type and nature of the activity (particularly breeding)

- A case involving 7 or more adult dogs – Council will always require the submission of a planning application in order that we can consider change of use

   So, planning permission may be required irrespective of whether the premises are to be run as a business. If it is to be a business then generally permission will have to be sought. (Note that the requirement for planning permission is quite separate from any need for a boarding or breeding licence, which may be required under other legislation.)

The SPG will also be a material consideration when determining planning applications for noise-sensitive uses, where the amenities of those uses could be significantly reduced due to the noise impact of nearby animal boarding and breeding premises.

1.3   Adoption

The SPG has been the subject of close liaison between the Council's Housing and Planning Services and Environment and Leisure Services. It has been prepared in accordance with the criteria set out in the Department of the Environment, Transport and the Regions' Planning Policy Guidance Note 12 'Development Plans' (paragraphs 3.15 to 3.17), and has been adopted by the Council following public consultation. The SPG supplements the Development Plan, is consistent with it and will be a material consideration carrying substantial weight in the determination of planning applications

1.4   Decision-making

Hence the SPG is for use in the decision-making process and it also provides useful advice to prospective applicants

2. Context

2.1 Minimising the adverse impact of noise

The Government has provided local authorities with guidance on the use of their planning powers to minimise the adverse impact of noise. This is set out in the Department of the Environment's Planning Policy Guidance Note 24 'Planning and Noise'. It outlines the considerations to be taken into account in determining planning applications both for noise-generating activities and for noise-sensitive developments. So PPG24 (UK planning guidance) provides a context for the Council's preparation and use of this SPG, relative to the principle of location for animal boarding and breeding establishments.

2.2 Noise-sensitive uses

In respect of noise-sensitive uses (be they existing or proposed), typically this will be housing but as paragraph 6 of PPG24 states – it can include hospitals and schools. Offices can also be noise–sensitive (see Annex 1 of PPG24). Regard will be had to the circumstances of the case.

2.3 Noise impact reduction

Paragraphs 13 and 14 of PPG24 highlight how engineering, layout and administrative measures can influence noise impact, and reduce it. Preferably the applicant will discuss these with the Council officers prior to submission of the planning application so the proposals will incorporate appropriate measures. The Council may need to secure measures through the use of planning conditions (paragraph 15 to 19 of PPG24 refer).

2.4 Development proposals

Within the adopted **South Holland District Local Plan** Policy E1 provides a broad range of assessment criteria for dealing with development proposals generally. Policy E1 seeks amongst other things to maintain amenity and resist pollution. This provides a policy context for this SPG. There will also be other considerations that are material to the determination of planning applications. However, the issue of noise impact is of particular relevance in the case of proposals for animal boarding and breeding premises.

2.5 Matters affecting noise impact

Noise impact can be influenced by a number of factors. Matters such as the management of such establishments, working conditions and animal welfare are primarily regulated by non-planning legislation. For example, existing premises may cause a level of noise impact so high that it can be counted as a 'statutory nuisance'. In such a situation the local authority has power, under environmental protection law, to serve notices requiring noise levels to be reduced.

2.6 Matters within planning control

This SPG can only deal with matters capable of planning control. As such it deals fundamentally with whether this particular land use is appropriate in a given situation. Also, it does not necessarily distinguish between individual types or breeds of animal.

2.7 Detailed method for assessing proposals for dog establishments

The SPG presents a detailed method for assessing proposals for dog establishments as they tend to give rise to more severe and commonly occurring noise impact than do establishments for other animals (such as cats). Nevertheless the underlying methodology will be relevant and used as a basis for assessing noise impact of the proposals irrespective of animal type.

3. Basis

3.1 Proven methods of measurement

There is no specific guidance nor recommended noise level standards relating to animal boarding or breeding establishments. In the absence of these, reliance must be placed upon proven methods of measurement and assessment published elsewhere.

3.2 Existing background level noise

In general, a noise is liable to provoke complaints whenever it exceeds the background noise by a certain margin or when it attains a certain absolute level. Noise levels at or below the existing background level are unlikely to give rise to complaints.

3.3 Relevant noise control documents

This fundamental acoustic principle underpins the guidance contained in the most relevant noise control documents, BS 4142: 1997 'Rating industrial noise affecting mixed residential and industrial areas' and BS 5228: Part 1 1997 'Noise and vibration control on construction and open site'. The methodology set out in this SPG is based on those documents.

3.4 Distance from noise-sensitive locations

Operational experience shows that the distance between an animal boarding/breeding establishment and noise-sensitive locations is key to the incidence of complaints. The distance required will depend upon the specific circumstances of the individual case, particularly the background noise level. So the SPG provides the procedure by which one can assess whether there is an adequate separation distance for a particular proposal. It provides safeguards to this particular type of commercial operation in any given location and at the same time ensures reasonable protection to nearby noise-sensitive premises.

3.5 Assumptions

The attached Technical Appendix, which forms part of the SPG defines the methodology to be used. It also explains the principles behind the various assumptions made to establish a consistent approach to what is, by its very nature, a variable source of noise. At the end of the Appendix are two case studies providing worked examples of the procedure.

3.6 Source noise data

The source noise data (in Figure D1 of the Technical Appendix) is extrapolated from measured data and is assumed to be representative of conditions existing at commercial kennels.

3.7 Separation distances

The separation distances evolved from the SPG assessment are consistent with those existing within the District where there is no history of complaints of noise nuisance.

4. Overview

4.1 To be submitted with application
The onus will be on the applicant to submit as part of the planning application:

- Indication of whether the premises are for boarding or for breeding (or both)

- The number of dogs, being the total number of boarders or in the case of breeding then the total number of adult dogs (NB. If the owner/operator of the premises intends to keep their own pet dogs on the site then these must be included in the totals given)

- Scaled plans of the design, layout and construction of the kennels and any runs proposed

- An indication of the intended occupancy of any dwelling forming a part of the proposals, and its relationship to the boarding and breeding operation

4.2 Matters assessed through the stage-by-stage procedure
These are the matters that will then be assessed through the stage-by-stage procedure set out in the Technical Appendix and may be controlled through the use of planning conditions on any permission granted.

4.3 Influences on noise impact
In addition to information provided by the applicant, the assessment procedure also takes into account the following influences on noise impact:

- The background noise level (so regard is given to existing noise levels at that location)

- Specific factors about the location of the proposal including the types of ground and any screening between the noise source and the noise-sensitive premises in the vicinity

- The influence of prevailing wind on noise impact

- Where there are already boarding and breeding establishments within the vicinity of the proposed premises and noise-sensitive locations then the cumulative noise impact of existing and new kennels will be used

TECHNICAL APPENDIX

Method for the assessment of dog noise from boarding and breeding establishments

Foreword

This assessment method is intended to provide supplementary planning guidance on the suitability of locations for dog boarding and breeding establishments with open-air runs. The standard will cover all new kennels and those established kennels seeking expansion, including any cumulative effects upon neighbouring noise-sensitive locations.

The propagation of airborne sound is highly complex, being influenced by a range of atmospheric effects, ground absorption or reflection and attenuation from barriers. In general, a noise is liable to provoke complaints whenever it exceeds the background noise by a certain margin or when it attains a certain absolute level. Noise levels at or below the existing background noise level are unlikely to give rise to complaints.

The methodology is that of assessing the specific noise level of the source, determined as an equivalent continuous A weighted sound pressure level (L_{Aeq}) against the existing background noise level (L_{A90}) at noise-sensitive locations.

For the purposes of this assessment unless otherwise stated, the relevant definitions and measurement procedures given in the following British Standards shall apply:

(i)   BS 4142: 1997   Rating industrial noise affecting mixed residential and industrial areas
(ii)   BS 5228: Part 1 1997   Noise and vibration control on construction and open sites
(iii) BS 7445: Part 1, 2, 3 1991 Description and measurement of environment noise

Interpretation

For the purposes of this assessment, the following additional interpretations and assessment criteria are to be used:

1. Background noise level (L_{A90})

Measurements to be made at a position close to a noise-sensitive receiver location in the open air and at least 3.5m/12ft from any reflecting surface other than the ground. Precautions shall be taken to minimise any interference on the noise readings from any sources such as wind, heavy rain, etc.

Measurement time intervals shall be sufficient to obtain a representative value of the daytime (0700 – 1900 hours) background noise level. The measurement time interval shall be at least 30 minutes comprising 10 minute periods of which the arithmetic average shall be taken as representative.

For multiple receiver locations where it is not practical to measure the background noise level at all receiver locations it will be acceptable to measure the background noise level at some other position (P) where is it presumed to be equivalent and report the reasons for presuming it to be equivalent.

All receiver locations shall be assessed according to their use classification.

2. Activity Noise Level - L_{Aeq}

Baseline source data is representative of 1 medium sized dog in the open air barking at a distance of 10m/32ft for a cumulative period of 10 minutes in any hourly period.

For noise assessment purposes the number of dogs barking on any site shall be assumed as:

- Boarding   Total number of dogs x 0.6

- Breeding   Adult dogs + 25% (puppies) x 0.5
  (for clarification purposes any decimal place shall represent 1 dog)

  Adult dogs to be determined as per the breed categories in **Table 1** (see the following page)

Operational constraints supported by planning conditions may be appropriate in certain cases it is assumed all dogs will be housed in insulated kennels during nighy-time. Where there is to be any deviation from the standard criteria a justification for doing so shall be reported

Table 1 - List of Breeds

Toy (Dog becomes adult at approx 6–9 months)	Small (Dog becomes adult at approx 9–12 months)	Medium Dog becomes adult at approx 12–18 months)	Large (Dog becomes adult at approx 18–22 months)	Giant (Dog becomes adult at approx 22 months)
BREEDS	**BREEDS**	**BREEDS**	**BREEDS**	**BREEDS**
Chihuahua	Basenji	Afghan Hound	Bassett Hound	Alaskan Malamute
Dachshund (min.)	Bedlington Terrier	Airedale Terrier	Belgian Shepherd Dog	Anatolian
English Toy Terrier	Border Terrier	Austrilian Cattle Dog	Bernese Mountain Dog	Shepherd Dog
German Spitz	Boston Terrier	Beagle	Borzoi	Bloodhound
Maltese	Cairn Terrier	Bearded Collie	Bouvier des Flandres	Bullmastiff
Miniature Pinscher	Cavalier King	Border Collie	Boxer	Great Dane
Papillion	Charles Spaniel	Cocker Spaniel	Briard	Irish Wolfhound
Pekingese	Dachshund (std)	Elkhound	Bulldog	Komondor
Pomeranian	Dandie Dinmot	English Springer	Bull Terrier	Mastiff
Poodle (toy)	Fox Terrier	French Bulldog	Chow Chow	Newfoundland
Yorkshire Terrier	Japanese Spitz	Hungarian Puli	Clumber Spaniel	Pyrenean
	Lancashire Healer	Keeshond	Curly Coated Retriever	Mountain Dog
	Lhasa Apso	Norwegian Buhund	Dalmatian	St Bernard
	Manchester Terrier	Pharaoh Hound	Deerhound	
	Pug	Pointer	Dobermann	
	Schipperke	Rough Collie	English Setter	
	Schnauzer (min)	Saluki	Estrela Mountain Dog	
	Scottish Terrier	Schnauzer (std)	Flat Coated Retriever	
	Sealyham Terrier	Siberian Husky	German Shepherd Dog	
	Shetland Sheepdog	Soft-coated	German Shorthaired	
	Shin Tzu	Wheaten Terrier	Pointer	
	Tibetan Spaniel	Staffordshire	Giant Schnauzer	
	Tibetan Terrier	Bull Terrier	Golden Retriever	
	Welsh Terrier	Welsh Corgi	Gordon Setter	
	West Highland	Welsh Springer	Greyhound	
		Whippet	Hovawort	
			Hungarian Vizsla	
			Irish Setter	
			Irish Water Spaniel	
			Japanese Akita	
			Labrador Retriever	
			Large Munsterlander	
			Maremma Sheepdog	
			Old English Sheepdog	
			Otterhound	
			Poodle (std)	
			Rottweiler	
			Weimaraner	
			Rhodesian Ridgeback	

Figure D1 - Dog Noise at 10m/32ft

No. of Dogs	Activity (L_{Aeq})
1	65.6
2	68.6
3	70.4
4	71.6
5	72.6
6	73.4
7	74.1
8	74.6
9	75.1
10	75.6
11	76.0
12	76.4
13	76.7
14	77.1
15	77.4
16	77.6
17	77.9
18	78.1
19	78.4
20	78.6
21	78.8
22	79.0
23	79.2
24	79.4
25	79.6

Acoustic Spectrum of 1 Dog Barking

Frequency (Hz)	125	250	500	1000	2000	TOTAL
DB (A)	26.0	38.5	60.9	63.1	55.4	65.6

3. Distance adjustment

Consideration should be given to the nature of the ground over which the sound is being propagated. Note: **Hard ground** is taken to refer to ground surfaces that reflect sound, for example, paved areas, rolled asphalt and surface water. **Soft ground** is taken to refer to surfaces, absorbent to sound, for example, grassland, cultivated fields or plantations. Where ground cover between the source and receiver is a combination of hard and soft, it is described as mixed. Soft ground attenuation does not apply for propagation distances less than 25m/82ft.

The effect of screening and soft ground attenuation should not normally be combined. Either the attenuations from screening and hard ground propagations or the attenuation of soft ground, whichever is the greater, should be taken. At distances over 300m/985ft noise predictions should be treated with caution, especially where a soft ground correction factor has been applied, because of the increasing importance of meteorological effects. Where there are clearly screening effects both at the source or receiver positions, some adjustment may need to be made.

For propagations over mixed soft and hard ground, additional attenuation due to soft ground (Ks – Kh) should be reduced according to the proportion of soft ground (e.g. for 25% soft ground 0.25 (Ks – Kh) should be used. Unless otherwise agreed, for calculation purposes the source point shall be taken as the geometric centre of the runs

Figure D2 - Distance adjustment K for activity L_{Aeq}

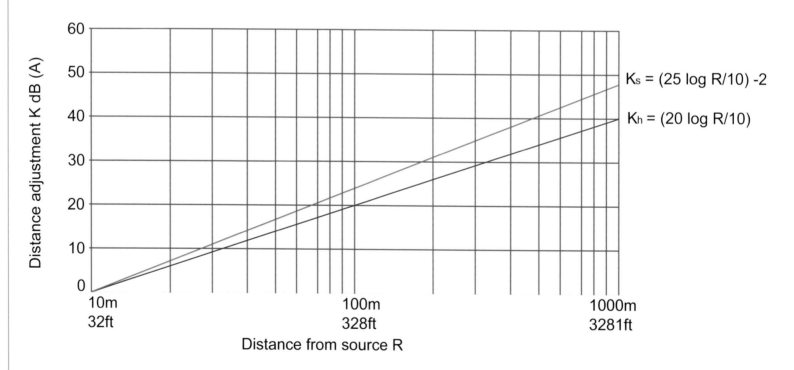

$K_s = (25 \log R/10) -2$

$K_h = (20 \log R/10)$

NOTE: K_s = Soft Ground K_h = Hard Ground

4. Screen effects of barriers (Figure D3)

The accurate determination of the effectiveness of a barrier is a complex process. Knowledge of sound pressure levels at separate frequencies and also of the geometry of the receiving positions in relation to the source and the barrier are required.

Calculations may be made in octave bands instead of 'A' weightings to provide a more accurate barrier attenuation - if the octave band sound levels and the positions of the sources, receiver and barrier are known. The acoustic spectrum in Figure D1 should be revised in accordance with the activity L_{Aeq} for the number of dogs being assessed. The barrier attenuation can be calculated from Figure D3. The result of this analysis should be logarithmically summed and weighted to provide an 'A' weighted level.

(As a working approximation, if there is a barrier or other topographic feature between the source and the receiving position, assume an approximate attenuation (reduction) of 5dB when the dogs are just visible to the receiver over the noise barrier, and of 10dB when the noise screen completely hides them from the receiver. High topographical features and specifically designed and positioned noise barriers could provide greater attenuation.)

Figure D3 - Screening effect of barriers

a) Illustration of path difference (a - b - c) introduced by a barrier

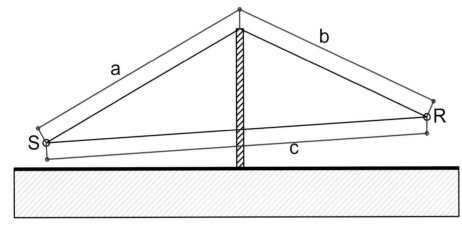

S = source 0.5m/20" height
R = receiver 1.5m/5ft height

b) Barrier attenuation at different freqencies of sound

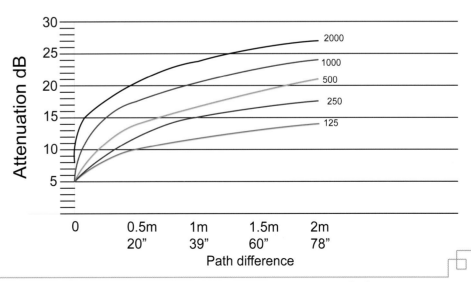

5. Prevailing wind direction (Figure D4)

In anything other than an idealised atmosphere, sound propagation (transmission) is likely to be subject to some degree of additional attenuation (reduction) or increase because of both atmospheric effects, and the direction of the noise source. For sound propagation (transmission) close to the ground, sound velocity gradients, (which can be caused by wind or temperature) have a big influence on noise levels received at a distance.

The prevailing wind for eastern England based on typical meteorological data is from within the 165 – 255 degree sector (Figure D4) and the receiver locations within the downwind 345 – 75 degree sector will potentially be subject to the greater impact. Receiver locations other than downwind of the noise source are likely to benefit from attenuated noise levels.

For the purpose of this assessment, a penalty correction of +3dB shall be added to specific noise level for noise-sensitive locations within the 345 – 75 degree sector (i.e. downwind of the prevailing wind sector).

Figure D4 - Prevailing wind direction

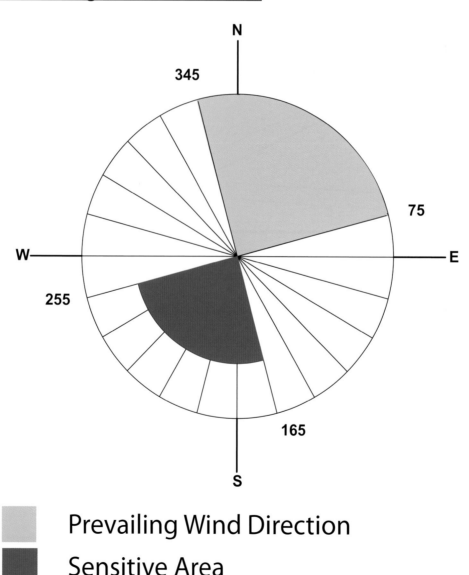

Prevailing Wind Direction

Sensitive Area

6. Cumulative Impact of Boarding and Breeding Kennels

Where there are existing kennels, or new kennels are proposed to be located within an area, each kennel unit shall be assessed separately and the resulting specific noise level values shall be logarithmatically summed to produce a cumulative value at noise-sensitive receiver locations, which shall then be assessed against the background level.

7. Assessment Criteria

The objective shall be that the specific noise level does not exceed the background noise level.

Assessment Method

Stage 1 Determine background noise level (L_{A90}) at the noise-sensitive receiver locations.

Stage 2 Determine number of dogs to be used for assessment purposes in relation to boarding/breeding.

Stage 3 Determine activity noise level (L_{Aeq}) from Figure D1

Stage 4 Determine the distance adjustments from Figure D2 for soft ground, hard ground or mixed ground

Stage 5 Determine the screening attenuations from Figure D3 and add this to the distance adjustments for either hard or mixed ground.

Stage 6 Using the greater attenuation value, subtract it from the activity noise level and determine the specific noise level at the receiver location.

Stage 7 Add the prevailing wind penalty correction (+ 3dB) to the specific noise-sensitive locations within the 345 – 75 degree sector (downwind of the kennels). Figure D4

Stage 8 Assess the specific noise level against the background noise level.

Stage 9 For cumulative assessment follow stages 1 – 7 for each kennel unit, and then having summed logarithmically, determine a cumulative specific noise value and assess this against the background level.

For examples see Case Study 1 and Case Study 2

Case Study 1

Boarding kennels housing 20 dogs with outside runs facing eastwards, screens along southern and northern elevations by 1.5 metre high walls.

Dwelling A: situated 400m/1312ft to the south-west where background noise level is 37 LA 90T.
Dwelling B: situated 400m/1312ft to the north-east besides a road where background noise level is 40 LA 90T.

Stage 1	Dwelling A: $L_{A90} = 37$ Dwelling B $L_{A90} = 40$						
Stage 2	Number of dogs (20 x 0.6 = 12)						
Stage 3 (D1)	Hz	125	250	500	1	2	L_{Aeq}
	1 Dog	26.0 +10.8	38.5 +10.8	60.9 +10.8	63.1 10.8	55.4 +10.8	65.6
	12 dogs	**36.8**	**49.3**	**71.7**	**73.9**	**66.2**	**76.4**
Stage 4 (D2)	400m (hard)	-32	-32	-32	-32	-32	
		4.8	17.3	39.7	41.9	34.2	44.4
Stage 5/6 (D3)	1.5m Screen (20m source point)	- 5	- 6	- 7	- 7	- 8	
		0.2	11.3	32.7	34.9	26.2	**37.3**
Stage 7	Prevailing wind correction for Dwelling B Specific noise level (37) + correction (3) = 40 L_{Aeq}						
Stage 8	Dwelling A: Specific noise level (37) – background level (37) = 0 Dwelling B: Specific noise level (40) – background level (40) = 0						

Case Study 1: Boarding Kennels (20 Adult Dogs)

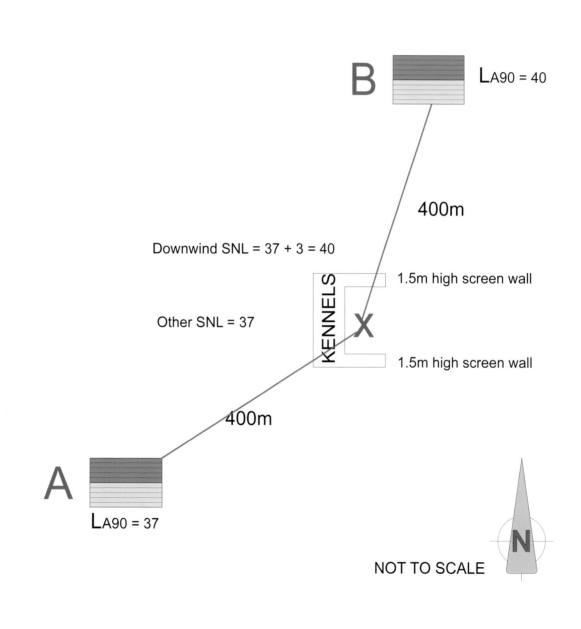

ROAD

B $L_{A90} = 40$

400m

Downwind SNL = 37 + 3 = 40

1.5m high screen wall

KENNELS

Other SNL = 37

X

1.5m high screen wall

400m

A

$L_{A90} = 37$

N

NOT TO SCALE

Case Study 2

Breeding kennels having 8 adult dogs with outside runs facing over open fields to the south.

Dwelling A: situated 150m/492ft to the north-east of the kennel building where background noise level is 46 L_{A90}

Stage 1	Dwelling A L_{A90} = 46						
Stage 2	Number of dogs (8 + 25% puppies) 2 = 10 x 0.5 = 5						
Stage 3 (Figure D1)	Hz	125	250	500	1	2	LA eq T
	1 Dog 5 dogs	26.0 + 7	38.5 +7	60.9 + 7	63.1 + 7	55.4 +7	65.6
		33.0	**45.5**	**67.9**	**70.1**	**62.4**	**72.6**
Stage 4 (Figure D2)	150m/492ft (hard)	- 23	- 23	- 23	- 23	- 23	
		10.0	22.5	44.9	47.1	39.4	**44.4**
Stage 5/6 (Figure D3)	2m Kennel Building (10m/32ft source point)	- 6	- 7	- 8	- 9	- 12	
		4	15.5	36.9	38.19	27.4	**37.3**
Stage 7	Prevailing wind correction for Dwelling A Specific noise level (41) + correction (3) = 44 L_{Aeq}						
Stage 8	Dwelling A Specific noise level (44) – background level (46) = **- 2**						

Case Study 2: Breeding Kennels (8 Adult Dogs)

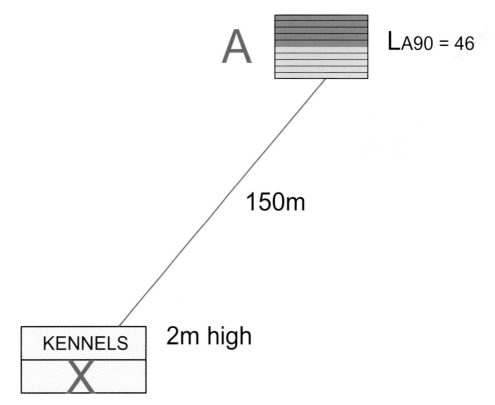

A $L_{A90} = 46$

150m

KENNELS

X

2m high

Downwind SNL = 41 + 3 = 44

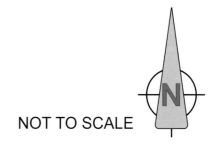

NOT TO SCALE

ASPECT AND SITE LAYOUT

Aspect

For temperate climates, all kennel buildings would face **south/south-west/east**. This means the dogs can relax in the warmth of the sun, and exercise runs catch the sun, helping to dry them out more quickly than if they were facing north.

This arrangement also means dogs and staff benefit from the warmth of the sun. South/south-west is ideal for the UK, however in hot climates, a directly southern aspect may be too warm.

Clearly, it is not always possible to ensure all the buildings enjoy maximum benefit from the sun, however, it is worth ensuring that some do.
Again, the design of the site should be flexible. For example, if a boarding establishment uses some of the dog kennels only during the winter months, ideally the warmer aspect kennels should be the ones that are used. You will need to play around with the site layout to ensure your kennels have the sunniest aspect, and ancillary buildings are in the most logical and practical place for daily activities.

Consideration of the individual site is important, and particularly so for coastal or mountainous locations.

Site Layout

The layout and design for your site will depend on many factors such as space, finances and any existing buildings that can be used.

The layout should encompass some very basic design rules that are applicable to all kennels. These are:

- **Security** - Buildings, theft of dogs and loss of dogs due to lack of inadequate safety measures

- **Access** - Ease of access for loading/unloading

- **Car parking** - Adequate car parking

- **Vehicle access** - Adequate access for large delivery vehicles

- **Expansion** - Suitable areas for expansion

- **Storage** - Suitable storage facilities and ancillary buildings close to the main centre of operation

- **Appearance** - A pleasing, professional appearance is always impressive to customers and clients; this can be achieved using suitable colours and materials and professionally landscaped areas

APPEARANCE

Make a good first impression.

A well-landscaped site will always enhance the aesthetic appearance of any building, and give visitors a strong initial feeling about your care, interest in your business and property, and ultimately in your care of their dogs.

FUTURE EXPANSION

Make the best use of space and appearance, without limiting your future options.

When planning and developing your site, always bear in mind that you may want to expand your business in the future.

This could be ancillary areas rather than increasing the number of kennels, and could include more play areas, residential accommodation, car parking - anything that you might want to include in the future.

SECURITY AND PUBLIC ACCESS AREAS

Clearly you do not want the public to have free access to the site, unless under supervision.

To be aware of who is on the premises, the design must channel all clients through a barrier system. Not only does this prevent unwanted visitors, it also secures the site, reduces disturbance to the dogs, and minimises the chance of a dog being let out either intentionally or unintentionally.

Security

Security is paramount for any animal establishment.

For commercial kennels, it is taken for granted by the dogs' owners that they are in a safe and secure environment.

The loss of a dog through poor security is tantamount to negligence and has the potential to damage your business.

The loss of a dog through escape is potentially the most serious and damaging of all circumstances you may encounter

---

It should become second nature to check all gates and doors to ensure that they are closed properly.

The loss of a dog might not be directly caused by you or your staff. Occasionally owners will bring their dog into reception by either carrying the dog in their arms, or without a lead – these are all potential areas for the loss of a dog at your premises. The end result could be potentially the same because the story becomes passed on or embellished, i.e. 'my dog escaped at that kennels' - this is not the type of publicity you want.

CAR PARKING

Larger kennels and welfare centres should have designated parking for staff and for the public.

Thought must be given to the number of staff that is likely to be employed and the availability of public transport. If the site is isolated and staff have no way of travelling to it except by their own car, adequate parking must be made available.

The number of spaces required for the public is often difficult to estimate, but a general guide would be parking for a minimum of six vehicles.

Some authorities adopt planning guidance for various activities, (e.g. residential, hotels, retail, etc). The closest category for kennels is veterinary establishments.

The recommendations for these are:

- 1 space per vet plus 2 spaces per vet for patients
- 1 space per professional staff
- 1 space per 3 non-professional staff

The space required for various types of vehicles is shown below:

VEHICLE TYPE	LENGTH		WIDTH		TURNING CIRCLE	
	Imperial	Metric	Imperial	Metric	Imperial	Metric
Small car	10 ft	3.05 m	4.5 ft	1.41 m	28.25 ft	8.6 m
Medium family car	14.5 ft	4.47 m	5.5 ft	1.71 m	34.25 ft	10.46 m
Large saloon car	17.5 ft	5.35 m	6.25 ft	1.90 m	41.5 ft	12.7 m
Van (1 tonne)	14.5 ft	4.4 m	6 ft	1.78 m	40 ft	12.2 m
Van (2 tonne)	19.5 ft	6 m	7.25 ft	2.24 m	43 ft	13.1 m
Dustcart (10.8 tonnes)	24.25 ft	7.4 m	7.5 ft	2.29 m	46 ft	14 m
Fire appliance (8.3 tonnes)	26.25 ft	8 m	7.5 ft	2.29 m	50 ft	15.2 m
3 axle skip lorry	23 ft	7 m	8.25 ft	2.5 m	57 ft	17.4 m
Rigid lorry (16.2 tonnes)	28 ft	8.5 m	8.25 ft	2.5 m	68 ft	21 m
Articulated lorry (38 tonnes)	49.25 ft	15 m	8.25 ft	2.5 m	39-50 ft	12–15 m

REFUSE AREA

This is another area that tends to be overlooked, often resulting in inadequate provision with dustbins being left around the site, creating a poor impression - and all due to lack of forward planning. However, before an area is dedicated, thought should be given to establish what method of collection is available for the disposal of the waste generated.

The most common systems used are:

- Plastic bags

- Standard Authority plastic wheeled bins – capacity from 90-330 litres

- Small skip type wheeled bins – capacity from 500-1,100 litres

- Open/covered skips, delivered/collected by purpose-built vehicles with capacities of 2,000-16,000 litres

Before a contract is placed with any supplier, questions to be asked are:

- What is the most suitable arrangement for you?

- How much waste will be generated?
  This will determine the size of the area to be provided, (as a general guide an establishment with around 40 kennels and 30 cat units will generate approximately 2,000-3,000 litres per week)

- Is the area accessible for the proposed collection vehicle?

- Can the area be isolated and screened off from the main buildings and public?

- Is the area accessible for the operators during unsocial hours, without disturbing the dogs or staff?

- What type of surface is available? Are there any steps or ramps?
  (It can be extremely difficult manoeuvring a full 1,100 litre bin down steps, or over gravel and soil)

- How frequent is the collection service?

- If plastic bags are to be used, some form of caging may be required to prevent dogs/foxes from damaging the bags

The latest Building Regulations in the UK – Section H6 of the Approved Documents states that:

> *"Adequate provision shall be made for storage of solid waste. Waste storing areas should have an impervious floor and also provision for washing down and draining the floor into a suitable system"*

Clearly this is highly dependent on the size of the development. However, it does need careful consideration.

On one recent project, the local authority insisted on the installation of a foul water drainage system in the open storage area – even though the waste bins are fully sealed with close fitting lids!

INCINERATOR

If you intend to install any form of incinerator, ensure you contact the local authority to establish what the current legislation is, and what permissions are required.

While the installation of an incinerator might seem a cost-effective solution to removing a large percentage of the waste generated on the site... beware. It has hidden costs and legal requirements, and may prove to be more problematical than first envisaged.

Incinerators come in many sizes and levels of efficiency; they all aim to achieve the same end result, which is to transform the waste into a less hazardous, less bulky or more controllable form. The problem with most of the waste generated from kennels is that is tends to be metal from cans of food (which could be recycled), blankets/bedding that have been soiled with faeces/urine, etc.

Most, but not all local authorities deem animal faeces and materials contaminated with faecal matter as clinical waste, and therefore not suitable for collection under normal refuse systems. However, this varies enormously and it is worth checking with local registered waste carriers to seek their views.

If planning to install an incinerator, ensure the supplier/manufacturer is fully aware of the type of material intended for incineration. This needs to be confirmed in writing.

You will also need to ensure that the burning of waste in your locality does not infringe upon any local or national environmental laws.

The basic options for incinerators are:

■ **Open burning/smouldering**
This is only suitable for burning clean, dry materials such as timber, paper, etc

■ **Non-fuelled prefabricated systems**
These are generally simple metal boxes with regulators and flues. These are most useful for burning general waste in a more controlled form than the above

■ **Fuelled prefabricated units**
These tend to be specialist systems for the incineration of specific waste and are designed for that purpose. This type of system is used in hospitals, research establishments, quarantine and other secure operations

Clearly, the cost of an incinerator and associative legal costs will substantially add to the expense. You will also need to include any costs to provide a room, cover for the incinerator, or fenced storage, etc.

5 DOG WELFARE

WE WILL NOW
FIND OUT JUST
HOW MUCH STRESS
FACTORS CAN
AFFECT DOG
WELLBEING & HOW
TO IMPROVE IT

DOG WELFARE REQUIREMENTS IN KENNELS

Whatever your reasons for wanting to build kennels, the dogs' needs and basic requirements are the same.

The most important factor for a successful
kennel facility is its care and management

No matter where you are in the world, all kennel management techniques should have similar aims:

- To ensure that adequate and nutritious supplies of food and water are available

- To provide a safe, warm, dry and stimulating environment for the animals in their care

- To protect from extremes of climate

- To provide health and veterinary care when required

- To allow and encourage dogs to display normal behaviour and make choices

- Freedom from emotional and physical distress

Owners are expecting a higher standard of care for their dogs and to spend more on this, scientific studies have emerged that are challenging us to look carefully at future standards and requirements – all of this contributes to the drive towards better care, choice of services and accommodation.

Focusing on What Dogs Need

It is important to understand what dogs need and the ideals to aim for, rather than merely complying with what was acceptable in the past, is currently in use, or the minimum legislation required. The problem with many existing kennels is that they have taken the 'minimum' requirements and read this quite literally as 'the standard' to achieve.

Even with little or no money for improvements, whether a
shelter struggling for funds or taking on an existing business,
with a little thought you can ALWAYS do something to
improve dog wellbeing and welfare in your kennels

One of the most important factors in creating a good facility to promote dog wellbeing and welfare is to understand what dogs need, what makes them happy, and which factors increase or reduce stress.

In this chapter, internationally renowned author and behaviourist Gwen Bailey generously shares her knowledge of how to improve life for dogs in kennels, as she has with countless charities, sanctuaries and organisations around the world.

GWEN BAILEY

Gwen Bailey has a BSc(Hons) degree in Zoology
Trustee for Battersea Dogs and Cats Home
Founder of Puppy School, a network of UK puppy trainers
www.puppyschool.co.uk
www.dogbehaviour.com

Gwen Bailey has successfully solved behaviour problems in thousands of rehomed dogs, helping to prevent dogs with behavioural problems being passed from home to home, and improving rehoming success rates. Gwen worked for a leading UK national animal welfare charity from 1988-2002 and pioneered the use of dog behaviour knowledge in the rehoming of unwanted animals and improvement of dog welfare in kennels. The first person to be appointed by a national animal welfare charity as an Animal Behaviourist, she eventually headed a team of behaviourists.

Gwen lectures at national and international conferences, runs training courses for staff at animal charities around the world and has written many books and education leaflets. Gwen is now working on preventing behaviour problems among puppies and to encourage friendly, well-behaved dogs for the future.

DOG WELFARE

Gwen Bailey

Dogs have feelings and emotions too, just like ours. Understanding them and catering for them is an important part of caring for their welfare. Good management can make up for less-than-perfect surroundings. The most important thing for dogs is to feel loved and secure. As long as they have their emotional and physical needs met, dogs don't have to live in a palace to be happy – but a dog can't be happy in a cold, wet kennel. So facilities are important, but not as important as the people who care for them.

Welfare is better described as a continuum from poor to good. Stress, disease and abnormal behaviour (such as inhibition of feeding) or engaging in repetitive behaviour (stereotypies) are all indicators of poor welfare. The absence of such indicators is, however, not sufficient to place the animal on the 'good' end of the welfare continuum.

Equating welfare to the absence of stress, disease and emotional distress would be equivalent to saying that when a human is not physically or mentally sick, that automatically means that s/he leads a happy and fulfilling life. That is not the case! The environmental and social conditions needed for good welfare vary from individual to individual, depending on their personality, previous learning experience, life stage and so on.

WELFARE STANDARD

In an effort to improve welfare, several humane groups and organisations responsible for animal care have embraced the scientific concept of the 'Five Freedoms' (Farm Animal Welfare Council www.fawc.org.uk/freedoms.htm).

The World Veterinary Association (WVA, 2000), advises that **provision of care in the form of the Five Freedoms is essential to animal welfare** and that every practical effort should be made to achieve them.

The five freedoms for companion animals are:

1. Freedom from thirst, hunger and malnutrition

2. Freedom from discomfort

3. Freedom from pain, injury and disease

4. Freedom from emotional distress

5. Freedom to express behaviours that promote wellbeing

The Canadian Council on Animal Care states that animal wellbeing encompasses both physical and psychological health, and recommends that environmental enrichment promotes a full and extensive repertoire of normal behaviour, while at the same time preventing the development of abnormal behaviour.

THE FIVE FREEDOMS

1: Freedom from hunger, thirst and malnutrition

To provide for this freedom, we need to ensure that dogs have access to, and take in, sufficient fresh water and nutritionally-balanced, palatable food daily. Sudden changes in diet should be avoided to prevent upsets and diarrhoea. Stressed dogs may find it difficult to eat and careful watch should be kept with efficient communication systems between staff to allow food intake to be monitored. For example some dogs will not eat or drink from metal dishes because they have become frightened of the noise they make against the floor.

2: Freedom from pain, injury and disease

To provide for this freedom, we must recognise behaviourial and clinical signs of disease and pain. Internal communication between staff must be efficient, and decisions must be prompt to ensure veterinary care is provided at the first indication that the dog is not well.

3: Freedom from discomfort

Comfort needs are dependent on age, health status, individual preferences, breed type and previous living conditions. To provide for this freedom, dogs must be provided with clean living conditions at the correct temperature, with natural light, good ventilation and comfortable bedding.

4. Freedom from distress

To provide for this freedom, we must understand the causes of stress in dogs, and be able to recognise signs of distress and take steps to remove or reduce stressors. We must also provide for a dog's psychological and physical needs, particularly in relation to social interaction with people or other dogs.

5. Freedom to express behaviours promoting psychological wellbeing

To provide for this freedom, we must provide exercise, play, mental stimulation and environmental enrichment to enable the dog to engage in the wide range of behaviours normally expected of dogs.

LIFE IN KENNELS 1

Imagine you are young, innocent and vulnerable.

You are taken away from all that is safe and familiar – without explanation.

Members of a different species who cannot speak your language take you and walk you into a building. As they open the door, you can smell, see and hear the distress of the others there. You are afraid to go in, but you are roughly dragged through the doorway and down the corridor.

Shouts and angry voices come at you from either side until you reach your cubicle. You are dragged inside and pushed back with a foot as you try to leave before the door is shut. You feel frightened and trapped.

You look around. There isn't much room. There is a hard plastic bed at the back, and the cold concrete floor is wet where the metal water dish was upset as you struggled to get out.

In the dim light, you look out through the wire mesh door and see hostile eyes watching you from across the corridor. It's cold and you curl up in your plastic bed feeling miserable and alone.

The walls are thin and noises from outside disturb the others in the building and raise the noise levels until your ears are hurting. This brings someone in who shouts loudly and sometimes bangs a broom against the wire-mesh doors.

There is no place to hide and you move back to your bed.

Days go past without you leaving this small space.

Every day, someone comes to clear up any mess you've made. Once you have made a mess, you have to sit in your bed to avoid stepping in it. They hose down the floor and walls, causing you to jump around to avoid being sprayed. It's the only exercise you get all day.

The floor stays wet and cold for hours afterwards.

Once a day, they throw in a metal bowl of a food you don't recognise and don't like the smell of.

The lack of exercise, stress, loneliness and change in diet are taking their toll and by the 2nd week, you feel terrible and develop diarrhoea and an ear infection. The vet is called and, after that, your sore ear is roughly man-handled once a day by unknown hands. You are shouted at if you don't hold still.

Occasionally, people are shown around. This causes great excitement and noise that hurts your ears but at least there is no shouting or banging with brooms. You look up expectantly but unfamiliar eyes stare in and move on.

Would you want your dog to be treated like this while you are enjoying your holiday?

Would you like your dog to be treated like this if anything happened to you and your dog ended up in rescue kennels?

LIFE IN KENNELS 2

Imagine you are young, innocent and vulnerable.

A stranger gets down to your level to make friends with you and feeds you nice things.

You are happy to go with them for a walk.

You are taken into a building that smells clean and fresh and where soft music plays. You sense there are others of your kind in the building, and that they are relaxed and happy, but you cannot see or hear them.

You are taken into a room that is light and airy, with a comfortable bed. There is room to move around, and different areas with views to explore.

Your new friend talks to you for a while to help you settle in before leaving. You feel a bit lonely but your bedding from home is there to snuggle into, familiar toys that smell of home are there too, and you are soon distracted by something you were given that is both chewy and tasty.

Just as you were beginning to get bored, your new friend comes back to take you for a walk.

You are able to burn off lots of energy and play games too, and you come back feeling relaxed and happy.

Later, a bowl of the food you are fed at home is brought, and you end the day relaxed and sleepy.

The next day, someone new comes to see you. They are happy and friendly and spend some time with you getting to know you. They play games with you and feed you tasty treats. Later, they come to take you out for another walk so you get fresh air and exercise and can settle down contentedly again for a while.

There is no noise and no disturbance so you can get plenty of rest.

Soon, you know the routine and can look forward to the next event that will break up the solitude. Sometimes, strangers are brought round. You move towards somewhere you can hide, but you can see that one of your friends is with them and so you relax, knowing they are safe to have around.

Your new friends are very important to you. They keep you safe, bring all the things you need, and provide you with love and support. They seem to understand you when you are feeling sad, worried, or happy and excited, and they try to make sure you are feeling okay at all times.

Thanks to them, you feel secure and happy and, now that you have got used to it, your new life is not too bad at all.

Is this how you would want your dog to feel while you were enjoying yourself on holiday?

Is this how you would like your dog to be treated if something happened to you and your dog ended up in a rescue centre?

EMOTIONAL AND PHYSICAL NEEDS

To be happy and content in kennels, dogs need the following:

Emotional needs:

- Adequate social contact, and to feel part of a pack

- A sense of the familiar

- Mental stimulation, and opportunities to play

- Choice over their environment

- A lack of stressors or somewhere to hide/feel safe

- Routine

- Special needs met

Physical needs:

- Familiar food

- Exercise, and space to move around

- Controlled temperatures

- Comfort

- Grooming

- Rest/sleep

- To go to the toilet

- Chews

EMOTIONAL NEEDS

Meeting emotional needs is usually more dependent on quality of the staff and time available than the quality of facilities.

Adequate social contact and to feel part of a pack

Dogs are highly social animals and having good social contact is essential to their feeling of wellbeing. Dogs that have been well-socialised with humans will need to bond with those looking after them, to avoid becoming lonely and depressed.

Research has shown that dogs are significantly less stressed if given pleasant human contact during the early days of their stay in kennels. It usually takes a dog 3 days to become accustomed to its new life.

Good quality human contact during this time is very beneficial and giving some 'getting to know you' time when the dog first comes in is essential for fast relationship development and for the dog's wellbeing. This also helps to reduce stress for the dog and the chance of injuries to staff when they have to start doing things to the dogs, such as putting a lead on their collar, feeding them, entering their kennel, giving medication, etc. Taking some time to get to know the dog before it is put in a kennel can also reduce the risk of kennel guarding later, particularly if staff approach with the dog's own lead that will smell familiar.

Throughout their stay, dogs need to be allocated sufficient time to receive love, fuss, attention and positive experiences with caring staff. For boarding kennels, this time and care should to be built into the price paid by owners and advertised to them so they know they are getting a good service. Hiring the right kind of staff, who genuinely care about animals, is essential.

In large facilities, continuation of care is important so a dog can get to know its carers and develop a relationship with them. Having many staff care for all dogs does not allow strong bonds to form. Allocating a small group of people to each group of dogs (if the facility is large) can lead to a much better life for the dogs in their care.

Dogs that have formed stronger bonds with other dogs may prefer to play/get to know other friendly dogs, or be content to spend time with the other dog in the family that came in with them. If dogs prefer the company of other dogs to humans, efforts should be made to provide them with another friendly dog with which they can play and interact daily under supervision. Socialising and mixing dogs from different households is not recommended unless with permission from the owner, and if there is a member of staff with enough experience successfully to choose which dogs will interact well. For some dogs, play time with other dogs is a great stress reliever and also a good energy release, but care needs to be taken and expert supervision is required.

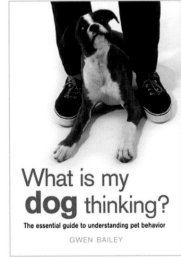

Alternatively, keeping two dogs from the same family together may provide both with much-needed company. While it is comforting for many dogs to be kennelled with a familiar dog, it is important to watch for signs that all may not be well between them once the authority of the owner is removed. Staff will need to be able to notice antagonistic body language and displays and may need to separate them to prevent fighting and injury. This becomes particularly important when dogs that differ in size are kept together.

The knowledge, ability and attitude of the kennel staff will have a direct effect on the wellbeing and welfare of the dogs in their care. Teaching staff how to understand dog behaviour and body language should be an important part of their training.

Further reading for understanding dog behaviour and body language:

What is my dog thinking? by Gwen Bailey

A sense of the familiar

A dog's main sense is the sense of smell. Until the dog is accustomed to the new life in kennels, the smell of familiar items can help them feel reassured. Providing bedding that owners have brought from home and the dog's own toys are an easy way to do this. Ensure owners know that there is a risk of these items being destroyed (reduce the chances of this by reducing stress levels in kennels using the ideas in this chapter).

To a dog's sensitive nose, disinfectant is a powerful smell. Making sure kennels are well rinsed after being disinfected can help to reduce the residual smell. Having a bucket and shovel outside each kennel specially for that occupant can help reduce the spread of disease and make it unnecessary to completely disinfect each kennel every day. This helps to save time, disinfectant and also improves life for the dog kept in the kennels, as well as helping to keep the kennel dry.

Small groups of dogs

Keeping kennel numbers low will also help. Dogs are more comfortable with living in small groups, rather than having to cope with large numbers of other dogs.

Mental stimulation and opportunities to play

Dogs will have varying requirements for play and mental stimulation depending on the age, genetics and previous experiences. Young, active dogs from working strains will generally need more than others. Providing for this by giving walks that incorporate sufficient games with toys will greatly improve the sense of wellbeing in kennelled dogs. In addition, reward-based training sessions will provide further mental stimulation for dogs that love to work.

Choice over their environment

The welfare of all sentient beings improves when they have the chance to make decisions about what to do. Providing an environment that allows them several options is beneficial. This can be achieved by having a sleeping area and a run attached so they can choose where they want to be, by providing different views from different places within the kennel, or using different height levels for them to climb or jump on. Providing toys and chews further enriches their environment and gives them more choices.

Routine

Animals find it easier to cope if rewarding experiences are spread out throughout the day. Structuring days so that food, walks, rest, play, etc comes at regular intervals can lead to calm, contented dogs. **More smaller feeds are better than one large feed, and fewer shorter walks and more shorter play sessions are better than longer ones**. They may be more labour intensive, but they can lead to more contentment and less excitement with resultant lower noise levels.

Special needs met

Each dog is an individual and some will have special needs such as those that are very young or very old, or those that need medication or nursing. Housing vulnerable dogs together where their special care can be managed more easily, and where they will not be upset by more boisterous ones makes sense if facilities are designed with flexible spaces.

WHY REDUCING STRESS IS SO IMPORTANT

Long-term stress will reduce the immune system's ability to fight disease so it is important that steps are taken to reduce stressors and make the dog feel more comfortable. In addition, staff are more likely to get bitten by stressed, fearful dogs, so it is important to tackle stress for health and safety reasons. **Having all staff make friends with each dog** will considerably reduce stress levels. Taking time to get to know shy dogs, and giving them time to make approaches at their own pace is essential for a good relationship to develop.

A lack of stressors or somewhere to hide/feel safe

Stressors can take many forms and are likely to be different for different dogs. A stressed dog will show body language and behaviour changes and staff will need to learn to recognise these.

Common stressors in kennels are:
- Strangers visiting the kennels (or staff that are not known)
- Aggressive dogs
- Loud noises
- Noxious smells
- Novel, unpredictable noxious stimuli (e.g. thunder, being squirted with water)

Anxious, worried or fearful dogs may show any of the following:
- Lowered tail
- Ears back
- Tense face
- Wide eyes or large pupils
- Rapid stress panting
- Yawning
- Weight on back legs, sloping forepaws
- Hiding behaviour
- Avoidance
- Aggressive behaviour
- Lack of interest in food and games
- Disinterest in social contact
- Repetitive behaviour such as pacing and circling

Thoughtful placement and careful management

Staff need to be aware of the stress caused to some dogs by the presence of other dogs. Partitioning between kennels so that dogs cannot see and bark at other dogs is important. Careful placement of the dogs in kennels can help to balance the needs of shy or fearful dogs by avoiding placing them next to aggressive or overpowering dogs, particularly if kennels have open mesh/bars/wire rather than solid partitions between the runs.

Staff also need to be sensitive to a dog's concerns about other dogs when moving them around the kennels, taking care to avoid aggressive or noisy dogs or using screening to prevent visual contact. Placing 'difficult' dogs at the end of a block to avoid having to take all the other dogs past each day can really help to reduce stress levels. For rescue kennels **where visitors are a constant source of disturbance, having somewhere to hide** can help shy dogs adjust and learn to be friendly more quickly.

Being sensitive to what stresses each dog, and avoiding such stress is important when considering their welfare. This will mean making the effort to think of individuals, for example, keeping entire male dogs in a separate block from females in season, or deciding not to take both into kennels at the same time.

PHYSICAL NEEDS

Meeting physical needs adequately is usually more dependent on facilities than management.

Familiar food

Changing a dog's diet should be a gradual process if upsets and diarrhoea are to be avoided. For this reason, it is better to store and offer food the customers have been feeding their dog prior to their arrival, rather than to feed the same food to all dogs. This brings management challenges but, in terms of welfare, changing food over slowly, or not changing it at all, is a better system than upsetting dogs' digestion at a time when all else is changing in their lives too.

Exercise and space to move around

Enough space to move around in the kennel to allow for self-exercising is important and a run attached to the sleeping quarters will make life more enjoyable and keep dogs fitter. This is particularly important for young, energetic dogs and those from working strains.

Controlled temperatures

Many pet dogs are used to living in centrally-heated or well-ventilated homes. Sudden departures from expected temperatures can cause welfare issues since the dog has only limited means of thermal self-regulation. A thick coat takes time to grow or shed. Dogs have a limited ability to get rid of excess heat, having no sweat glands, and constant panting is particularly tiring.

Comfort

Most dogs prefer to lie on soft bedding, and the provision of sufficient bedding is particularly important for thin-coated dogs such as Greyhounds, and for under-weight, or old dogs.

Grooming

Dogs with long coats need to be kept tangle-free, and it is better if this is done in short, happy sessions rather than one long difficult one just before the dog is going home. All dogs benefit from regular grooming sessions, and if owners are asked to bring the dog's own brushes from home, the familiar smell that accompanies them can add to the feeling of security during the first days.

Rest/sleep

Dogs benefit from having a kennel routine that allows for quiet rest periods after exercise or food, during which no one goes into the kennels and there is no disturbance. Sound-proofing may be necessary for kennels to cut down on external noise and disturbance. Visitors should be restricted to set times of day, and shown around in groups if possible, to minimise disturbance.

To go to the toilet

Dogs will search for substrates, such as grass, that they have become familiar with to toilet on. For house-trained dogs, lack of such a substrate at a time when they need to go can cause them great distress. Regular walks on grass (the substrate preferred by most dogs) at times when they would normally toilet are beneficial, and can help keep the kennels clean.
In addition, feeding them on food they have been used to will help to keep them regular, and help to prevent 'accidents'.

Chews

Chews provide a much needed 'occupation' for dogs with nothing to do. The risk of choking may be an issue, and supervision may be necessary depending on what is offered.

Sudden change in diet

Changes in feeding times

New, unfamiliar routine

Lack of control over environment, particularly
in bare or cramped kennels

Confinement frustration

Lack of mental stimulation

Boredom

Lack of opportunities to play

STRESS FACTORS

Presence & proximity of other dogs

Lack of sufficient social contact

Presence of and handling by strangers

Absence of owners

Lack of familiar smells

Temperature difference

Lack of physical comfort

No access to outside

No access to normal toileting substrate

Lack of exercise

Loud noise

Unfamiliar noises

Unfamiliar smells

Nowhere to hide if frightened

Lack of continuity of veterinary care

NOW YOU KNOW
THE IDEAL SIZE
YOUR KENNELS
SHOULD BE, WE
WILL LOOK AT THE
MINIMUM LEGAL
REQUIREMENTS

KENNELS LICENCE REGULATIONS

Always remember that legislation notes suggest the
absolute **M-I-N-I-M-U-M** standards
and are open to a great deal of latitude

United States, Canada and the Rest of the World

Legislation varies enormously between states/regions, and it would take another book to list them all.
However, it is easy to find out requirements with which you will have to comply – just ask your local authority. You will be able to find this out from the animal warden, animal control officer, or the licensing/permits office.

United Kingdom

Boarding Kennels

The Animal Boarding Establishment Act 1963 requires all establishments to be licensed by the local authority (except where it is an ancillary business or animals are kept according to the Animal Health Act 1981 requirements). You must not be disqualified from keeping animals. Boarding establishments are defined as the carrying on at any premises (including a private dwelling) of a business of providing accommodation for other people's dogs.

CIEH 'Model Licence Conditions and Guidance for Dog Boarding Establishments' 1993.
This publication's aim was to provide a framework for all local authority inspectors, to ensure that a consistent approach was implemented nationwide for kennel sizes, systems for hygiene control and standards.

The local authority has a duty to inspect annually and issue a licence for all boarding kennels. The inspectors normally come from the Environmental Health Department, this being the obvious choice as they are used to inspecting food outlets, restaurants, etc. **However, not all authorities have adopted the guidelines as policy.**

It has been accepted that it is impossible to bring all of the boarding establishments up to the required standard overnight, and this will need to be phased in over a period of time for **existing** businesses. For **new establishments**, there is an expectation that all of the conditions will be met before a licence is granted.

Cautionary Note:

- **Where an existing establishment has a licence and the property is sold**, it should be borne in mind that the new owner might be required to upgrade the kennels at the outset. Clearly, this will have serious financial implications and will require careful research

TEMPERATURE

The guidelines quoted for a minimum and maximum temperature range are as follows:

COUNTRY	MINIMUM		MAXIMUM	
UK Boarding	10 ℃	50 ℉	26 ℃	79 ℉
UK Quarantine	7 ℃	44.6 ℉	none given	
Australia	15 ℃	64 ℉	27 ℃	69.8 ℉
New Zealand	15 ℃	59 ℉	22 ℃	72 ℉
CANADA				
British Columbia	18 ℃	64 ℉	none given	
USA				
Colorado	10 ℃	50 ℉	32.2 ℃	90 ℉
Louisiana	10 ℃	50 ℉	29.5 ℃	85 ℉
Missouri	10 ℃	50 ℉	29.5 ℃	85 ℉

In order to achieve the temperature ranges shown above, the design, construction and materials used will all have an effect. Other factors such as geographical siting will also have an effect on either the minimum or maximum temperatures.

SUGGESTED MINIMUM KENNEL SIZES

I would always *strongly* advise full height kennels (full height for humans). Full height allows easy access for staff for cleaning and the cost is minimal to achieve this. It also provides easier and safer access for staff when dealing with nervous or difficult dogs. It also provides a more natural, room-like and 3-dimensional interest for the dogs by adding different heights to watch what is going on and areas to hide in or under. If there is the opportunity to move to a different level, dogs will take it.

My Suggested Sizes:

Having been involved with many organisations that all have their own requirements, ideals, building costs and budgets – for a temperate climate, the following style and sizes are recommended:

Ideal Style: Semi-outdoor/semi-indoor (views and fresh air available)
Ideal Height: Full-height, walk-in kennels of 2m/6ft 6" MINIMUM

MINIMUM Sizes:	Imperial	Metric
Indoor sleeping area of: **PLUS...**	6ft x 6ft (36 sq ft)	1.8m x 1.8m (3.2 m²)
Semi-outdoor exercise run of:	6ft x 8-10ft (48 – 60 sq ft)	1.8m x 2.4-3m (4.3 – 5.4m²)
COMBINED TOTAL:	84 – 96 sq ft	7.5 – 8.6m²

The above sizes provide a good compromise in terms of the dogs' needs, building costs, staff time, and are suitable for two dogs. However, larger kennel units (over and above the recommended minimum sizes) are also an excellent promotional and talking point, and bring **tremendous** impact and choice for customers.

It is well worth considering constructing even larger kennels (e.g 8ft x 8ft/ 2.4m x 2.4m) if space and budget permit it. It will be in the best interest of the dogs, staff and business to do so because of the financial and lifestyle advantages. We are now seeing new kennels being built with sleep areas of up to 10ft x 10ft/3m x 3m, which are proving to be extremely successful as more exclusive and upmarket dog kennels/hotels - catering for a new and untapped market.

No matter what size the kennel, the biggest benefits are seen where dogs receive LOTS of human interaction (grooming, playtime and attention away from kennels), which helps combat the effects of stress and makes for much happier and more relaxed dogs and owners

International Minimum Kennel Sizes for Combined Sleep/Exercise

Clearly, there is a major difference in what is deemed a satisfactory level and standard of space:

Country	HEIGHT	Sleep	Run	TOTAL
Recommended	6ft 6" – 7ft 10" 2 – 2.4m	6ft x 6ft (36 sq ft) 1.8m x 1.8m ($3.2m^2$)	6 x 8–10ft (46-58 sq ft) 1.8m x 2.4–3m ($4.3m – 5.4m^2$)	82 – 94 sq ft 7.5 – $8.6m^2$

United Kingdom

Country	HEIGHT	Sleep	Run	TOTAL
Boarding (CIEH) (sleep + exercise combined)	1.8m/6ft	$1.9m^2$ 20 sq ft	$2.4m^2 – 3.3m^2$ 26 – 36 sq ft	$4.3 – 5.2m^2$ 46-56 sq ft
Quarantine (DEFRA) *Any dog entering a quarantine facility stays in that kennel for 6 months and is **never** let out*	1.8m/6ft	$1.4m^2$ 15 sq ft	$3.7 – 7.4m^2$ 39.8 – 79.6 sq ft	$5.1 – 8.8m^2$ 54 – 94 sq ft

UK Quarantine – It is clear to see in the sizes shown for quarantine (and remember, this is from the *Voluntary* Code of Practice – many kennels do not even reach this standard) that the **sizes are totally inadequate** to provide the dog with freedom and space to allow natural behaviour.

United States of America

Country	
Louisiana and Missouri	Primary enclosures for housing dogs shall provide a minimum floor space for each dog equal to the mathematical square of the sum of the length of the dog in inches, as measured from the tip of its nose to the base of its tail, plus 6" - expressed in square feet. e.g: Length of dog in inches + 6" x length of dog in inches + 6" ÷ 144" = minimum square footage per dog

Canada

Country	HEIGHT	Sleep	Run	TOTAL
British Columbia (District of Mission)	7ft 10"/ 2.4m	15.9 sq ft/ $1.48m^2$ (minimum width of 4ft/ 1.2m)	40 sq ft/ $3.7m^2$ (minimum width of 4ft/ 1.2m)	
Ontario (Municipality of Whitestone)		25 sq ft/ $2.3m^2$	32 sq ft/ $3m^2$	

Australia

Country	HEIGHT	Sleep / Run / TOTAL
Australia	1.8m	Height of dog at shoulder: 300mm/1ft and above: $2.5m^2$ (26.9 sq ft) below 300mm/1ft: $1.5m^2$ (16 sq ft)

CASE STUDY:
21ST CENTURY DOG APARTMENTS

Organisation:	San Francisco SPCA
Location:	USA, California, San Francisco
Kennels Type:	Indoor
Kennels Function:	Boarding
Number of Kennels:	18 dog and 67 feline apartments
Apartment Size:	Average 12ft x 12ft, and 9ft high
Year Built:	1998 (ARQ Architects)

www.sfspca.org

THIS GROUNDBREAKING, STATE-OF-THE-ART ADOPTION CENTER IS ONE OF THE MOST BEAUTIFULLY DESIGNED ENVIRONMENTS OF ITS KIND IN THE WORLD. DOGS ENJOY SPACIOUS APARTMENTS WHERE THEY ARE SHOWN TO THEIR BEST ADVANTAGE

Maddie's Adoption Center photographs by Jane Lidz and Hiroshi Shimizu

MADDIE'S ADOPTION CENTER ~ SAN FRANCISCO SPCA

The San Francisco Society for the Prevention of Cruelty to Animals was founded in 1868. It was the fourth SPCA established in the United States and the first to be located west of the Rockies, and has long been a national leader in the humane and compassionate treatment of animals. Maddie's Adoption Center is named in memory of the canine companion of Cheryl and Dave Duffield, President and CEO of PeopleSoft. The Duffield Family Foundation provided the lead gift of $1 million for the project as a tribute to their cherished miniature schnauzer, Maddie.

Maddie's Adoption Center has proved to be an unqualified success. Suddenly, some of the hardest-to-place animals are finding new homes in record time, thanks to the center's unique new training programmes, architectural design and public appeal. The groundbreaking $7 million facility is 27,000 square feet and can accommodate approximately 200 animals awaiting adoption.

Maddie's was considered to be revolutionary when it opened in 1998, and it still is, even today. The Adoption Center is a brand new concept in animal sheltering, where the dogs live in light, airy apartments with cosy beds, furniture, rugs and toys. Constructed to incorporate an already existing building, the design and philosophy of Maddie's is today emulated across America and around the world. It is even included in several San Francisco guide books as a 'must see' tourist destination!

A SHELTER FOR THE 21ST CENTURY

The difference between Maddie's and a typical shelter is noticeable from the moment a visitor enters the lobby. It is a spacious, inviting area filled with natural light from the floor-to-ceiling picture windows, and it offers comfortable furniture featuring animal motif cushions, plants, and a large, flat-screen television showing SF/SPCA-produced animal advice DVDs. On the verandah, market umbrellas shade tables and chairs for people who want to relax outside, or talk over their decision about adoption.

What would you do differently?

- Use less glass 'everywhere' because the upkeep is constant and costly

- The sealed concrete floors have not worn well, and have been replaced in several areas with ceramic tiles

- Locks would have been installed on the doors of the animal rooms. Visitors are not allowed inside the rooms without permission and accompanied by a staff member. However, it is difficult to monitor all the rooms all the time. Some closed circuit cameras have now been installed

- A public address system and internet cable would have been installed during construction

- The shelter could use more people/office space

- Install half frosted/half clear glass panels in the doors between dog rooms, useful to prevent the dogs seeing their neighbours and becoming over-stimulated (see addition of temporary opaque adhesive panels right)

What are you most pleased with?

Maddie's Adoption Center has exceeded the Society's most hopeful expectations. From increased adoptions, including many hard-to-place dogs and cats, to reductions in the animals' length of stay, Maddie's has been an unqualified success!

UP CLOSE AND PERSONAL

PREPARING FOR NEW LIVES

All the animals at Maddie's Adoption Center initially go through an intake process that includes medical evaluation by veterinarians from the Society's Community Veterinary Hospital, and behavior assessment by skilled staff trainers and behaviorists. Every animal adopted from the Center is altered, prior to adoption, at The SF/SPCA Spay/Neuter Clinic.

Maddie's Adoption Center illustrates how homeless animals can be sheltered and prepared for new lives. It's an environment where dogs and cats are treated with respect, and where their dignity is reflected in their surroundings and the care they receive. Gone are the cellblock-like dog kennels and steel cat cages of a typical shelter. In their place are comfortable dog apartments and cat condominiums. Every room is like a room at the Ritz.

Dogs on Lassie Lane live in typical San Francisco Victorian and Spanish style apartments. Natural light streams from windows and skylights, and toys and TVs offer entertainment and stimulation. All of the animals' rooms have specially designed acoustic insulation and air circulation systems to keep them quiet and fresh-smelling at all times.

The result is an environment that prepares the animals for the transition from shelter to home. It is also an atmosphere that is conducive to adoption.

Every one of the lovable dogs and cats awaiting adoption at The San Francisco SPCA receives safe refuge, extensive medical care and abundant amounts of love. They are all assessed by expert trainers, and, if warranted, given extra socialisation and behaviour training to prepare them for their new homes.

At this state-of-the-art adoption center, dogs enjoy play sessions with other dogs, and head out on daily walks with volunteer dog walkers. Cats reside in deluxe kitty 'lofts' and are visited 'in house' by cat-socialising volunteers who brush, pet and play with them.

> *"The atmosphere at Maddie's is conducive to adoption, and prepares dogs for the transition from shelter to home"*

LIFE ON LASSIE LANE

The dog apartments are along 'roads' with facades evocative of San Francisco neighbourhoods. This design reinforces the original goal of providing a more 'home-like' setting for each dog. Above Lassie Lane is an 'acoustic cloud' – a special sound buffer that reduces the noise of barking dogs. Additionally, the walls of all the dog corridors are not flush. This is a noise-reduction feature, as are the floor to ceiling, retractable drapes in each hallway.

To buffer sound inside the rooms, specially formulated plaster was used on the walls and an anti-microbial fibre finish put onto the concrete floors to eliminate bacteria. Center drains in all the dog rooms make hosing and cleaning easier. In addition, a state-of-the-art air filtration system pulls air out from floor level to reduce any unpleasant doggie smells.

MORE FEATURES

Another interesting setting at Maddie's Adoption Center is the upstairs Solarium. An airy, spacious room, it has picture windows and doors that open on to a small outdoor terrace. The Solarium serves as a combination board room, staff meeting place and volunteer training room. Next to the Solarium is a Rotunda, which was designed to allow in lots of natural light.

Underneath the adoption center is a very large multi-purpose room that can be divided into three sections, with floor-to-ceiling sliding doors. This room is used for dog training sessions and play groups. The floor is covered with rubberised material for easy washing and for quietness. An overhead sound buffer also reduces dog noise.

While they are residing at Maddie's Adoption Center, all the shelter dogs receive one-on-one, reward-based obedience training with SF/SPCA trainers, often in the multi-purpose room. Some lucky shelter dogs are chosen to be project dogs for The SF/SPCA's renowned Academy for Dog Trainers. Their adoption is put on hold, and for six weeks they spend a large portion of each day being trained by their student mentors. This is a win-win situation for the dogs and their eventual adopters.

SAN FRANCISCO SPCA

FEELS LIKE HOME

DOG APARTMENTS

The animal apartments at Maddie's Adoption Center are spacious but cosy, with picture windows, artwork on the walls, and soft furniture to sink into. Natural light streams through skylights, the sun is warming and there's always something diverting to watch – birds, people, or even a video. All the apartments have specially designed acoustic insulation and air circulation systems to keep them quiet and odor-free at all times.

Great care has been taken to make the environment in the dogs' living quarters comfortable and relaxed. The roomy interior of each of the 18 shared apartments (holding from 1-5 dogs) is designed to look and feel like a real home, complete with non-chewable furniture, low hammock-style dog beds, dog crates, artwork and an occasional television set. Visitors are able to observe each dog, up-close and personal – something that is not easy in a conventional shelter. Each apartment also has a 'sniff hole' where interested adopters can formally introduce themselves with the smell of a hand before they actually meet a dog.

The canine apartments open onto multi-function interior courtyards where the dogs can socialise together in groups. In addition, these courtyard spaces between dog apartments provide a temporary home for the dogs while their apartment is being cleaned, or they are used to separate them so that a potential adopter can meet a particular dog, alone.

Because these areas are used for 'get-acquainted' and play sessions, they also provide an opportunity for an adopter to observe how a particular dog interacts with other dogs, not easy in a conventional shelter. The courtyard skylights supply natural light, and exhaust fans provide ventilation.

Each animal's daily activities are educational, fun and rewarding, making his or her placement in an adoptive home successful and long-lasting. It's a wonderful experience for the dogs. They're happier and they're seen to their best advantage. SF/SPCA adoption counsellors and staff match potential owner/guardians with cats and dogs suitable to their lifestyles. The Society's Adoption Outreach Program also takes shelter pets to shopping centers, business districts and community events so the animals can be seen by more potential adopters.

THE MADDIE'S MODEL

In the 12 months after Maddie's Adoption Center opened in 1998, there was a 20 percent increase in adoptions and a 50 percent decrease in the length of stay of an animal at the shelter. The adoption rate has since evened out; in 2006-2007 The SF/SPCA found homes for 3,217 dogs and cats. In 2007 its live release rate for companion animals was 97 percent. In one of the most beautifully designed environments of its kind in the world, Maddie's Adoption Center brings people and animals together to find each other.

> *"An unqualified success, suddenly some of our hardest-to-place animals are finding homes in record time"*

VISITORS' REACTIONS

The Director of Adoptions at Maddie's remembers visitors and adopters making comments such as "*This place is better than my home*" and "*I'd love to live here!*"

POSITIVE FEATURES FOR ADOPTERS

Because the animals are viewed in a home-like environment it's easier for adopters to picture them in a home. Visitors can also see the animals better because they, and the animals, are more comfortable. Many visitors have commented that they don't like going to typical shelters, but they enjoyed the experience of Maddie's. A great number of visitors thank the staff for taking such good care of the animals. There are also many conducted tours of the facility, including for young school children participating in The SF/SPCA Humane Education Program.

POSITIVE FEATURES FOR STAFF & VOLUNTEERS

Many of the staff and volunteers, who are highly qualified and have a great deal to offer, will not work in traditional shelters because it is too difficult for them to function in such an environment. Staff enjoys working at Maddie's Adoption Center, and because they are more comfortable, the animals are happier, too. At Maddie's opening ceremony, employees expressed their personal appreciation to Mr Dave Duffield, who provided the lead gift to build the facility, for their very special workplace that his gift had helped make possible.

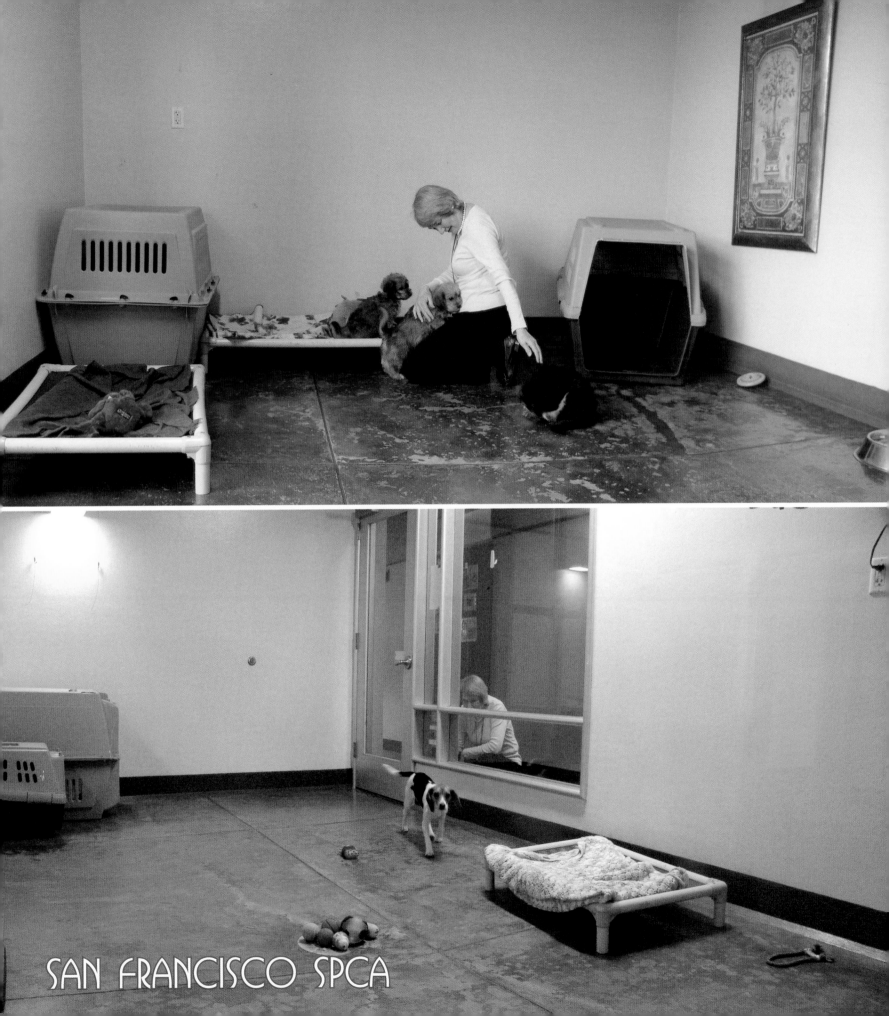

SAN FRANCISCO SPCA

SAN FRANCISCO SPCA

SAN FRANCISCO SPCA

THE TREND TOWARDS LARGER ACCOMMODATION

There has been a trend to provide larger accommodation, particularly for new commercial, rescue and sanctuary work.

The reasons for this are:

- Allows better facilities for dogs (e.g. shelving at various heights to provide a more stimulating environment, and enough room for a seat to make volunteers, owners or potential owners more comfortable)

- Ease of working for the staff. (We recently visited a (licensed) boarding kennels of low standard and hygiene with 2ft/60cm mould growths on the concrete slabs – the manager was a rather portly gentleman who could just about squeeze in and turn around in the 3ft/1m wide kennel, so it is no wonder cleaning was difficult)

- Greater increase in multi-dog households

- Shows the dog in a more natural environment, and hopefully more relaxed

- Is excellent PR and makes good business sense, particularly for commercial establishments when advertising

- The move to have 'something different' and 'better' is leading towards greater prevalence of large 'suite' kennels

Single or Double Dog Kennels

A major manufacturer of prefabricated kennels systems, has stated that the majority of commercial boarding kennels installed have generally been sized to **accommodate two dogs** (a double kennel). This makes perfect sense once it is understood that approximately 40% of dogs will be in pairs and, as well as providing flexibility in the kennels, it looks more generous to clients for single dog use.

The reasons for making all kennels 'double' (suitable for two dogs) are:

- Approximately 40% of UK/USA households have two dogs, or more

- Minimal build cost difference between single or double kennel sizes

- Greater public appeal and perception of the property

- More flexibility for offering greater space or for multi-dog families

- More space for the single dog

- Greater flexibility to the owner

- Ease of working for the staff

- It is far easier to take good photographs of dog kennels that are large

CASE STUDY:
LARGE SUITE ACCOMMODATION

Organisation: Canine Country Club
Location: UK, Cornwall/Devon
Kennels Type: Semi-outdoor
Kennels: 15 boarding
Kennel Sleep Size: 2.4m x 2.4m (8ft x 8ft) and
2.4m x 3.3m (8ft x 11ft)
Kennel Run Size: 2.4/3.3m x 4.2m (8/11ft x14ft)
Year Built: 2007
www.caninecountryclub.co.uk

A NEW, RURAL BOARDING KENNELS WITH LARGE SUITES UP TO 22FT/6.7M. THEY ENJOY THE SUCCESS OF BEING A HIGH QUALITY BUSINESS WITH A HOME-LIKE FEEL, WITH LOTS OF SPACE FOR BOTH QUIET REST AND FUN PLAYTIMES

CANINE COUNTRY CLUB

CHANGING THE IMAGE OF KENNELS

Jackie and Tim Ferrier are pioneers in the world of boarding kennels, being the first to build such large rooms (8ft x 8ft/11ft sleeping areas with 14ft runs) to such a high standard of building. Wanting only the best, the building is traditionally constructed to 'human' standards with insulated cavity blockwork (good insulation keeps buildings warm in winter, cool in summer), trussed rafters with a slate roof to give it high class aesthetic qualities, and low maintenance and running costs.

Like many aspiring boarding kennel owners, Jackie and Tim's thoughts about the possibility of owning such a business started a number of years before the actual reality of becoming kennel owners.

Having always had dogs of their own, with parents living nearby who could look after them – the thoughts of finding a suitable boarding establishment had never been an issue.

However, in 2000 Jackie, the family and her parents went on a cruise – this meant that suitable accommodation had to be found for the dogs. Jackie had her first experience of viewing boarding kennels:

"*Wow, what a shock – what a disappointment. How could much-loved dogs that live along side us both day and night be expected to live in tiny, dark, smelly, noisy, damp, cold spaces with little or no exercise, while we have a wonderful luxurious holiday?*"

In the end Jackie settled for a pet sitter, believing this to be the better option after her experience of viewing local kennels. This option proved to have its own problems and the reality of having the dogs in their own home created additional issues with neighbours complaining about the pet sitter, and her dogs being left for lengthy periods of time.

On returning, they vowed never to leave their dogs again.

> *"When you get clients driving 15 hours just to come and look at the kennels before booking their dog in, it speaks volumes!"*

I CAN DO BETTER

This story is so familiar, and one we hear over and over again – "*I can do better*". It is typical of the caring people we work alongside, people who have been involved with animals – in Jackie's case it was racehorses.

Like many of the clients we deal with, Jackie's story is based on a desire to provide a facility for owners who have to leave their dogs, but want to go away and enjoy their holiday, knowing that their dogs are being looked after on a more personal level, with quality time and interaction on a one-to-one basis in a spacious, home-like environment.

Jackie first approached Kennel & Cattery Design in September 2005 having found our website. From the outset it was very obvious that she was going to be a unique client, determined to construct kennels to an extremely high standard.

Given her experiences when viewing established boarding kennels, she soon realised that it would be impossible to purchase an existing business that had the standard and design of kennels that they wanted to build.

Jackie and Tim lived in Hampshire and after visiting several estate agents with a list of their requirements for a suitable property where they could construct kennels and that 'ticked all the boxes'. They quickly realised that the cost of such a property in Hampshire far exceeded their budget. The search radius was broadened to the South-West of England.

The property had to fit a list of requirements, such as a minimum of 5 acres of land, no neighbours, situated close to a main road and to be a visually appealing location from a customer's point of view.

Eventually a suitable property was located in Cornwall. They made an offer – it was accepted – it was really happening.

IN A LEAGUE OF THEIR OWN

THE DESIGN BRIEF

During the intervening period Jackie was in regular contact with us to discuss design options, practical issues such as services, drainage, etc. The design finally chosen was an 'L' shape. The reasoning behind this was to minimise the stress and noise, and to create a building that was functional, while at the same time providing a facility that was simply in a league of its own. This fitted with Jackie's design brief and her commitment to provide a kennel facility that offered so much more than anything she had seen elsewhere.

Finally, they moved into their new property in January 2006 and applied for planning permission 2 weeks later. At the parish council meeting Jackie explained why they wanted to construct such a facility; fortunately, all of the council members supported it wholeheartedly.

Unfortunately, the property straddles two county council borders; this meant that Cornwall Council had to liaise with Devon Council. The consultation process ended up taking six months; eventually a 'yes' decision was given. The only objection the council received was from a neighbouring kennel owner! Fortunately the council ignored this.

PROJECT MANAGEMENT

Neither Jackie nor Tim had ever undertaken such a large project. Initially they obtained quotations from local building contractors. The aim was to use the main contractor as the project co-ordinator. Based on finance, they decided to undertake the project management themselves, employing the various trades as and when they were required.

During the regular telephones calls made to us during the construction stage, it soon became obvious that this option was not as advantageous as they had first imagined. It is not until you undertake such a project that you realise exactly what is involved in project-managing a build. Without a formal contract, with no overall plan with timescales, and the issues with sourcing suitable materials in the correct time period, it proved to be a project with many ups and downs.

As Jackie commented on several occasions 'dealing with contractors was an entirely new language and took a period to adjust to'. Being gentle people, they also found it very hard dealing with contractors not pulling their weight. After eight months with many ups and downs, the project was completed.

EXCEEDING EXPECTATIONS:

Jackie and Tim are delighted with their end result and say that the building has exceeded all their original expectations. The building has 15 suites with double-glazed UPVC doors, underfloor heating with warm, vinyl floor coverings. The large size of the rooms and the design of the building make it an extremely calm, quiet and relaxing atmosphere to live and work in. This combined with the low number of dogs allows for lots of individual attention – is a winning combination which their customers delight in. There were also 'hidden' rewards for building such high standard dog-friendly accommodation, including things like how much easier the cleaning routine is, not only because of the vinyl finish, but also that there is little 'mess' to clear up. The dogs are very relaxed in their own private and quiet spaces, have comfortable, warm sleeping areas and get taken out several times a day. They behave as if they were at home, waiting for their late night or early morning visit outside.

The high quality of the kennels attracts a definite 'type' of customer who has rarely taken a holiday since having dogs, or who have rescue dogs who they feel have been through enough in kennels already. Their customers tell Jackie they are lucky to have found somewhere so special for their dogs, where the low numbers mean there is time to develop relationships with them – but most of all, time to care for them. Customers immediately understand that the love and dedication behind creating such a special and unique business is applied to everything, from the care of the dogs to their website diaries.

When we asked Jackie and Tim how they felt after operating for six months, their reply was simply: "*We love the fact that we are appealing to people just like us who have never left their dogs before. It is a lovely feeling to know that all of these people are happy to leave their precious dogs with us, and it makes the journey to get where we are now all the sweeter. Our passion for dogs started this project and to us nothing can be better than getting up each morning, in the most stunning location and entertaining and loving dogs all day – does it get any better than this? We don't think so!*"

Having visited the site on several occasions it is clear what they have achieved is a credit to them both; the quality they aimed for has been achieved, their initial vision and sheer determination has given them a kennel facility that sets them apart and has been so welcomed by their clients.

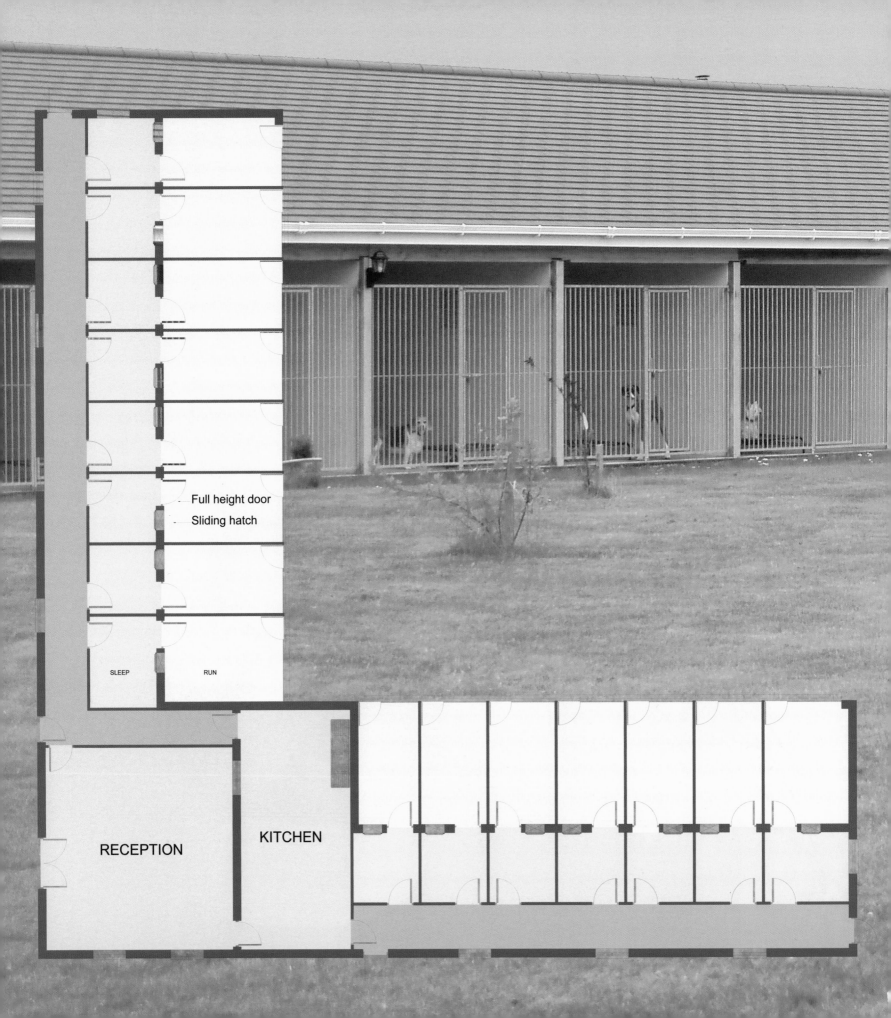

Full height door

Sliding hatch

SLEEP   RUN

RECEPTION   KITCHEN

CANINE COUNTRY CLUB

STATUTORY LEGISLATION

The scale of project has an impact on the level of infrastructure required, and it can also affect the level of legal requirements to be complied with.

In reality, the legislation shown on the following pages could apply to any new or existing development. However, the requirements for a smaller-scale project will be less onerous than for a larger-scale project. It is obvious that regulations cannot be listed for every county in every region in every country. Like kennel buildings, regulations will be similar (certainly between the UK, USA and Canada), although the wording may be slightly different.

In this chapter are listed regulations that kennel owners may need to observe in the UK, but there will be equivalent regulations in many countries. Many are a matter of common sense, even if there are no similar regulations for that country. Following are examples are the more common regulations with which you may need to comply.

You will see what kinds of responsibilities you may have from glancing through this chapter, such as:

- Building regulations, gas, electric, fire risk, emergency lighting, asbestos

- Health and safety regulations, accidents at work, protective equipment, working at height

- Construction, demolition, design and management

- Environment protection

- Disability discrimination

Statutory Obligations

All businesses are compelled to comply with certain legal obligations and regulations, irrespective of the size of the business; these regulations apply to both the employee and the employer. Like all legislation, the rules are complex and constantly changing; therefore only an overview is given of the relevant legislation to ensure that the employer is aware of the effect of the main legislation.

Full guides to the UK legislation can be obtained from HMSO Publications www.tso.co.uk and specialised publications such as Croner's www.croner.co.uk.

Building Regulations

Building Regulations are totally separate from planning permission. Although the Building Control Department may be housed in the same building as the planning authority, they are two self-governing bodies, totally independent of each other. Generally, under normal circumstances all schemes require Building Regulation approval. However, it is worth checking with the Building Control officer to establish whether all your proposed development will require permission.

Note: Building Regulations can be somewhat of a 'grey area' in the UK. It is worth checking with the Building Control Officer to seek their views on this.

Under Class III of the UK Building Regulations (Greenhouses and Agricultural Buildings) there are exceptions that allow for some relaxation in the requirements. These are:

- Buildings used for agricultural purposes, or principally for the keeping of animals:

  - sited not less than 1.5 times their height from any building containing sleeping accommodation, and
  - provided with a fire exit that is not more than 30m/98ft from any point of the building

These two points give an extremely useful loophole for the owners of any new development. However, consideration should be given to ensuring that the structure is safe, has adequate fire alarms and protection, and has adequate fire escape provision.

What is Building Control?

Building Regulations require that buildings, which are erected, extended, altered or which have a material change in their use, are capable of performing to minimum standards.

These standards are set to protect the health, safety and welfare of people; to conserve energy, and to prevent contamination of land and water. To ensure that these standards are met, you are required to inform the Building Control office of your intentions. Your architect, surveyor or builder will normally address the specific technical requirements of the regulations; however, there is no reason to stop you from dealing with the department yourself.

In most circumstances involving a commercial business or operation, the Building Control officer will primarily be interested in:

- Insulation values of the building

- Fire protection

- Heating source type, e.g. gas/oil boiler, electricity, etc

- Drainage – foul and surface water disposal

- Structure stability, foundations and ground conditions

- Access and fire escapes

Construction (Design and Management) Regulations 2007

CDM normally applies to existing UK businesses and in particular larger scale projects that will be longer than 30 days or involve more than 500 person days. The aim of the regulations is to promote better safety standards and health and safety provisions for construction workers. The responsibility for enforcing these regulations lies with the Health and Safety Executive. The regulations place specific duties on all parties involved with the development, i.e. client, design professionals, contractors and subcontractors. Projects which involve CDM notification to the Health and Safety Executive would normally have professional advisors, e.g. architects, that will advise the client and manage the legislative requirements of the Act.

Demolition

It may be necessary to demolish existing buildings on a newly acquired site. The reasons for this are usually to clear part of the site for development, or to remove or make safe any existing structures in an unsafe condition. The law regarding demolition is very specific and should not be taken lightly, with statutory requirements that must be adhered to. For any large-scale demolition, expert advice should normally be sought. Generally, consent to demolish a building is not required under the Town and Country Planning Acts, the exception to this being for a listed building. However, a person intending to demolish a building or part of it must give notice under section 80 of the UK Building Act 1984 to the local authority.

The Building Control section of the local authority usually undertakes the control of such work. The notice usually takes the form of a letter describing the impending work and a site plan showing the location and the building.

In addition to the Authority, the owner or his/her agent must also notify:

- Any utility boards, i.e. gas, electricity

- The owner/occupiers of any building adjacent to the building concerned

Personal Protective Equipment at Work Regulations 1993

Personal Protective Equipment (PPE) means all equipment (including clothing affording protection against the weather) intended to be worn or held by a person at work and which protects against one or more risks to health, safety and welfare.

The main items of PPE for the kennel owner would include such items as aprons and gloves (isolation), eye protection (mixing disinfectants), etc. It is designed to be personal protective equipment for an individual, not for communal use. The person given the equipment should have suitable provision to secure the equipment away after use. It is normally the 'last resort' and only to be provided where engineering controls and safe systems at work do not effectively control the risks identified.

The problems associated with PPE are:

- Protects only the person wearing it

- Maximum levels of protection with PPE are seldom achieved; in practice the actual level of protection is difficult to assess

- May restrict the wearer's movements, visibility, hearing and provide additional weight to be carried

Health and Safety at Work Act 1974

The broad aims of the Health and Safety at Work Act 1974 are essentially:

- **To secure the health, safety and welfare of persons** at work.

- **To protect persons other than employees** from risks at work, e.g. those living or working near the business or those entering the premises in the course of business

- **To control dangerous substances** in terms of acquisition or use

- **To control emissions** into the atmosphere from the workplace

- **Failure to comply with the Act**, or any regulations made under it, is a criminal offence and the employer, or even the employee, may be prosecuted

- **Health and Safety Policy Statement**
  At present any employer who has five or more employees must prepare a written statement of his general policy on health and safety. This policy will evolve and take into account changes in management, legal requirements and technological changes

Duties of Employees – Sections 7 and 8 of the Health and Safety at Work Act 1974 require every employee to have the following responsibilities:

- Take reasonable care for the health and safety of himself and other persons who may be affected by his acts or omissions at work, and as regards any duty or requirement imposed on his employer, or any other persons to co-operate with him, so far as is necessary to enable that duty or requirement to be performed or complied with

- No person shall intentionally or recklessly interfere with, or misuse, anything provided in the interests of health, safety or welfare in pursuance of any of the relevant statutory provisions

Accidents at Work

The legislation regarding accidents at work in commercial premises is contained in the Reporting of Injuries, Diseases and Dangerous Occurrences Regulations 1995 (RIDDOR). The aim of these regulations is to ensure accidents that occur in the workplace are investigated and, where possible, remedial measures are taken to avoid recurrence.

An accident is normally defined as one of the following and is reported to the Health and Safety Executive (HSE):

- Fatal accidents and major accidents/conditions

- Incidents where as a result of an accident connected with the workplace, people not at work are injured and have to be taken to hospital for treatment

- An incident where a person not at work suffers a major injury as a result of work being carried out and has to be treated at a hospital

- Dangerous occurrences and accidents that cause more than three days of incapacity absence from work

- Certain work-related diseases

- An accident includes any non-consensual act of physical violence suffered at work

Disability Discrimination Act 1995

It is unlawful for service providers to treat disabled people less favourably than other people for a reason related to their disability. Service providers have been obliged to:

- alter practices, policies or procedures that make it unreasonably difficult for disabled people to use their services

- provide alternative methods of making their services available where the physical features of their premises make it unreasonably difficult for disabled people to access services

- provide auxiliary aids and services to assist disabled people to access goods and services

The extent of adjustments that a service provider is obliged to make will depend on a number of factors; these include the level of activity, financial resources and the disruption the adjustment will cause.

Being Aware

The DDA classes someone as disabled if they have a physical or mental impairment that has a substantial and long-term adverse effect on their ability to carry out normal day-to-day activities. In addition to clients who use wheelchairs (a very low percentage), or who have mobility problems, there are millions of potential clients affected by some degree of hearing loss, learning disabilities, visual impairment, mental illness or more common conditions such as arthritis. The most important barriers to access for disabled people arise from the physical features of premises, from staff communication and training, and from the business policies and practices that service providers adopt. To achieve full access, it is as important that staff are aware of the various disabilities as it is to remove physical barriers to access such as steps, poor signage and dangerous and damaged pathways. A common sense approach towards individual needs, combined with minor adjustments, can make a dramatic improvement. Remember that around 3% of people are born with their disability, and around 83% of disabled people become disabled during their adult life.

Making Adjustments to Your Premises

Service providers have to make 'reasonable adjustments' to their premises so that there are no physical barriers stopping, or making it unreasonably difficult, for disabled people to get and use their services. The DDA requires that you make changes when it is unreasonably difficult for disabled people to use your services, not solely when it is completely impossible to use services. The definition of 'unreasonable' means whether the time, inconvenience, effort, discomfort or loss of dignity experienced by disabled people in using the service would be considered unreasonable by other people if they had to endure similar difficulties. Possible adjustments will depend on the scale of service you provide, practicality, disruption, cost compared with turnover. These factors will vary from kennels to kennels. A feature that is deemed reasonable for you to adjust might not be deemed reasonable for another business provider to adjust.

In circumstances where a person with a disability cannot gain access to a business because of the presence of a physical barrier, the business is obliged by the legislation to consider one or a combination of the following options:

- The removal of the feature that prevents the disabled person gaining access
- Alter the feature so that it no longer has the effect
- Provide a reasonable means of avoiding the feature
- Provide a reasonable alternative method of making the service in question available to the disabled person

Some of the main areas of concern and potential difficulties for disabled visitors are:

- **Car parking** – lack of dedicated parking
- **Main access door** – too narrow or too heavy to operate
- **Cluttered reception areas**
- **Signage** – outdated and poor signage with lettering too small to read
- **WCs** – without adequate door widths and emergency communication facilities

There are actions that can be taken by all businesses to minimise issues, and awareness is one of the critical factors.

There are simple actions that can be taken that do not cost money, such as:

- Not allowing able-bodied staff and visitors to use the disabled parking bays
- Keeping corridors and doors free from clutter and obstacles
- Not using disabled toilets as storage areas
- When speaking to a disabled visitor who is wheelchair bound, it is far better to pull up a chair and sit next to them. This is not only polite, but also more comfortable for both parties
- If the centre is busy and noisy, it is far better to talk to a visitor with a hearing impairment by moving to a quiet part of the reception or preferably to an interview room

The aim is to allow the disabled person to remain as independent as possible and to enjoy the visit as much as an able-bodied person

Environmental Protection Act 1990

The UK Environmental Protection Act 1990 (Part III) draws together most of the statutory nuisances from earlier legislation, and amends some of the definitions and rationalises them. Under the 1990 Act, there is a duty for every local authority to *"cause its area to be inspected from time to time to detect any statutory nuisances which ought to be dealt with"*. Areas of concern that may affect the kennel owner might be noise, smell, conditions of premises, waste materials (e.g. cans, litter, animal waste) not suitably contained that might attract vermin and flies, and any other nuisance.

Duty of Care

Under Section 34 of the Environmental Protection Act 1990 all producers of waste are compelled to dispose of it in such a manner so as not to endanger public health or the environment; this is known as 'duty of care.'

All waste produced on the site has to be transported by a registered carrier and disposed of at an authorised facility.

Under The Environmental Protection (Duty of Care) Regulations 1991 a mandatory system of transfer notes was introduced. Under normal circumstances all waste will be collected by arrangement either by the authority or a local, registered carrier. The definition of waste produced by kennels is under review; therefore it is worth checking with the local authority to clarify local policy (see the chapter on Environmental Legislation).

Gas Safety Regulations

The Gas Safety (Installation and Use) Regulations 1994 were introduced to try to prevent and reduce the amount of dangerous gas appliances in use; these include fires, cookers, boilers, laundry equipment, etc.

The regulations are complex, but the basic guidelines are simple: to ensure that any gas appliance or installation pipework at a place of work is maintained in a safe condition. It is the duty of any person who owns a gas appliance or any installation in a premise, or part of a premise, let by him, to ensure the appliance and installation is in a safe condition. A registered and qualified person should check the appliance and installation annually. A record should be kept of the inspection and of any recommendations made or works carried out.

Electricity at Work Regulations

The Electricity at Work Regulations 1989 were introduced in April 1990 and were designed to take into account changes in technological developments and, more importantly, brought a legal compliance to all.

Inspections

It is a legal requirement that the premises provide a safe environment for staff, public and any other visitors, and that an inspection of the entire wiring system is carried out every three to five years. Obviously, a new installation that has not been modified or tampered with is far safer than an installation that is 30 years' old and has had several modifications over this period.

Portable Appliance Testing

The testing and recording of electrical portable appliances is a procedure that is normally carried out every 12 months for most light commercial operations; it is a legal requirement. Each appliance and if applicable its power lead is tested by a suitably-trained person or electrician; on completion of the test it will either pass, or fail and need corrective works. Once these works have been carried out, it will be tested again and either pass or fail. Once a 'pass' standard has been reached, this will vary for each appliance. A label will be stuck/attached to the appliance with its own unique number or code for identification purposes. The details should be logged either in a book or on a computer disk, and this should be kept in a safe place.

Control of Substances Hazardous to Health Regulations 1994

The Control of Substances Hazardous to Health Regulations 1994 (COSHH) applies to potentially harmful substances. The COSSH provisions cover practically all substances harmful to health at work, e.g. disinfectants, waste, etc.
The act is divided into six main provisions:

1. **Assessment -** No employee should be exposed to substances hazardous to health unless an assessment has been carried out. Data sheets provided by the chemical manufacturers will provide the general information required

2. **Prevention or control -** Once substances hazardous to health have been identified, the employer must prevent or control it by various means such as substitution, elimination or ventilation, etc

3. **Maintenance and testing of equipment -** Employers must ensure employees use any control measures in force. The employer is responsible for ensuring all equipment is inspected, tested and a record kept of this

4. **Monitoring -** Employers must monitor employees who have been exposed to hazardous substances

5. **Health surveillance -** If employees are exposed to substances that may have been a contributory factor to ill health, e.g. dermatitis and disinfectants, it may be appropriate to arrange a health surveillance programme. This can range from a full medical check to self-**inspection**

6. **Information, training and instruction -** Employees exposed to hazardous substances must be given adequate training, information and instruction to know the risks involved to their health and how to use control measures

Control of Asbestos at Work Regulations 2006

This latest piece of legislation is one that all businesses in the UK need to be aware of.

Asbestos first became noticeable in the 1960's when it was recognised that exposure to asbestos fibres had potential and deadly consequences. Asbestos is still found in many households and businesses today. In reality it is still an extremely useful product. It was used extensively in housing for insulation, fire-proofing materials, thermoplastic floor tiles, rainwater guttering and roofing materials as well as a wide range of commercial applications. It was used extensively in construction during the 1950's until the early 1980's, and even up until 1999 in some cement-sheet based products.

The current legislation requires the following in non-domestic premises:

- To survey and to determine whether asbestos-containing material is present (the presumption is that the material will contain asbestos unless it is proven otherwise)

- Assess the amount and condition of the material

- Make, record and keep up-to-date records of the location

- Assess the risk of the material and how the risk will be managed

- Review and monitor the situation

- Provide information to anyone who is likely to come into contact with the material

- Due to the complexities of this regulation, any business should take professional guidance

See www.HSE.gov.uk for more information.

Work at Height Regulations 2005

The Work at Height Regulations 2005 must to be considered by all businesses. Falls from relatively low heights, up to 2m/6ft 6" still remain the single biggest cause of workplace deaths and one of the main causes of major injury.

The nature of many roofing materials used in kennels often means it has to be cleaned to remove algae and vegetation, etc. The fragile nature of many roofing materials will, in many cases, not support the weight of a person; obviously this is potentially lethal.

The aims of the regulations are to:

- Avoid work at height where possible

- Use work equipment or other measures to prevent falls where working at height cannot be avoided

- Where the risk of a fall cannot be eliminated, the use of work equipment or other measures to minimise the distance and the consequences of a fall should one occur

- The use of mechanical lift platforms has become the mainstay for many operations that in the past were carried out by the use of ladders

For further information see www.hse.gov.uk/falls

Fire Precautions (Workplace) Regulations 1997

On 1 December 1997 the Fire Precautions (Workplace) Regulations took effect, with explicit requirements for every organisation with five or more employees to carry out a written fire risk assessment. The assessment is to ensure that all areas of potential risk have been identified. In the main this will cover:

- Identification of the areas where fires are likely to occur, and risk assess for those areas
- Provision of measures to minimise the possibility of a fire starting
- Ensuring that fire protection systems, escape routes, etc. allow escape to a safe place

Every area should be assessed separately and a judgment should be made with regard to the type of combustible materials and possible sources of ignition, types of doors, i.e. should standard doors be replaced with fire-rated doors, availability of fire extinguishers, etc.

Fire Protection

Generally the main areas of concern are: fire alarm system, emergency lighting, fire-fighting and protection.
Most kennel buildings by their very nature do not represent a significant fire risk; the solid nature of construction and the lack of inflammable materials all reduce the risk. This, combined with a non-smoking policy and regular electrical wiring checks, will minimise the risk. The normal procedure when applying for Building Regulations Approval is for the officer concerned to pass a set of the plans to the Fire Brigade. The plans will be assessed and recommendations made for any specific requirements; for most small kennels the minimum recommendation would possibly be for portable fire extinguishers or fire doors with overhead closing devices. Insurance companies may also stipulate the level of equipment required for a particular location and operation. Even if your building does not come under the requirements for Building Regulations or Control, it is good business policy to install basic fire protection as it may save lives.

The basic elements for domestic and small commercial operations can be divided into three elements:

- Fire detection and alarms systems
- Emergency lighting
- Portable fire fighting equipment

Fire Detection and Alarm Systems

There is a vast range of systems available on the market from simple battery-operated, stand-alone units to fully integrated systems linked to intruder alarms. The level with which your insurance company and the fire authority are satisfied will depend on the layout of the centre, the size of the building, the number of staff employed and any high-risk operations that might be carried out. However, most animal welfare establishments and kennels are classed as low-risk properties and therefore do not normally require a sophisticated system. The purpose of fire detection and alarm systems is to act as an early warning system. The more time there is to take the appropriate action, the less likelihood of serious damage or loss of life.
Fire detection should not be viewed as an unnecessary expense, a waste of time or something that may never be used; the sooner a fire is detected, the more chance of limiting the damage. The cost of installing a basic system is an extremely small percentage of the overall project cost. The minimum requirement is a battery-operated stand-alone unit, which will give an audible alarm in the region of 90dB. Clearly this type of unit has its limitations and this must be taken into account when looking at the site layout, distance of the kennels from any residential property, etc. A more permanent solution is to install a basic system of heat/smoke detectors linked to a control panel with manual call points and an external audible alarm. A 'zoned' system allows a staff member to go directly to the fire zone without having to spend time looking for the fire.

Emergency Lighting

The aim of emergency lighting is to indicate the emergency escape routes, to show changes of direction, to show where the fire alarm call points and fire extinguishers are located and also to enable emergency work to be carried out or completed. The types of lighting available are:

- Some luminaries with emergency battery back-up
- Wall-mounted plug-in, battery-operated units
- A central battery system, which powers all of the luminaries
- A back-up generator capable of providing power to all the lights
  This has the added benefit of being able to provide power to enable the rest of the site to continue to function

Because of the relatively simple construction and layout of most single-storey kennels, the normal requirement is for a very basic mains-supplied system, which covers legal requirements and enables basic duties to continue during a power cut.

Portable Fire-fighting Equipment

The installation of portable fire extinguishers is a legal and usually an insurance requirement. Most kennels will have only this type of equipment installed; the installation of fixed, centralised, monitored systems will not be required for most single-storey buildings with good external access points. The type and number of extinguishers required is dependent upon the size of the premises and the risks of fire involved; advice should be sought from insurance companies, extinguisher suppliers, and the fire officer. When talking about fire extinguishers we are dealing only with small isolated fires that can be extinguished quickly and safely; we are not concerned with large fires that have engulfed an entire room or a more extensive area. Once a fire has reached this latter stage the only safe action is to vacate the building and call the Fire Brigade.

- **Wall-mounted extinguishers** – These fire extinguishers come in a variety of sizes and substances for use on different types of fire and materials. Advice on the most suitable for your needs should be discussed with your insurance company or provider

- **Hose reels** – Recommended particularly for floor areas in excess of $800m^2$/8611 sq ft. Extremely effective on certain classes of fire, they deliver an unlimited supply of water, and with sufficient mains pressure can deliver a jet of water in excess of 6m/20ft. A standard hose is 30m/98ft in length

- **Fire blanket** – This is used to smother small fires involving liquids and organic materials, and would normally be installed near cooking appliances

All of the above appliances need to be sited in the most suitable place, generally:

- As close as possible to any fire risk
- Close/adjacent to doorways and on escape routes
- At the same location in identical buildings
- Near 'fire points'
- Away from extremes of temperature

The extinguishers need to be securely fixed to walls, approximately 900mm/3ft above the floor. This will prevent the base from rusting, particularly in wet environments, and also prevent them being used as 'door stops'! They should be visible at all times and staff should be aware of their location and, more importantly, how to use them. It is pointless having extinguishers on the premises if none of the staff can operate them. Most supplying companies will offer an annual inspection to ensure that the units are fully charged and capable of working; this can also be an ideal time to train staff to operate an extinguisher. It is surprising how difficult some people may find the procedure of discharging an extinguisher.
ANY form of practice might make the difference between a minor fire and a major disaster.

These Kennels were Funded
by
The Late Mrs Coco Markus

These Kennels were Opened
by
HRH the Duke of Gloucester KG GCVO
on
29 April 2003

7 KENNEL STYLES AND DESIGNS

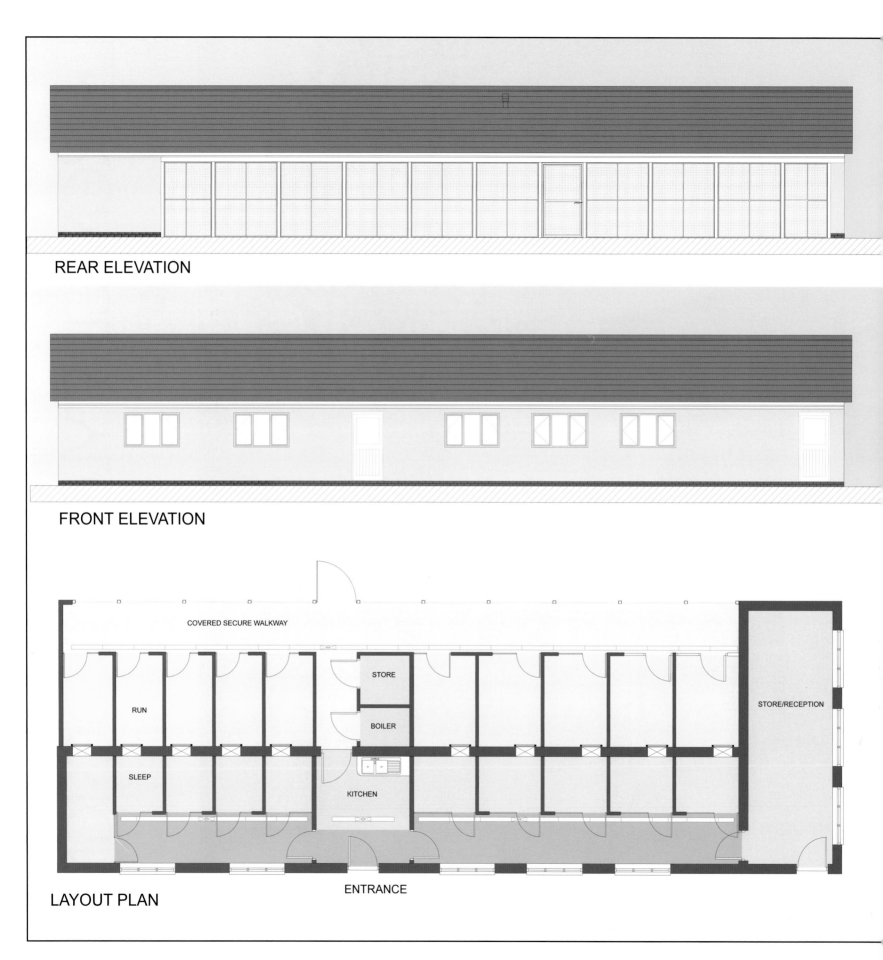

REAR ELEVATION

FRONT ELEVATION

COVERED SECURE WALKWAY

STORE

STORE/RECEPTION

RUN

BOILER

SLEEP

KITCHEN

LAYOUT PLAN

ENTRANCE

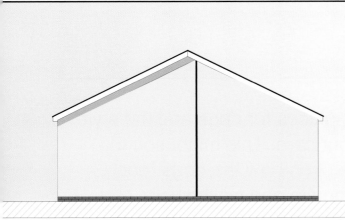

END ELEVATION

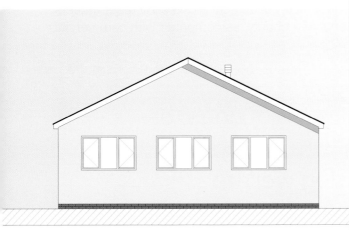

END ELEVATION

CONSTRUCTION MATERIALS

ROOF = dark grey insulated steel profile
WALLS = cream rendered blockwork
WINDOWS/DOORS = painted softwood
METALWORK = galvanised finish

BUILDING SIZE = 25180mm x 8420mm

rev.	date	details

Client:
David Key

Project Title:
New Kennel Building

Drawing Title:
Planning Elevations & Layout

Drawn:	Scale:
Date:	Drawing Ref:

Kennel & Cattery Design
PO Box 146
Chipping Norton
Oxfordshire
OX7 6WA

Tel: +44 (0) 1608 646454
www.kenneldesign.com

This drawing is the Copyright of
Kennel & Cattery Design

DRAWING DETAIL INFORMATION

Visualisations for the Owner

The 3Ds, layouts and elevations shown in this book have been shaded to help you visualise the different areas within a building (i.e. sleep, run, ancillary rooms, corridors) and think through how the different designs will work for your requirements and site.

For large developments, they can also be a useful aid for planning/zoning

Planning/Zoning Drawings (left)

However, the architectural designs for planning/zoning permission have a different focus. The authorities are concerned with how the building will look on your site, the scale of it, the materials you intend to use. The elevations and layout shown left are typical of the type of detail required for submission to the local authority (i.e. elevations, layout, sizes, facing construction materials) and would need to be to scale for an application. **These DO NOT show specific design detail for construction purposes**

Construction Details for Builders (below)

For physical construction, pricing and building control, your builder will need a set of drawings to scale, and written specification with detailed information on the materials to be used, the size of openings, specialist products to be used (i.e. setting out of measurements, angles, drainage, services, floor construction, placement of doors, hatches and windows). **These MUST show specific design detail for construction purposes.**

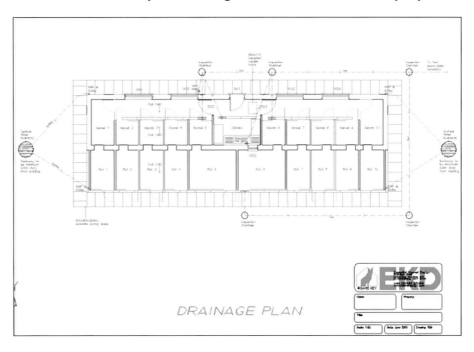

DRAINAGE PLAN

KENNEL STYLES AND DESIGNS

As already discussed, kennels can be very traumatic places for dogs and the style of design has to be suitable for the type of dogs in your care. This might sound obvious, but different designs can have a marked effect on how the dogs react, settle into the kennel routine, and ultimately on their health and wellbeing.

The designs shown in this section are primarily aimed at commercial kennels, rescue organisations and charities. In so far as the 'best' kennel design, there is no single design of kennels or layout that is suitable for all sites. All requirements are different, and this is particularly noticeable when looking at the requirements of a charity, as compared with commercial establishments.

Not all designs are suitable for all types of dogs, or businesses. This chapter will help you understand how different designs affect dog welfare

---

Organisations providing long-term or permanent stay facilities will tend to have their own requirements, and additional welfare aspects will need to be taken into consideration when designing this type of faciity.

The size and design will be influenced by financial restrictions, the land area available, proximity of neighbours, the number of kennels to be built, planning issues, and any existing buildings that may be used. The ultimate standard and image you portray, and also any business statement to make to customers can be incorporated into the design. Equally important will be environmental aspects such as areas with extremes of temperature (hot and cold), wind, rain and altitude, and all these aspects should also be taken into consideration.

However, often it is the financial restriction that has the greatest influence on the number of kennels constructed.

Generally, commercial kennels will be **full height (i.e. minimum height of 2m/6ft 6")** and have a sleep area with direct access to an **attached exercise run or toiletting area**.

Dogs NEED to have sleeping and eating areas separate from toiletting areas. (Even with indoor-only kennels, the separation of these two areas is easily achievable)

Kennel Styles:

The different styles available:

- Indoor
- Outdoor
- Semi-outdoor (this is the ideal)

These three styles will have a significant impact on the choice of kennel design.

Kennel Designs for Dog Welfare

Designs listed in order of preference for dog welfare:

1. Single Line

This is the best option for dog welfare and quieter kennels, as it **prevents dogs facing each other**, and allows easier management of dogs within the building (reduces negative excitement and redirected aggression) but it is slightly more expensive to build.

- Straight line
- L shape
- U shape
- Square

2. Double Line

This is the most cost-effective design, but there are disadvantages as the **dogs are facing each other**. Many of the disadvantages with this design can be reduced by **increasing the corridor width** to a minimum of 1.8m/6ft and even greater benefits can be seen with larger widths, e.g. 3m/10ft. Further improvements on this design can be made by **incorporating full height walls** (dividing and corridor walls) **offset with glazed doors** (offset from the opposite kennel) to make the dogs feel more secure and give a greater level of privacy and seclusion, that naturally reduces stress

3. Circular

Although 'different' and a visually appealing idea to humans - this is **the worst design for dog welfare** for organisations which have a high turnover of dogs unused to the kennel environment.
All dogs are facing each other, which leads to greater levels of stress, negative excitement and greater noise levels. Experience shows that this type of design can produce the highest levels of noise.

Final design and configuration can dramatically alter the appearance of the building and affect how the dogs react.
If you would like to see and hear just how much difference each of these designs makes to dog welfare and noise, visit:
www.kenneldesign.com/videos

Corridor width of 1.8m/ 6ft which feels spacious in a single line kennels with lots of natural daylight

Corridor at 3m/10ft wide giving a spacious, open feel in a double line kennels
Also note that kennels are offset and angled to reduce the number of dogs facing each other

CORRIDORS AND WALKWAYS

Consideration should be given to ensure that adequate width is provided for walkways, access and safety corridors.

Corridor and Walkway Widths

The minimum width to consider is 1.2m/4ft, with a preferred width of 1.5m/5ft.

When running a busy rescue, sanctuary or upscale boarding kennels, it is worth considering increasing this to a minimum of 1.8m/6ft, as this will allow two wheelchairs to pass each other.

Whatever width is decided upon as being the most suitable and cost-effective, it should be a clear width, without obstructions such as radiators, fire hoses, display stands, etc. The width of the corridor could be a building regulations requirement for a large charity.

For double-line kennel designs it is evident that a wider corridor (in excess of 1.8m/ 6ft) does have dog welfare benefits. Even without finding scientific studies to back this concept, experience has shown how successful it is in practice.

The final decision comes down to personal preference, space and budget available, and how kennels access for staff and visitors wil be managed.

Corridors at 1m/3ft look and feel cramped, worsened in a dark setting with small windows

INDOOR KENNELS

Indoor kennels are more common in America and Canada (and other countries with extremes of climate or greater use of industrial buildings). This style is also favoured by some organisations and individuals where noise is, or is likely to be, an issue with neighbours, or where conversions of existing buildings have taken place.

There are some additional considerations that have to be taken into account. The main areas of concern are ventilation and lack of natural lighting. However, providing these have been considered at the design stage and adequate allowance made, there is no reason why this design should not be as successful as any other. Indeed, given the lifestyle of many pets, this type of building will be closer to their normal environment than a sudden or dramatic change such as very open kennels subject to extreme weather conditions.

This style (if constructed properly with good ventilation and natural lighting) is equal to other designs for short-stay periods. Indoor kennels can have the same design characteristics as all the other styles mentioned in this chapter (e.g straight line, L-shaped, U-shaped, square, double or circular) but the difference is there is no immediate contact with the outside environment (i.e. mechanical ventilation rather than natural fresh air).

Special considerations for indoor kennels are:

- Adequate ventilation to be taken into account when the building is running at full occupancy

- Adequate natural light

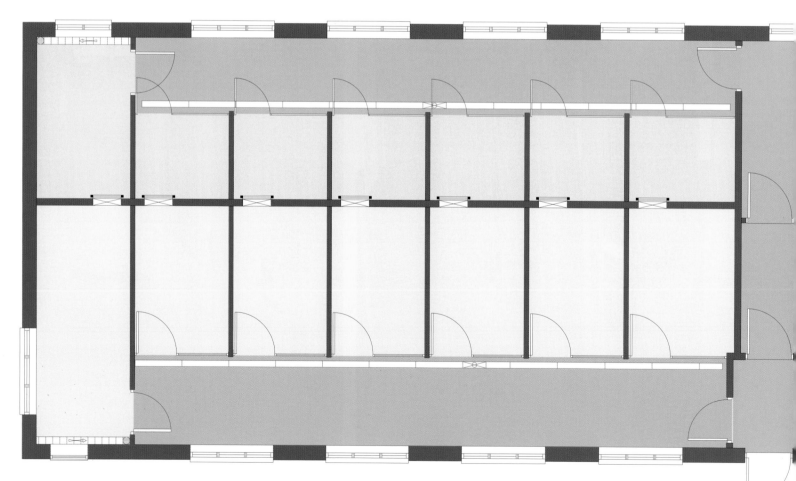

Advantages:

- Temperature control in areas with extremes of climate

- Where a quiet external environment is required (e.g. for neighbours)

Potential Disadvantages:

- Higher environmental control costs, i.e. air-conditioning, enhanced ventilation, fully mechanical heating and cooling (a backup system for large developments might also be required)

- Lack of ventilation/fresh air

- Lack of daylight, or poorer quality of lighting

- Lack of an outlook for the dogs

- Higher risk of disease

Indoor Style - Single Line Straight

The layout shown below overcomes many of the potential disadvantages, with a design that allows windows to be opened to allow fresh air into the building. It also addresses potential noise issues by allowing the noise to be handled in a more controlled manner, making it more manageable.

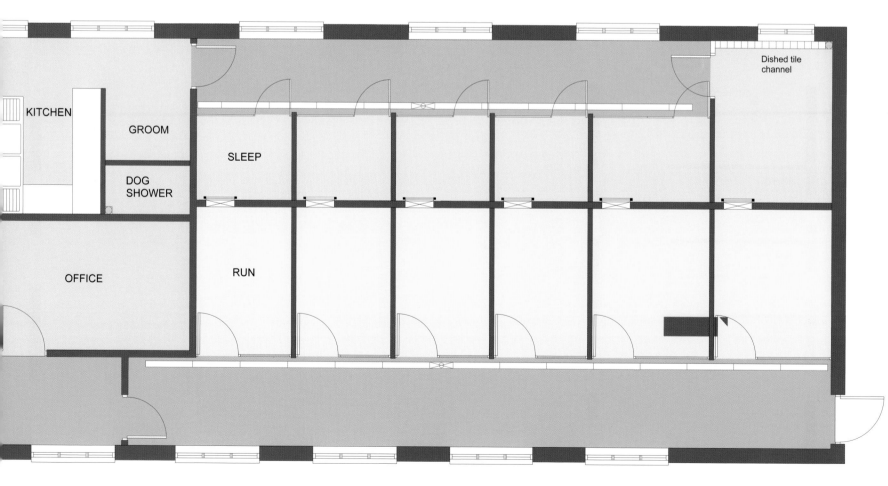

LAUNDRY
&
BOILER ROOM

KITCHEN

SLUICE

FEMALE WC

KITCHEN

Isolation 1

Isolation 2

Isolation 3

STORE

MALE WC

GROOMING ROOM

FOOD STORE

EQUIPMENT STORE

Indoor Style - Single Line U-Shaped Design

This layout shows an indoor style kennels with large sleep areas only (no attached exercise run) and was designed for a specialist **police dog** training centre.

The brief was for indoor kennels (to reduce noise externally) and the fact that the dogs were working and undergoing an intensive training programme meant the kennels were acting purely as overnight sleeping accommodation, with the dogs out working all day.

The extra large sleep areas were 3.5m x 1.7m/ 12ft x 5ft 7".

The single line design (dogs not facing each other) was chosen to reduce the levels of negative excitement, possible redirected aggression and provide a secure environment that allowed the dogs to relax more easily.

The building incorporated kitchen, laundry, grooming and stores as well as a separate isolation wing.

This was a building for a specialist need, designed to accommodate the client's unique requirements for the type of dogs in their care, all of whom were out exercising, training and working all day long.

This design would NOT be suitable for a commercial or rescue kennels because it does not allow the dogs separate toileting area

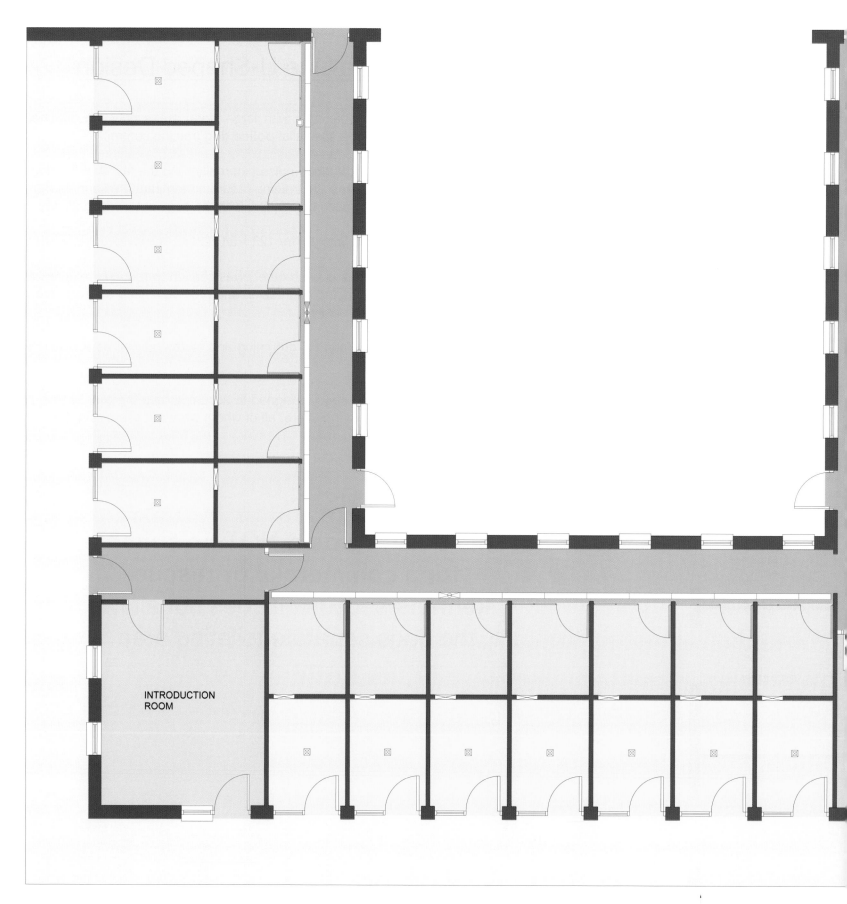

INTRODUCTION
ROOM

Covered walkway

Dog
Shower

KITCHEN

CE AREA

STORE

Indoor Style - Single Line U-Shaped Design

This layout shows another variation, but a more traditional design with adjoining sleep and run areas - suitable for rescue or boarding kennels.

OUTDOOR KENNELS

Outdoor kennels have many similarities to semi-outdoor kennels. They have an external run or toilet area with an attached sleeping area. The difference may be clarified by the way the sleep area is entered. For an outdoor kennel, the sleep area is entered externally via the exercise run.

This design is more common to working dog kennels (e.g. gun dogs).

Advantages:

- **Modular system**
  Often utilising timber as the main construction material (NOT permissible for licensed boarding establishments). This design also lends itself tor construction from traditional materials such as blockwork.

- **Ventilation**
  This design allows excellent levels of ventilation and generally a good views for dogs

- **Natural light**
  Allows good levels of natural light

- **Cheap** to construct

- **Quick** to install

Disadvantages:

- **Safety**
  The major disadvantage with this design, particularly for charities, sanctuaries and commercial boarding kennels is that the sleep area has to be entered via the exercise run (toiletting area). This means that the staff have to either remove the dog when cleaning, or control the dog.

  This is fine when the dog is well-behaved and its temperament known, but for organisations dealing with strange dogs with unknown temperaments, this can pose safety issues for the staff.

- **Cold for Dogs, Staff and Visitors**
  The major disadvantage with this system, particularly for sanctuaries and charities, is that it tends to be cold for the staff and visitors; this can have a marked effect on rehoming figures and number of visitors, etc. This is often exacerbated by the fact that the indoor sleeping section is warm, and the dogs are quite happy to stay indoors and out of sight!

SLEEP

RUN

COVERED WALKWAY

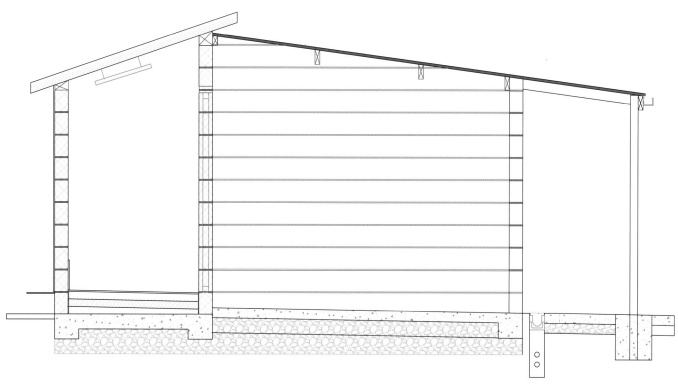

SEMI-OUTDOOR KENNELS

Semi-outdoor kennels have heated indoor accommodation and individual, covered exercise runs with the front face open to the atmosphere. Each kennel is entered individually from a service corridor.

There are design options that allow access to the external exercise run from the internal corridor; these differences can be seen in greater detail in the following layouts/plans.

This design forms the backbone for the majority of designs throughout the world. The layout and design can come in many configurations; it is generally the most cost-effective and flexible design, and provides many of the required features for the dogs' welfare, staff ease of working and public access. Favoured by many commercial kennels, charities and sanctuaries as it offers better viewing from the public's point of view, and usually plenty for the dogs to watch. It also allows staff to work and discuss potential adoptions/bookings with clients under cover and in the warm in the colder months (or cool in the warmer months, especially if air conditioned)

The semi-outdoor design is generally the most cost-effective and flexible design, and provides many of the required features for dog welfare, staff ease of working, and public access

---

Designs listed in order of preference for dog welfare:

- **Single line**
  This is the best option for dog welfare and quieter kennels, as it prevents dogs facing each other, and allows easier management of dogs within the building (reduces negative excitement and redirected aggression).

- **Double line**
  Some of the disadvantages with this design can be reduced by increasing the corridor width to a minimum of 1.8m/6ft and even greater benefits can be seen with larger widths e.g. 3m/10ft. Full height walls (dividing and corridor walls) offset with glazed doors (offset from the opposite kennel) to make the dogs feel more secure and give a greater level of privacy and seclusion, which naturally reduces stress

- **Circular**
  Although 'different' and a visually appealing idea to humans - this is the worst design for dog welfare. All dogs are facing each other, which leads to greater levels of stress, negative excitement and consequently noise.

  Final design and configuration can dramatically alter the appearance of the building and affect how the dogs react.

If you would like to see movies and hear how much difference each of these designs makes to dog welfare and noise, visit www.kenneldesign.com/videos

Semi-outdoor design with full height door to the exercise run

SINGLE LINE DESIGN

The biggest benefit of single line design is that dogs are not facing any dogs opposite their sleep area. The benefits are many, including the provision of a more private, secure area for the dogs, reducing noise, stress and frustration, and creating a calm, relaxing environment.

This design substantially reduces noise levels, and therefore improves dog welfare. It also reduces the risk of complaints from neighbours, makes a noticeably more pleasant working environment for owner, staff, clients and adopters. The calm, comfortable and relaxing environment makes the experience a world apart from typical expectations, and this quieter environment encourages more bookings, more volunteers, and potential adopters to stay longer (which will naturally increase rehoming rates and levels of donations).

Site layout should be designed to maximise welfare benefits. For example, the enormous benefits of this design will be ruined if another kennels is built opposite, so that the dogs all face each other, or if an exercise area is placed in front of the kennels. The concept of the single line design is to stop the stress and frustration (negative excitement) of seeing other dogs.

The single line design can be a straight line, L shape or U shape. The advantages of using L or U-shape is that it reduces the overall length of the building, this naturally breaks up the building into smaller zones. This provides a building with a high degree of flexibility (e.g. keeping the single line style, but fitting shorter building lengths onto a more compact site) and ensures a smaller number of dogs in any one area.

The single line design is the most beneficial to dog welfare

Advantages:

- Offers a more personal, upmarket feel of a quieter, smaller development - which naturally lends itself to a higher income or rehoming rate

- Modular style that can be extended or reduced and suitable for a variety of sites

- Looks less imposing than a double bank style (this might be a planning consideration)

- Less noise and stress as the dogs are not facing each other

- The building can be orientated to face the sun in cooler climates (e.g. south/south-west in the UK) to give the dogs benefit of sunlight, and help dry the kennels faster

- The sections can be of unequal length if required, to suit the plot of land, or for aesthetic reasons

- Non-animal related operations can be carried out without going into the main kennel sections

- Soft landscaping increases the aesthetic qualities and removes the harsh look often associated with kennels

- Individual sections for different types of dogs, e.g. elderly, puppies, nervous or large and boisterous

Disadvantages:

- More expensive pro rata to construct than a double bank

- Limited practical length of building (e.g. a straight line with 20 kennels will be in excess of 35m/115ft in length)

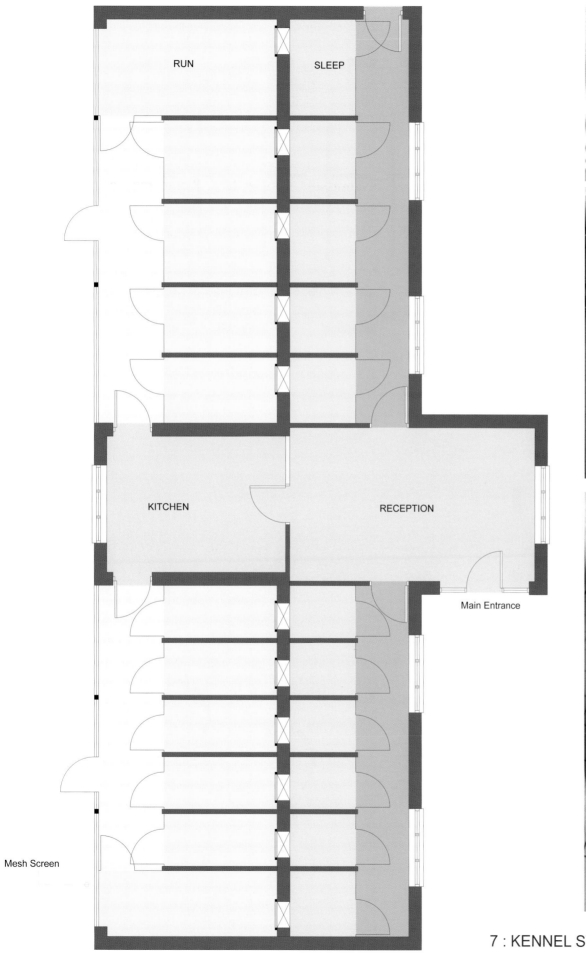

RUN

SLEEP

KITCHEN

RECEPTION

Main Entrance

Mesh Screen

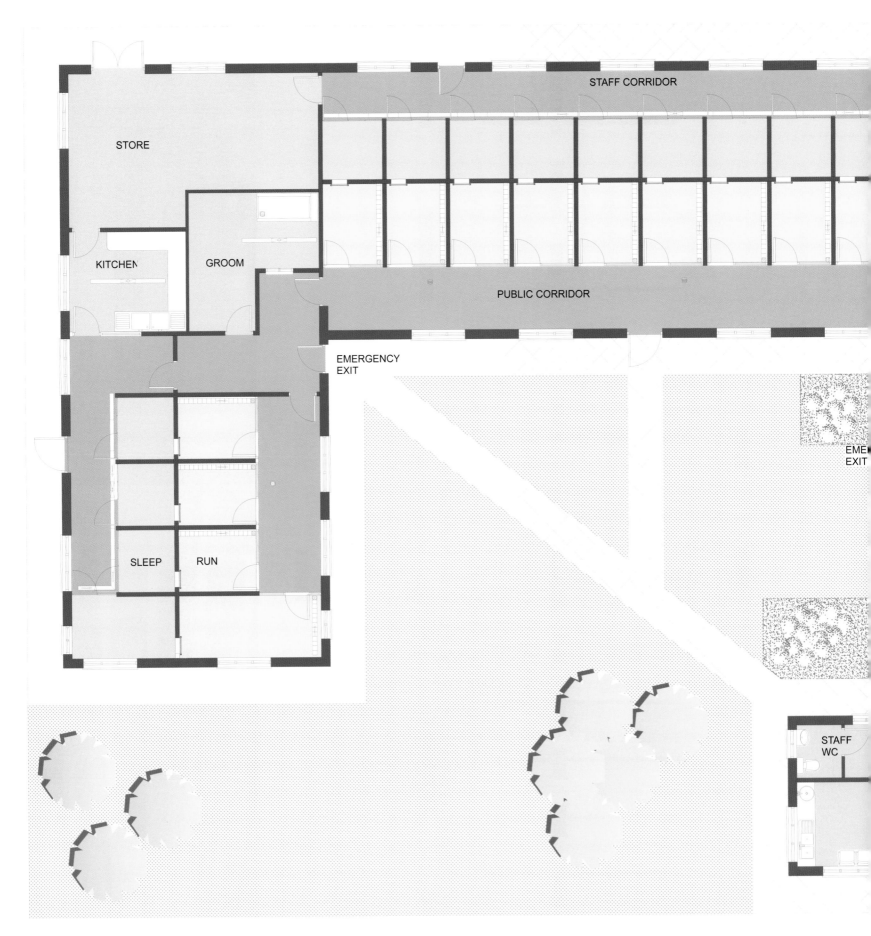

STAFF CORRIDOR

STORE

KITCHEN GROOM

PUBLIC CORRIDOR

EMERGENCY
EXIT

EME
EXIT

SLEEP RUN

STAFF
WC

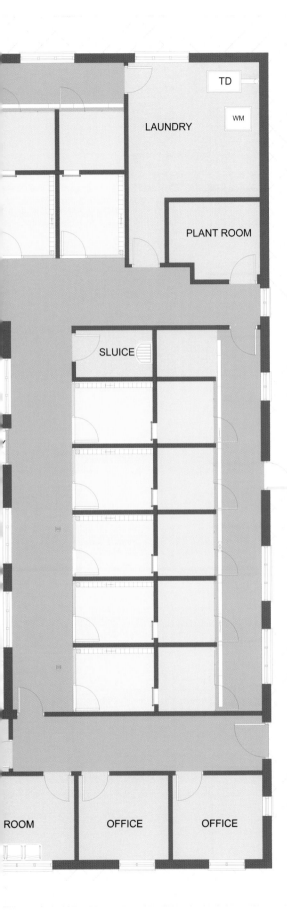

TD

LAUNDRY

WM

PLANT ROOM

SLUICE

EMERGENCY
EXIT

ROOM

OFFICE

OFFICE

MAIN
ENTRANCE

Single Line - U Shaped

This 20-kennels design was a proposal for a charity as its next generation style of kennels, encompassing all of the latest welfare ideas, ease of use for staff and staff facilities, and much more welcoming to visitors.

This building could easily be adapted as the design is very flexible. For example, the office and staff room space could easlily become a retail area, grooming, etc as it is right next to the entrance.

There is a fine line between calling this an indoor or a semi-outdoor design. The design could still be considered semi-outdoor, (even though the public corridor is behind blockwork and glass rather than open mesh) because there are doors and windows that can be opened whenever required.

This design would reduce the levels of noise externally. This makes it suitable for noise-sensitive sites.

This design has individual rooms (full height dividing walls) for improved dog welfare and to provide a more relaxing environment for the dogs.

Given the large number of visitors all year round, the decision was taken to provide an indoor corridor for visitor comfort and to encourage them to spend more time at the kennels, which would hopefully lead to more dog adoptions.

For a more traditional semi-outdoor design, the corridor could be constructed using mesh instead of blockwork and glass.

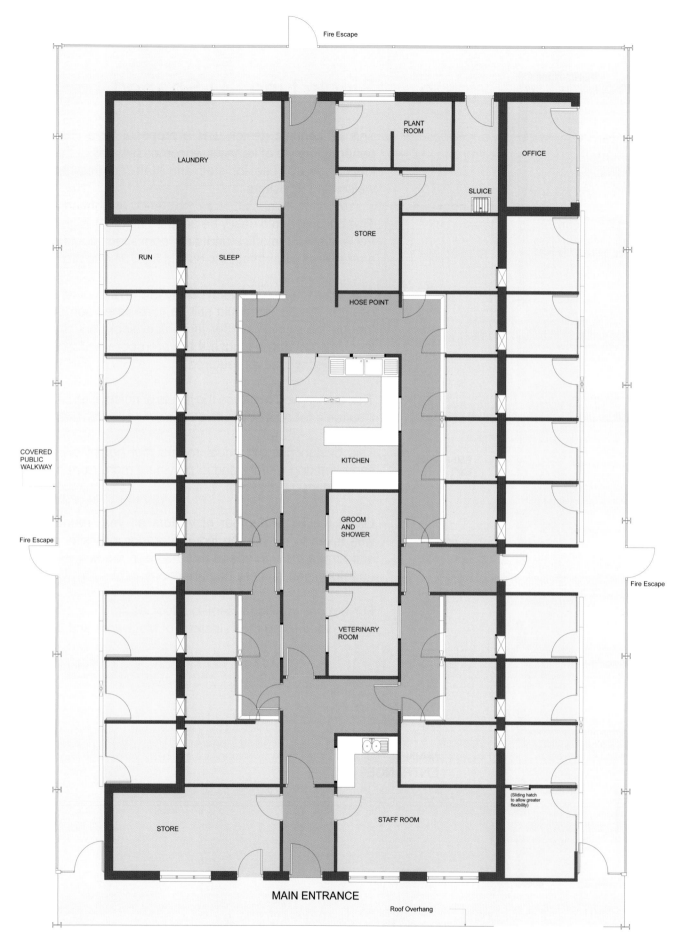

Fire Escape

PLANT ROOM

OFFICE

LAUNDRY

SLUICE

STORE

RUN

SLEEP

HOSE POINT

COVERED PUBLIC WALKWAY

KITCHEN

GROOM AND SHOWER

Fire Escape

Fire Escape

VETERINARY ROOM

(Sliding hatch to allow greater flexibility)

STORE

STAFF ROOM

MAIN ENTRANCE

Roof Overhang

Single Line Design: Square

The images opposite and below show a large square design. Although it might look as if it is a double line, it is still classed as a single line because no dogs are facing each other. The central core incorporates all the ancillary rooms such as kitchen, office store, grooming, etc.

These 3D images were for a concept proposal to see how some of the issues for concern (such as lighting and ventilation) could be satisfied. After careful consideration this design was abondoned in favour of a straight single line, which removed the problem of the building size being so deep (the single line is more flexible, it will fit on restricted sites far easier than a large building like this).

This change of direction illustrates exactly why the design of the building is so important when considering requirements not just for now but for the long term. What at first may seem an ideal design may not work practically for you. There may be a better design that satisfies all your requirements and site constraints.

For areas where building size is not a concern, this is a design that has many benefits, providing critical areas such as ventilation and natural lighting are considered carefully.

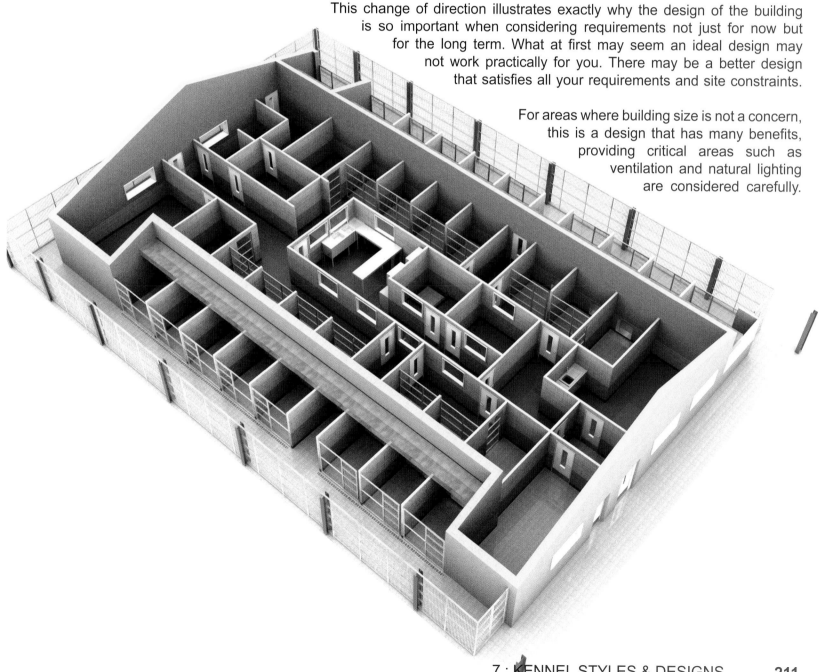

DOUBLE LINE DESIGN

This has been the traditional style for may years, and even today still proves to be a design that has many benefits to the owner, but less for dog welfare. It is a versatile design that will suit a variety of sites. Owners like the fact that the design is symmetrical, fits in well on a compact site, and tends to be used to house a larger number of dogs - and pro rata it is cheaper to construct than a single line design, as there are more services in one area and in closer proximity (drainage, etc).

The benefits to the owner have to be balanced against the dog welfare concerns (when designed to hold a large number of dogs, continual change-over of dogs, dogs get used to each other, then new dogs are brought in and the process starts again). As with all designs, good management systems (responding to the dogs' needs) plays a major part in dog welfare.

There are ways to improve dog welfare by having a wider corridor, solid full-height walls between the kennels and internal corridor walls (providing a more secure environment for the dog, and allowing privacy or space to hide from other dogs). The use of glass doors (offset from the opposite kennel door) provides a more room-like feel (more like an environment a pet dog is used to) which also helps reduce noise and disturbance from other dogs, and allows in more light.

The double-line design is the most cost-effective to build.
To improve dog welfare, care should be taken to
minimise the number of dogs who can see each other

Advantages:

- Modular style that can be extended to suit the individual's needs

- Cost-effective

- Can be sub-divided into smaller units. This is an important welfare issue

- Straightforward design and construction methods

Disadvantages:

- Will generate extremely high levels of noise and disturbance when used to hold large number of dogs – further reading in the chapter on dog welfare.

- Little privacy for old or nervous dogs

- For milder climates like the UK - only one aspect will face south/south-west

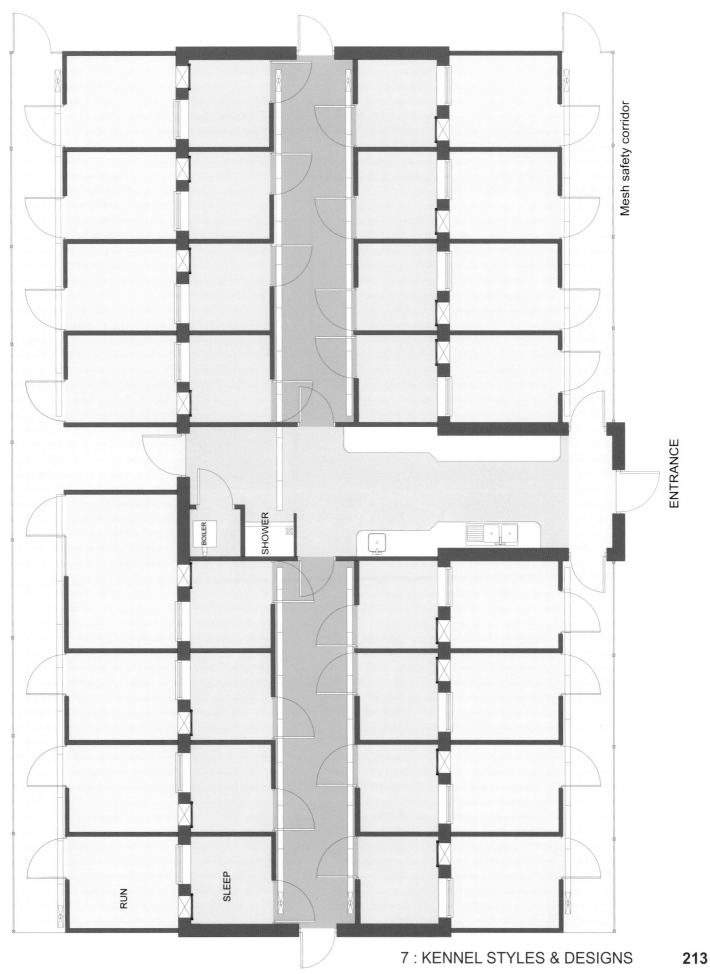

RUN

SLEEP

BOILER

SHOWER

Mesh safety corridor

ENTRANCE

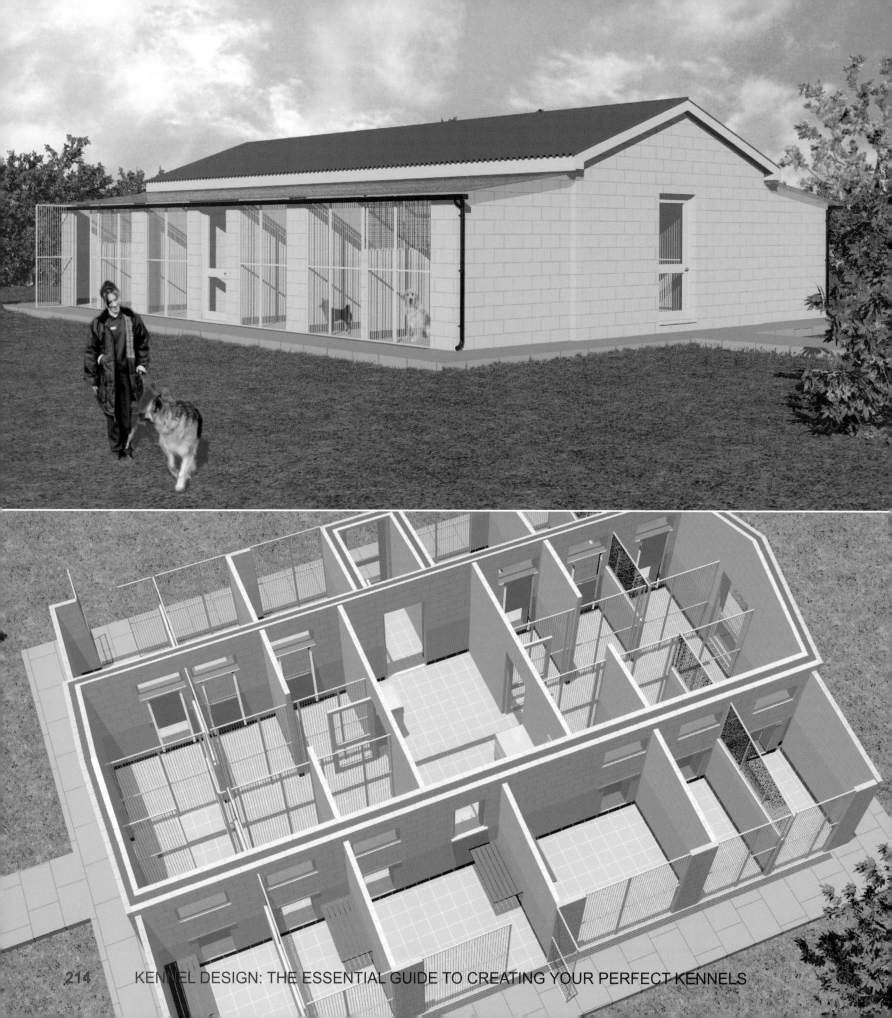

The 3D images opposite show one of my standard kennel designs (see Gentian Hill case study page 30)

This 12 kennels building is very flexible - it provides varying room sizes for different sizes or numbers of dogs. The central kitchen divides the building into 2 segments which can be zoned. For example, one side could be for small, elderly or nervous dogs and the other side for larger, active dogs.

A secure area must surround the kennels - either a covered walkway (ideally), or external fencing to create security.

The photo on this page shows the sleeping area of kennels built to this design. To improve welfare the metalwork could be replaced by solid walls and a glass door.

CIRCULAR DESIGN

The design is generally based on a 12m/39ft circle; this is normally divided into 12 equal segments, giving 11 kennels and a kitchen area/entrance. The system can be seen in a prefabricated form as well as more traditional brick and block construction method.

The design on the right shows fewer kennels and a kitchen and vet/groom room and shows how any design can be adapted to suit requirements.

This design is stressful to dogs who don't know each other and in kennels that have a continual turnover of dogs (i.e. rescue and boarding)

Advantages:

- Simplified heating and ventilation system

- Ease of staff use

- Suitable for permanent-stay dogs or dogs used by specialist operations such as assistance dogs.

Disadvantages:

- Styling, this will not suit all locations

- The standard design necessitates staff having to go outside the main building to gain access to the exercise runs

- Limited space for ancillary rooms

- The site needs to be securely fenced due to the lack of a safety corridor

- Large numbers of dogs facing each other; this substantially increases the noise and stress levels

- The floor can be difficult to construct properly to ensure the correct falls are maintained

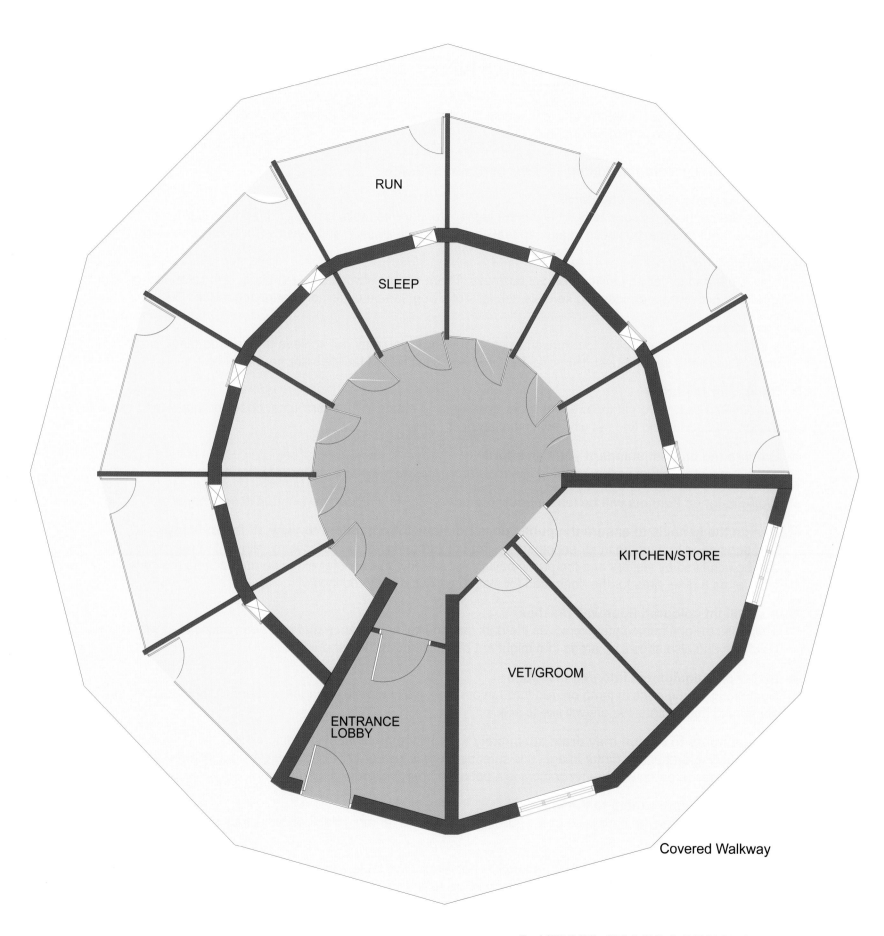

RUN

SLEEP

KITCHEN/STORE

VET/GROOM

ENTRANCE
LOBBY

Covered Walkway

SUMMARY FOR MODERN KENNELS

By now, it should be clear how modern, efficient kennel buildings are designed to take into account the needs of the staff in parallel with the dogs' needs and requirements.

To summarise, the guiding principles for modern kennels are:

- **Fewer kennels - higher standards**
  There are so many reasons to build fewer but higher standard kennels, ranging from dog welfare, noise levels, staffing requirements, business image, appeal - and your own lifestyle and reasons for wanting to work with dogs

- **Security**
  This is paramount for any animal-related business. There should always be a minimum of 2 safety doors, and ideally 3. For owners of boarding kennels, the loss of a dog can be extremely damaging to their business

- **Plan ahead**
  It is not always cost-effective to refurbish existing buildings; you may not achieve the desired result with a design and layout that is second best. Purpose-designed and constructed facilities are hard to beat

- **Design for the future**
  A greenfield next to you at the present might be a housing estate in 10 years' time; check potential land use with the local authority and find out who owns the land

- **Build to the highest standard you can afford**
  Experience proves that well-constructed kennels are easier to maintain, clean and offer better disease control

- **Well-designed kennels will be less labour intensive -** this is a hidden benefit that is not immediately apparent

- **Design the kennels to ensure the public does not have total freedom to view all the buildings**
  The dogs need to have an inner sanctum free from disturbance; this is particularly relevant to rescue centres. This can be achieved by visitors and the public having access only to the outer exercise run, leaving the central/inner corridor as a quiet area for the dogs, and for staff to carry out daily routines

- **Install light coloured floor/wall finishes**
  This reflects light, immediately removes the dark 'prison-like' appearance that has been associated with animal buildings and also shows up areas that might not be as clean as they should be

- **Install play equipment into exercise runs**
  Something for the dogs to jump on, run through or climb; it all helps to enhance and enrich their environment and is something that visitors/owners will like to see

- **Design floors to ensure they drain adequately** to avoid the problem of standing water.
  A dry building presents a better image, it is safer as there is less chance of slipping, and it also reduces the risks of some viruses (a damp warm environment is a potential breeding ground for disease)

- **Provide soft landscaping to the site**
  This will help soften the hard lines of the buildings and give a far more aesthetically pleasing site

- **Unusual features**
  If you want to install a particular feature and it is not readily available, speak to a specialist company about your idea – it is surprising how willing most companies are to find a solution for you

The designs mentioned in this chapter represent some of the latest thinking and advances for kennels.

Everyone involved with dogs will have their own ideas on the best way to house them; there is no single way that is correct; different methods work for different people, locations, types of dog, etc.

One thing is certain, although some of the latest kennels have come a long way and are a great improvement over kennels built 10 years ago, they are still evolving and will continue to do so for many years. The improvements and modifications of design might be only minor, but added to some basic well-proven systems and designs, matters can only improve.

Moreover, everyone can learn something new - whether it is a system, method or procedure to improve, enhance or make easier. Kennel requirements are the same worldwide, so it makes sense to incorporate good ideas to make life in the kennels as pleasant and happy as possible.

Ideas can be taken from other countries, welfare research, or from other kennels (boarding/rescue/show, etc) where there is always something new to learn, an improvement to find, or a problem to avoid

---

Always be on the lookout for ideas that will improve your kennels and raise standards.
To be successful, all businesses need to evolve

To keep in mind when building kennels:

1. Consider fewer kennels with bigger sizes
   Trends for modern/designer homes and commercial buildings are for larger rooms with plenty of light and space.

2. Consider natural daylight and ventilation
   These have health benefits and feel much more welcoming

3. Consider high quality, it will pay in the longer term.
   Don't skimp on materials - in the long term it will cost you more. Build to the best standard you can for your budget, even if this means reducing the initial number of kennels.

4. Consider the image you want to create
   Your image is made up of many areas including building quality, materials and finishes, staff attitude and aesthetics. Neutral colours have a calming effect, reflect more light and look more professional. This affects your income, occupancy/rehoming rate and number of recommendations/return visits you receive.

5. Plan ahead for the future
   What will you want to do with the business in 10 years time? The larger the kennels, and the more robust the structure - the higher the value of the property when you come to sell, and it will sell faster rather than languishing on the market for months or years

AGORA
management

Design

Agora Management is a professional practice providing a full range of building advisory and design services ranging from: project management, architecture and quantity surveying, to mechanical and electrical services and CDM co-ordination

South Elevation 1:150

North Elevation 1:150

East Elevation (Front) 1:100

West Elevation 1:150

DogsTrust

The elevations (above) show just one new build project that we have been involved with.

The brief from the Dogs Trust was to prepare an architectural design for a large rehoming centre which, whilst residing in a designated Green Belt area, also provided the charity with maximum visibility on a prominent site. The resulting design merged the local vernacular aesthetic with some contemporary elements and materials in order to meet a potentially conflicting set of requirements. Acoustic concerns were also addressed by the careful use of soft landscaping and the selective placement of sound absorbing materials and enclosures.

PROFESSIONAL DESIGN & ADVICE

ABOUT AGORA MANAGEMENT

Agora Management Limited is a professional design and management practice involved with a wide range of animal-related projects, our clients range from private individuals, veterinary surgeries and hospitals to charities; both small and large.

All of our projects are bespoke and are tailored to suit our clients' requirements; these may be entirely new, multi-function developments on greenfield sites, through to extension and refurbishment works on existing buildings.

Agora can assist at the initial concept and feasibility stages, to advise and provide a variety of solutions to enable clients to make the best possible use of their resources; whether financial or logistical.

Having been involved with a large number of specialist animal projects, this experience enables us to 'stand back' and take a more pragmatic look as an outsider. This ability enables us to advise our clients on the best long-term strategy for their building or site.

The options might suggest that it would be financially more prudent to demolish and construct from new, equally, it might be that a major refurbishment programme would achieve the client's brief and provide the best viable solution.

Dogs Trust Kenilworth Centre (see large photo page 314)

The Blue Cross Bromsgrove Centre (case study page 420)

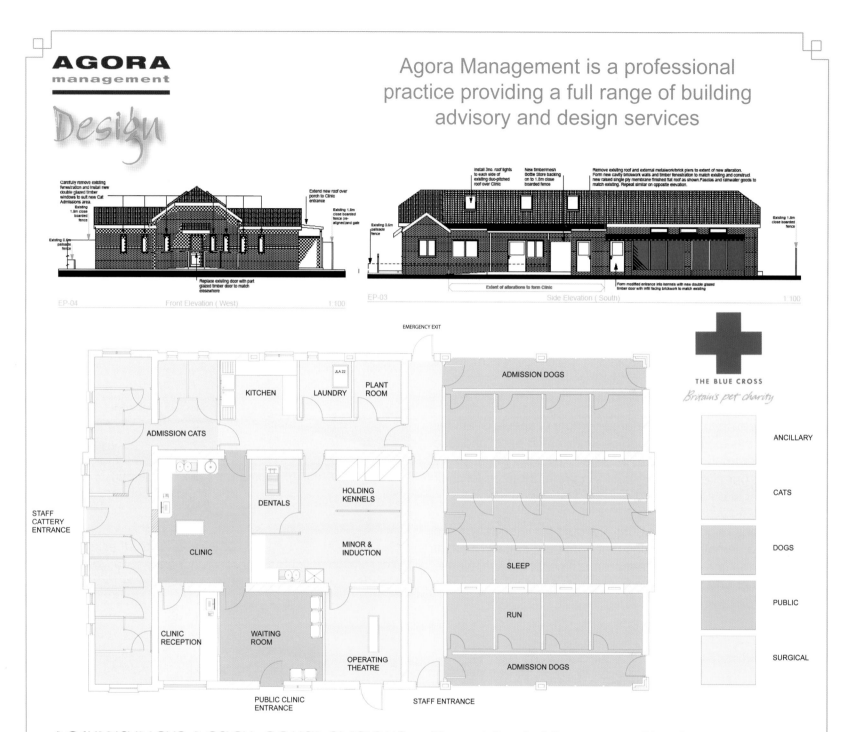

Agora Management is a professional practice providing a full range of building advisory and design services

THE BLUE CROSS
Britain's pet charity

ANCILLARY

CATS

DOGS

PUBLIC

SURGICAL

REFURBISHMENT DESIGN CONSIDERATIONS

The plans above show just one refurbishment project we have been involved with. The design brief from The Blue Cross Animal Welfare Society was to look at cost and feasibility of converting an existing outdated 20 kennel building to provide a new cat admissions, dog admissions and a public welfare clinic, with a full operating suite.

This project included many areas we specialise in, such as dog and cat accommodation, public and veterinary suites.

The existing building was traditionally constructed and structurally sound, but it had many disadvantages for the charity in terms of its layout, design and dog welfare considerations. Also, the charity wanted to incorporate this phase of the works into a larger, longer-term strategy. Planning ahead is a major consideration for any large development, and certainly for charities to ensure that they have made the best possible use of their resources. In this case the building provided the client with all of the required parameters. The final design incorporated a practical, functional working design with dedicated working areas/zones.

AGORA MANAGEMENT

BACKGROUND TO THE COMPANY

Agora Management is a friendly and helpful practice, formed in 1998, to provide a full range of building advisory and design services ranging from project management, architecture and quantity surveying to mechanical and electrical services and construction, design and management co-ordination. The members of our practice are mature, qualified professionals with a wealth of experience in the building industry, who will take any project through from initial concept design to completion of construction on site.

Whilst we are able to provide a comprehensive service on projects of any nature, we have a particular specialisation in animal welfare facilities, be they rehoming centres, boarding kennels and catteries, veterinary centres or hospitals. Many of our clients have charitable status and are very pleased with the assistance we can provide for their fund-raising campaigns in the form of valuing, and providing appropriate images of individual elements of the proposed projects, to enable the campaigns to be suitably focused.

Our growing list of clients, all of whom we are delighted to be associated, includes:

- Battersea Dogs and Cats Home
- Cats Protection
- Dogs Trust
- National Animal Welfare Trust
- RSPCA
- SSPCA
- The Blue Cross
- The Guide Dogs for the Blind Association
- Wood Green Animal Shelters
- We also provide services to individual organisations such as the Raystede Centre for Animal Welfare (Sussex), Haven Veterinary Practice (Great Yarmouth), Northlands Veterinary Hospital (Kettering), and are proud to have been the project managers of the Dogs Trust Highway Farm Centre (see case study page 274).

SOME OF OUR PROJECTS

Agora Management were project managers assisting in the control and design development of the projects shown in this book, including:

- Battersea Dogs and Cats Home (page 268)
- Blue Cross Bromsgrove Centre (page 420)
- Dogs Trust Highway Farm (page 274)
- Dogs Trust Kenilworth (photo pages 236 and 314)
- See more of our projects on pages 264-273

TO FIND OUT MORE

If you have a building need, be it a new development, the alteration of an existing facility or a change of usage to animal welfare, it is our genuine belief that we can assist you regardless of its location and project scale. Our professional dedication and knowledge has been fundamental to our success and growth. Our current clients in the animal welfare fraternity view us as a practice able to respond to all their building needs in a timely, thoughtful and economic fashion.

If anything that we have discussed within this book is of interest to you, or of help, but you would like to take it further, we would be more than delighted to assist. We endeavour to treat all our clients with the respect that they deserve being fellow professionals within their own field. We appreciate that your project is your own, we therefore do not differentiate on the size of a project and we will offer the same quality of service. Indeed, our reputation has spread across the Channel, and we now have the pleasure of working in mainland Europe.

In the first instance, we invite you to contact our Managing Director, Alex Darvill (who has worked with David Key, the author of this book, for many years) to arrange an initial meeting and discussion:

AGORA
management

Alex Darvill
Agora Management Limited
12 Kings Court, Willie Snaith Road
Newmarket, Suffolk CB8 7SG
Tel: +44 (0)1638 560343
www.agoramanagement.com

ANCILLARY BUILDINGS

The type and number of ancillary buildings and areas required will depend on the scale of the business, the type of dogs being housed, whether residential accommodation is needed for staff, etc.

The following list shows some of the more utilised facilties in the kennel environment:

- Reception
- Laundry
- Grooming
- Veterinary
- Hydrotherapy
- Storage
- Holding
- Isolation
- Admissions
- Socilisation and quiet areas for special needs dogs
- Covered play areas

RECEPTION

This is normally the first building that clients will go to, and is extremely important. Not only can it function as an office, shop, etc, but it is the first impression of the property that most people will have. The design and size can be as elaborate and spacious or as simple as required.

To highlight how flexible/versatile a reception area can be, here are some other uses for it:

- ## Reception counter/desk/table
  An area is needed where the public can fill out documents, sign cheques, etc. The installation of electrical sockets is a normal requirement for calculators, cash tills, internet access and computers

- ## Holding room for dogs that are being discharged
  This can be part of the veterinary inspection room if required. The purpose is to provide a clean, quiet area away from the main kennels, and gives the opportunity to hold dogs if an owner is going to turn up late or has been delayed

- ## Manager's office
  This is often a dual-purpose room, not only serving as a quiet area in which to retire to concentrate on office paperwork, accounts, etc. but also offering a suitable room away from the main building to discuss private matters with owners and staff

- ## Sales area
  The installation of a sales area is common practice for boarding kennels and welfare centres; it can provide an easy form of additional income. The sales goods can be basic items such as toys and dog treats through to bulk sales of dog food

- ## Staff accommodation
  Are staff required to live on site? If so, how many? The building of accommodation above the reception can serve a dual role: it utilises space, it provides additional security for the site and is a cost-effective method of providing accommodation. One disadvantage of this is that the staff are always above a source of activity, even on their days off. This can limit the type of staff employed

- ## Public and staff toilet
  A public toilet is highly practical. It is normally a planning requirement to provide a disabled toilet.
  It is always preferable to try to provide separate toilets for staff and clients

- ## Staff room
  With heating, washing facilities, hot/cold water, fridge, microwave and soft furnishings. It can be of great benefit for staff to get together over coffee to chat and discuss the centre's activities

- ## Staff shower
  A showering facility is becoming a standard fitting for large charities. It shows a positive attitude to health and safety issues

- ## Veterinary inspection room
  This can be part of the main reception, or incorporated within the kennels

LAUNDRY

The issue of laundry equipment, type of bedding to be used and infrastructure services should be addressed at the outset of the development; it should be considered as an integral part of the project.

The problems associated with cleaning animal bedding can be a major source of irritation, expenditure, time and energy to the kennel owner who has not addressed this issue. The end result could be unsatisfactory arrangements that in the long term are often more costly. Correctly addressed, this problem becomes just another part of normal day-to-day activities leaving you to concentrate on the more important issues. The installation of suitably sized laundry equipment is essential for any modern animal establishment using fabric bedding. The provision of a laundry will depend on the type of bedding used.

The three most common options available are:

- Special dog beds, or dogs' own beds from home

- Vetbed® (PetLife International Ltd www.vetbed.co.uk)

- Blankets, sheets or towels

Image and practicality play a major part in the choice of bedding

Which option to be used is a matter of personal choice, availability and cost. From a practical and personal point of view, the proprietary **vet bedding or dog bedding** is recommended. The **advantages** are is that it is light, hygienic, easy to wash, dries very quickly, provide high levels of comfort for the dog and is aesthetically pleasing. The **disadvantage** is the high initial cost. However, given that some dogs will destroy or chew bedding, having a variety of suitable bedding is a good idea, and it must be accepted that occasionally bedding will have to be thrown away.

The use of blankets/sheets/towels is a close substitute. For rescue centres, it is surprising how easy it is to obtain old bedding free of charge. The **disadvantage** over vet bedding is that larger pieces are required to provide the same level of padding and comfort, and it takes considerably longer to dry. **This can be a major problem when faced with a large quantity of washing.**

Whatever the bedding chosen, you will need a suitable washing machine/s to cope with the loads being generated on a daily basis.

Standard domestic washing machines and tumble dryers will not normally be adequate for larger establishments, and will not be able to cope for a prolonged period of time. The only answer is to install commercial machines.

The size of the machine/s will depend on the scale of business you have and the layout of building. It is suggested the minimum size washing machine should be 8kg/18 lb.

Legal Issues

In recent years in the UK and America concerns have been voiced by the water supply companies about possible contamination to main water supplies with back-siphonage or backflow from washing machines, showers and hosepipes. For full details please see Water Supply Regulations in the chapter on Environmental Legislation.

A standard domestic machine does not have the built-in backflow prevention measures of the commercial machines.

At present in the UK the water supply companies are carrying out surveys of kennels, catteries, stables and veterinary surgeries to see if these establishments comply with current regulations and standards.

Service Requirement

Washing Machines

For large commercial machines above 9kg/20lb - to operate efficiently and effectively they will normally require a three-phase electricity supply.

If a site does not have a commercial three-phase supply, the manufacturers can downgrade the machine to a single-phase. However, this needs to be clarified before the machine is purchased. Another option is to install a converter; this allows a three-phase machine to be run off a single-phase supply.

Tumble Dryers

The larger tumble dryers are normally operated by gas and require a single-phase electricity supply. The larger (above 8kg/18lb) machines are not economical operating via electricity.

If there is no mains gas supply to your centre it is well worth considering installing an LPG tank. This would overcome the problems of installing a large commercial machine/s.

Typically the commercial tumble dryers have capacities of between 8kg/18lb to 22kg/50lb. There are far larger machines but these do tend to become prohibitively expensive.

The new generation of large tumble dryers have the S.A.F.E (Sensor Activated Fire Extinguishing systems). This system has been design to eliminate serious fires, which can start in tumble dryers. The fires are normally due to lack of maintenance, spontaneous combustion, or small loads that have been over-dried.

If a fire starts in the drum, sensors detect changes in the temperature and activate a sophisticated water vapour system into the rotating drum. This ensures that the risk of damage to the property is eliminated.

Special Note for Rescue Charities and Large Commercial Operations

Typically charities and large operations install one central laundry room for the entire site. This system allows the installation of single, larger capacity machines and is cheaper pro rata than having smaller machines located in different buildings around the site.

The main costs are the services requirement to the individual buildings and the purchase of additional machines.

The disadvantages of a centralised system are that it does not offer any flexibility if a machine breaks down. It will also involve the staff having to take dirty bedding to one central point – for a large site, or a site with varying ground levels, this can have health and safety implications and can also be a drain on staff time.

Equipment Provider

Commercial companies, such as JHC can provide a range of machines to suit your requirements. They have options to lease or purchase outright all their range of machines.

Another very important aspect to consider when choosing a provider is whether the company can offer a full back-up and maintenance service. If the company cannot provide a back up service, it is strongly recommended that you look elsewhere.

Helpful Hints:

- Try to ensure that the laundry area has at least one external wall, this will allow the tumble dryer flue to be directly vented to the outside. This gives the most cost-effective installation and improves the efficiency of the machine. It also allows easy installation of adequate ventilation or 'make-up' air

- Try to keep large machines on the ground floor for ease of access and installation

- Ensure that the entrance door is at least 926mm/3ft wide, as this will allow the installation of the larger machines without having to remove doorframes, etc

- If the laundry is in a large commercial centre or charity, the door must have at least half-hour fire resistance

- Install a floor drain outlet within the laundry area, this will allow any water to drain away from wet bedding or floods

- A solid, concrete floor is needed for all commercial machines

- Do not try to mix the laundry area with the boiler room - blanket fluff and boilers are not compatible!

- Ensure the equipment you purchase complies with local water by-laws (see the chapter on Environmental Legislation)

GROOMING

All commercial kennels and rescue centres should have a good dog bathing facility for general use. A professional grooming business is another way of increasing your income without increasing the number of kennels.

The key factors are:

- Good supply of hot water

- Adjustable temperature thermostatically controlled shower, with good water pressure for efficient bathing

- Ease of use for staff. The photos below show either full height walk-in systems or a tiered system. Both these systems are much easier and safer to use than enclosed tub systems. It is more relaxing for the dog, probably what they are used to at home, less enclosed, and the lifting implications for staff are reduced

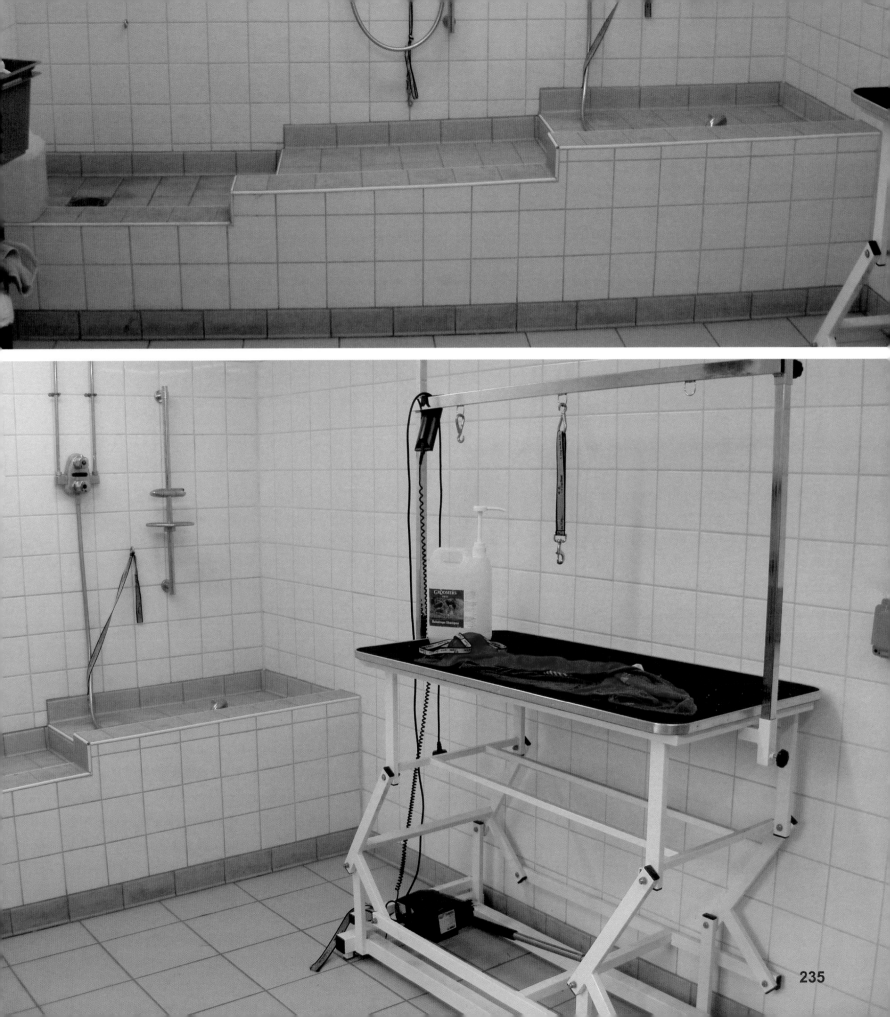

VETERINARY

The scale of the veterinary facility required will be higher for a charity than for boarding kennels. For a large commercial facility, the provision of a dedicated quiet room for veterinary inspections is well worth considering. A smaller facility could also make use of a veterinary room to examine a dog prior to admission, for weighing (useful for obese or nervous dogs) or for monitoring health.

Examination room (below) and full veterinary hospital suite (opposite) designed and project managed by Agora Management (see pages 220-223 and 264-273 for more information).

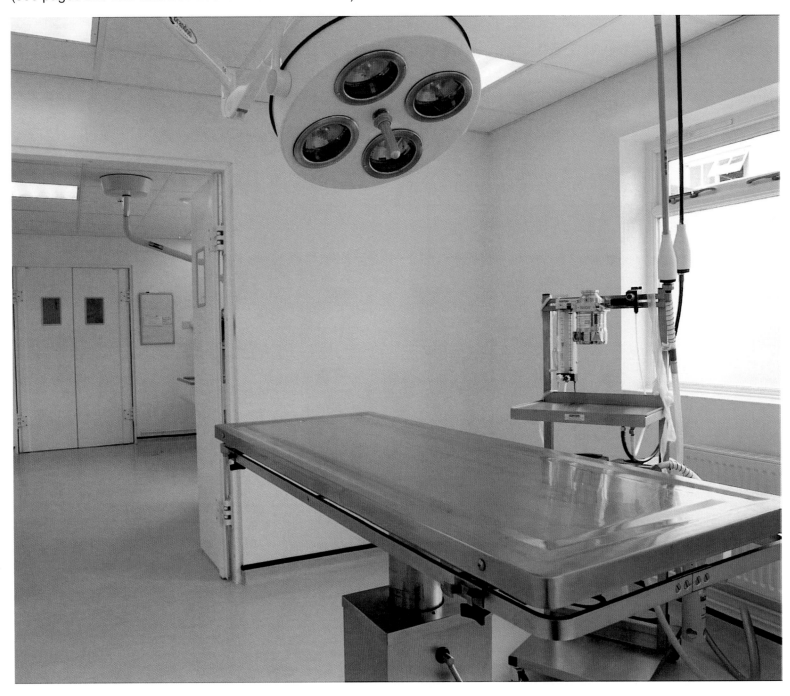

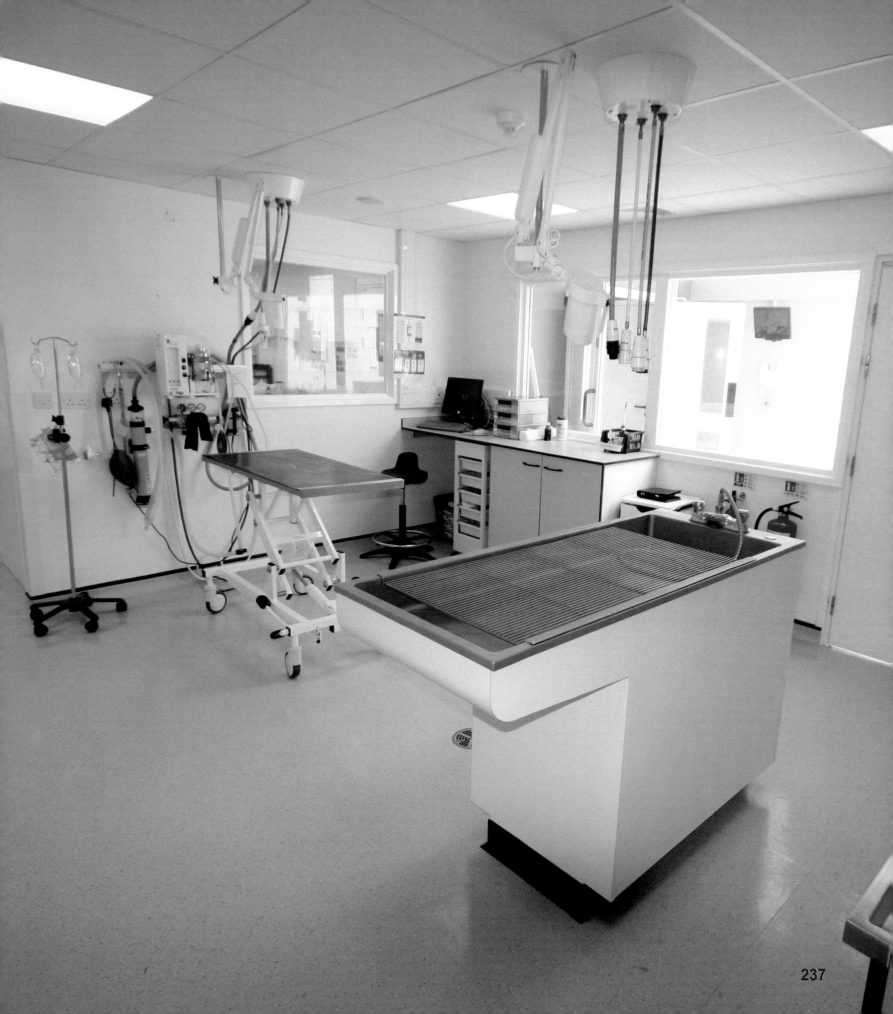

HYDROTHERAPY

Hydrotherapy has been used for many years for high-performance and high-value animals such as racehorses and racing greyhounds. However, in recent years it has become widely available for the family pet with numerous individuals and veterinary surgeons offering this facility.

It is well proven that hydrotherapy (swimming or walking with resistance against water) can bring a wide range of benefits to dogs with a range of conditions – especially those suffering from lower limb and joint problems.

Swimming is an excellent form of exercise, it allows and encourages the dog to carry out a full range of limb movements without having to support the full weight of its body. This promotes healing and strengthens the muscles.

The hydrotherapy session will the tailored to suit the dog's needs – there is no one set programme. The sessions will generally be short to start with, and gradually build up as the dog's level of fitness improves.

STORAGE

This is an area that is much underestimated. The problem of not providing suitable and adequate storage can be extremely tiresome. Ideally, there should be two types of storage: One for the bulk deliveries (food, etc), and another small facility close to the core working areas. The facilities should be large enough to provide dry, vermin-free storage and have suitable access for vehicular and pedestrian traffic.

The building will need to have a range of suitable shelving to help make full use of it. This is normally in the form of purpose-designed warehouse shelving systems, floor pallets, or secure bins with lockable lids. Another important aspect to consider is the off-loading of deliveries and moving of supplies once on the site. Apart from the time factor, the health and safety of staff must be considered.

Below left: Having taken over an existing business, this owner is struggling to find enough storage space. Another problem is that the kitchen is a considerable distance from the kennels, wasted time and frustrating for staff, particularly in bad weather.
Below right: Proprietary racking keeps everything tidy and easy to find.

HOLDING KENNELS

Holding kennels are temporary housing facilities used primarily by commercial kennels and are for short-term temporary use (up to 24 hours) used during changeover times (usually at weekends).

Holding kennels have advantages for the kennel owner, but they must be used with care and not as a matter of course in order to increase the number of dogs that can be held.

The standards for these kennels should be the same as for the main boarding kennels (i.e a good size, hygienic, washable, well-ventilated, etc).

The UK's CIEH give the following minimum sizes:

- 2.5m^2/25ft^2

- Generally, holding kennels should not account for more than 25% of the total number of residential kennels

ADMISSIONS KENNELS

Admissions kennels are mainly used as an intake facility by charities and used for 7–14 days. They are used to assess the dogs' health and allow them to settle into the new environment, which is calmer than the main rehoming kennels.

The aim of admissions is to minimise the risk of an outbreak of disease in the main rehoming building, preventing temporary closure. They have a clear and defined use for welfare centres and sanctuaries, which have to **admit dogs from unknown backgrounds and keep them until the incubation period for common diseases has passed**.

To work effectively the building should be totally self-contained (i.e. separate access, hot water, utensils and, if possible, staff), with no cross-over with the main rehoming kennels.

Obviously the number of kennels required is dependent on the total number of dogs coming into care. If the average monthly figure for dogs being rehomed is 60, then the number of admission units will be approximately 30, this taking into account that the dogs will be in this unit for 14 days.

Obviously, several factors should be taken into account before such a unit is constructed, these being:

- **Cost implications**

- **Planning and space restrictions**

- **Time considerations**
  How long will the dogs be kept in this building, type of animals coming into care, do they have a documented background and have they been vaccinated?

- **Waiting list**
  If you have to close, what happens to the dogs on your waiting list? Is there an alternative sanctuary/centre for them to go to?

- **Financial**
  Can you afford to keep the dogs for an extended period of time?

- **Staff**
  Can you afford the additional staff to run this unit?

ISOLATION

All animal establishments are normally required by the licensing authority to have an isolation facility to contain and prevent the spread of infectious diseases.

In the UK, for example, the Chartered Institute of Environmental Health (CIEH) insist on the following requirements:

- One isolation unit for up to 50 dog kennels, and pro rata above that

- A minimum separation of 15ft/5m from any other animal units in existing facilities, and 33ft/10m for any newly constructed animal buildings

Thought should be given to ensure that the isolation kennels are of an equal standard, if not higher than the main kennels

The reasoning behind this is simple: an isolation kennel needs to be thoroughly cleaned and disinfected after each use to prevent any cross contamination to future users. The cleaning process may involve the use of mist spraying, steam cleaning or chemical means, and the construction should take these issues into account.

It is always a contentious point as to how many isolation kennels are needed. The requirement should be judged on the type of facility constructed and the type of animal being cared for.

Commercial Kennels Isolation

Many kennel owners who are caring for fully vaccinated animals argue passionately that there is actually no requirement for an isolation facility. They feel that if an animal is unwell it should be with the vet and receiving full, professional medical care. This is better for the dog. For the owners it removes any potential legal implications and is far more responsive in the event of medical complications.

Obviously, this assumes that the veterinary surgeon has 24 hour cover, has the correct facility to hold and isolate dogs with possible infectious diseases, and is willing to provide this service.

Rescue Kennels Isolation

In an ideal world, it would be better to have two separate buildings with at least 2-3 kennels each.

Again, the reasons are simple: there is no point in putting a dog that is simply 'looking off colour' into the isolation building with another dog that is obviously ill and receiving veterinary treatment.

It is far better to adopt a flexible approach with more buildings. This enables you to segregate the animals and, hopefully, prevent any cross-infection.

Clearly, if you have a major outbreak of a virus/disease that has infected a large percentage of the dogs in your care, a few isolation kennels will be totally inadequate.

Obviously the isolation facility should be totally self-contained, with its own access, hot water supply, protective clothing, food supplies, food bowls, cleaning utensils and grooming/shower facilities.

Ideally, the person responsible for this unit should not be working with healthy animals. If this is not possible, then high standards of 'barrier nursing' should be employed, with the use of washable PVC coveralls, wellington boots and disposable gloves.

All these measures will create additional work, and are not always guaranteed to be 100% effective. However, without them, the problems will be much, much worse.

For any rescue or charitable organisation, having adequate isolation is ESSENTIAL

SOCIALISATION/REHOMING AREAS AND HOME-LIKE ROOMS

A great idea - the addition of at least one room providing a home-like atmosphere.

It is worth thinking about the inclusion of a home-like room in every form of kennels. These are flexible rooms that can also be used for staff/owner relaxation, talking to dog owners and taking bookings or details, interviewing and even a spare office.

You will always find a use for another room!

Inclusions could be anything that mimics the environment of home that dogs will be used to, such as television or radio, comfortable sofas to relax with humans or by themselves, plenty of choices for resting areas and being able to look out of windows, playing tapes of friendly and familiar home sounds, dog furniture and toys, home-like furnishings (e.g. pictures, paintings, ticking clocks, mirrors, ornaments, etc) as well as dog-friendly furnishings such as fixed or movable benches – and of course a big benefit is the greater increase in space.

Rescue Centres: Socialisation and Rehoming Rooms

One benefit for rescue centres is in providing a safe, relaxed area for potential owners to get to know a dog better, and for the dogs to be able to relax and show their true personality in a familiar environment. The biggest benefit may be for quiet or more difficult-to-home dogs who are finding it hard to adjust to life in kennels, where just being able to relax with a familiar human will be highly beneficial.

This type of area could be an existing room, perhaps an office or staff room with sofas and a kitchen area. Socialisation rooms have proven to be of great benefit for dogs (who have shown improvement, especially on being introduced to a carer one-to-one in this more familiar, less sterile environment) without the distraction of other animals nearby, and more organisations are seeing the benefit of this flexible option.

Commercial:
Home-like Rooms

There is no reason why home-like rooms could not be used in commercial kennels.

As with rescue centres, many dogs will benefit from this. The licensing authority may require certain conditions to be met (cleaning/disinfection, disease risk, solid barriers etc.) where other dogs are present. But if this need is incorporated as a separate room or building, it will also be more flexible for discussions with clients.

Covered/Indoor Exercise Areas, Play Rooms and Play Barns

Large, separate covered or indoor exercise areas can be highly beneficial for most dogs, but particularly for sanctuaries and welfare organisations where dogs can be kept for longer periods of time, or as permanent residents. As will be obvious by now, even the sizes recommended for accommodation will not allow a young, fit and active dog sufficient space. One way to overcome this is to construct a 'play room'. This can be as simple or as extravagant as desired. Some charities have developed this idea and have provided highly exciting, stimulating and welcoming rooms for the dogs and visitors.

The advantages are:

- Allows for greater freedom and natural behaviour of the dogs

- Allows members of the public the opportunity to sit in a room with the dog and get to know them better (this is generally not practical or feasible with standard size accommodation)

- Provides greater flexibility – an extra room, and/or somewhere to provide another option to reduce stress in dogs

- A large playroom or playbarn can be used for training, agility, one-to-one time, open days, etc

- Provides an indoor exercise area ideal for use in bad weather

- Provides excellent public relations

Obviously the main concern in creating such an area is one of hygiene and suitable surfaces that can be disinfected. However, given that the dogs should be vaccinated, fit and healthy before using this type of facility, the risks are minimised, as the health background of the dog is known. **The advantages of this type of facility far outweigh the practical issues in these circumstances**, and provide a greatly improved and more natural environment for the dogs.

9 PROJECT MANAGEMENT

MANAGING BUILDING PROJECTS AND CONTRACTORS

Many kennel owners and charities/sanctuaries will at some stage in their business life have to improve, refurbish or construct buildings.

This is either due to the need to expand, or to replace dilapidated and sub-standard premises. It can be an exciting and fulfilling time; but it can also be a difficult time. The aim of this chapter is to help you prepare, and to avoid common problems.

New premises that are tailor-made for your particular business can enhance and improve operating efficiency, reduce costs and send out the correct message to potential clients that you are taking your business seriously and are prepared to invest in its future.

Making the initial decision that purpose-built, tailor-made premises are the way you wish to move forward can be time-consuming, but the end results will obviously be more satisfactory and give greater long-term benefits to your business.

There are many questions that need to be asked, for example:

- How much can I afford to spend on the project?

- How will it be funded?

- What are my main goals and priorities?

- How long will the work take?

- Will I have to shut down the existing kennels to allow access?

- Do I need to construct all new buildings, or can I convert some existing ones?

- Can the work be carried out in phases?

Generally, **building from scratch** offers the best opportunity to create facilities that match **your** particular needs and aspirations

LONG-TERM COSTS

Before embarking on a new-build project, alternative options should be explored and long-term cost implications considered. These might be building related, but sometimes it may involve a more radical approach such as a site relocation to larger or more suitably located premises.

New-Build versus Conversion

Generally, new-build is more expensive than conversion, but this can depend on several factors, such as the condition of the existing premises (particularly for large cost items such as foundations and structural stability), government tax implications and possible tax savings, etc.

> Adapting existing premises is **always** a compromise and might not be the solution for your particular site

New Build

Once you have decided that new-build is the option for your business, some fundamental issues need to be resolved:

Project Brief
Even if you choose to construct the buildings yourself, it is essential that you have a clear understanding of:

- What you are trying to achieve, and what you expect from the buildings

- How they will fit on your site

- The materials to be used

- The overall cost of the project

- What is their anticipated useful working lifespan?

Site Survey
If you are constructing a building, particularly on a difficult site (e.g. unusual ground conditions, sloping site, etc) it is worthwhile investing in a full measured survey of your boundaries and existing buildings. A scale of either 1:500 or 1:200 is normally sufficient to show building lines, etc. In the UK, a simple method of obtaining fairly accurate plans showing boundary lines and footprint of existing buildings is to purchase a Superplan from Ordnance Survey. These come in a range of scales and can be used for planning purposes, plotting for additional buildings, etc.

Ancillary Cost Items
Often these tend to be overlooked, as the main focal point tends to be toward the animal buildings only. It is essential to look at **all** areas that make up the working environment. These can be storage buildings, drainage, adequate and safe access, demolition of redundant buildings, additional insurance and any legal conditions that might be imposed by the statutory authorities. Such ancillary items can be expensive, and need to be taken into account in the overall project cost.

Choosing your Building Method

Most commercial kennel projects are (in construction terms) fairly straightforward and uncomplicated buildings, and this allows the use of a wide range of building options (procurement)

The following methods are the more common used by most kennel owners. There are other methods available, but they tend to be for more specialist projects:

- ■ **Owner Self-Builds**
  The owner has the necessary skills and time to construct the buildings him/herself.
  This is obviously the cheapest method, with the owner carrying out the building works and employing local subcontractors for the more specialist trades as and when necessary.
  This method also means that the owner locates and purchases all of the required materials

- ■ **Manufacturer Installs**
  To use a prefabricated (pre-manufactured) buildings system.
  If a prefabricated building is to be used, it would be sensible and generally more cost-effective, to allow the manufacturer to install it, as they are used to erecting their own product. This will also mean that you have some redress if the building develops any problems at a later date. Typically, a manufacturer will want the base and groundworks prepared by others. Once installed, it is usual for the owner to then carry out finishing works such as plumbing and electrics.

- ■ **Owner Subcontracts**
  The owner employs all local subcontractors on a direct labour method.
  This is normally a mixture of the owner purchasing some of the larger items directly (such as concrete blocks, roofing materials, etc). For smaller, more specialist items such as electrical and plumbing fittings, it might be preferable to let the contractors purchase these (in fact, they might insist on it).

- ■ **Building Contractor**
  To use a main building contractor, typically a small/medium sized, local construction firm.
  This can either be self-managed, or managed by either a surveyor/architect or project manager

- ■ **Architect/Designer Technician**
  To employ a surveyor/architect/designer to design, project manage and issue interim payment schedules for the duration of the project.
  This is a common practice for larger-scale developments and does provide an additional level of safety and comfort. However, there is an additional cost penalty attached to this option.

- ■ **Design and Build**
  This is where a main contractor designs the building for you and constructs it from day one to completion

Further Deciding Factors

Flexibility:

- Self-build

- Manufacturer installs

- Owner subcontracts

Clearly these methods allow the most flexibility, with the option for the owner to stop/start the project as funds permit, or to alter the specification, without incurring any contractor-related penalties that might be imposed when using an architect.

Design Work:

- Owner subcontracts

- Building contractor

- Architect/designer technician

With these methods it is assumed that a greater level of design work has been carried out to enable the contractor to accurately cost the project.

Normally this takes the form of detailed drawings showing various elevations, setting out plans (giving the correct sizes for the building, kennels, etc), section drawings (giving heights and the required pitch of the roof) and materials to be used.

All these details will normally form part of the planning application. Any planning authority will want to see what the building will look like externally in terms of size, material choice and textures.

Common Route – Using a Main Building Contractor

Assuming that you have opted to use a main building contractor as your preferred method to construct kennels, and that you have had some detailed plans drawn up by another party, here are some of the things that should be considered during the construction period:

Construction Cost

The Contract Price is the lump sum given by the builder.
It is essential to establish exactly what has been costed before the contract starts and to have any queries or 'grey' areas ironed out.
Often it is the lack of detailed information that may account for any unexpected final increased costs.

Materials

Have a clear understanding of the materials you wish to use.
Most general builders will not know **why** you want to specify a particular product, when there are many alternatives available. Using unsuitable materials will produce a building that cannot cope with the daily wear and tear.

Contract Documents

All documents used in conjunction with the project should be made part of the contract documentation. These might include detailed drawings, survey plans, existing services on the site, and should all be used by the builder to ensure that they have covered all areas of work to allow the completion of the buildings.

Start Date and Contract Period

These are mutually agreed dates between the contractor and owner.
Dates should be realistic and take into account weather conditions, how much access the contractor is given, any restrictions that might apply, etc.

Payment

The method of payment to the builder should be agreed before the contract commences.

Three methods often used are:

1. Interim or fluctuating payments

2. Fixed or stage payments

3. Lump sum payment

As most new construction is likely to last more than four weeks, most builders will want to use either methods 1 or 2.

The advantage of fixed or stage payments is that the owner will know beforehand the likely monthly costs. Again, these costs would need to be discussed and agreed with the builder prior to work commencing.

Variations

All variations to the project will have a cost implication, either +/-
There is nothing unusual in varying minor items in the project; even with the most detailed schemes there are always areas of work that have to be altered.

The main point to remember is that any variation should have a cost set against it BEFORE the work commences, and this needs to be recorded by both parties and signed for. This will help prevent problems nearer the end of the project if the builder asks for additional payments for work that has not been agreed.

Special Conditions
These might be:

- **Building Regulations/Control**
  Who is responsible for payment and co-ordination?

- **Access**
  How is the builder going to gain access to the site? Who will pay for any damage to grassed/paved areas caused by heavy machinery?

- **Contractors' Claims**
  Building is an unpredictable profession; as a client you **must** be prepared for things **not** to go to plan

- **Facilities**
  Use of your facilities (e.g. toilets, kitchen, electricity, water, etc)

Additional Claims

If the builder submits a claim for additional money that has not been discussed, it is essential that you investigate the claim and do not simply reject it out of hand.

Contract

A contract document will not eliminate all the above problems, but will provide a framework agreed by both parties. This provides a basis of understanding that will hopefully remove many of the problem areas and issues that can dominate and spoil projects.

The Federation of Master Builders has a selection of easy-to-use contracts that can be downloaded from its website, or purchased. See www.fmb.org.uk

PROJECT DEVELOPMENT COSTS

Clearly, before you embark upon a project you will need to know what the final cost is going to be.

It is not uncommon for the peripheral items to be overlooked, or indeed some of the more general items such as connection to the mains sewage system, electricity upgrade, water supply, etc.

The following list shows some of the main items that should be taken into account when preparing your budget for any development. Clearly this is not exhaustive, but is merely indicative of the different areas/items that should be taken into account.

It is recommended that you obtain at least **three quotations** for your project.

The easiest way to get contractors to provide you with like-for-like quotations (to ensure consistency) is to provide a 'specification' of your requirements (sizes, materials, access, utilities, etc).

Please see www.kenneldesign.com for more detailed information on Building Specifications and Building Cost Pricing documents.

Sample Project Development Cost Sheet

FEES	£/$	EXTERNAL WORKS	£/$
Planning Permission		Car park	
Building Regulations		Lighting	
Architect		Landscaping	
Quantity Surveyor		Fencing	
Structural Engineer		Road signage	
Mechanical/Electrical Engineer		Spoil removal	
Land Agent		Landscaping	
Land Surveyor		**Sub-total:**	
CDM Planning Officer (Construction, Design and Management)			
Infrastructure costs		**EQUIPMENT**	
Electricity		Laundry equipment	
Gas		Pressure washer/steam cleaner	
Water		Water hose/fittings	
Drainage		Fire prevention	
Specialist Contractors (e.g. asbestos removal)		Office/staff room furniture and fittings	
New buildings		Computer	
Sub-total:		Telephones and intercom	
TEMPORARY WORKS		Kennels furniture (e.g. benches,beds, bowls, dishes)	
Fencing/security		Music system	
Accommodation		Safe/security box	
Services (e.g. gas)		Vehicle	
Sub-total:		**Sub-total:**	
MAIN BUILDINGS			
Reception			
Kennels			
Isolation			
Sub-total:			
PROJECT TOTAL:			

Individual Buildings – Cost Comparison

We have already looked at the overall development costs. However, it is also worth looking at the individual building costs.

If you are obtaining quotations from a builder, (whether for a simple concrete base or a complete building) – it is always worth breaking down the quotation into smaller components

---

Breaking the quotation down will make it easier for you to see how the builder has arrived at his final figure, and will help you to compare the difference between various quotations. It will also allow you to see if any major errors or omissions have been made in their pricing structure.

A typical example of the information you should be asking for is:

Pricing Document		
REF:	**ITEM**	**COST**
1	Provisional dayworks	
2	Preliminaries	
3	Substructure	
4	Solid floor	
5	Roof construction	
6	Roof cladding	
7	External walls	
8	Windows and doors	
9	Internal walls	
10	Wall and ceiling finishes	
11	Plumbing services	
12	Electrical services	
13	Specialist services (e.g. galvanised metalwork)	
14	External works	
15	External services (e.g. water, drainage, electricity)	
16	Profits and Overheads	
		Total:

Project Flow

These guidelines apply to ALL projects:

Project identified

Project scheme feasibility, preliminary costings

Client approval to basic scheme, detailed design

Planning submission
(The client has the option to wait until planning approval is granted
before committing to further design work.
Equally, if the planning authority does not have any major objections
to the proposed scheme, detailed design work can proceed in order to save time)

Tenders invited

Tenders received

Tenders approved

Financial approval

Project phase

Other Issues to be Considered

Getting Started
At the initial meeting with the architect/surveyor/designer, the general principles of the scheme will be discussed, any cost restraints set out, and a fee agreed.

Fees
The fee can either be a fixed amount (this is more normal for **smaller contracts**) or a percentage of the total contract sum. It is normal for an architect/surveyor to outline the stage payments required, and other services that are not included in their fee (e.g. structural engineer). **Larger contracts are paid on a monthly basis**; the architect issues interim certificates after consultation with the supervising officer or quantity surveyor. The certificates represent the value of the work completed to date. It is normal practice for a retention of 5% to be withheld at this stage. **At the end of the building stage (practical completion) half of the retention will be paid. At the end of the Defects Liability Period**, the contractor will have rectified any defective items. It is at this stage that the final certificate is issued and the remaining retention paid.

What you want
Prior detailed thought about what you want from the buildings/layout, can bring about a major saving in time and money.

Alterations
Alterations can be made at any time, but it is good policy to have ironed out any major revisions before work commences.

Services
Where refurbishment work is undertaken, there can be a significant disruption of services. These areas should have been addressed during the early discussions with the architect; indeed to comply with CDM (Construction, Design and Management) Regulations, all aspects of the project will need to be taken into account. It might be necessary to provide temporary services (e.g. water, electricity) all of these having a cost implication.

Contract
The Contract document comprises working drawings, specification/bill of quantities, health and safety plan, signed Contract.

Site Meetings
Site meetings are normally on a monthly basis, but they can be as often or as few as required. Normal practice is for all amendments and alterations to be issued by the architect, direct to the contractor. This avoids confusion and keeps costs in order.

Neighbours
Ensure you inform neighbours of your plans. If planning permission is submitted, most authorities will inform them.

Whenever a development is proposed, it is human nature to be wary of it. Therefore, it is essential to keep neighbours up-to-date with your proposals

UK Party Wall Act 1996

The Act covers England and Wales. However, there are similar issues for Scotland. One item to take into consideration when planning your site layout is how close the development will be to your neighbour's boundary. Generally, if the distance is less than 6m/20ft, then consideration will need to be given to this Act.

The Act has implications for all building owners intending to carry out work which involves:

- Work on an existing wall shared with a neighbour
- Building on the boundary with a neighbouring property
- Excavating near a neighbouring building

The basic elements of the Act requires the owner who intends to carry out the work to notify in writing all adjoining owners about the works involved. This must be done at least two months prior to any work commencing.

A useful website for further information is: www.odpm.gov.uk

Planning

It is important to obtain as much information as possible before submitting your application. Study the local planning policy. If planning is granted, ensure you comply with any conditions imposed as many authorities employ enforcement officers. The role of this officer is to ensure that developments are carried out in accordance with the planning permission granted.

End Value

It is worth considering the end value of your property before embarking on major and expensive developments.

Decision-making

Plan ahead and try not to leave making decisions about the design, materials, etc until the last moment.

Services

Ensure that any required services are available (e.g. water, gas, electricity and drainage) before commencing work. Also check to see what the lead times and costs will be to bring these to your site – such costs can be prohibitive.

Building Materials

Ensure that you know the standard of materials to be used before any confirmed orders are placed.

Ground Conditions

Ensure you establish the ground conditions before commencing work. Many projects suffer additional costs and delays due to unknown ground conditions. Have trial holes dug well in advance of the development as this will allow an engineer to give guidance on suitable foundations, etc. It also allows any additional costs to be factored in.

Budget

Ensure that you have sufficient budget, including a contingency. You will need to keep a constant eye on the cost of the project to ensure that you don't have an unexpected claim at the end of the contract.

The main difficulty is cash-flow.
It is surprising how quickly money can drain away. Having to stop the project due to cash-flow problems can result in lengthy delays in getting the builders back to complete any outstanding work. A programme of works showing the various stages and potential costs at each stage is essential for large-scale projects as it allows better cash-flow.

A contingency allowance will normally be
around 7% – 10% of the total project cost.
(The percentage is generally higher for refurbishment work).

Key Decisions

Ensure that you have a full input to any key decisions. Even when you employ an architect/surveyor you need to ensure that the building is suitable for your requirements. You are the expert in what you want from your kennels.
Take advice – but ensure you possess enough relevant knowledge to make your own informed decision.

Builders

Any reputable builder will not be available immediately – most are booked for at least three months in advance. This is particularly the case for smaller companies employing a work force of 5 – 20 staff.
Larger contractors have more flexibility, but they may be more expensive.

Grey Areas

Some items are difficult to finalise at the early stages of a development. It is essential to continue to carry out any relevant research to ensure that the project is not delayed.

Insurance

Ensure that you inform your insurance company
of any new development

If you have taken the responsibility for the construction, it **must** be insured as it progresses. If a main contractor has insured the project during construction, you will need to notify your insurance company once the practical completion stage has been reached.

WHY PROJECTS GO WRONG

There are numerous reasons why projects go wrong, cost more, and take longer to complete than originally envisaged. The majority of projects are, on the whole, largely successful in terms of the completed building.

No project is 100% successful, no matter who is running it, or what the budget is. The majority of kennel buildings work extremely well, although there might be a few teething issues, or design issues that can be improved.

For major companies (such as retail parks or food companies) constructing a large number of developments each year with the same materials, construction methods, design layouts, etc, it is far easier for them to get it right as they have already been through their 'learning curve'. However, for the majority of kennel owners and welfare organisations, each building is a prototype and therefore bespoke. This clearly invites potential problems.

The main reasons for client dissatisfaction are:

■ Cost

Clearly, expenditure over and above what has been set aside for the development is a concern.
To go into a project without any form of contingency is extremely unwise.
The reasons for cost increase can be minimised by doing your homework before committing to the project.
The majority of additional costs are often attributed to poor ground conditions (such as collapsing trenches, contaminated ground, additional drainage, steep sites where more material is excavated than allowed for).
The costs can also be affected by external influences that you have little control over, such as the local planning department. It might be that they insist on a certain type of material that is more expensive than you have allowed for. In most cases it is quicker and easier to accept their requirements and move the project along.

■ Contractor

The choice of Contractor is critical to ensure that the quality is correct, the costs given are fair and accurate, and the contractor is the correct company for your project. Too large a company and it will be more expensive, too small a company and they probably won't have the resources to cope with the project

■ Client

Quite often it is the client who is the worst offender.
Simple things such as altering the specification halfway through the project, or including extra items, all have financial implications. It is perfectly acceptable to make changes. However, you need to know the cost **before** the work is carried out, to ensure you are not presented with a substantial claim for additional costs at the very end of the project

Time
Most projects will run over the contracted time period. This is not uncommon.

However, you need to keep on top of this and find out the reasons why the contractor is behind his schedule. A small overrun for a contractor who has worked diligently and thoughtfully is something that has to be lived with. It is often a small price to pay for a completed project that has can be moved into straight away, one that you are happy with and has few snagging items (a snagging list is compiled prior to the building contractor finishing, but there are minor items of work not completed or finished to your satisfaction e.g. mastic joint not completed, area of decorating not up to standard).

The problems normally arise with smaller contractors, who have taken on too much work and are juggling several contracts at the same time without the resources to complete any one project. This can be a major issue, and particularly so for a kennel owner who has booked dogs in on a set date.

The other reasons for overrunning the scheduled time are often associated with long lead times, and delivery for metalwork and specialist items. Many of the suppliers of specialist animal products tend to be individual, smaller companies who often have to quote lead-times in excess of **12 weeks**; this can lead to major issues, particularly on smaller projects.

Utility Companies
Again, this is another area that can result in the project running over the scheduled time. If the project requires a new utility supply (e.g. electricity) the lead times are lengthy. Quite often the contractor has little power to influence the provider and simply has to wait.
If new utilities are required, these need to be identified and requested at the earliest opportunity.

Summary for a Successful Project
The aim for the successful completion of any project is:

- Be on budget

- Be on time

- Have a building that is to the required standard and specification, and meets your expectations

- Avoid claims and legal disputes with the contractor, planning officials and neighbours

- Be fair but firm with builders. Any claims for additional payments should be investigated to establish their validity. It might be that the claim is honest and fully justified

- Avoid legal arbitration if at all possible. The only winners from this route will be the legal representatives.

PROFESSIONAL PROJECT MANAGEMENT AND ARCHITECTURE

Alex Darvill, Agora Management

PROFESSIONAL PROJECT MANAGEMENT

It cannot be stressed strongly enough that the building industry is complex – it is one in which we are deeply involved, and extremely experienced. The likelihood is that the unaided layman will fail to deal adequately with the procurement, management and financial rigours of his project. For example, a 'Design and Build' method will fail miserably if there is an inadequate detailed brief and the absence of a skilled professional to guide the prospective building owner in all aspects of this particular method.

A professional project manager will spend as long as is necessary to develop a client's initial design brief into a final concept, that will provide a pleasing, functional and robust facility. At Agora Management we tailor our services to suit the circumstances of each project, which is essential to ensure the right balance of time, cost and quality is provided.

A wide and detailed knowledge of building materials and of practical design issues such as ours enables a building to be modified to each client's needs, and to any limitations that the proposed site may place upon it.

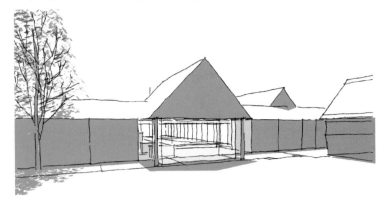

PRACTICAL CONSTRUCTION ISSUES

Building any form of animal housing is a specialist area, and this knowledge is something that can only be obtained by continually working and developing in this sector. Mistakes are easily made due to lack of knowledge, and it is often left to the client to outline the project brief and specifications.

PLANNING APPLICATIONS

There are many pitfalls in making a planning application.

Again, specialist knowledge will come into its own here – as a wide and detailed knowledge of planning legislation and environmental issues is essential (it has proved vital to many of our clients), and is an area in which we have an exemplary record of dealing with such complex issues. We find our previous experience invaluable and act as precedents/case studies, which pay dividends in achieving planning success.

BUILDING REGULATIONS REQUIREMENTS

Building Regulations define the amount of carbon dioxide emissions permitted from the heating and other energy-consuming services of new and altered buildings. Control measures, such as solar shading, can have significant impact upon both cost and a building's appearance and hence may have planning implications if not considered early enough.

We therefore advise our clients of the design options that will best meet Building Regulations, or exceed current standards by a defined amount, by producing a Simplified Building Energy Model (SBEM) at the planning stage from our intelligent three-dimensional design models.

> "Planning is bringing the future into the present so that you can do something about it now."
>
> *Alan Lakein*

Agora Management is a professional practice, providing a full range of building advisory and design services ranging from: project management, architecture and quantity surveying, to mechanical and electrical services and CDM co-ordination

AGORA
management

We employ a 3D imaging package as a service to aid the client in visualising their proposed development. This enables clients to see any chosen part of the building, just as if they are standing in it or next to it.

DESIGN DEVELOPMENT PROGRAMME & BUILD ESTIMATE

A TYPICAL DESIGN DEVELOPMENT PROGRAMME:

The typical design development programme shown here turns the project from an academic concept into a reality – it is actually happening!

The client can see how he fits into the design process and can consider such matters as the date from which the contractor's entitlement to periodic payment will begin.

Typical larger project Build Estimate

AGORA management

Elemental Budget Estimate / A. THE WORKS	Est'd Cost	Est'd Cost Sterling £	Est'd Cost Euro €	Est'd Cost USA $	Notes
1.00 The Building					
a. Substructure	£27,500				
b. Frame	£10,000				Prov'l sum pending design
c. Upper floors and stairs	£15,000				
d. Roofs	£35,000				Incl prov'l sum £3,000 for screen planting
e. External walls	£27,5?0				
f. Windows and external doors	£18,?0				
g. Internal walls	?,7?				
h. Internal doors and screens	?,?00				
i. Wall finishes	?9,?0				
j. Floor finishes	£?,5??				
k. Ceiling finishes	?,000				
l. Fittings	£3?,500				Prov'l sum pending design
m. Services and lift	£160,000	£416,500	€ 545,199	$792,974	Prov'l sum pending design
2.00 External Works and Services					
a. Demolitions and site clearance	£6,000				
b. Hard Landscaping	£7,500				
c. External structures	£27,500				
d. Soft Landscaping	£1,750				
e. Mains service connections	£12,500	£55,250	€ 71,930	$105,190	Prov'l sum pending design
3.00 Drainage					
a. Surface/foul water		£7,500	€ 9,764	$14,279	Prov'l sum pending design
4.00 Sub-total A		£479,250	€ 623,936	$912,444	
5.00 Estimated preliminaries cost		£92,500	€ 120,426	$176,111	
6.00 Sub-total B		£571,750	€ 744,361	$1,088,555	
7.00 Estimated OH&P margin		£42,881	€ 55,827	$81,642	
8.00 Sub-total C		£614,631	€ 800,188	$1,170,196	
9.00 Contingencies (taken @ 10%)		£61,463	€ 80,019	$117,020	
10.00 Estimated Total Cost @ 1Q/08		£676,094	€ 880,207	$1,287,216	
say		£677,000	€ 881,386	$1,288,940	

B. GENERAL NOTES:

1.00 All figures are current @ 1Q/08 and exclude VAT, professional fees and planning/Building Control fees

---

DESIGN DEVELOPMENT — AGORA management

ID	Task Name	Start	Finish
0	DESIGN DEVELOPMENT & CONSTRUCTION PROGRAMME	10 Dec '07	29 May '09
1	A: Not Starting Drawings Until We Have Received Planning	10 Dec '07	29 May '09
2	Planning Submission Drawings	10 Dec '07	16 Jan '08
3	Planning Submission	17 Jan '08	17 Jan '08
4	Planning Period	18 Jan '08	13 Mar '08
5	Expected Planning Approval	14 Mar '08	14 Mar '08
6	Client to Instruct Working Drawings for Bills of Quantity	17 Mar '08	25 Mar '08
7	Working Drawings	26 Mar '08	21 May '08
8	Bills of Quantity	22 May '08	19 Jun '08
9	Tender	20 Jun '08	20 Jun '08
10	Contractors Tender Period	23 Jun '08	18 Jul '08
11	Contractors Tender Return	21 Jul '08	21 Jul '08
12	Mobilisation	22 Jul '08	04 Aug '08
13	Start on Site	05 Aug '08	05 Aug '08
14	Construction Period	06 Aug '08	29 May '09

Page 1 — S/Programmes/DesignDevelopment

A TYPICAL LARGER PROJECT BUILD ESTIMATE

As against a one-line, lump sum estimate, an elemental estimate of the type shown here helps the client to understand how the design of each element of the project affects its estimated cost.

This format is crucial in our being able to provide alternative estimates for individual elements of the project as the design is reviewed and developed.

AGORA management

SPECIALIST KNOWLEDGE FOR PROJECTS

PLANNING AND ENVIRONMENTAL ISSUES

Professional project management also needs to be extremely conscious of environmental issues, particularly in respect of considerations such as planning, contaminated ground, waste disposal and the recycling of rainwater. Our policy is always to open, and maintain, a dialogue with the relevant authorities and to work very closely with them to resolve all issues that may arise. Our record in this respect is exemplary.

Whilst there may be particular reasons (perhaps related to planning or to a client's image) why a building must have a certain external style, we remain conscious of the need to provide value for money and to strike a balance between the function of a building (which is paramount), and its form (which is an aesthetic consideration specific to each project).

ANIMAL WELFARE

At Agora Management we ensure that our knowledge of all legislation and guidelines relating to animal welfare is current, so that the facilities for which we are responsible are fully compliant.

It is important to keep up-to-date with animal welfare regulations and issues to stay one step ahead. The new Animal Welfare Act has recently been amended in the UK.

Our expertise extends from canine, feline and equine rehoming centres to aviaries, guide dog training centres and veterinary centres and hospitals. We are also closely involved in the development of specialist metalwork products for the kennelling aspects of such facilities.

SUITABLE MATERIALS FOR KENNELS

Comprehensive knowledge of suitable building materials and design considerations is vital and enables us, at an early stage, to advise on the nature and layout of a building that is likely to suit a client's brief and budget. Our knowledge of materials suitable for animal welfare facilities is vast, and is constantly being updated so that we can ensure the right material is specified – not only for reasons of its initial cost, but also for its likely maintenance needs.

CLIENT ISSUES

At Agora Management, we view all projects with equal care and consideration, and are very mindful of budgetary constraints. We provide financial advice and control, from initial concept design through to the settlement of the contractor's final account, to the closing of the project.

Skills in advising and organising on behalf of a client ensure that the best method of build procurement for a particular project under consideration can be chosen.

Our expertise in planning, programming, management and negotiation has proved invaluable in ensuring that projects are completed within the contractually-dictated timescale and budgetary constraints. We also have experience of the design and construction of multi-use sites (i.e. those with different organisations sharing the same site), and not only of new buildings on new sites, but also of converting and adapting existing buildings, some listed. Close liaison with the relevant authorities is essential – not least where consent for a change of usage is required.

We believe very strongly that the initial design concept and budget costings we offer to our clients are of paramount importance, as they set the benchmark by which all subsequent advice may be judged, and on which a client may base initial funding approval.

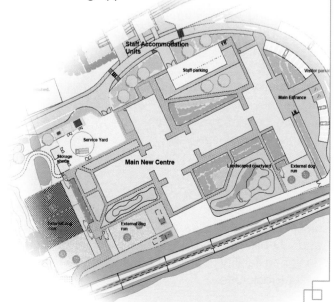

CLIENT CASE STUDY

BATTERSEA DOGS AND CATS HOME BRANDS HATCH

In 1860 Mrs Mary Tealby, concerned by the number of animals roaming the streets of London, opened 'The Temporary Home for Lost and Starving Dogs' in a stable yard in Holloway. The Home moved to its present site in Battersea in 1871, and was renamed The Dogs' Home Battersea. The Home started taking in cats in 1883, following an individual donation of £500. In 1885 Her Majesty Queen Victoria became patron of the Home, and it has remained under royal patronage ever since. In July 2002 the organisation changed its name to Battersea Dogs and Cats Home.

The Home started to spread its wings in 1898, opening additional, country facilities in Hackbridge, Surrey, where Sir Ernest Shackleton kennelled his sled dogs before setting out on his second Antarctic expedition. Bell Mead Kennels in Windsor were acquired in 1978 and are now known as Battersea Dogs and Cats Home, Old Windsor. The former boarding kennels near the Brands Hatch motor racing circuit in Ash, Kent were purchased by the Home in 1996. Both satellite centres receive lost and abandoned dogs and cats from the local area and from the other centres, including from Battersea Dogs and Cats Home in London. Their purpose is to provide temporary shelter and care before rehoming the animals into caring and permanent new homes.

As the former kennels at the Brands Hatch site became unusable, plans were drawn up to completely redevelop the site and Agora Management Limited were appointed to assist. The redevelopment provides for 50 dog kennels and 23 cat pens.

The quality of life offered to the animals is of paramount importance and therefore, whilst the numbers of kennels and cat pens may seem limited, a wide variety of sizes and designs of enclosure allow behaviour assessments and any subsequent training to be undertaken, with minimal stress to the animals concerned.

The steeply sloping site influenced the final layout, with two distinct kennel blocks providing intake, isolation, rehoming and behavioural assessment with training in a purpose-designed facility. Cats are housed in the lower ground floor of Block One.

Due to acoustic restrictions relating to the prominent, elevated location, kennels feature enclosed 'run corridors' with carefully detailed timber louvered and glazed screens to restrict the break-out of noise whilst permitting the free-flow of air for natural ventilation. The cat pens mirror this approach with a mixture of glass and mesh fronts and are large enough to allow potential new owners to spend some time with the cat on a one-to-one basis.

Block Two, although similar in size to the 37 kennel unit Block One, provides **13 distinct kennels for stressed or nervous dogs**. These are **much larger than the current statutory kennel size**, to give the dogs more space to acclimatise to new surroundings and to ensure safe handling by staff.

Four distinct Dog Training Rooms are used for one-on-one sessions, and a large communal covered and heated run meets socialisation needs. **Attention to detail** by the design team and client has seen the inclusion of some very practical features, such as projecting nib walls to each kennel front to ensure that when staff visit or view a dog, they remain out of sight of neighbouring dogs, greatly reducing stress and noise.

PROJECT MANAGER'S COMMENTS

"*This challenging and exciting scheme made the best possible use of a difficult site. BDCH had purchased a larger plot of land in a neighbouring field, which was level and perfect for a new building. However, we were unable to obtain permission to build in this field as it was felt that this would move the centre closer to the nearby built-up area in the village.*

"*It was then decided to build at the top of the hill and new plans were designed and priced. Inevitably, to build on the heavily sloping site meant much larger construction costs for BDCH. One large building at the top of the hill presented far too many problems with regard to split levels, so the final design of two 'L' shaped buildings placed on top of the hill enabled the under-croft of Block One to be used as the cattery.*

"*To enable the centre to remain operational during construction, temporary kennelling facilities were installed for the duration of the works, and the contractor given a separate point of access for deliveries, plant and workmen to remove potential disturbance and conflict of use.*

The quality of life offered to animals at Brands Hatch is of paramount importance. Agora Management Limited were appointed to assist with the redevelopment to provide for 50 dog kennels and 23 cat pens.

Utilising 3D modelling and rendering software, all members of the Design Team and Planning Authority are able to visualise and understand the proposals upon the actual site before commencing works.

"Once completed, the existing staff accommodation building was refurbished and the temporary kennelling sold on to help another animal welfare charity, thereby allowing the full extent of the car park to be finished.

"There was some local opposition to the possibility of an increase in dog numbers. Most of the objections were, as is often the case, due to a lack of information and knowledge about modern dog kennelling. Local residents felt that there might be a rise in dog numbers, which would in turn increase activity, noise, offensive smells, etc. but this is not necessarily the case if a building is well designed.

"Ease of cleaning, better sewage facilities, better acoustic materials used and a higher specification of building materials greatly improves the effectiveness of a building."

PROJECT REVIEW

Apart from the difficulty building on a very heavily sloping site and the need to create another construction access for the contractor (so as avoid a conflict of contractors vehicles and clients visiting the site), the whole project progressed fairly quickly once planning had been approved.

Planning itself had proven to be the biggest task over a three-year period. There are a number of complexities in planning restrictions these days relating to sewage, building materials, acoustics, and water and flood risk assessments. Therefore, in the early stages, the extensive discussions with local planning officers were time-consuming.

Once final approval of the drawings from the client and the local authority had been received, the Project Manager and his team progressed to tender. Using local contractors this was fairly straightforward.

The use of temporary kennelling kept disruption to a minimum, and the proactive decision to seek a purchaser for the modular kennels once redundant ensured that a valuable resource was re-used. This also proved to be a very cost-effective method and should be considered wherever new building works may impede upon existing facilities.

On this particular project, close co-operation between all parties produced a good workable programme to provide temporary kennelling, construction access and reduce costs to the client for this unique rehoming centre.

AGORA
management

3D

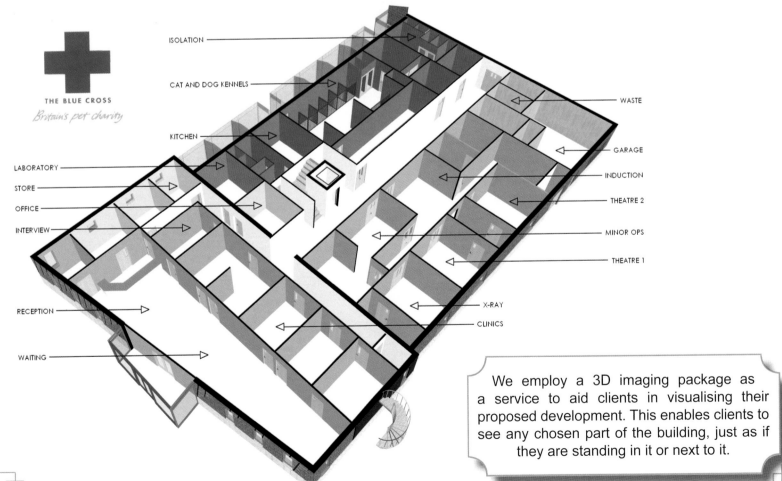

THE BLUE CROSS
Britain's pet charity

ISOLATION

CAT AND DOG KENNELS

KITCHEN

LABORATORY

STORE

OFFICE

INTERVIEW

RECEPTION

WAITING

WASTE

GARAGE

INDUCTION

THEATRE 2

MINOR OPS

THEATRE 1

X-RAY

CLINICS

We employ a 3D imaging package as a service to aid clients in visualising their proposed development. This enables clients to see any chosen part of the building, just as if they are standing in it or next to it.

VETERINARY CARE AND HOSPITAL DESIGN

In our experience, we have found that today's clients include within their establishments varying standards of veterinary care, and that larger organisations have increased and **updated their veterinary facilities to provide the best surgical and medical care for all of their animals**.

Increased veterinary facilities obviously provide greater flexibility to deal with the changing situations that arise from when an animal is received and whilst it is homed.

Larger centres are able to offer full veterinary care including holding and recovery rooms, preparation areas, and theatres, each providing a host of new equipment such as scrub sinks, dental and operating tables, X-ray facilities and, in some cases, full autoclave and surgical equipment racks for invasive treatment to animals. Even smaller centres and single shelters within the United Kingdom are now including within their rebuild a **small veterinary room; some incorporating an adjacent small theatre for minor operations**.

When designing a veterinary suite, consideration should be given not only to the flow of the patient from the waiting area through to holding, preparation, theatre and back into recovery, but also the cleanliness of design and the use of materials: the avoidance of 90 degree junctions, clean wipe-down services with aseptic paints and finishes should be adopted wherever possible.

Experience in this area of animal care facilities is vital for a highly efficient working veterinary suite, and this has taught us that 'cheapness is dearness' in the long-term when creating a veterinary suite, and attention to detail is essential.

We have worked with David Key, (author of this book), for many years, and you can see more of our projects and designs on pages 220-223.

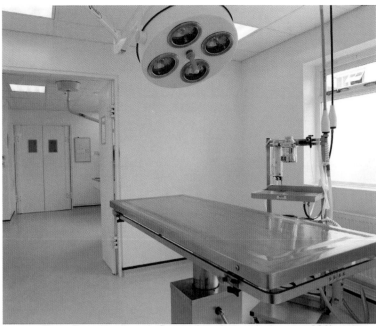

Dogs Trust Kenilworth Centre (see large photo page 236)

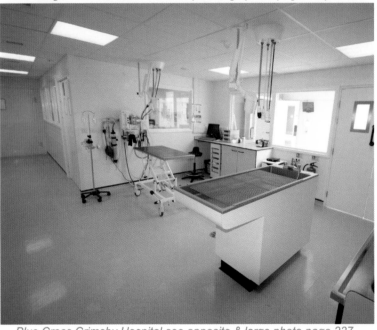

Blue Cross Grimsby Hospital see opposite & large photo page 237

AGORA
management

Alex Darvill
Agora Management Limited
12 Kings Court, Willie Snaith Road
Newmarket, Suffolk CB8 7SG
Tel: +44 (0)1638 560343
www.agoramanagement.com

CASE STUDY:
A BIG PROJECT

Organisation: Dogs Trust Highway Farm
Location: London, UK
Kennels Type: Semi-outdoor
Kennels Function: Rescue and Rehoming
Number of Kennels: 75
Kennel Size Sleep: 1.8m x 2.4m /6ft x 8ft
Kennel Size Exercise: 1.8m x 2.4m/6ft x 8ft
Year Built: 2006

www.dogstrust.org.uk

DOGS TRUST WANTS TO SOLVE THE
PROBLEM OF WHY THERE ARE SO MANY
UNWANTED DOGS, AND SEEKS TO ACHIEVE
THIS THROUGH PRACTICAL MEASURES
AND AWARENESS-RAISING INITIATIVES TO
EDUCATE AND INFORM DOG-OWNERS

DOGS TRUST HIGHWAY FARM

Dogs Trust is the largest dog welfare charity in the UK and has a world-renowned reputation for dog welfare. Its Highway Farm rehoming centre at Harefield in West London is their flagship, one of 17 centres across the UK, and is capable of housing up to 140 dogs on the 13 acre site.

CLEVER KENNEL DESIGN

The kennels are a single line design arranged around central landscaped courtyards, with seating areas to allow visitors to spend more time with the dogs they are thinking of adopting. The more time spent with the dogs, the more the true nature of the dog comes out on a one-to-one basis, and the more successful the partnering is likely to be.

To secure planning consent for the site, one of the conditions for planning permission was that the charity had to restore the existing Grade II Listed oak-framed barn. A great success, this stunning building now provides a highly functional space for lectures, meeting rooms and is an integral part of the facilities.

The kennels provide lots of natural light through the glass-fronted corridors opening onto the courtyards. Wide-opening windows and doors in the corridor allows natural ventilation, and an open, garden room feel which brings nature indoors.

SCALE OF DEVELOPMENT

The building footprint for this centre is one of the largest of all the Dogs Trust centres, and is partly attributed to the single line design. The layout follows the success of the angled kennels on some of their other centres, but here it has been modified in line with planning conditions to reduce the ridge height of the buildings.

The layout, with its integral courtyards, reduces the impact of the scale and gives the centre a very relaxed, welcoming feel and great character that belies its size.

New Dogs Trust centres are packed with special features and are filled with natural light, so the dogs for rehoming feel happy and stress-free when waiting for adoption

I LOVE PEOPLE!!

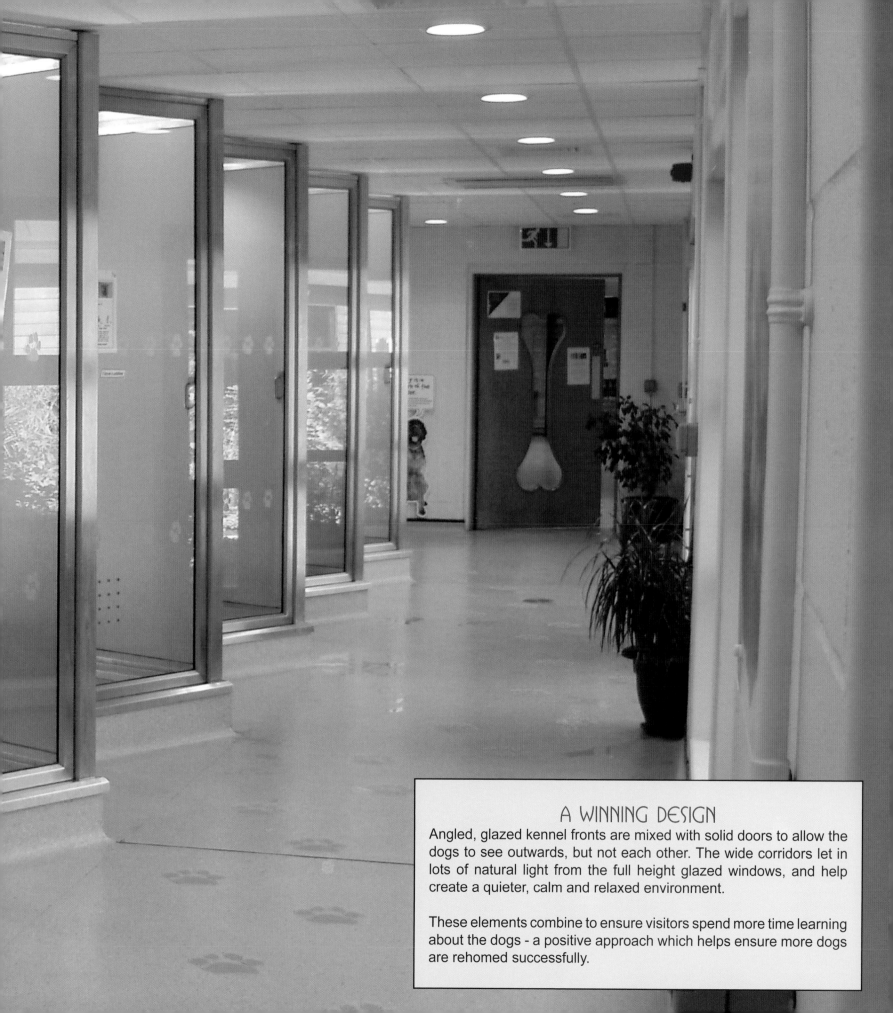

A WINNING DESIGN

Angled, glazed kennel fronts are mixed with solid doors to allow the dogs to see outwards, but not each other. The wide corridors let in lots of natural light from the full height glazed windows, and help create a quieter, calm and relaxed environment.

These elements combine to ensure visitors spend more time learning about the dogs - a positive approach which helps ensure more dogs are rehomed successfully.

BEYOND THE KENNELS

Manager Richard Moore is responsible for this busy centre with its 31 staff. Richard described how he found working at this brand new facility for the first 18 months. He says: *"Compared to operating a previous centre with a circular design kennels, this is much quieter - a fact I put down to the single line and improved design which has so many welfare benefits to the dogs. The cleaning regime is far easier."*

When asked what other features he would have liked to be incorporated within the design, Richard said he would like more kennels in admissions/reserved dogs because of the higher rehoming rate at this centre. He is also a keen advocate of having a socialisation kennel within reception to showcase the more sociable dogs that thrive on human company.

THE IMPORTANCE OF PLAY

Dogs Trust not only focuses on excellent dog-friendly design but also on the peripheral areas that provide wellbeing for the dogs. These include multi-surface free run areas, for example you can see 3 of the 6 large open exercise areas (opposite page, photo below left) showing a combination of grass, sand and concrete to provide different textures and playing areas for the dogs.

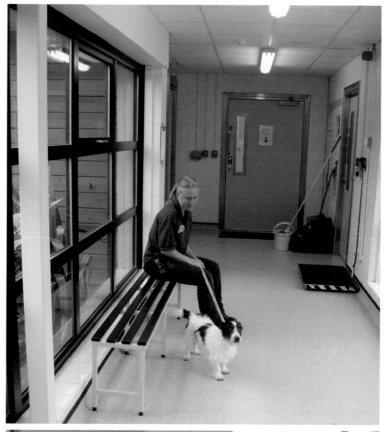

A GOOD SIGN

Dogs Trust excels at providing friendly and educational elements that are eye-catching and fun. These elements include welcoming signage, pawprints and highlight signs to guide visitors around the kennels, and poster-sized prints of their mission statement (photo bottom left) to real-life sized dog images with thought-provoking messages.

This reinforces the charity's strong, positive image and identity, leaving visitors with a lasting impression of the charity's care of, and passion for successful dog rehoming.

DOGS TRUST HIGHWAY FARM

10 CONSTRUCTION MATERIALS

EXTERNAL CONSTRUCTION MATERIAL CHOICES

Although typical animal buildings tend by their very nature to be utilitarian, it is surprising how they can be transformed and aesthetically improved with the correct choice of materials, colours and subtle architectural detail.

The construction style and choice of materials for your proposed development will depend on several issues; the location, the position of the site (e.g. on top of a hill or areas with restricted planning). All locations pose their own difficulties and restrictions, some more onerous than others.

The local planning authority will probably insist that any new development be sympathetic and in keeping with the style for that locality. All of these issues will need to be discussed with the planning authority at an early stage. It is pointless having plans drawn up for the development that will be totally unacceptable to the planners.

In areas of outstanding natural beauty or restricted planning the choice might be very limited, with the local authority perhaps insisting on the use of natural stone common to the area. The end result is higher costs for the development.

The costs involved with any construction project have increased considerably over the past few years, and it is not uncommon for many animal buildings constructed out of brick/block to cost similar amounts to those for domestic housing.

The nature of animal accommodation means the rooms are generally smaller than those in houses, which has cost implications. The ground works involved for brick/block constructions are similar to those for a house; consequently the costs are similar. The roof construction, whether it is tiled or insulated steel sheeting, is also the same for a kennel building as for a house. Combine all of these factors with boiler-fired central heating systems, and it is easy to see how the costs can be greater for animal accommodation.

Many of the companies offering prefabricated systems will normally offer some level of design work as part of their package. Clearly this can be a very attractive deal.

Once the building construction method approaches the more traditional methods (i.e. brick/block), it is not unusual to find that the client has employed the services of an architect or surveyor. This can be either to design and submit plans suitable for a planning application, or to design, project manage and oversee the entire development.

Ultimately, the deciding factors are often financial, size of the development, how confident the client is in dealing with builders, difficult site or ground conditions, and the type of image you wish to portray.

BUILDING CONSTRUCTION MATERIALS

Kennel construction materials fall into the following categories:

- Prefabricated units

- Steel and timber frame buildings with insulated panel infills

- Brick, block, stone, poured insulated concrete

- Conversions of existing buildings

Within the above categories there are numerous design and material options available.

Obviously, the choice of construction method is a primary and fundamental issue. The choice will have planning, cost, logistical, ease of use, and longer term issues such as maintenance and potential re-sale value if the business is sold.

All of the above materials and systems will work; however, they all have advantages and disadvantages.

Advantages and disadvantages can often be matters purely of personal preference, and are often associated with the overall design, availability and quality of construction materials used, and local labour.

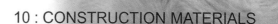

PREFABRICATED UNITS

The use of UPVC for kennels has increased over the past five years. The reasons for this are:

- Well-known and familiar product for replacement doors and windows that is quick and easy to assemble

- Easy to clean and non-porous

- Professional and clean appearance

- Is generally supplied in a white finish. Alternative colour options are available, but are more expensive (these are only used on the external face with white still being used internally)

What to check:

- There are large variations in cost/quality between manufacturers, for what at first appears to be the same product.

- The product may expand slightly during periods of **prolonged heat**. Although this can be an irritation if doors/windows temporarily do not close smoothly, it does settle down again when the temperature cools

- Careful consideration of the manufacturer's specification is essential to establish the differences and to compare like-for-like. For example: compared with 25mm/1" polycarbonate opal/bronze-tinted roof sheeting, the heat-shield coating option can double the cost. This isn't noticeable when you see the products, but on a hot day you would certainly feel the difference in temperature with the heat-shield system preventing high internal temperatures

- Looks extremely smart in a traditional construction, or in a building conversion. Can look more obtrusive when used as a stand-alone building in certain settings, (landscaping obviously helps any building 'settle in')

- Websites and brochures should be checked for the number of existing customers who are happy to recommend the manufacturer. It is much more valuable to learn from those who have used an established product for a number of years and still highly recommend a manufacturer (having tested the product out with a multitude of dogs and staff in all weathers and seasons), rather than comments immediately after installation or before use.

The quality of the material, advice, design and aftercare service varies **enormously** between manufacturers.
It is strongly recommended that you speak to and visit existing customers who are using the product on a daily basis.

Next we will look at a case study of a rescue. A direct comparison (same site, dogs and staff) can be made between the existing kennel problems, and the design features which make the new kennels work extremely well. By understanding and learning from the problems with their original typical older style kennels, they were able to create a new, better facility with markedly less stress, noise, cleaning and visitor issues. The benefits of their modern UPVC kennels by highly recommended manufacturer Pedigree Pens speak for themselves. The benefits to dogs, staff and visitors using good design and stress/noise reduction ideas applies to all kennels - whether prefabricated or traditional build.

CASE STUDY:
A WINNING COMBINATION FOR DOGS AND PEOPLE

Organisation: Dublin SPCA
Location: Ireland, Dublin
Kennels Type: Indoor/Semi
Kennels Function: Rescue
Number of Kennels: 20
Unit Size Sleep: 1410mm x 1530mm/4ft 6" x 5ft
Unit Size Exercise: 1410mm x 2440mm/4ft 6" x 8ft
Date Built: 2007

www.dspca.ie

A BUSY SHELTER JUST OUTSIDE A
MAJOR CITY IMPLEMENTED ITS IDEAS
AND PHILOSOPHIES WITHIN NEW COST-
EFFECTIVE KENNELS. THEY CREATED
A QUIET, CALM AND WELCOMING
ENVIRONMENT FOR DOGS AND ADOPTERS

DUBLIN SPCA

The Dublin Society for Prevention of Cruelty to Animals was established in 1840 and is the oldest and largest animal charity in the Republic of Ireland. The Society was based in Dublin City from its formation up until 1990, then moved to the suburbs, and generations of Dublin people were familiar with it as 'The Dogs and Cats Home'. In 2003 the Society moved to its current location, formerly the Pine Valley Golf Club.

Over the years the Society's kennels and cattery facilities had been seen by other Irish welfare groups as role models and it strived to provide the best possible facilities for the animals in its care, based on the funding available. With each change in premises, great efforts were made to build the best, but affordable, facilities. When the Society moved to its first purpose-built premises in 2003, the cattery, isolation unit and surgery were perfect for their needs, but within 2 years they realised the kennels were already too small and had some major unforeseen problems, particularly with high noise levels.

The kennels were typical of the day. The building was built using a steel frame, with block walls, rendered with plaster outside, and pointed on the inside. Each kennel unit was constructed with blocks, and the usual metal frame door and grills, with a sleeping area and a dedicated run outside. Viewings of the dogs for rehoming by the public was from outside and only staff were permitted inside the kennel block. Inside, the building was noisy, with a metal roof and bare blockwork failing to provide any noise absorption. It was also cold and at times quite odorous, despite underfloor heating and a large air extraction and heating system. Staff found it difficult to clean to a satisfactory level due to the metal grills of the kennel doors and rough painted blockwork. In bad weather, the outside of the kennels was not suitable for people to view the dogs as it could be cold, wet and windy with no protection from the elements, and they were not happy to let the public into the noisy interior.

So in late 2006 General Manager Jimmy Cahill decided to start researching new facilities for the dogs, with an easy-to-clean environment and to reduce noise levels. He was also looking for an easy-to-view, visitor-friendly environment where the dogs could be seen from inside a warm, comfortable and all-season facility. Their ideal design was a building that was maintenance-free, inexpensive, warm and attractive inside, but that also fitted in with the existing buildings. It was decided that purpose-built kennels within a basic barn type frame were to be constructed, and to be fitted out with custom-built kennels, rather than building from scratch.

In Jimmy's extensive research, he came across Pedigree Pens who would build kennels to fit their requirements. The total build time took just 17 weeks from start to finish, and the kennels themselves were fitted in just a few days. Pedigree Pens provided all the staff to fit the kennels, and have been extremely helpful in their aftercare service.

Jimmy says: "*We have found the new rehoming kennels have made a vast difference to the number of dogs being rehomed on a monthly basis. The public are much happier to view the dogs in a bright and airy indoor environment, which, though it is not totally noise free, is a great improvement on the previous kennels. The old kennels are now being used for dog rehabilitation and treatment.*"

Jimmy is extremely proud of the new light, warm and inviting kennels, in particular how quiet and calm they are, and says:

"By providing the best possible kennelling and viewing facilities, potential adopters can see dogs at their best. The increase in the numbers of dogs being rehomed is testament to the happier environment provided for both dogs and people alike"

Above: The old kennels were noisy, cold and open to the elements ,which made them stressful for dogs and unwelcoming for visitors

DUBLIN SPCA

UPVC ACCOMMODATION

Paul Collins, Pedigree Pens

KENNELS AND CATTERIES

In today's discerning market there is a need for high quality, hygienic, low maintenance facilities. This strategy is important in order to market and establish your business correctly, not only because of customer demands, but also to comply with increasing local authority regulation requirements.

Over the last ten years we at Pedigree Pens have worked closely with our customers and built up extensive knowledge in assisting people starting up a kennel or cattery business. It is an essential part of our strategy to work closely with our customers on an ongoing basis, as this ensures our customers are happy and also provides us with a continuous programme of design and development.

We are chosen for our quality construction materials, in-depth knowledge, and **our full design service.** We can provide statements to assist **planning issues**, **offer advice** on advertising and marketing strategies, courses and even provide a free business support service via our website, which lists our customers' business details, such as address, contact details, photographs and website addresses. This helps to generate new business for them, because if anyone searches the internet for a cattery in a specific county, the search engine will identify our website, through which customers can be contacted by pet owners.

We have helped over 80 boarding and rescue centres start up

Our customers want the highest quality of boarding accommodation to provide the highest standards of comfort, hygiene and security seen in the boarding industry. Due to the emphasis on these high standards, they are able to charge higher fees for this level of service.

STARTING A NEW KENNEL OR CATTERY

We would suggest that our boarding units are installed as small and exclusive developments (ideally 10 to 30 double-size units) and are focused towards the more discerning pet owner who is prepared to pay a premium for a high quality service and environment. **Our pens can be installed as complete buildings, or within an existing or new building**.

The cost of the pens can usually be covered by sales in the first year of trading, and possibly by the end of month eight!

SUCCESS AND EXPANSION

The majority of our installations are listed on our website and each one is running very successfully, achieving repeat business year after year. Many of our customers are so successful within the first two years of opening that they contact us again looking to expand their business further.

Choosing a Pedigree Pens installation means that you will be offering a service with the highest standard of accommodation, which more and more customers demand these days. Serious direct competition is unlikely to exist, as there are certain to be boarding establishments within your local area which offer a much lower standard of accommodation.

We can manufacture to your exact requirements, and we can supply you with:
- Freestanding pens
- Convert existing buildings
- Fit out a new building

FREESTANDING PENS

1

When starting a cattery, many people use the land adjoining their home. Where this is the case, we can install freestanding pens (the units are fitted to a level concrete base), e.g:

1. Patz Catz Cat Hotel: 10 double 'penthouse' style pens located in Hampshire

2. Cloughfields Cat Hotel: 'L' shape formation consisting of 15 double size pens located in Sheffield

2

3. Imberpark Cattery: 14 double size 'walk-in' pens located in Middlesex and 10 minutes from Heathrow

4. Templeogue Cattery: 30 double size pens located in Dublin, Ireland

5. Beechcroft Cats Hotel: Cattery consisting of 30 'walk-in' style pens located rurally in Cardiff

3

Below: Dublin SPCA: 20 kennels installed within a new steel-framed building (see case study on previous pages)

4

5

CONVERSION

You may have existing farm buildings or outbuildings that you wish to convert. In this case we can convert the existing building into a new kennels or cattery, requiring just the shell of a building to install under cover. Pens are installed internally and usually have a flat roof, e.g:

1. The Blue Cross Tiverton: Conversion creating 20 pens for this rescue centre located in Devon
2. Dublin SPCA: Rehoming kennels fitted within a new steel-framed building. Dublin, Ireland

NEW BUILD

Pedigree Pens frequently fits out new buildings. We work closely with contractors, provide: doors, divisions and rooms on individual requirements, and our expertise, e.g:

3. Heathrow Airport (Animal Reception Centre): Kennels and cattery for quarantine and passport pets
4. The Mayhew Animal Home: Dog socialisation playroom. London
5. The Blue Cross Lewknor: Fitted out divisions, doors and rooms to create new cattery. Located in Oxfordshire

Below: Play room at The Mayhew Animal Home in London

CONVERSION & NEW BUILD

1

2

3

4

5

PEDIGREE PENS

RESCUE & REHOMING

We also manufacture and install high quality, insulated boarding kennels and catteries for rescue centres, examples of which can be seen at many of Britain's leading animal charities such as Cats Protection, The Blue Cross, RSPCA, and The Mayhew Animal Home.

In particular, Blue Cross and Britain's RSPCA have worked closely with us to ensure that their exact requirements for animal housing have been met fully for their long-term needs. Different styles of pens can be viewed at our Gloucestershire showroom (M5 Junction 9) – directions available from the website.

Some of our customers:
*   Blue Cross
*   Cats Protection
*   Dublin SPCA
*   Heathrow Airport Quarantine
*   Lincoln University
*   Mayhew Animal Home
*   RSPCA
*   Wiltshire College
*   Wood Green Animal Shelters
*   and over 50 boarding
        establishments

ABOUT PEDIGREE PENS LTD

We are a BS EN ISO (British Standards Quality Assured, UK) registered company and specialise solely in the manufacture of

PVCu animal housing and have done so since 1993. We have hundreds of installations throughout the UK and Ireland for commercial boarders, rescue centres and private households.

Our experience in this field is second to none. We are original sponsors of the UK's CIEH (Chartered Institute of Environmental Health) Model Licence Conditions for Cat Boarding Establishments.

PRODUCT QUALITY AND STANDARDS

With a clear objective: to raise standards for animal care in the private and public sectors, we have developed our exciting range of pet accommodation to address issues of hygiene, security, comfort, maintenance and longevity.

Our products are manufactured to meet increasingly high expectations and individual requirements, in addition to providing designs which have been carefully developed over the years.

All our frames are made from PVCu which is highly regarded for its self extinguishing properties. The modular design of our pens allows for installation of any number of units from just one or two to a hundred or more and means they can be installed at a later date to accommodate your expansion plans.

If you have any questions, please contact Paul Collins, our Managing Director, at:

happy dogs & cats habitats!

Pedigree Pens Ltd
A2 Northway Trading Estate
Northway, Tewkesbury
Gloucestershire GL20 8JH, UK
Phone & Fax: +44 (0)1684 299567
www.pedigreepens.com

STEEL AND TIMBER FRAME BUILDINGS

Steel Frame

Typically steel frame buildings are used for larger developments, particularly with wide cross sections. The reasons for this are ease of construction, structural and strength issues, and economies of scale.

A steel frame building still provides a support for the roof covering. All of the external and internal walls and flooring are the same as solid construction. Consequently the cost will still be the same. Another advantage of using steel frame is that it allows the roof to be constructed early in the build (whereas a solid construction the walls support the roof and so they have to be built first). Getting the roof on early gives a major advantage, in that work can carry on even in inclement weather.

Timber Frame

Depending on the style and design of the kennel building the use of timber framing is another option. For countries that suffer extremes of climate (particularly cold), it is likely that the timber frame construction method will be common to the area, and consequently the materials and labour will be more readily available. Another advantage for such locations is that the frames are pre-manufactured and do not involve wet trades e.g bricks/blocks. This means that they are not subject to delays due to bad weather.

Note:

The framing will need to be clad and sealed with a waterproof, impervious material. Timber frame is more suited to the single line design of kennels than the double as it removes the framed areas out of the main dog/wet areas.

BRICK, STONE, BLOCK AND POURED CONCRETE

A traditional, solid construction method of building is always the most appealing option. The more home/house-like appearance has strong appeal for many clients.

Solid buildings are generally a bespoke option for a particular site or client requirement, and offer the most options in terms of design and architectural flair. From marketing, business and public appeal points of view, this type of construction gives the impression of a professional, long-term commitment and feels more 'solid' and secure.

Also, bear in mind that a traditional building is a more tangible and flexible asset at a later date, should you wish to sell the property, or convert the building to another use.

The reasons for using this traditional method of construction and materials might be due to:

- Personal preference
- Design options and material choices
- Planning requirements

Certainly the design options are virtually limitless with these materials and do allow and provide for a greater degree of design flair. However, kennels constructed using brick/block or poured concrete are the most expensive of the options to build.

CONVERSIONS OF EXISTING BUILDINGS

If designed correctly, some of the most appealing kennel buildings are often found in conversions of existing buildings. However, to ensure good functionality with an existing building, it does require skill and imagination to ensure the project works well.

A careful cost analysis should be taken for a larger project to see if any benefits will be gained in major refurbishment of an old building as compared with a new build.

CASE STUDY:
BUILDING CONVERSION

Organisation:	Nottinghamshire Police Force
Location:	UK, Nottinghamshire
Kennels Type:	Semi-outdoor
Kennels Function:	Police Dog Training Centre
Number of Kennels:	10
Kennel Sleep Size:	2.2m x 1.8m/ 7ft 2" x 6ft
Kennel Run Size:	2.2m x 4.2m/ 7ft 2" x 13ft 7"
Year Built:	2005

www.nottinghamshire.police.uk

A REFURBISHMENT, EXTENSION AND CONVERSION OF AN EXISTING BUILDING HAS PROVIDED THIS POLICE FORCE WITH A KENNEL FACILITY THAT PROVIDES SPACE & FLEXIBILITY FOR THE DOGS AND HANDLERS, WHICH GREATLY ENHANCES DOG WELFARE

NOTTINGHAMSHIRE POLICE FORCE

In 2005 Nottinghamshire Police took the decision to upgrade its existing kennels at its Headquarters. The original brief was to demolish the existing building and ancillary areas and construct a totally new building with all of the ancillary services and rooms required to keep both dogs and staff happy. A preliminary scheme was drawn up that encompassed all the Dog Section's requirements.

The key elements of the brief were:

- Reduce the levels of stress in the dogs

- Good levels of natural lighting, energy efficient heating with simple operation

- Can be cleaned quickly and efficiently with surfaces that dry fast

- Ease of operation for dog handlers

- Remove some of the existing trees surrounding the site to allow more natural light and allow more air movement around the building

- Improved staff welfare and storage facilities

- Better drainage to the external exercise run areas

- Comply with all current animal welfare legislation

SCHEME 1

After drawing up some concept proposals, it became apparent that the cost and scale of development for the proposed project was going to exceed the budget allowance. In addition, at the time of the discussions there was a great deal of uncertainty for all the Police Forces in the UK over possible mergers to create larger regional forces. Given the cost implications and merger uncertainties, a second scheme was drawn up to utilise as much of the existing structure as possible.

SCHEME 2

The second scheme was drawn up and fully specified; this was submitted to six contractors for competitive tendering. The tender process is always a slightly nervous time for every kennel build, with the uncertainty of whether your budget allowance will be adequate to cover the project.

In this case we had a group of three contractors who had similar costs – this is always a good indicator. The tender was finally awarded, with a 12-week construction programme that was deliberately kept tight to ensure that the dogs were off site for the shortest time possible.

MANAGING THE PROJECT

Even a relatively small project of 10 kennels takes time and effort to ensure that it runs smoothly. There are decisions that have to be made constantly. The majority are simply part of the construction process, but some are related to unforeseen issues that arise. These have to be addressed as they arise if the programme is to be kept on schedule and cost.

Dealing with conversion projects does tend to have more issues and require a greater degreee of flexibility by all parties, to ensure that the project runs smoothly. The main contractor proved to be extremely helpful throughout the entire project and pro-active in his attitude to unforeseen problems.

What are you most pleased with?
Phillip Ellis of Nottinghamshire Police explained:
"*I am pleased with refurbishing an old dilapidated kennel building into a clean, fresh, modern kennelling facility built on time, within budget, and that everyone is happy with.*"

What would you do differently?
"*I don't think we would do anything differently!*"

CONSTRUCTION WORK

The work involved the removal of the existing timber kennels, which had been constructed inside the main timber frame, and the removal of the entire existing floor.

A new floor was laid with correct falls (slopes) to ensure that the water drained into the grated channels (the photo opposite page bottom right clearly shows the step arrangement). This ensures that the wash-down water runs into the drainage system. A concrete and timber-clad extension was also constructed to create dry secure storage for dog food and equipment.

Other works included improved staff welfare, new external exercise runs, both grassed and concrete, new fencing, pathways and re-felting of the main timber structure.

QUALITY FINISHES

Inside the kennels the floors and walls were tiled using 300 x 300mm/ 12" x 12" vitrified tiles. A lightly textured tile was used on the floor to help prevent dogs and staff from slipping; whereas a smooth tile has been used on the walls.

High level radiant cassettes heat each kennel with individual thermostats. This flexibility will allow the handlers to set the level of heating appropriate for their dogs.

Like the majority of Police Forces, Nottingham uses a mixture of breeds. However, on the whole these tend to be German Shepherds, Malamutes and Springer Spaniels.

A number of the kennels have had mesh tops fitted to prevent dogs from escaping. Even though the internal walls are 2 metres high, this would not be sufficient to prevent some of the younger dogs from climbing over.

Although this is a simple, cost-effective measure, it will stop a dog from trying to climb over. It also removes the risk of possible leg injuries by jumping down into confined areas, or dogs getting their legs trapped in the mesh doors.

WELFARE CONSIDERATIONS

Other measures incorporated are windows between the sleep and exercise run to allow the dogs to see out when locked in, and raised platforms in the exercise runs. Again, this is a feature the dogs gain great benefit as it provides a more 3-dimensional aspect to the environment.

FRESH AIR

The building has a simple multi-port ventilation and extraction system to ensure there is a constant supply of fresh air.

The project went extremely well and the end result has given a practical, efficient building and one the handlers are extremely delighted with.

The photographs clearly show what can be achieved with some lateral thinking, good materials and a building contractor who is prepared to put that extra amount of effort in.

When the kennels opened, the press nicknamed it 'Barkingham Palace'!

ROOF COVERINGS

Natural daylight, heating, artificial lighting and ventilation are all an integral part of any building design, each dependent upon the other.

The advantage of economy from natural lighting (e.g. roof lights) has to be balanced against the disadvantages of poor thermal and sound insulation, and solar heat gain. However, the glazing should be of sufficient area to provide suitable and adequate daylight to give a uniform light level to the entire working area.

Animal buildings with **excessive** areas of single glazed roof lighting can give rise to higher levels of solar gain during the summer months; this can be a major concern for any kennel owner.

Obviously, having a dark building is not the answer.

UK Tip:

The Chartered Institute of Environmental Health (CIEH) suggest that the temperature should be a minimum of 10°C/50°F and a maximum of 26°C/79°F. The UK over the years up to 2008 has experienced **temperatures exceeding the maximum for prolonged periods** during the summer months.

Cautionary Note:

- Once the ambient temperature reaches these high levels, older, poorly insulated, badly ventilated buildings with large areas of single glazed roof lights will be noticeably affected by solar gain
(like leaving a car with all windows closed in strong sunlight),
often resulting in highly distressed dogs… or even worse.

Roof Materials

The type of material used will depend on the construction method and kennels style and type.

In addition, if the building is subject to Building Regulations/Control, you will have to prove that the materials used reach the criteria for U-values (the rate at which heat is transferred through an element of the building).

Obviously the roof structure to the main sleeping area needs to be fully insulated, to prevent condensation/heat loss during the winter, and solar gain during the summer

---

If the building does not have to comply with Building Regulations/Control, there are more options available. However, it must be remembered that insulation works both for cold climates in retaining heat, and also in hot climates to prevent an excess of heat build-up.

Two main types of roofing for traditional type construction are:

■ Slate and tiles

■ Profiled sheet coverings

Slate and Tiles

Traditionally, roofs on smaller buildings were constructed using either slate or concrete tiles. The coverings are fixed to timber roof trusses or purlins (roof structure), with pitches of at least 22°. For aesthetic qualities, and areas with particular planning restraints, these materials are still used for traditionally constructed buildings.

The covering materials are generally poor insulators against transfer of heat. This problem has been overcome by the use of insulating materials such as glass-fibre matting and expanded PVC, the insulation is laid between the ceiling rafters.

The insulating layer will act to reduce the heat loss from the building to the roof space, and also reduce the heat gain from the roof space into the building. These finishes are normally associated with traditionally-constructed buildings.

Profiled Sheet Coverings

The advantage of steel as a material for roof covering is its favourable strength-to-weight ratio, making it both practical and economic to use. The other main advantage of this type of covering is the lower pitches at which it can be laid e.g. 5°. The roof is normally a sandwich construction, with the insulating material between the outer top sheet and an inner lining sheet. The insulation thickness ranges from 40mm/1½" to 100mm/4".

The sheets come in many styles, profiles, materials and colours. Most have a lifespan in excess of 40 years, with the major manufacturers giving a 30 year guarantee.

Note:

Any 'sandwich' roofing system should be certificated to its fire safety properties. Many of the larger UK companies will provide roofing systems that come with a Loss Prevention Certification Board (LPCB) LSP1181 test certificate

Profiled Sheet Materials

■ **Hot-dipped galvanised**
This is a method of applying a coating of zinc to the sheet as a protective barrier against the elements. The disadvantage of this sheet is that it is only available in one finished colour, silver/grey, which tones down over a period of time to a dark grey

■ **Plastic coated steel sheets**
Most plastic coated steel sheets look very much the same. However, the quality of the coating and the types of coating vary enormously, and this results in varying lifespans and costs. It is important to realise the type of coating the sheet has. The coating serves two purposes; it provides an additional protective barrier, and also introduces a wide range of colours to the standard sheets. The effects of ultra-violet radiation will gradually bleach the pigment in the coating over a period of years

Cement sheets

Often incorrectly referred to as asbestos roof sheeting.

The sheets are made from a mixture of natural fibres with alternating layers of cement and water. The wet mixture is then rolled flat or formed into corrugated sheets and steam-cured to harden it. These cement sheets are used extensively for agricultural, storage and industrial buildings.

During recent years, the introduction of colour coatings has improved the aesthetic quality of this system and made it more acceptable as a form of roof covering for smaller buildings.

Note:

Cement sheets once contained asbestos fibres. However, since March 1998, all new, British-made roofing sheets are asbestos-free. The use of asbestos is now illegal. Sheets manufactured before this date will contain approximately 12% of white asbestos. This point should be taken into consideration if demolitions have to be undertaken.

If asbestos is discovered, then expert advice should be sought; this will take into account the Health and Safety aspect and the legal requirement for the removal and disposal.

Asbestos in good condition is perfectly acceptable. If the sheeting is secure and in good condition, it can be left in place. It is only when it has to be worked on, removed or is damaged that the legal issues have to be considered.

Warning:

- If single-sheet system is used without any form of insulation, be prepared for **extremes of both hot and cold temperatures in the kennels**

- Single-skin metal roofing is **extremely noisy** during rain or periods of hailstones.

- Typically, a single-sheet system would ONLY be used over exercise runs or a covered play area. When used over a heated building, it has to be an insulated, double-skin system

Exercise-Run Coverings

All materials are used to obtain the maximum transmission of light (e.g. glass, and flat or profiled transparent or translucent sheets) but offer little resistance to the transmission of sound or heat.

The roof structures of most animal buildings consist mainly of solid roof materials, e.g. tiles, high performance boarded roofing membranes or profiled sheet with the inclusion of a few rooflights to allow some natural light in.

However, it is the exercise-run roof covering (whether this is an integral part of the building as used by most charities, or a freestanding structure as is the norm for most boarding kennels) that tends to be the area of concern to most owners.

Because of the general use of single skin products, the extremes of weather are most noticeable in the exercise runs, i.e. too hot during the summer months. As said before, the problems associated with high temperatures are more difficult to correct than those with low temperatures.

The main systems used for prefabricated roof lights to the exercise runs are:

Glass

- In the kennel environment, glass would normally be used only in proprietory framed systems i.e. roof lights.

- Glass has poor mechanical strength and therefore requires the strength of metal glazing bars, set comparatively close together. Today, the main use of glass is for smaller, preformed dormer type double-glazed window units. These provide excellent light and ventilation levels

Profiled sheeting

- **UPVC**
  This is one of the **cheapest** of the translucent plastic materials used for roof lights. It has **reasonable light transmission** (77%), **reasonable impact and scratch resistance**. On exposure to solar gain, it has a useful life expectancy of around 25 years. However, it will **discolour with age** to give a yellow/brown colour. Over this period the **light transmission will be markedly reduced**. It tends to become very **brittle** after a short period and can **crack** very easily if walked on to carry out maintenance

- **GRP**
  Glass reinforced plastic – similar to UPVC in terms of appearance, impact resistance and strength; however it **does not have the light transmittance of UPVC**, with only 50%-70%

- **Polycarbonate**
  Is generally manufactured as double, triple or five-walled systems. It has **good light transmittance** (88%), is **extremely strong and durable** and has **good weathering qualities**. It is the **most expensive** of the plastic materials used, and is often used in situations where glass would be damaged

  Its main use is in domestic conservatories and is available in either **clear or bronzed** tint finish. The installation of a twin/triple wall system with a bronze tint or heat shield coating will help reduce solar gain, and provide a more controllable working environment. **It is highly useful as a covering over exercise runs**

The methods commonly used are:

Single Solid Sheet

Advantages

- Cost-effective and easy installation

Disadvantages

- Will be affected by extremes of temperature
- Metal sheeting increases noise reverberation

Single sheet translucent sheeting

Advantages

- Cost-effective and easy installation

Disadvantages

- Will be affected by extremes of temperature
- Does not provide areas of shade for the dog

Part solid – part translucent (single)

Advantages

- Cost-effective
- Easy installation
- Provides shade for the dog
- Is generally an acceptable form of covering for most situations

Disadvantages

- Will be affected by extremes of temperature
- Can be noisy when it rains or hailstones

Polycarbonate Multi-wall System

Advantages

- Relatively easy installation
- Excellent insulator and will provide protection from solar gain, particularly sheeting with a heat shield or bronzed tint finish
- Extremely strong and durable
- Has a smooth finish that makes it easy to clean
- the long-term benefits of durability and lower maintenance costs are considerable

Disadvantages

- As with all finishes, initial slightly higher cost (for the better quality and durability and lower long-term costs)

Helpful Hints

If you have existing kennels with large areas of translucent sheeting, and experience problems with excessive heat during the summer months – then you need to take action.

Short-term solutions

The normal method is to paint over some of the roof lights with a white or solar reflective paint. Although this is only a temporary measure, it will rectify a major problem for a while. A more expensive measure is either to replace some of the sheeting with solid/insulated boarding, or to spray/paint one of the specialist solar reflective coating products over the top.

The long-term solution

Replace it with a better quality system.

Summary

The multi-wall polycarbonate coverings offer the most long-term advantages for the kennel owner

THERMAL INSULATION

HAVING THE
CORRECT LEVEL
OF INSULATION
HELPS KEEP YOUR
KENNELS WARM IN
WINTER AND COOL
IN SUMMER

THERMAL INSULATION – WARMTH AND COOLING

Increasing costs make it important to conserve fuel and reduce heating bills and this means greater levels of insulation in buildings; this applies to all buildings from domestic to industrial. To provide adequate levels of thermal comfort, it is accepted that walls, floors and roof should provide resistance to excessive transfer of heat.

Thermal Transmittance – U-Values and W/m²K

Thermal Transmittance is the rate at which heat is transferred through an element of a building and is called the thermal transmittance or U-value. The lower the U-value, the better the insulation, and the lower the heat loss. U-values are expressed in W/m² K (watts per square metre) temperature differences between internal and external temperatures.

The UK Building Regulations set maximum thermal resistance values for non-domestic dwellings as:

- Walls   0.35 W/m² K

- Floors   0.25 W/m² K

- Roofs   0.20 W/m² K

- Windows and doors   2.0 W/m²K

Helpful Hints:

- It is worth checking with Building Control to establish if any of the new buildings will be exempt from Building Regulations. The interpretation of the regulations varies with each local authority. From experience, this 'grey-area' applies to new buildings that are purely for animal use and do not contain any form of habitable rooms for humans (e.g. staff rooms or kitchens). This point is worth considering, particularly if you own a boarding kennels, as this 'grey-area' could reduce your building costs considerably by removing the inspection fees and additional legal requirements

- If your building is subject to Building Regulations or Control, it is worth noting that **many of the prefabricated systems cannot achieve the necessary U values required.** One governing factor is the level of heat that will be used in the building. If this is below 25 watts per m², it might be below the requirement for Building Regulations

- The type of construction will determine what materials can be used for insulation. The table opposite shows some of the more common types of insulation used in brick/block type buildings

Insulating Materials

Insulating materials keep a building warm but also help to keep it cool.

The most common materials used to provide insulation for walls, ceilings and floors are:

MATERIAL	THERMAL CONDUCTIVITY and DENSITY	
Polyurethane	0.023 W/m°C	20 kg/m³
Polystyrene	0.037 W/m°C	15 kg/m³
Mineral fibre	0.032 – 0.038 W/m°C	16 kg/m³

It is easy to see how polystyrene and polyurethane are highly-effective insulators; this combined with their low weight, makes them highly suitable for both wall, floor and roof insulation.

Generally, because of the higher insulation qualities of polyurethane insulation products, they do not require the thickness of mineral wool to achieve the same U-values. The mineral wool and polyurethane products tend to be the more common ones used in the UK and USA. The type of insulation used will depend on the method of construction. All of the above systems are suitable for brick and block construction, which has a cavity between the inner and outer materials. Obviously, the better the insulation, the warmer/cooler the building will be.

> Insulation products not only help to keep the building **warm** during colder periods, they also **help to keep the temperature down** during hot periods

The amount of insulation is something that cannot be overlooked. When it is cold, it is easy to turn on the additional heating that should be standard in every kennels. However, in hot weather it is extremely hard, particularly over short periods, to reduce the temperature. High temperatures can be more harmful to animals than cold.

Cautionary Note:

Vermin: most rodents will attack polyurethane and polystyrene insulation. If you live in a rural location, or suffer from rodent damage, it will be better to use fibreglass as an insulating material, as this does not seem so attractive to rodents.

Choosing an active dog.

Fire exit

12

FINISHING MATERIALS

CHOOSING THE
RIGHT FINISHING
MATERIALS FOR
YOUR KENNELS
WILL MAKE
CLEANING AND
MAINTENANCE SO
MUCH EASIER

FLOOR FINISH CONSIDERATIONS

Any form of finish used in the kennels has to start with a suitable base such as concrete, screed, or concrete planks.

The top-wearing finish has to be resistant to water, urine, faeces, disinfectant as well as durable, quick drying, long lasting and tough enough to withstand everyday wear and tear

Unfortunately, floor finish is so often the cause of complaint of many kennel owners, where a suitably durable surface has not been specified.

Main criteria when specifying flooring systems are:

- Hygiene

- Safety

- Durability

- Cost

Factors to be considered when choosing flooring:

- Cleaning

- Floor Slope

Note:

The use of drainage systems will need to be discussed with your local authority. It is not acceptable to have foul drainage that simply runs into the ground, without it being collected and channelled into a recognised system. Although this is commonly seen in many older kennels, it does not comply with current legislation.

CLEANING SYSTEM COMPATIBILITY

Before you decide on the type of floor you wish to install, it would be wise to consider your cleaning regime.

The cleaning regime, the amount of water and the disinfectant used can all have an effect on the product over a period of time. There are arguments as to the best methods for cleaning animal buildings, and whether using large amounts of water provides the best solution.

Generally, most of the following products will be suitable for the majority of kennels and, providing they have been correctly installed, should provide an easy-to-clean and suitable surface. For rescue kennels, this particularly applies to sanctuaries that use large amounts of water and pressure washers. For further details see the chapter on Drainage, Kitchen and Cleaning.

Incorrectly specified, a floor finish can, at the very least, be aesthetically spoilt or, at the worst, destroyed.
Liquid will rot timber in a VERY short time.

Below: timber door frame rotting away because of hosing and cleaning

FLOOR SLOPE

If a floor is laid with a fall, this is normally achieved using a sand and cement screed over a concrete slab base. The final wearing/finishing material then covers the screed.

For floors to be self-draining (i.e. the water runs naturally into the drainage channel without too much mopping, etc) the fall must be a minimum of 1:60, and ideally 1:50

Obviously, the fall can be increased to create a more pronounced slope to provide better water run-off. However, this has to be set against the increased material and labour costs involved, and comfort of staff walking on a slope all day. Even with a fall of 1:60, some water will remain and may need to be mopped up.

The final choice of wearing surface is normally decided by the required image and aesthetics, noise considerations, finances, type of construction, method of construction (e.g. self-build or main contractor) and the amount of use the kennels will receive.

By approaching this decision with a flexible attitude, you should be able to specify the correct product for your requirements.

Undoubtedly, a cheaper product cannot be expected to last indefinitely, but as long as this has been taken into consideration and resources and time are made available to carry out any remedial works, this should not be a problem. However, in the case of a large animal welfare charity that operates at full capacity throughout the year, it is extremely difficult and time-consuming to have to empty and close down kennels to carry out maintenance works.

The correct choice of suitable materials for your situation is probably one of the most important decisions you will have to make.

An incorrect choice can make life extremely difficult and expensive in the long-term with unplanned remedial works, and floors that are unhygienic, resulting in bad odours and damp conditions

FLOORING CHOICES

Flooring types (in order of cost, durability and aesthetic appeal):

- Tiles

- Vinyl

- Resin floor sealers and coatings, resin screeds

- Polymer, granolithic and concrete screeds

- Painted concrete

Recommendations for High Usage Kennels

The correct floor for your situation is an important decision that needs to be taken at an early stage. Flooring can improve the aesthetics and provide a more hygienic, and easy-to-clean building. As there are so many choices, it is particularly important for kennels with high usage to make the right choice of flooring, one that will be able to cope with the wear and tear of dogs, staff, cleaning routines and visitors.

My first recommendation for organisations with HIGH usage would be vitrified tiles as being the most suitable long-term solution to the flooring problem. They stand the test of time, and, when cleaned they look like new.

On opening a technical catalogue, it can seem a little daunting at first, with all of the R and V values for industrial and barefoot areas. Obviously there is always a compromise in terms of aesthetic qualities, cost and personal preference. However, at the time of writing, a tile with a R10 rating is a good all-round tile for the kennels environment.

For two rescue kennels and a veterinary hospital constructed in 2005, the tile specified for all three projects was the 'Nature' floor range manufactured by Pilkington. This tile has been used by the charity for a number of years and at the time of writing, still offers a good compromise in terms of cost, durability and slip resistance. (This is a 300 x 300 x 9mm (12" x 12" x ½") tile that has a R10 rating)

My second recommendation for organisations with HIGH usage would be polyurethane screed

This has similar installation costs to tiles, but is quicker to install and lay, can be coved up walls and also used on walls as a covering material. The disadvantage with this option is the floor will have a tendency to stain.

Recommendations for High Usage Corridors and Ancillary Rooms

Vinyl makes a superb finish for these areas, it is quick to lay, can be coved up walls and helps reduce noise and reverberation.

Tiles

An excellent material for aesthetic, longevity, durability and hygienic qualities.

When talking about tiles, we are concerned only with unglazed, vitrified (non-porous) tiles with low water absorption qualities to class BI.

The choice is critical in ensuring that the product is suitable for the environment in which it is to be used.

All ceramic tiles are manufactured from natural sources (i.e. clay, felspar and quartz) and have been used extensively in industrial, commercial and health care applications for many years. During the 1980's there was a trend to use alternative, seamless finishes to improve the hygienic qualities, hence the increase in resin-based systems. However, with suitable grouting and disinfectants, any concerns relating to their use in animal accommodation and harsh environments are totally unfounded. Independent research carried out by Lancashire Polytechnic, and also by Campden Food and Drink Research Association has shown that floor and wall tiled surfaces have a biological integrity at least as good as competitive materials.

Tile Advantages and Disadvantages

Advantages:

■ Uniform finish

■ Durable and virtually maintenance free
(Having specified tiles for use in animal buildings for over 20 years of constant daily wear, they still look pristine and remain hygienic, and I've never had to carry out any remedial works)

■ Range of colours and slip-resistance

■ Resistance to most acids and alkalis (all of the kennels installed with suitable tiles have not suffered in terms of discolouration or staining; which cannot be said for resin based systems)

■ Highly suitable for hot water power-washing

■ They are not affected by solar radiation, which means they are fade-resistant

■ Simple installation, providing that the screed has been laid to a good standard

Disadvantages:

■ High initial cost (this is applicable to all quality finishes that will stand the test of time)

■ Slower installation times as compared with resin-based systems

■ High R and V values (slip-resistance and water displacement) can be difficult to clean (you will need to find a good compromise between slip-resistance and ease of cleaning). This applies to all floor finishes.

Slip-resistance in Tiles

Some floors have higher risks of slipping on than others.

There are a number of contributing factors:

- Type of material used

- Presence of water, fats or disinfectants

- Physical movement in confined spaces

- Type of footwear used

All these matters will influence the slip-resistance of a floor.

At present only Germany has set standards of slip-resistance for floors in commercial, industrial and barefoot areas (barefoot area is a term used to describe wet areas such as showers, changing rooms, etc). It is likely that this will become the standard used by all European Union countries in the near future.

The system used by the German government to **assess and measure the level of slip-resistance is known as the 'R-value'** for commercial and industrial uses, and A, B, or C value for barefoot areas. The higher this value, the more slip-resistance the tile has.

The **capacity to displace water and dirt is measured and known as the 'V-value'**. The higher the V number, the greater the space between the studs (tiles with a raised profile). The values are V4, V6, V8 and V10. Obviously the greater the space between the studs and the deeper the profile, the greater the amount of water that can be dealt with before the floor becomes dangerous, but the more difficult it is to clean.

Slip-resistance in Commercial Applications:

SLIP ANGLE°	R-VALUE
From 3° to 10°	R – 9
From 10° to 19°	R – 10
From 19° to 27°	R – 11
From 27° to 35°	R – 12
More than 35°	R – 13

Barefoot (Wet) Areas:

SLIP ANGLE°	V-VALUE
Minimum slip angle – 12°	A
Minimum slip angle – 18°	B
Minimum slip angle – 24°	C

Vinyl Sheeting

For dog hotel owners, corridors and ancillary rooms this is an excellent material.

Dog hotels and upscale boarding kennels and assistance dog kennels will tend to get dogs out of the kennels a lot more. This means that there is little/no mess within the kennel. The dogs in these situations are more relaxed in the home-like environment and therefore are less destructive and settle better. This enables the owner to use an industrial quality vinyl to greatly improve the aesthetic qualities of the building.

The commercial quality sheets available have been used extensively in canteens, kitchens and hospitals for many years – and of course privately in the home. They are available in different grades, patterns and with varying degrees of slip-resistance, this being achieved by the use of profiles, or with silicon carbide and aluminium oxide particles incorporated within the finish (as shown in the textured, sparkly finish in the photo opposite).

Advantages:

- Quiet - helps reduce noise reverberation
- Warm for dogs to lie on
- Will feel familiar to dogs if they have this flooring at home
- Enormous range of colours, patterns and textures
- Can be coved up the wall for improved hygiene
- Joints MUST be heat welded to form a continuous, hygienic and watertight finish – this should _always_ be specified

Disadvantages:

- Can be damaged by sharp objects
- It melts on contact with cigarettes – but you should obviously not be smoking in kennels anyway

Vinyl sheeting has many applications for the kennel owner, it is aesthetically pleasing and extremely versatile, and can be coved to form hygienic and watertight junctions.

Note:

Vinyl is totally waterproof and can be pressure-washed; some are also suitable for steam cleaning.
However, the type of cleaning needs to be identified at the outset to allow for heat welding of joints, suitable silicone sealing around doors, etc, to prevent water from getting under the sheet.

Before installation, ensure that the substrate (screed) is dry, and ensure the flooring contractor checks before installation - otherwise vinyl will lift or bubble

Resin Floor Systems

■ **Resin Floor Sealers (50-100 microns)**
These systems are the **minimum** required to satisfy the UK's CIEH and provide a non-porous, washable and hygienic surface. They can be either be water or solvent based. These systems are generally applied over concrete or sand/cement screed to harden and reduce dusting. Unlike paint systems, these products produce a chemical reaction and are **bound into the matrix of the floor surface** giving a durable, hard-wearing and dust free surface.
Advantages: easy, economical to apply, retards the penetration of water, oils, etc.
Disadvantages: will need subsequent applications.

■ **Resin Floor Coatings (150-300 microns)**
Unlike the floor sealers, these tend to be classified as paints and **remain on the surface** of the sub-base. These paint systems can be either single or two-pack applications, and come in a range of guises and colours.

■ **Resin High-Build Coatings (300-1000 microns)**
These have similar qualities to the coatings in Category FeRFA 2 (see table opposite). Obviously, the thicker finishes at 1000 microns will be more durable than 300 microns.

■ **Resin Multi-Layer Coatings (>2 mm)**
These multi-layers, also known as 'sandwich' systems have good slip resistance and a matt finish. They are the minimum requirement for use in kennels to achieve a durable surface that won't require remedial works for a number of years.

■ **Resin Flow Applied Flooring (2–3 mm)**
Flow-applied coatings, or self-smoothing coatings are generally two-part systems. Although still relatively thin, they should last approximately 10 years before remedial work is required. The inclusion of a fine aggregate into the finished surface is something to consider; it will help prevent staff and visitors slipping. The coarseness of the aggregate is a personal decision, but a general guideline is to try to achieve a finish similar to that of orange peel. Too coarse, and it will hold the dirt and be difficult to clean, too fine and it will be of little benefit.

■ **Resin Screeds (4-6 mm)**
It is normal for a polyurethane screed to be laid to an average thickness of 4mm to 6mm, applied with a steel trowel. The **cost** for this type of screed starts to become noticeably more expensive compared with a coating. However, correctly installed, a polyurethane screed will provide a durable, hygienic finish and last for many years.

Resin Flooring Classification:

Advantages:

- Gives a seamless and hygienic finish
- Semi-gloss finish
- Full range of colours
- Cost-effective
- Slip-resistance (achieved by the number of back-rollering operations carried out)
- Fast installation
- Does not require sealing coats, enhancing its durability

Disadvantages:

- Can look industrial
- The quality of the system and finish is highly dependent upon the quality of contractor. Also, the finish may vary throughout the building, even using the same contractor and product
- Limited durability. This is subjective and influenced by external factors such as correct preparation, product choice, cleaning regimes, use, etc
- Unevenness in the underlying layer will reflect in the coating
- Can be damaged by hot/cold pressure washer
- Discolouration e.g. disinfectants/urine

Category	Description	Notes
FeRFA 1	Floor Seal	2 coats up to 150 micron final thickness
FeRFA 2	Floor Coating	2 or more coats at 100 micron each
FeRFA 3	High-build Floor Coating	2 or more coats at 300-1000 micron final thickness
FeRFA 4	Multi-layer Flooring	Floor coating or flow-applied, multi-layers to >2mm, aggregate dressing
FeRFA 5	Flow-applied Flooring	2-3mm thickness, self-smoothing, smooth or dressed surface
FeRFA 6	Screed Flooring	>4mm thickness, heavily filled, trowel finish, usually surface-sealed
FeRFA 7	Heavy Duty Flowable Flooring	4-6mm thickness, aggregate filled
FeRFA 8	Heavy Duty Screed Flooring	>6mm thickness, aggregate filled, trowel finished, system applied, impervious throughout
Federation Resin Flooring Association, UK		

Summary of Applied Resin Floor Systems.

These systems have many good features; they have been used extensively in factories, hospitals and breweries for many years and continue to be used. They have failed in kennels environments primarily because of incorrect specification.

However, the new generation of polyurethane and epoxy products offer more flexibility and improved wear quality. They also appear to give better finished results without some of the concerns and issues often associated with the early epoxy-based systems. The matt finish of many of these products is useful when considering the anti-slip properties of the floor. I now feel more comfortable in specifying these for use in animal accommodation.

A compromise system that has greater aesthetic qualities are the epoxy quartz products at around 4mm thickness;, however, instead of using an epoxy seal (this can be affected by urine and disinfectants) use a polyurethane seal.

If you choose an applied finish, whether it is a simple paint or an expensive screed, these are some of the points you should consider:

- Use a reputable company and ensure that they make a site visit to familiarise themselves with the particular project and any problems that might occur, (e.g. epoxy screeds do not allow for any movement, while polyurethane screeds have a small amount of flexibility). This is an important point, particularly when dealing with buildings that have shown signs of movement

- Explain fully what the product is to be used for, and how much use it will receive. Obtain a written guarantee from the manufacturers stating that the recommended product will achieve the required standard

- Ensure that the company visits the site to check that the substrate is suitable for their product

Polymer finish in the exercise run

Polymer, Granolithic and Concrete Screeds

Polymer

Polymers are based on cement and selected aggregates with a liquid copolymer additive. They are better known for their applications for industrial situations, particularly in wet areas such as breweries and fish processing, and are not particularly well known in kennels applications.

Advantages:

- Can be laid as a thin screed, suitable for repairing old or damaged concrete
- Simple installation
- Jointless in small areas
- Anti-slip aggregates can be incorporated
- Resistant to oils and acids
- Suitable for wet environments
- Suitable for steam cleaning
- Range of colours
- Cost-effective
- Can be used externally

Disadvantages:

- Tendency to stain (as shown opposite)
- The quality of the finish is dependent upon the operative to ensure a uniform finish
- The cost can be greater than polyurethane screed products

Summary

Although not widely used for kennels, it can be used to overcome problem or damaged areas.
Polymer has been used to overlay some damaged and rough concrete exercise runs, and it has proved to be extremely durable and easy to clean.

However, there are cheaper and more aesthetically pleasing products available.

Granolithic

This is a natural material based on cement and selected aggregates; it is normally laid with a minimum thickness of 50mm. It is a durable and long-lasting surface. However with time, some dusting may occur (see photo top right). To prevent this and increase its durability, an application of sodium silicate hardener is normally applied. Sprinkling the surface while still wet, with carborundum powder, will add a degree of slip resistance. Its main use today is in commercial and industrial applications.

Advantages:

- Extremely durable and does not damage easily

Disadvantages:

- **Cost -** High initial cost

- **Aesthetics** - As this is a cement based product, it has the same dull grey/brown colour as concrete

- **Quality -** In order to provide a satisfactory finish a high level of skill and supervision is required. It also requires careful attention to detail to prevent cracking and crazing at a later date

- **Porous -** Will need some form of sealing agent, or it will stain

- **Cost -** Similar to Polymer finishes

Summary:

Although it is used in industry, it has **little to offer the kennel owner.** Its poor aesthetic qualities and specialist application has meant that alternative products have superseded it.

Concrete

Concrete is often laid as the finished or wearing material. Although it is a durable product, it still needs to have a sealing coat applied to prevent water and urine from soaking into the surface (see photo below right). **Concrete flooring without a sealing coat is unhygienic and if used daily, the unsealed concrete will never dry out properly - and it will SMELL.** Its aesthetic and durability qualities can be increased by adding colouring and waterproofing during the mixing process

Advantages:

- Easy to install

- Cost-effective

- Readily available

- Will withstand heavy usage

Disadvantages:

- Is liable to crack over a period of time

- Poor aesthetic qualities (in standard colour) - suggest looking at the use of a through coloured concrete system

- Will stain and smell if unsealed, or not maintained

Porous concrete showing signs of staining

Damaged concrete that has been patched

Painted Concrete

No matter what quality of paint used, it WILL flake off after an extremely short period of time. This means that the concrete is no longer sealed, so this leads to damp, unhygienic floors that look unkempt - and will SMELL.

Below: the paint flakes off in this brand new kennel build after only 3 months
Right: despite multiple coats, the paint still flakes easily, leaving a porous and unsightly floor that will smell

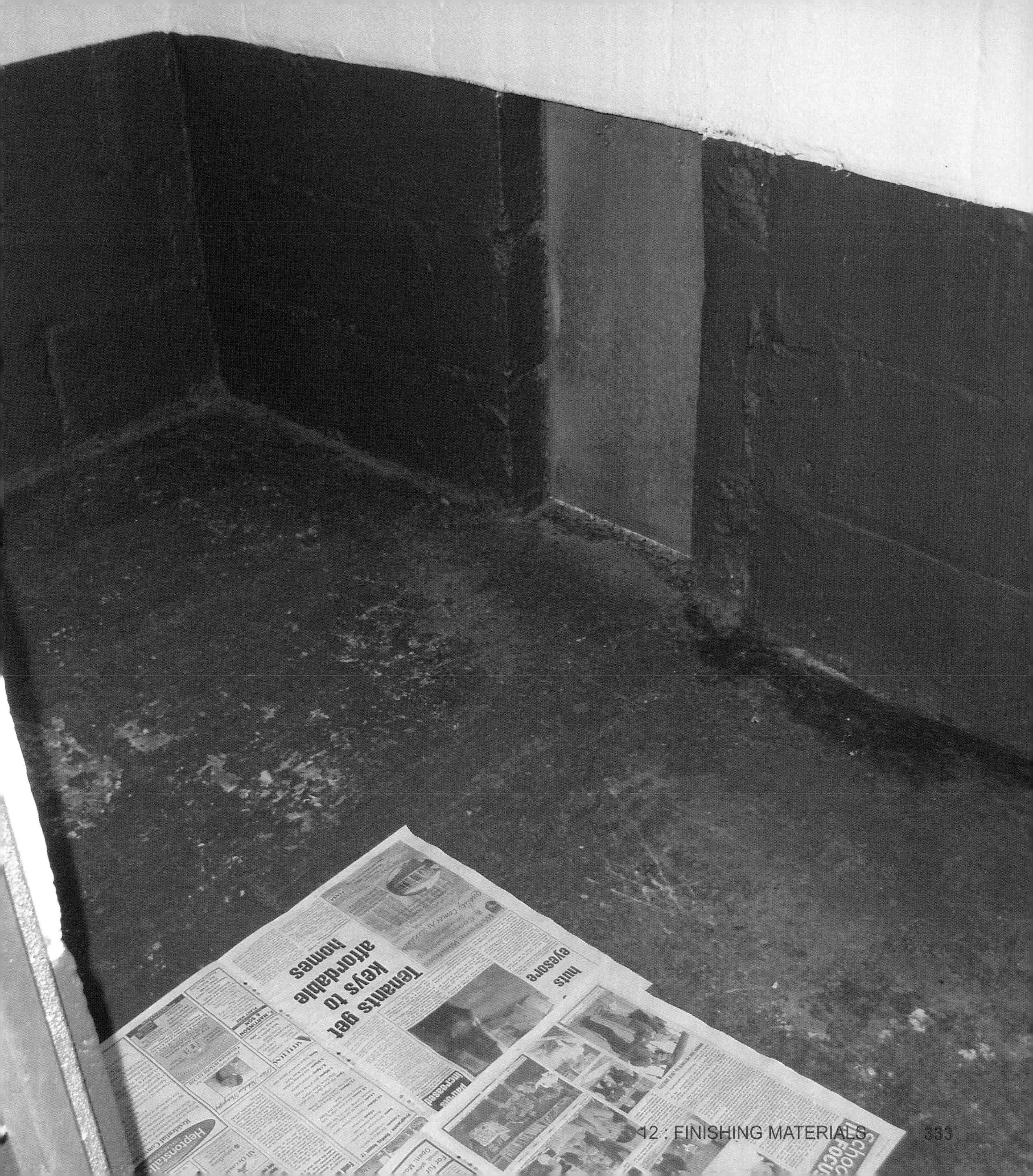
Tenants get keys to affordable homes
eyesore

Covings (Required for all Flooring Types)

All kennels should have a 'sealed' junction between the wall and floor sections.

This is normally achieved in one of five ways:

1. **Tiles**
   All manufacturers have floor systems that allow for the use of a sit-on, traditional flush fitting or flush-fit coved skirting, with internal and external angles. Providing the layout has been designed to accommodate these finishing pieces, they work extremely effectively. The finishing pieces can be expensive and care should be taken to ensure that they have been included with the main flooring cost, and not looked upon as an extra

   Helpful Hint:
   Ensure that the flooring contractor allows for the necessary expansion joints between the vertical/horizontal, and also in front of floor drainage channels

2. **Polyurethane**
   This system is extremely effective; it is basically a mixture of fine aggregates and epoxy resin, which is formed into a smooth, coved skirting, normally 50mm/2" high. It is a quick and relatively cheap system, can be retro-fitted to any floor, it is extremely durable, jointless and gives a professional finish

3. **Vinyl Skirting**
   If vinyl flooring is fitted, the most hygienic finish is to continue the flooring material up the wall, to a height of approximately 300mm/12". At the junction of the wall and floor a preformed plastic cove is fitted to remove the 90° junctions

   Helpful hint: An alternative is to fit a plastic skirting. However, this is normally glued on and there is always a gap between the skirting section and the floor/wall

4. **Sand/Cement**
   Sand/cement can be used in a similar fashion to that of epoxy. It is easy to install, cost-effective and can be painted to give a more professional appearance. If you opt for this system, ensure that you use fine-grained sand, and add PVA to the mixture to ensure a smooth finish that is strong and waterproof

5. **Mastic Joint**
   The cheapest and most cost-effective option is to apply a mastic joint between the two surfaces. There are a number of suitable compounds available. However, it is strongly recommended that you use one of the hard-setting mastics. This is harder for the dogs to claw out, but it will require **maintenance**

On the next pages there are some examples of different floor types and covings.

Above: Vinyl

Above: Sit-in coved tile

Above: Vinyl with capping strip

Above: sit-in coved skirt tile

Above: tiled floor with tiled upstand (skirting) with mastic seal to floor/wall joint and top of tile

Above: sit-in coved skirt tile

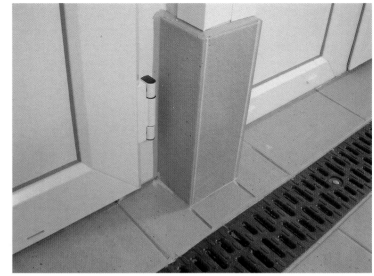

Above: tiled floors with tiled upstand and mastic joint

Above: polyurethane floor

Above: vinyl floor in public corridor

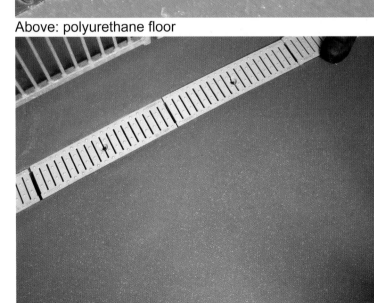

Epoxy resin floor

Tiled floor

Above: tiled covings to tiled floors

Above: vinyl sheeting

Concrete/granolithic flooring (left) and concrete flooring (right)

12 : FINISHING MATERIALS   **337**

WHY FLOORS FAIL

The quality of the finished wearing surface is very much dependent upon the quality and preparation of the sub floor and foundations. Any shortcut in these areas has the potential for failure of the building and floor system.

Failures in the foundations and floors are generally the most difficult and costly to remedy

Poor quality workmanship in floor screeds can have issues for the thinner-wearing surfaces such as vinyl. The thinner the wearing surface, the more noticeable any defects and variations will be.

Foundations

Any building requires foundations that are adequate to ensure its stability. Without suitable foundations, any building is liable to move over a period of time. It is essential for any permanent brick/block or concrete constructed building to have foundations suitable for the size and weight of the building and local ground conditions. It is important to take into account the amount of vegetation around the building, the proximity and type of trees, the type of soil and other issues such as old mine workings, etc. Also the removal of large trees has a noticeable, long-term effect on local ground conditions.

On sites that have firm, shrinkable clay soil, it is not uncommon to find that foundations have to go down to a depth of 1m/3ft. A local structural engineer is the best person to advise on the suitability of foundation types and depths. Any concrete slab base should have a well-consolidated base, and allowance made for expansion and contraction.

New concrete and screed bases

One of the main reasons for the failure of wearing finishes is moisture in the substrate. In order to prevent failure of the screed and wearing surface, it is essential that the substrate be allowed to dry out properly prior to the wearing surface being laid. The timescale required to reduce the level of humidity in the substrate will vary depending on the building design, the thickness of the slab, the ambient temperature, special concrete mixes, etc.

The general guide time for drying is 1 day per millimetre of thickness of substrate.
On this basis, a concrete slab of 150mm/6" thickness with a 75mm/3" sand/cement screed could take 225 days.

Obviously, this is not practical for most construction projects. In extreme cases, the use of suppressants can be used. The general guide for the laying of finished products is to ensure that the substrate has a moisture level not exceeding 75% Relative Humidity. To ensure the RH levels, a Hygrometer should be used. The readings need to be taken over a 72-hour period to give an accurate result.

Damp proof membranes

All concrete bases should have an effective damp-proof membrane (DPM).
If you are carrying out remedial works to an older building, particularly one that has an agricultural history – check to see if it has a DPM. If in doubt, ask a local builder to carry out some investigative work to establish if one has been installed.

Paint finish flaking off the concrete

Poor quality concrete breaking up - not able to withstand the constant cleaning regime

Movement

Any flooring product should allow for any flex or movement. A rigid screed won't allow for flex and will crack. Any limitations of a floor finish should be discussed with the manufacturer.

Contaminants

Any contamination in the substrate (this relates particularly to buildings that are being converted and adapted from previous uses) could affect the finished product. This needs to be checked with the contractor before any works commence, and the necessary corrective works undertaken.

Movement joints

Any movement in a building will cause the wearing finish to crack. In order to help combat this, movement joints need to be installed. The guideline is for a movement joint around the perimeter of the building and at 4.5m/15ft centres. This should be 6mm/ ¼" wide, and run through the depth of the concrete slab, screed and wearing surface.

Screed thickness

The sub-screed needs to have an adequate depth and strength to support the imposed loads, and provide a suitable surface on which to lay the wearing surface.

Product not correctly specified

The correct specification for the environment in which the product is to be used in is essential. This becomes critical if you need to use power washers and steam cleaning machines.

Temperature

Most of the resin-based systems require an environment that is dry, with a temperature of 15°C/59°F or above.
A reputable company will not lay these products if the environmental conditions are unsuitable.

Work quality

All of the above products require good quality workmanship to succeed.
It is essential that before the final wearing course is installed, you determine the quality of the concrete or screed sub-base. As previously mentioned, for the installation of vinyl finishes and thinner resin-based systems (up to 6mm/ ¼") any undulations in the floor surface will show, or could affect, the quality or thickness of the final wearing surface. Obviously with a thicker wearing surface finish of 12mm/ ½" any undulations can be disguised in the final finish.

Open joint caused by movement

Resin screed breaking away from step

During the installation of the sub-base, and before the final wearing surface is laid, use a straight edge to see how good the quality of the workmanship is, and how true and level the floor has been laid.

Above: a well-laid floor (i.e. continuous fall without undulations)

Above: an incorrectly laid floor, showing a hollow in the corner of the run and consequently this is a urine/water trap

Above: the same incorrectly-laid floor as the below left photo opposite. Water is running away from the drainage channel instead of towards it. The dry area in the foreground should be the 'lower' level and water should be draining towards you.

KENNEL DIVIDING WALLS AND PARTITIONS

All caging and dividing panel systems used for commercial kennels and welfare centres should provide security, be hygienic, and be easy to clean; they should also be non-absorbent. Equally important they should provide the dogs with an area they feel secure in, and cannot be touched or overlooked by dogs in the adjoining kennel – as this can lead to stress and possible injury, and increases the risk of disease.

Solid dividing walls and panels not only act as the physical 'walls' that create the structure, but also help reduce noise, stress and act as disease prevention or reduction barriers.

The UK CIEH states that *"Partition walls between kennels must be of solid construction to a minimum height of 1.2m/4ft"*. **Although this height is suitable for small dogs, it is not a sufficient height for kennels holding larger dogs.**

The method is still seen in the majority of kennels i.e. a solid lower section with mesh above. Once you spend time in a variety of kennels it soon becomes obvious that the different methods used to divide kennels and exercise runs does have a marked effect on how the dogs react – again, this is all part of improving dog welfare and making the building a more comfortable and enjoyable place to visit or work.

There should be NO DIRECT CONTACT between dogs from different households.

Walls between kennels should be solid
(e.g. not open mesh) to prevent nose-to-nose contact, risk of disease and fight injuries

Having been witness to an appalling injury sustained by a dog, which lost half of its tail after being chewed off by a dog in the adjoining kennel, it is important to emphasise that dogs should be kept separate between kennels.

Given the animal welfare issues of using open mesh dividing panels and the potential for accidents such as mentioned above, it is important to use full height walls in excess of 3m/6ft 6".

Note:

There is an argument for having mesh at high level in the exercise run in **countries with consistently high temperatures**, as this will allow for improved ventilation across the top of the exercise runs.

The decision on which option is right for you will be decided by dog welfare considerations, personal preference, the design and construction of the building, the type of dogs being housed, and the business image to be portrayed.

The more common systems used are:

- ### Brick and Blockwork

  This is still my preferred choice for traditionally constructed kennels. The disadvantage is that the brick or blocks have to be sealed to prevent the ingress of water, urine, etc. This has always been the weak point for this type of construction method. **Historically** the choice has been to use a cheaper masonry or emulsion type paint and expect to re-coat every 2–3 years.

  A much better alternative is to coat the wall with the more expensive resin-based paint, render, coating or tile. All of these work extremely well, providing the blocks are good-quality paint grade with a close-knit texture, and are thoroughly dry before applying any system. Another alternative that offers the best coating system is a fibreglass-based product. This is cost-effective and produces a hygienic, easy-to-clean surface that is extremely hardwearing.

- ### UPVC and Plastic Board and Panels

  The range of suitable plastic type panels available is immense. These products are durable, hygienic and easy to clean. Most of these products have to be fitted into a robust framework to provide the necessary support - typically this would be constructed using either galvanised or stainless steel metal or UPVC. The advantages with this type of product is that they are self-finished i.e. they do not require any form of finishing-paint type product, they are warm to the touch, and have a 'solid feel' to them. These are all important features to enhance the dog welfare qualities and provide a more pleasing, quieter and relaxing building.

- ### Fireproof Board

  There are numerous cement-based panels available that fall into this category. Generally they have smooth surfaces that provide an excellent surface for the final finish. These boards are porous and therefore require a surface coating to make them non-porous. These boards come in a variety of thicknesses, but for the kennel environment a thickness of 10–12mm/ ½" is recommended. Again, they have to be supported in a framework to provide the necessary strength.

- ### Galvanised Metal Sheet

  This is the cheapest of all systems, it is readily available and easy to install and has been probably the most common material and system used in the majority of kennels in the UK. When compared with the other systems mentioned, it is extremely outdated, and if you are aiming at a more upmarket kennels or trying to improve dog welfare, it is not the system for you.

  The noise levels generated when a dog jumps up against the panel are extremely high. When watching dogs in kennels with this type of system it is easy to see how dogs, once they hit the panel and the dog in the adjoining kennel reacts (either by barking or jumping up at the panel), this triggers negative excitement with increased barking and consequently, noise. These all combine to waste energy and increase levels of stress. **Installing much better systems will markedly reduce these problems.**

- ### Open Mesh/Chainlink Fencing

  Areas of major concern with chainlink fencing as kennel partitions are:
  - The risk of aggressive dogs attempting to fight through the fencing
  - There is direct nose-to-nose contact which increases the risk of injury and spread of disease
  - Increased stress because of the open environment
  - Easily damaged by chewing (once a section is damaged it loses its strength and integrity for the entire panel)
  - Does not provide a secluded environment for dogs, therefore substantially increasing stress and noise
    (it is not unusual to see a row of kennels with chainlink partitioning for the entire length of the kennel run, meaning all the dogs can see each other, further increasing stress and therefore noise)

> Dogs will be less stressed if there is privacy and somewhere they can hide from a neighbouring dog if desired

Above: high specification (smooth) block painted finish

There should be
NO DIRECT CONTACT
between
dogs from different
households

This photo shows how easily chainlink is damaged and ripped away from the frame, leaving dangerous sharp edges.

This presents risk of disease, stress, injury and infection to the dogs, added veterinary fees for the owner, will not encourage clients to tell their friends - and will never make the most of the potential income.

From an aesthetic point of view, there are far superior alternatives that will set your kennels apart, and remove the prison-like feel

This photo shows how the kennel owner has tried to overcome the problem of having open mesh between the kennels.

The low blockwork wall has been added, but chainlink is still above it. Although this will help a little - it is still too low to stop dogs being able to jump up or see each other.

The owner has then attached boarding over the chainlink to remove the issues of nose-to-nose contact, aggression, and to provide more secluded areas for the dogs.

It would have been far better to have constructed the dividing walls as full height blockwork from the outset - for less cost and inconvenience

WALLING FINISHES FOR BRICK AND BLOCK BUILDINGS

The range of products suitable for walls is virtually endless.

The primary aim of over-coating concrete block and cement based panel walls or any porous finish, is to improve the hygienic qualities of the building, i.e. to prevent dirt, faeces, urine, and bacteria/viruses being ingrained in the open, porous nature of block.

The second benefit is to improve the aesthetic qualities of the building. Most concrete blocks tend to be dull grey or brown in colour, but with suitable finishes these can be dramatically improved.

Helpful Hints:

- If you are planning to apply a paint finish to concrete block work, ensure that you specify a high-quality paint-grade block. A coarse, open textured block is not suitable for a paint finish; even with three or four coats, the open texture will be difficult to seal, difficult to clean, and will not give a long-lasting, pleasing appearance

- However, if you intend to apply ceramic tiles, then the cheapest block will be sufficient

The more common wall finishes are:

- Fibreglass coating

- Masonry paint

- Single or twin-pack epoxy or polyurethane systems

- Rubber based paint

- Standard paints

- Plaster skim finish

- Tiles

- Cladding materials (e.g. vinyl sheeting or plastic boarding)

- Engineering bricks

We will now look at these wall finishes in detail.

Fibreglass Coating

Fibreglass is an excellent product. It is a wet-applied system for use on blockwork walls and any solid wall surface. The product has been used extensively in the dairy industry for many years - and is still the main system for dairy parlours, etc due to its hygienic and easy-to-clean qualities. The smooth finish is rounded around corners, giving a professional, upmarket look.

I have used it myself on 60 kennels and am delighted with the results, it's proven to be an excellent product. The cost is higher than paint, and less than tiling - but you'll only ever have to apply it once. As you can see in the photo below, the thickness and smooth, glossy finish of the fibreglass coating (butter yellow) is far superior than the standard painted finish.

Masonry Paint

This is probably the cheapest system on the market that is suitable for both interior and exterior use in kennels. Most are water or acrylic based, easy to apply and can be applied during most conditions.

The large range of colours and types available enables you to choose a suitable product for either new or refurbishment work. If you opt for this system for interior use, ensure that you specify a smooth, sheen finish; this will make it far easier to clean.

Below: paint on good-quality fairfaced blocks

Plaster Skim Finish

This finish, which is normally seen in domestic houses, can give an excellent finish to concrete block walls. This will give a uniform, home-like finish, which will need to be decorated to seal it and provide a finished system. Clearly, this has a cost implication.

This type of finish would be more suited to an upscale dog hotel where the cleaning regime is mop and bucket, rather than hosepipe. If you want to use pressure washers or large volumes of water; this is not a suitable finish for you.

Below: a plaster wall finished with emulsion paint

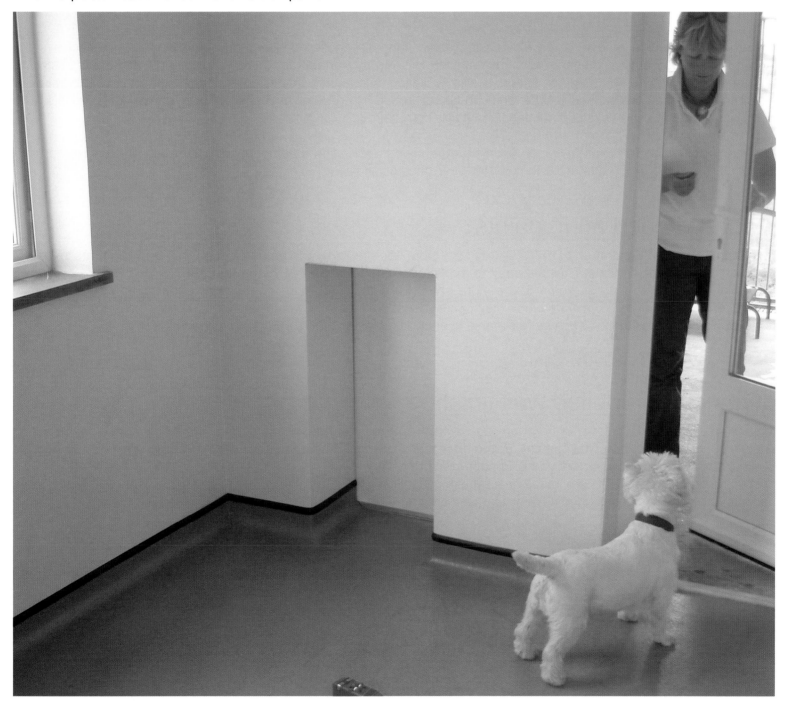

Single and twin-pack epoxy/polyurethane paint

Like the floor coatings, the number of systems available in this category is immense, with a large number of companies all selling what appear to be the same product, and this is where the problems start. Most of these systems require a **higher level of application with better preparation and cleaning** than for masonry paints. Correctly specified, they provide a tough, hard-wearing, chemically-resistant finish. There is a wide choice of colours. However, they are **more expensive** than many other paint systems.

Acrylated rubber

This product has been used extensively for industrial and commercial applications for many years. It is a single-pack system, for non-skilled application and is normally brush applied; it is **highly suitable** for damp environments and areas subject to frequent washing down. The range of colours is slightly limited, although it is sufficient for most situations. Unlike epoxy or polyurethane finishes, the surface is softer and **can be scratched** by persistent animals, although I have not found this to be of any major concern and any minor damage can easily be repaired.

It is an **expensive** product and has very **strong fumes** during application. It is not suitable for applying to a building that cannot be emptied of dogs, due to the fumes. However, once dry, it is fine.

Standard decorating paints

The standard paints found in any DIY (do-it-yourself) store such as vinyl silk emulsion, eggshell and gloss are excellent products for use in the kennels. They are **easy to apply, cost-effective, and easy to maintain**.
They might not last as long as some of the more specialist paints. However, due to their relatively low cost and easy application, it is simple to redecorate when they become scuffed. Most are water-based and do not give off strong fumes during application. This makes them more suitable to apply in buildings that already have dogs in them.

Summary of applied wall finishes

You should ensure that whatever system you choose is suitable for your requirements. I would strongly advise against using a new product from an unknown company. **Remember that when the time comes for redecorating, you need to be able to purchase the same product as you originally used.**
Most of the professional paints are based on a system of application, i.e. matching primers and undercoats with two or three topcoats; they have been designed as a system, and are therefore not suitable for mixing and matching.

Something that cannot be emphasised strongly enough:
whatever system you use,
always remember to keep the data sheets
or record of the product

Acrylated rubber paiint (cream) on blockwork,
with tiling to lower section

Tiles

Tiling is usually carried out to a height of approximately 1500mm/5ft - this being the main area of cleaning, wear and tear. Above this height a quality masonry paint is sufficient. Tiling is expensive in the kennel environment due to the smaller areas to cut around (e.g hatches).

Cladding finishes

There are some excellent materials available for cladding, e.g. vinyl sheeting, plastic cladding, resin-bonded boarding. In order to prevent ingress of water and urine, these materials generally need to be professionally fixed and sealed.

Engineering bricks

This is an alternative to applied finishes. This system gives a durable finish that does not require any future maintenance. Obviously, if you opt for this system it needs to be identified at the outset of the contract. Generally, engineering bricks are used to construct division walls due to their smooth, easy-to-clean finish, but they can also be used throughout the entire building if required. The choice of colours in engineering bricks is limited (e.g. beige, red or blue tend to be the standard colours). This might seem rather drab, but with suitable floor and wall finishes above the engineering brick it can work extremely well. **In order to prevent staining of the mortar, a waterproofing agent will need to be added** during the construction stage; an alternative is to paint the joints with a clear epoxy sealer.

Cautionary Note:

I feel that this is an outdated system and can look very 'prison-like' in large buildings.
If you choose this system, be aware particularly when constructing single-skin walls, that **only one face will be true and smooth**. Bricks are not totally square and symmetrical, each will have small variations. Although this can be evened out by the mortar joint, the other face will be slightly more irregular. This leaves you with two options: either you accept this, or you construct a wall two bricks deep (225mm/9") by placing bricks back-to-back (irregular sides together), giving you two even outer faces.

Galvanised and glass run to puppy area

KENNEL FRONTAGE AND DOORS

One of the most important areas to get right with kennel doors and side screens is to ensure that the **gap under the door** is no more than 15mm/ ½". This is sufficient to allow wash down water to drain freely underneath, without leaving too large a gap (where dogs can get their legs under) or insufficient gap to allow water to drain away.

The ideal gap for doors and side screens is 15mm or ½"

DANGER - Too Large a Gap

Danger to dogs: Given the opportunity, dogs will lie with their legs stretched out in front of them, and will naturally be interested in watching what is happening outside the kennel. If a dog rises too quickly (e.g. after hearing a sudden noise, or being surprised), there is a great risk of a dog breaking its front legs due to trapping their legs under the door.
Danger to people: a rail across the door can easily be a trip hazard for staff, and makes it more difficult to clean through.

DANGER - Too Small a Gap

If there is an insufficient gap to allow drainage. Liquids will seep under the panel and sit there. Even with an excellent cleaning regime - it will still be impossible to prevent a build-up of stale foul water.

Below: this photograph shows BOTH problems - too high a bottom rail on the door, and the front panel sitting directly on the tile without drainage clearance.

The potential danger of broken legs

Adequate clearance for drainage AND dog safe but trip hazard for staff

Adequate clearance for drainage, dog AND people safe

DOOR FRAMING SYSTEMS

Framing systems make an enormous difference
to the look, feel, style and image of kennels

Traditionally all types of kennels used metal door frames and metal chainlink, mesh or bar infills - giving kennels the **prison-like** look associated with typical dog faciltiies.

However, with a greater emphasis on dog welfare requirements, and changes in the pet market (driven by dog owners' desire for more upmarket products, food choices, and services), today the focus is on **improving the quality** of the facilities and **providing more options**.

Today, forward-thinking kennel owners and dog owners both want to have kennels that are more home-like and friendly, and provide a more familiar home-like environment for dogs that naturally reduces stress levels.

Framing types (in order of cost and aesthetic appeal):

- Stainless Steel
- UPVC/PVCu
- Galvanised Steel
- Aluminium
- Powder Coated Steel
- Painted Metal

All systems used for commercial kennels and welfare centres
should provide security, be hygienic and easy to clean,
and should also be non-absorbent.

Equally important - they should provide dogs with an area they
feel secure in, and not overlooked by dogs in an adjoining
kennel, as this can lead to stress and possible injury

Stainless Steel Door Frames

This material is the most expensive of all of the metal systems. However, it is a **highly suitable** product for the kennel environment and has a **gleaming finish** that looks smart, ultra-modern, hygienic and aesthetically pleasing.

The major difference between stainless steel and galvanised steel, is that with stainless steel there is no protective barrier or coating to break down. This is an option chosen by those looking to get away from the 'prison-like' appearance associated with heavy bars.

Stainless steel is often seen in veterinary hospitals, upscale dog hotels, rescue centres, and luxury kennels where the owner is aiming for a high quality, professional appearance that sets them apart from others - and will keep its gleaming appearance.

Above: stainless steel frames and glass infill

Above: stainless steel frames and bar infills in a stable door

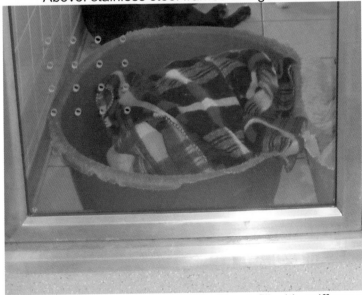
Above: stainless steel frames & glass infill with sniff zone

Above: stainless steel frames and glass AND bar infills

UPVC Door Frames (Unplasticised Polyvinyl Chloride)

Use of this product has increased noticeably over recent years, particularly for commercial kennels and charities. The 'home-like' look, especially when combined with full height 'rooms', provides a more upscale image to the public, and a more relaxing environment for dogs and staff due to the environment dogs are used to as a family pet.

Its uses are pretty much limitless, ranging from doors and partitions, right through to complete kennels. The doors and partitions can have a mix of infill types such as glass, mesh or combinations of both.

However, the size of any mesh infill should be the same as previously mentioned in the metalwork section.

Hot Dipped Galvanised Door Frames

Galvanising is a process where all the metal is dipped into a tank containing molten zinc. This forms a chemical bond with the metal, which ensures a protective, durable coating. The **finish is a dull silver-grey, darkening to a deeper dull grey** over time.

This coating (providing it is not broken, e.g. damage by tools or inferior coating application during the dipping process) will last for many years without showing any signs of deterioration. For this reason this system is still the most cost-effective solution for the kennel owner who wishes to use a metal bar or mesh finish.

Galvanised metal is the most widely used system for the majority of kennels in the UK.

Aluminium Tubing/Box Section Door Frames

Aluminium tubing has been used because it is cost-effective, fast to install, lightweight and non-rusting. A system commonly seen in typical establishments in the USA and Canada, the tubular section is used with chainlink infill.

Plain Metal with Paint Finish Door Frames

This is the cheapest system in the short-term. New metal that has had a coloured paint finish looks bright, clean and gives a professional appearance. However, this won't last. The paint will flake off after a relatively short period of time; this is most noticeable on the lower sections as these are the areas that receive the most damage from mops, urine, washing down and disinfectants. After a short period of time the metal will have heavy rust deposits, be unhygienic, have poor aesthesic qualities and will require remedial work. The remedial work normally involves replacement; this is where it becomes expensive in time and labour; once rust has taken hold it is impossible to remove.
Note the degree of rusting after 15 months

Powder Coated Steel Frames

A spray-applied finish available in a range of colours, this coating will eventually flake or chip off in heavy-duty areas. If applied it should always be applied over galvanised metalwork to ensure that rusting doesn't take place.

Note this system is great for adding colour to public areas - but is NOT robust enough for dog contact areas

INFILL SYSTEMS FOR DOOR FRAMES

Infill systems make an enormous difference to the look, feel, and image of kennels AND improving dog welfare conditions

Infill systems (in order of cost and aesthetic appeal):

- Glass
- UPVC/PVCu
- Stainless/Galvanised Steel Mesh/Bar
- Powder Coated Steel
- Painted Metal

Glass

The increased use of glass and steel in the kennel environment is one that has many advantages.

The main use of glass is for the kennel doors as compared with dividing partitions. Glass will need to be contained in a frame. Typically this would be in UPVC, stainless steel or aluminium. This system is found in **premier facilities** such as dog hotels and upscale kennels. It is also used in welfare facilities as a way of improving the welfare requirements, reducing the risk of spread of disease, and increases the secluded feel in the dog's area from visitors (no direct contact - when hands are pushed through caging it increases the chances of potential adopters being bitten).

The disadvantage is that it will require more maintenance in the form of cleaning than some other methods. The advantage is that glass will actually get cleaned!

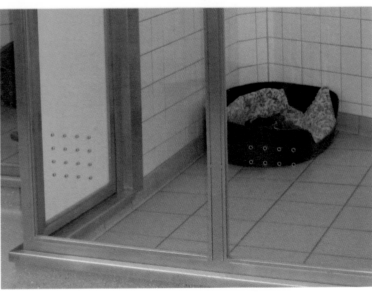

UPVC and Plastics

The use of UPVC (Unplasticised Polyvinyl Chloride) has increased noticeably over recent years, particularly for commercial kennels and charities. Its uses are pretty much limitless, ranging from doors and partitions, right through to complete kennels.

The doors and partitions can have a mix of infill types such as glass, mesh or combinations of both.

However, the size of any mesh infill should be the same as previously mentioned in the metalwork section.

Mesh Specification

The design and specification is really your choice, but as a general guide – the recognised **standard size** is for 50mm x 50mm (2" x 2") weldmesh with a frame of 25mm x 25mm x 2.6mm (1" x 1" x 12 gauge) box section.

Bar Specification

An alternative to weldmesh is to use a vertical bar infill. This is slightly more expensive than the mesh and its use is a matter of personal choice. The bars are normally spaced at 50mm (2") with horizontal strengthening ribs to provide additional support.

Chainlink Fencing

Chainlink has been used because it is readily available and fast to install. It is a system commonly seen in typical establishments in the USA and Canada with a galvanised tubular frame and chainlink infill. Although chainlink provides some security, its use as a dividing partition does not offer any of the positive dog welfare elements found with a solid partition.

Above: stainless steel bar

Above: galvanised bar and mesh

Above: galvanised bar

Above: typical finish for chainlink showing potential for injury

SLIDING HATCHES

These are used in semi-outdoor style kennels where the dog has the choice of being in either the run or sleep area, this is accessed via a sliding hatch or 'pop-hole'. The same materials shown for division panels are generally suitable for hatches. Traditionally in the UK the majority of hatches have been manufactured from single-sheet galvanised metal.
Single sheet metal is a poor insulator of heat/cold, it is extremely noisy when dogs scratch it or when being operated by a member of staff. **Using single-skin metal sheeting for hatches is an outdated system with many disadvantages. There are far better and more modern alternatives available** in the form of plastic panels with insulation. These are lighter, quieter and easier to operate.

The size of the hatch is partly dictated by the size and breed of the dog using it. Obviously for charities and boarding kennels a compromise has to be made. As a guide, the use of two sizes of hatch is sufficient.

The sizes are:

- 600mm wide x 750mm high/ 24" x 29.5"

- 600mm wide x 900mm high/ 24" x 35.5"

There are a number of 'dog doors' on the market; these are basically larger versions of a cat flap. These doors are generally made of plastic with a hinged top section or split in the middle. The advantage with this type of door is that it **retains the heat** in the kennel, rather than letting it all escape through the hatch. For colder climates this is well worth considering.

A 'cheap' alternative is to install clear PVC strips on the external face of the run. These strips are used extensively in commercial cold and freezer rooms. The strips reduce the level of draught entering the building and help retain heat. Ideally make the strips removable for dogs that have great fun in seeing how many pieces they can chew them into!

FULL HEIGHT DOORS

For giant breeds it is extremely useful to have at least one kennel, with a larger sliding hatch, or a full-height human door or stable door.

For upscale kennels and dog hotels, we are now seeing more full-height doors used between the sleep and exercise areas. This can be instead of, or as well as a sliding hatch. A glazed full height door will also let in a lot more light, making the kennels feel brighter and more welcoming.

However, it is recommended to have at least one kennel with a sliding hatch as well. This would provide staff security for dogs with aggressive tendencies.

Having a full-height door changes the look and feel of the kennels, as well as providing additional flexibility for staff. The continuing strong trend towards home-like or hotel-like rooms and dog-friendly environments means full height doors provide a more appealing and upmarket appearance.

With larger kennels there will be room for both a door and a hatch on one wall. Smaller sized kennels may prefer to install a hatch within the door to save space.

ENVIRONMENT CONTROL

LIGHTING, HEATING, COOLING AND FRESH AIR PROVIDE SIGNIFICANT BENEFITS TO DOGS, STAFF AND CLIENTS

ENVIRONMENT CONTROL

In this chapter, we look at the environment within the kennel building:

- Lighting

- Heating and cooling systems

- Ventilation

- Risk of disease (increasing/reducing factors)

- Condensation/dehumidification

LIGHTING

Any building with lots of natural daylight and sunlight will always feel more inviting.

Daylight and Sunlight

Clearly, the amount of natural daylight entering the building will have a marked effect on the amount of artificial lighting required. Whatever form of lighting is provided, it has to be adequate for safe and effective working at any time of the day or night. Recent advances in lighting technology can give energy savings of approximately 30%, especially when compared with installations more than 10 year's old. **Sunlight is also a natural killer of viruses and bacteria; this, combined with natural ventilation, can go a long way to reduce the incidence of disease.**

Try to aim for a minimum of 20% natural daylight inside the building.

Internal Lighting

Consideration should be given to ensure there is suitable working light for cleaning, disinfecting and daily routines. Of all systems available, fluorescent tubes are regarded as being the most suitable for most animal accommodation. They range from 1.2m/4ft to 2.4m/8ft and come in either single or double fittings, are low-maintenance, cost-effective and with an operating life of 5,000-15,000 hours. The fittings can have integral emergency lighting if required. Fluorescent fittings with 2D fittings (low energy) provide supplementary lighting and offer the most flexible of systems. The 2D fittings are generally of the 'bulkhead' type and are often used in individual dog kennels, or as illumination for open walkways.

Helpful Hints:

- If specifying fluorescent tubular lighting, it is well worth spending a little extra to purchase the dust/vapour-proof enclosed unit. Apart from being easier to clean, this type of unit will withstand being splashed by over-enthusiastic staff using hosepipes.

- Change to the new smaller 26mm/1½" diameter tubes. The older 38mm/1" are approximately 8% more expensive to run. The new 26mm tubes will fit into your existing holders without modification

- Fluorescent fittings with high-frequency ballast are the most efficient. Although more expensive to buy, they have energy cost savings of around 15%

External Lighting

There should be suitable amenity lighting for external walkways, car parking, etc.

HEATING AND COOLING SYSTEMS

The CIEH recommend a kennel temperature of between 10°C/50°F and 26°C/79°F. All factors, such as the size of the building, its insulation qualities and the time of the year it is in use, will influence the type of heating system installed.

Temperature regulations for other countries:

- UK Quarantine   7°C   44° F – No maximum given
- UK Boarding   10 - 26°C   50 - 79° F
- Missouri, USA   10 - 29.5°C   50 - 85° F
- Colorado, USA   10 - 2.2° C   50 - 90° F
- Australia   15 - 27°C   59- 80° F
- New Zealand   15 - 22° C   59 -72° F

The decision on the type of heating system to install in the kennels needs to be taken at an early stage. It is often dictated by the services available locally, (e.g. mains gas) and/or the type and design of the building (e.g. semi-outdoor or indoor kennels). In older properties, the heating is often one of the last items to be upgraded, frequently relying on infrared heat lamps, or the occasional floor-standing electric fan heater. It is not always the cost of upgrading these systems that prevents the work from being undertaken; often it can be the problem of choosing the most suitable system and physically carrying out the work.

Whichever system is used, it must be convenient, have a suitable service back-up, be adequate for the purpose for which it is intended, and be easy to use. It is pointless having an over complicated system that the staff do not understand.
It is also worth considering the amount of use the heaters will receive. If an isolated building is only used for a few weeks a year, then an expensive boiler-fired heating system will not be the most cost-effective or suitable.

Heating systems commonly in use:

- Infrared and ceramic heat lamps
- Radiant heating panels
- Electric fan heaters
- Quartz halogen heaters
- Night storage heaters
- Boiler-fired high level fan convectors
- Domestic radiators or tubular heating pipes
- Underfloor heating (electric and wet system)
- Solar energy
- Air conditioning
- Heat recovery

Infrared and Ceramic Heat Lamps

This system uses several types of bulb, such as red heat bulbs, ceramic heat lamps and dull emitter bulbs. Since the heat is radiant, the animals feel the warmth immediately. All have been around for a long time and are still commonly used for cats, dogs, poultry and particularly pigs. The infrared rays given off are similar to those given off by the sun.

The **advantages** of this system are that it is relatively cheap to install, simple to use, and cost-effective when used in small numbers. The **disadvantage** is that lamps are designed to provide a direct heat over the animal; they do not provide an effective level of warmth to the building or room, unless they are installed in adequate numbers or wattage.

Most charities tend to use them for young or frail cats as a **backup** to the main heating system.

If choosing to install this system, ensure you use ceramic or dull emitters are used, they are far safer and stronger than the red bulb variety, which **tend to explode when splashed with water**. All electrically operated equipment needs to be correctly installed at high level, out of the animal's reach and to have a suitably protected electrical supply.

The disadvantages of using heat lamps are:

- They do not provide the 'luxury' image that today's market demands

- The building won't have an overall feeling of warmth, (it is only the dog that receives the warmth in the sleep area)

- There is a danger of scalding the dog if the lamp is too close. Generally, they need to be fitted at least 2m (6'6") above the head of the animal

Radiant Heating Panel

Radiant panels provide gentle long wave heat that can be used either as the sole source of heat or to supplement other systems. The panels use low temperature electric heating elements; these are normally installed at ceiling level.
The **advantages** with this type of system are that there are no moving parts, no maintenance, and are cost-effective to install.

Electric Fan Heaters

Unlike infrared heaters, an electric fan convector is suitable for room heating, particularly for large areas. The industrial varieties come in a range of powers from 2kw to 25kw. They are usually wall or ceiling-mounted, simple to use, normally with a built-in thermostat and provide instant heat.

The **disadvantage** with these units is the cost of running them; four heaters at 6kw each are extremely expensive to run. The other disadvantage with a moving air type system is that it can blow airborne diseases around.

Quartz Halogen Heaters

These units are often specified where there is a need for localised heat or immediate warmth. They are commonly used in industrial and commercial applications in premises that are lightly constructed, naturally cold and have poor insulation. They are also used in large buildings, which need to have only a small area heated.

Night Storage Heaters

A modern night storage heater is slim at not more than 170mm/7" deep, and is an efficient form of room heating. These appliances are cost-effective, being charged during the night on cheaper electricity; controllable and correctly sized they can give off high levels of heat. For certain applications, they are highly recommended. **Advantages** are for use in staff rooms, and rooms that house perishable goods which need to be kept damp free. They can be used in the kennels environment providing they are raised off the floor by approximately 300mm/12", to prevent water and urine from corroding them.

The **disadvantage** associated with them in a kennels environment is that during the early evening when it starts to get cold the heaters are losing their heating capacity; they will not be recharged until after 12.30 am. Without any additional form of heating, this could lead to the building being too cold for a period of time. For this system to work cost-effectively, an 'off-peak' (white meter) electricity supply will be required.

Boiler-fired High Level Fan Convectors

These units are normally found in industrial buildings, warehouses and large areas requiring a good, uniform level of heating. Unlike electrical fan convectors, these units require a boiler, either gas or oil fired as they operate on high temperature hot water. They have a finned tubular heating element, with a fan to improve the circulation of warm air. In addition to providing heat, they can also be used during the summer months as a cooling fan. The important point to remember when specifying such units is to **check the level of noise they produce when working**; it is important to have the quietest unit available.

There are some concerns about the possibility of dust, germs, airborne viruses, etc being blown through the building with this type of system. Even though this has not proved to be a problem, **it is far more suspect as a source of possible disease spread than a still air system**.

Domestic Radiators

Most modern panel radiators are constructed using light gauge steel, pressing-welded together. Heavy cast iron units are also available and are used extensively in homes and offices. Radiators, like boiler-fired fan convectors, require some form of boiler to provide the necessary hot water for them to operate. An alternative to radiators is tubular heating pipes. These are normally 50mm/2" diameter and extremely durable.

However, they have the **disadvantage** of not being aesthetically pleasing. A major concern if they are mounted at low level, is a risk of dogs trapping their legs behind the pipes, if the pipes do not have a protective cage over them.

For kennels, the radiators should be lifted slightly higher above the floor than normal (approx 400mm/16-18") to prevent the base from rusting from urine or cleaning/disinfection.

The advantages of radiant heat are:

- Gives a greater feeling of warmth with a lower air temperature; this achieves about a 15% saving in fuel costs

- A system with which any heating engineer is familiar with

- It warms the whole area of the building where used, making it more pleasant to work in and to visit.

- The location of the radiators will partly depend on the design and style of the building. For single line kennels this system works extremely well.

Underfloor/Radiant Heating (Electric and Wet System)

Having used several methods, I am convinced that underfloor heating is the most convenient, efficient, practical and suitable for animal accommodation. It has low running costs, risk-reducing factors for disease, a luxury, aesthetic appeal, and anyone who has underfloor heating at home knows how dogs love to relax on warm floors!

There has been a significant increase in the use of underfloor heating (UFH) in recent years. This is because of cost, easier installation, improved product quality, aesthetic qualities (it is hidden) and cheaper running costs. It is not a new technology, as the Romans pioneered its use. There are two main types of system, either warm water flowing through pipes, or electric cables. Underfloor heating can be used throughout the entire building, or be combination of underfloor and radiators.

Electric

Underfloor heating has a higher capital (purchase/installation) cost than most other forms of electric heating; however, correctly installed, it should last for many years without requiring maintenance. It can also be self-installed by a competent DIY'er. This system normally comes as sealed pads of varying sizes or lengths of insulated cable in a mesh mat, laid to the required areas. The running costs for electric underflooring will be slightly higher than for a wet underfloor system (that is boiler-fired) - but running costs are lower than radiator systems (savings of a least 15%).
Electric systems can be powered by 'greener' systems, e.g. ground source heat pumps which use the ground's constant temperature by converting and transferring this heat into buildings to power underfloor heating and water (see page 388).

Wet system

During the 1960's wet underfloor heating became popular for a short time. Its popularity did not last for long; it proved to be unreliable, difficult to maintain and had to be run at extremely high temperatures, particularly with poorly-insulated buildings. Since then it has evolved considerably with the use of polyethylene and aluminium pipes and better-insulated homes.

Only 60-70% of the sleep area should have underfloor heating to allow the dogs to choose a cooler area if they prefer

---

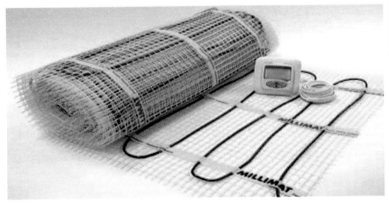 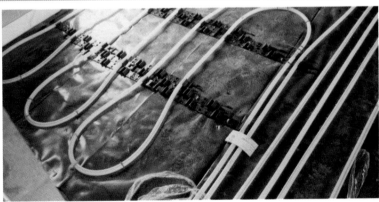

Underfloor/radiant heating - advantages and disadvantages

Advantages:

- Aesthetically pleasing, with no obvious source of heat

- Low running costs, with savings of more than 15% compared with radiator systems. This is achieved by heating the dense thermal mass (concrete slab). Once the slab has reached the desired temperature, the thermostat cuts off the supply, and the slab remains warm for a long while - hence the cost and energy savings

- Only 60-70% of the kennel sleep area should have underfloor heating - this ensures there is a cooler spot available according to the individual dog's preferences or needs

- The heat is distributed evenly across the floor; this helps to dry the floor extremely quickly after cleaning

- No moving parts

- The electric systems are easy to install

- No air being moved or pushed around by fan convectors; some consider this the most beneficial advantage (e.g. less risk from airborne diseases such as viral cough)

Disadvantages:

- Higher capital costs to install

- The floor needs to be well insulated to provide an effective output

- The system is less responsive to changes in ambient temperature. For buildings that are in constant use throughout the winter months, this is not an issue. However, it takes longer to bring the room up to the required temperature, consequently it takes longer to cool down. This is because it heats up the concrete base, which has a dense thermal mass

- Most of the electric systems cannot be run on cheap off-peak electricity

- Space has to be available for the manifold (control) system

Helpful Hints:

- Leave approximately 30% of the sleeping area free of heating. This allows the dog some freedom to choose either a warm or slightly cooler area

- Ensure there are detailed drawings of the areas covered by the cables or pads. This might be extremely useful for any future works that might be carried out, particularly if fixing new metalwork to the floor

- Check with the manufacturer that it is suitable for the wearing surface (e.g. vinyl)

- If installed with a tiled finish, ensure that the adhesive and grout are compatible

- Check on the guarantee of the pipe if installing a wet system

- Use the manufacturer's design service. This is normally part of the package if purchasing a wet system

- The wet systems work best with modern, condensing boilers and good floor insulation

Mechanical Ventilation with Heat Recovery (MVHR)

With the ever-increasing costs of fuel, there has been a drive to use less energy, and equally to use more cost-effective and efficient heating and ventilation systems. Heat recovery is one off-the-shelf option available.

A heat recovery system attached to a mechanical, whole-building ventilation system can recover approximately 40% – 60% of the heat that would otherwise be wasted. The basic operation of the system is to use fresh air that is brought into the building; this passes through a heat exchanger and picks up the heat recovered from the stale air.

The warmed air is then ducted to other parts of the building.

These systems are generally modular and can incorporate other elements such as: comfort cooling, air conditioning, air filtering and dehumidification. In order for these systems to work properly they need to be fully designed by a competent company, and to take into account the special requirements of animal buildings (which might not be fully apparent).

Critical points outside normal design issues are:

- Separating the intake and exhaust terminals to ensure that there is no crossover of contaminated air

- Ensuring that the units have accessible and easy-to-clean filters. Dog hairs are very fine and can cause significant maintenance issues if the filters are not cleaned regularly

- Ensuring the operating noise level of the system is known

AIR CONDITIONING

The aim of air conditioning is to control and maintain a building's environment. This covers all aspects from heating, cooling and ventilation to humidity control.

There are two basic types of air conditioning, either single zone packaged units or complete systems:

■ ## Single-Zone Packaged Units
Single-zone packaged units are used for single rooms through to complete building systems.

■ ## Complete Building Systems
Complete systems are normally fitted during the construction stage. They are an integral part of the design, and design parameters are calculated on the location of the building, its size, insulation values, etc. Retro-fitting (installing at a later date) a full building system does not generally work as well.

The aim of any system is to ensure that it is designed for your particular situation, building size and location. All these requirements should be discussed with your design company or heating/cooling engineer or consultant.

Both systems tend to be used for indoor-only designs or for consistently hot climates. The issues are exactly the same as with MVHR.

If installed correctly, these systems can provide a fully controllable environment covering humidity, warmth, cooling and ventilation. However, they are more expensive to install and do require a greater level of maintenance than standard boiler-operated heating and ventilation systems.

For smaller boarding kennels and rescue organisations in temperate climates (particularly those using semi-outdoor designs), these systems are over-complicated, and it would be better to look at some of the other options mentioned earlier.

GREEN ENERGY

All of the previously mentioned systems are conventional fossil-fuel based. Given the high costs of fuel, and the drive to find greater energy efficiency and alternative systems to replace or reduce the dependency on fossil fuel based systems, the three 'green' technologies commercially available that have merits for the larger kennel owner/operator are:

Solar Hot Water Heating

This system has certainly gained prominence in the domestic market, and is normally associated with providing hot water. As with all such ventures the cost of installation has to be weighed against the time it takes to pay back the initial costs. It is worth looking at any government grants that may be available.

A conventional system uses solar collectors, through which water is circulated, heated and then piped to a well-insulated storage tank. The solar panels are normally sited on the roof of the building, although they can be mounted in any convenient location.

Ground Source Heat Pumps (GSHP)

Heat pumps or 'nature's free energy' as they are also known, operating from solar energy stored either underground or from the ambient air temperature. This is one of the more expensive systems available with high initial capital costs, but as with any good system - longer-term benefits are lower running costs, helping the environment, increasingly of great interest to customers, and provides a green, caring and upmarket image which will be part of your unique selling point.

The advantage is that the running costs are approximately half those of oil-based heating systems, and can be used to power underfloor heating and also water.

There are three important elements to a GSHP heating system:

1. ### A ground loop
   This is comprised of lengths of pipe buried in the ground. The pipe is filled with a mixture of water and anti-freeze, which is pumped round the pipe absorbing heat from the ground.

2. ### A heat Pump
   This has three main parts:

   - The evaporator – this takes the heat from the water in the ground loop

   - The compressor – this moves the refrigerant round the heat pump and compresses the gaseous refrigerant to the correct temperature needed for the heat distribution circuit

   - The condenser – gives up heat to a hot water tank that feeds the distribution system

3. ### A hot water heat distribution system
   Due to the lower temperatures produced by the system, the heat given off is ideally suited to underfloor heating systems rather than a standard radiator based system. The system produces water at 60°C/140°F; underfloor heating systems require a temperature of approximately 45°C – 50°C/113°F – 122°F.
   A radiator system runs at a temperature of approximately 80°C/176°F.

Biomass Boilers

Wood or wood pellet boilers have been popular in Scandinavia for a long while. They are becoming more widely available in the UK.

There are a number of issues that must be considered when planning this type of installation:

- Ease of use – these are not as convenient as gas or oil-based supply systems

- Size and location of boiler and storage of fuels

- Fuel availability

With all of the above systems, calculate the initial capitals costs and compare with the longer-term savings, (bearing in mind what grants are available to make the installation costs more attractive), what the payback period is likely to be, the servicing and maintenance that will be required, and the many long-term benefits to the environment and to your business.

KENNEL DESIGN: THE ESSENTIAL GUIDE TO CREATING YOUR PERFECT KENNELS

VENTILATION

Adequate ventilation in any kennels is of paramount importance

The primary aims are:

- Removal and dilution of airborne animal diseases such as viral cough

- Reduction in humidity levels

- Removal of carbon monoxide

- Removal of odours

- Not to create excessive draughts

It is generally recognised that any system utilised in animal accommodation has to be supplemented by mechanical means to ensure control.

Air Changes Per Hour

The number of air changes per hour is the rate at which the air in the building is expelled, and replaced with fresh air from outside.

The general guide used is approximately 4 – 6 changes per hour, with the option to boost to around 8 if required during a period of disease outbreak.

Under normal operating conditions we have found that the 4 – 6 changes per hour is sufficient.

As most of the disease problems occur during the warmer summer months or when the kennels are full to capacity, the capability to boost the ventilation rate is a desirable option. What must also be taken into consideration is the style and design of the buildings, the number of visitors who have access into the animal units (which increases the risk of disease transfer), the type of dogs being admitted (e.g. strays or fully vaccinated pets), and the number of dogs housed.

All these factors will have a significant effect on the frequency and severity of disease outbreak.

The following examples are design and performance criteria set by some of the leading animal welfare organisations:

- ### Universities Federation for Animal Welfare
  Recommend a minimum ventilation rate of 10 – 12 air changes per hour.
  It also recommends the use of negative pressure systems, with fan speeds maintained below 0.25 m/s to avoid discomfort from draughts

- ### The Humane Society of the United States
  Recommend a rate of between 8 – 15 air changes per hour

Practical Issues

In reality, the majority of domestic kennel owners and animal welfare organisations operating rehoming centres will choose a basic ventilation system.

For buildings without full climate control, there will be great difficulty in achieving the higher levels of ventilation required (i.e. 10 – 12+ per hour in normal animal welfare environments) particularly during the colder months.

To maintain the required temperature within a building that has high levels of extraction, the heat-producing equipment has to be increased in size, capacity and sophistication to balance these two opposing actions. The costs involved in trying to balance these requirements can be considerable, and need to be fully designed and engineered to achieve a balanced system.

VENTILATION SYSTEMS

Ventilation systems in use:

- Natural ventilation (Passive)

- Natural inlet with mechanical extract

- Positive input ventilation (PIV)

- Heat recovery ventilation

- Mechanical multi-port extraction system

The design, type of system and your own particular requirements will vary enormously. Often the determining factors will be cost, amount of use, building type and construction method.

Below: a mechanical multi-port extraction system

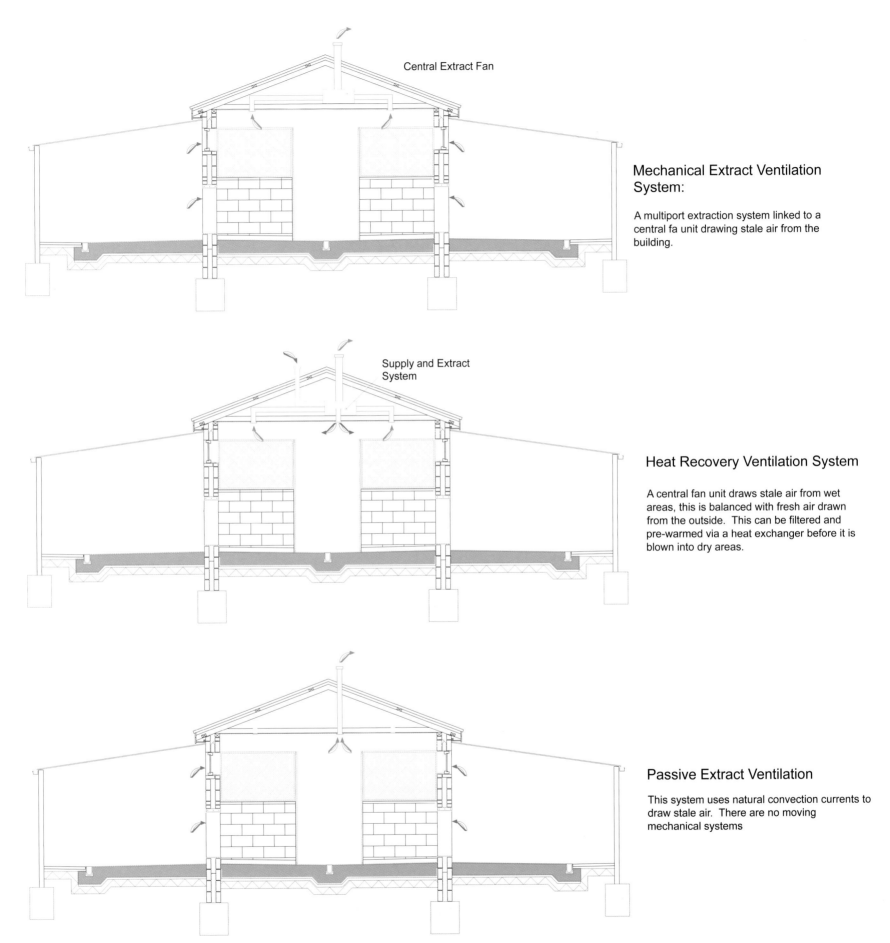

Mechanical Extract Ventilation System:

Central Extract Fan

A multiport extraction system linked to a central fa unit drawing stale air from the building.

Heat Recovery Ventilation System

Supply and Extract System

A central fan unit draws stale air from wet areas, this is balanced with fresh air drawn from the outside. This can be filtered and pre-warmed via a heat exchanger before it is blown into dry areas.

Passive Extract Ventilation

This system uses natural convection currents to draw stale air. There are no moving mechanical systems

Natural Ventilation (Passive)

This is the simplest and cheapest method available to the kennel owner. Natural ventilation is often described as either cross ventilation or passive ventilation (stack effect).

- ## Cross Ventilation
  This utilises openable windows, doors and dog hatches, etc, which transfer laterally across the building

- ## Stack Effect
  This utilises the principle that as hot air rises and warms, it becomes less dense than the surrounding air, (this is know as convection). It is dependent on the wind and air temperature (warm air rises) which creates a stack effect. If there is no wind and the temperature inside the building is at the same temperature as the outside, natural ventilation will be less positive.

  The utilisation of the 'stack effect' is well known and is exploited in operations that generally have consistently high internal temperatures such as poultry houses and foundries. Passive stack ventilation systems are not totally effective in summer time when the external temperature may exceed the internal temperature. To be totally efficient the system has to be designed for your particular application and location. The prevailing environmental conditions need to be taken into account as low or fluctuating conditions can have a detrimental impact on system operation.

  Due to the relatively low ceiling height of most commercial kennels, the small amount of heat given off by dogs (as compared with large poultry houses and large animals such as cattle) and its lack of controllability, **this system has little to offer the kennel owner**.

Natural Inlet with Single Fan Mechanical Extract

This is the most common type of system and is generally used in domestic kitchens, veterinary rooms and public conveniences, etc. The extractor fan creates negative pressure on its inlet side, causeing the air inside the room to move towards the fan, and then displaced by fresh air coming from outside. This is probably the most widely-used system in animal accommodation; it is cost-effective, simple to use, can be controlled and will remove odours and condensation. Its main use is for single rooms.

Positive Input Ventilation systems (PIV)

Fresh air is impelled into the building, thereby creating a positive pressure; the contaminated air is expelled by natural seepage through windows, dog doors/hatches, etc. In its basic form, this system uses warmed air in the roof space, this applies only to buildings with a 'cold roof' design. If the building has a 'warm roof' design (as is common with a lot of animal buildings using composite steel sheeted roof systems) then consideration needs to be given to ensure that cold air is not forced into the building. This has further complications in locations with freezing, cold weather conditions.

Heat Recovery Units

These simple units, while providing excellent ventilation rates, also recover some of the removed heat from the room/building. The design of the system ensures there is no cross-contamination of extracted stale or contaminated air, with fresh incoming air. These units have their limitations and need frequent servicing, particularly in kennels, to ensure that the filters are clean, allowing the unit to function to its maximum capacity.

Mechanical Multi-Port Extraction System

This is basically a natural inlet with mechanical extract, which uses a multi-port outlet system.

MY PREFERRED SYSTEM:

Having tried many systems, in terms of cost-effectiveness, ease of servicing and maintenance, ease of installation and proven benefit, the multi-port extraction system is still my preferred choice.

A ducted system connected to multi-port, ceiling-mounted extraction grills, all connected to a high performance acoustic fan. The flow is provided by gaps around the dog doors/hatches, etc and door trickle ventilation. This type of system has proven to be extremely beneficial in reducing the overall incidence of disease outbreak and also a reduction in the severity of the outbreak. The system allows for uniform extraction over the entire area of the building. The mechanical systems are more expensive to install, but offer more controllability over natural ventilation systems.

Consideration Points:

- Use manual time clocks and control systems. The fully electronic humidity switches do not allow staff the desired flexibility to override and boost the system

- The extraction fan should not have an in-line filter (built-in) on the extraction side of the unit, as this only increases the maintenance

- Any extraction port should have a fully adjustable cover grill to allow some control over the extraction levels

- For glazed kennel doors, fit trickle ventilators at high level (1.75m/6ft) above the floor, or around the door (to a maximum of 10mm/¼" to ensure dog safety). This will allow some movement of air within the kennel. This also allows a supply of replacement air. If the system has a particularly high extraction rate, this will need to be catered for in the design to ensure a free flow of air

- Ensure that expelled air is not forced into, or on to, other kennels

Summary:

There is a commonly held belief that simply increasing the number of air changes will prevent the risk or spread of disease in the kennel environment. This is simply not the case. There are many other contributing factors that can help reduce, and equally increase, the incidence of disease outbreak. With the need for welfare organisations to allow the public to view their animals, and with the continuing influx of new animals, it is inevitable that there will be periods when the building has to be closed down to control the risk of disease.

Non-airborne Diseases

It must be remembered that ventilation will not provide protection from other diseases that are not airborne. Reducing the risk of direct contact diseases such as Parvo, or the indirect contact diseases such as enteritis, is equally important. Other factors such as intermediate surfaces known as fomites e.g. contaminated hands, cleaning utensils, clothing, etc., can all play a part in the disease control issues. ,

The ventilation aspect cannot be considered as a stand-alone aspect of the building design. It has to be an integral part of the overall building design, cleaning routine and the management control system at the centre. It is pointless spending excessively, purely to achieve the higher rates of ventilation/exchange. The costs of installing expensive, high maintenance and oversized heat-producing equipment (for what could be very limited use) could be considerable.

This factor becomes more noticeable given that the vast majority of disease incidence tends to occur during the summer months when the heating is normally switched off.

CONDENSATION (DEHUMIDIFICATION)

Many kennels are too wet or damp. The reasons for this are obvious: water from over-zealous cleaning processes, damp bedding, uncovered exercise runs, porous materials, etc. All these factors contribute to a poor environment in which to house dogs; a damp environment is a breeding place for viruses and germs.

Condensation is a problem that affects many buildings, not just kennels. It is particularly noticeable during the winter months, and at night, when the temperature falls, the humidity rises and condensation forms.

Your bathroom window is a good indicator of the problem. When running a hot bath on a cold day, it will not be long before the inside of the window is heavy with running water. The air we breathe is like a big sponge; the warmer the air, the more water in the form of vapour it can absorb. As soon as the air is cooled for any reason it contracts, and has to unload its absorbed water on to the cold surface - this is condensation (dew).

The materials used in modern kennels are not the most beneficial to counteract this problem; the cold, hard finishes of tiles or sealed block work readily show the problem.

The fundamental principle of minimising condensation as a result of high humidity is to maintain a balance between the ventilation, the heating and thermal properties of the building.

To combat the problems associated with condensation often requires taking various levels of action; each stage has to be carried out separately, allowing measurement of how effective it has been. Heating, ventilation and humidity should be looked at as a whole and not as isolated elements; approaching the problem in this manner should give excellent results.

If heating and ventilation alone do not correct the problem of condensation, there are two choices:

- ## Dehumidification
  These simple units can be of great advantage to any property owner and are used extensively for drying new houses, basement cellars and for keeping document stores dry. They come in a range of sizes and extraction levels, are cost-effective, give excellent results and are simple to operate and maintain

  The basic principle of the system is that moist air within the building is drawn over a heater coil, ensuring it deposits its condensed water, which is then drained away. During this process the latent energy of the water vapour is recovered and is recycled back into the air as it leaves the unit. This warmed air can be a useful source of heating for the building. Correctly sized, a dehumidifier will reduce your heating and ventilation costs and at the same time improve the kennels environment by removing excess moisture from the air

- ## Building Construction and Management Technique
  Look at the construction method and fabric of the building (e.g. old, outdated building, rising damp), and also your management techniques (e.g. cleaning, amount of water used, etc).

RISK OF DISEASE – INCREASING AND REDUCING FACTORS

To minimise the risk of disease outbreak and spread, some other factors have to be taken into consideration, as ventilation alone will not prevent disease outbreaks. Factors affecting the risk of disease:

Risk Increasing Factors:

- Large numbers of animals housed in one area
- Poor management
- Poor staff awareness and control systems
- Dark, damp buildings
- Public access to all areas
- Poor quality and unhygienic surfaces and finishes
- Stressed and bored animals, lack of environmental enrichment
- Poor cleaning regimes
- Draughty buildings
- Buildings that are subject to extremes of temperature

Below: the dark interior corridor of an old, outdated kennels

Risk-Reducing Factors

- Fewer dogs in any one area, with a maximum of 20 kennels per building preferably split into sections.

- Happy, relaxed dogs having lots of human contact with plenty of options to play, and interact with staff to stimulate dogs both physically and mentally

- Good management

- Good staff awareness and training

- Buildings that have good cross-ventilation, with the correct number of air changes across the entire building (not just in isolated pockets near windows)

- Animals have access to natural daylight/sunlight (sunlight is a natural killer of viruses and bacteria)

- Reducing the amount of shared air

- Providing a stimulating environment

- Quality finishes that allow the building to dry quickly, thus ensuring the environment is dry

- Type of cleaning regime (excessive use of water can create additional problems)

- Type of heating system (having used several methods I am convinced that either underfloor/radiant heating types are the most convenient and suitable for animal accommodation)

- Smaller, more individual buildings

- Providing public zones to restrict access to some areas

KENNEL DESIGN: THE ESSENTIAL GUIDE TO CREATING YOUR PERFECT KENNELS

WHY ENRICH THE ENVIRONMENT?

Kennels are an unnatural environment, and can be extremely stressful. Therefore the more that can be done to 'enrich' and improve the environment to help dogs adapt, the more they will be able to express natural behaviour, allowing them to settle and relax into the daily routine.

Environment enrichment comes in many forms, some elements will be part of the physical kennel construction, some will be external aspects away from the kennels and some will be due to dedicated and enthusiastic staff. Whatever form of enrichment you use, it is a win - win situation, with more relaxed, calm, less stressed, quieter and far happier dogs.

'Enriching' the environment can be done by providing for the following needs:

- ## The importance of getting dogs out of the kennels
  Getting dogs out of the kennels is one of the most beneficial ways to improve dog wellbeing

- ## Contact and interaction with familiar faces
  Kennels worldwide have stated that maintaining continuity of staff has a noticeable and positive effect on the dogs. This can be provided by playing, grooming, stroking and just spending time together

- ## Hiding – somewhere to feel safe and relax
  Dogs entering a new environment will need time to adapt and settle in. For some dogs, the provision of a blanket over the door, a high-sided bed or box will allow the dog to hide away until s/he feels more confident. The design of the building and the number of dogs housed will have noticeable effects on how dogs settle.

Somewhere to hide: ensure you include this fundamental requirement for shy dogs to help them settle in quickly

---

- ## Provide different levels and vantage points
  Resting places above ground level allow dogs to relax and rest comfortably in safety, away from cold and damp floors. Again, allowing the dogs to express their natural behaviour is all part of reducing their stress levels. Different levels and vantage points can easily be provided by beds, chairs and benches. Elevated platforms provide somewhere to observe the surroundings, and this can be achieved easily with benches or raised areas

- ## Provide choices and interest
  Having the freedom to 'make choices' about where to rest or what to play with should be provided to further help reduce stress. The aim is to make the best use of the space available, introduce different toys or equipment to provide interest. Change something daily to provide novelty and something to explore. In a natural environment dogs would be able to show natural behaviour such as searching for food, hunting, exploring, and surveying their surroundings. Hide treats or provide interactive 'clever' toys and puzzles to give dogs something to think about

- ## Encouraging and allowing dogs to use all their senses
  Use ingenuity to provide novel ways to encourage dogs to think and become more active by using all their senses (sight, smell, sound, taste, touch)

This chapter will provide you with some ideas on how to put all of these essential requirements into practice daily.

THE IMPORTANCE OF GETTING DOGS OUT OF THE KENNELS

Environment enrichment comes in many forms, some elements will be part of the physical building and have a cost implication, and some will be due to dedicated and enthusiastic staff. Whatever forms of enrichment you use, it is a win-win situation, with more relaxed, calm, less stressed, quieter and far happier dogs. Kennels can be very stressful environments for dogs and can also be very boring. The more you can do to promote and generate interest in the dogs to explore and play, the happier the dog will be.

Off-lead Exercise

Although a few people frown upon the idea of having large secure open areas where the dog can run free, this is generally from a disease and hygiene point of view. It has to be remembered that exercising dogs on the lead also uses the same areas routinely, so the same concerns apply. However, **the benefits to the welfare of the dog are immense**.

Dr Robert Homes writes:

Free-Running Exercise Outside the Property.
"*Providing dogs with at least once, and preferably twice, daily free-running (off-lead) exercise outside the property is wonderful stimulation for dogs; using energy, getting fresh air and exercise gives a sense of wellbeing. This does not mean following owners who are running, cycling or driving. It means letting them run free as the wind to sniff wildlife/ other dogs scents, urine and faeces, race around, play and follow their noses. In other words, to behave like dogs.*

"*This is far more stimulating than free-running in the back-yard. Incidentally, big back yards can be just as boring as little back-yards, as most dogs have many hours per day to become familiar with all the features.*"

To put this into some context, if you take your dog somewhere new, whether it is the beach, another person's house, park, etc, s/he will 'come alive'. They will be interested in every part of the building with its new smells, sights, sounds and objects.

Obviously the free-running area has to be secure – safety and security must be a top priority for every kennel owner. The level and intensity of exercise has to be balanced and tuned to the dogs' individual requirements. For an elderly dog or one that only ever had the freedom of a small back yard, the freedom of a large area could be too much initially. This is a management issue, and one that should not preclude the provision of this type of facility.

The size and scale of the area will depend on several factors such as the amount of free land available, financial implications to securely fence an area, and the numbers of dogs that will be housed. Obviously for a centre with a large number of dogs it would be impractical to simply have one exercise area. For a large scale operation it would be better to have more areas. This has the advantage of allowing any areas that have become waterlogged or too muddy to be rested.

Lead-Walking

As we have already mentioned, the aim is to remove the dog from its kennel environment for short periods each day. This can also be achieved by lead-walking. It provides the dogs with different sites, sounds, and allows interaction with people – these factors are critical. For a welfare centre or sanctuary the use of volunteers as dog-walkers is beneficial to all. It is a win - win situation for the volunteer, as they are able to take part in an activity that has health and wellbeing benefits, it provides additional pairs of hands for the centre, and allows the dog more time away from the kennel environment.

Play Equipment

As can be seen from the photographs in this book, the exercise areas can be fitted out to include a wide range of things for the dogs to jump on, jump in and over, investigate and explore.

CONTACT AND INTERACTION WITH FAMILIAR FACES

Developing a relationship with the same person or people is important. Consistency in the relationship is vital to dogs – new people can be a source of anxiety or stress.

The experiences dogs have previously had of people, their confidence/extrovert/introvert nature, whether they have been in kennels before, and their normal routine and activity level will all be factors in how quickly they settle in - and what sort of relationship you will have with them.

Owners form a strong bond with their dogs. They can also get over-attached to their dogs, and dogs can get over-attached to their owners. Some dogs will be very independent, and others will have a much more dependent relationship. If the owner is upset at leaving the dog, it may cause extra stress in the dog, over and above being 'moved' to the new environment of the kennels. Educate owners to allow plenty of time to take their dog to the kennels so they are not in a last minute panic and short of time. Otherwise, the owners' stress will be communicated to their dogs, and it is better if they are left relaxed and happy. When owners leave, try to get them to be positive and matter of fact, rather than consoling, so their dog understands there is nothing to worry about.

You should **never** force a dog into doing anything - it is much better to let him/her come to you of their own accord to help establish trust. Kennel owners can help both dogs and their owners in a variety of ways, all of which are about establishing trust. Feeding a dog helps establish a relationship with the carer, therefore we can use this knowledge in the kennels by providing treats, talking to the dog in a soft voice whilst providing food, and spending more time with dogs in their first few feeding times, when it is crucial to get them to start eating away from home.

Customers notice much more than you may realise. The amount of care and attention shown to the dogs in person, how proud the kennel owner is of their facility, what supportive and enriching elements the kennel owner has to help the dogs settle in, knowledge and experience, a kind and empathetic nature and of course the image the kennel establishment presents, and promotional material such as the website - all these things come together to create clients' perception of your facility.

Some ideas for human interaction:

- Keep the same carers looking after the same dogs, continuity is important

- Ensure the longer-term carer provides the first few meals, it helps to develop a relationship quickly

- Provide treats on the first few visits to help establish a positive relationship

- Talk in a soft voice

- Always use the dog's name

- Allow time to play with the dogs, using favourite toys

- Allow time to stroke and groom the dogs, for wellbeing

- Find out as much as you can about the dog's temperament, likes and dislikes (create a dog profile), this will help ensure you do positive things for the dog that don't cause stress

- Spend as much time with the dogs as you are able to, this will help the dog place his/her trust in you

Stimulate all dog senses in the kennels to provide a fuller life while they are with you, and help them settle in quickly.

HIDING/SOMEWHERE TO FEEL SAFE AND RELAX

The more open the kennels are, the more essential it will be to provide a private, safe area for dogs. Older style kennels with greater numbers of dogs tend to be more open and much noisier. Giving dogs seclusion and choices about places to rest will encourage them to settle.

Consider kennels with hard, cold, rough surfaces - the provision of a choice of somewhere to rest will encourage dogs to use them. Where no comfortable option is given, the dogs have no choice but to stay alert or tense as there is nowhere to relax. This may sound like common sense, but think for a moment - how many kennels have you seen where any form of bedding or resting place is provided within the exercise run? (Rubber matting typical in equine establishments is ideal).

Ideas for places to hide:

- Cardboard boxes with 'doors' cut out, or travel carriers

- Blankets draped over open mesh/bar kennel fronts

- Plastic/disposable dog/child play centres

- Beds with high sides

- Off-the-floor bedding

- Raised benches (dogs can sit on or hide under them, draping a blanket over the bench creates a private space)

- Provide choices - different beds, blankets or towels, different materials

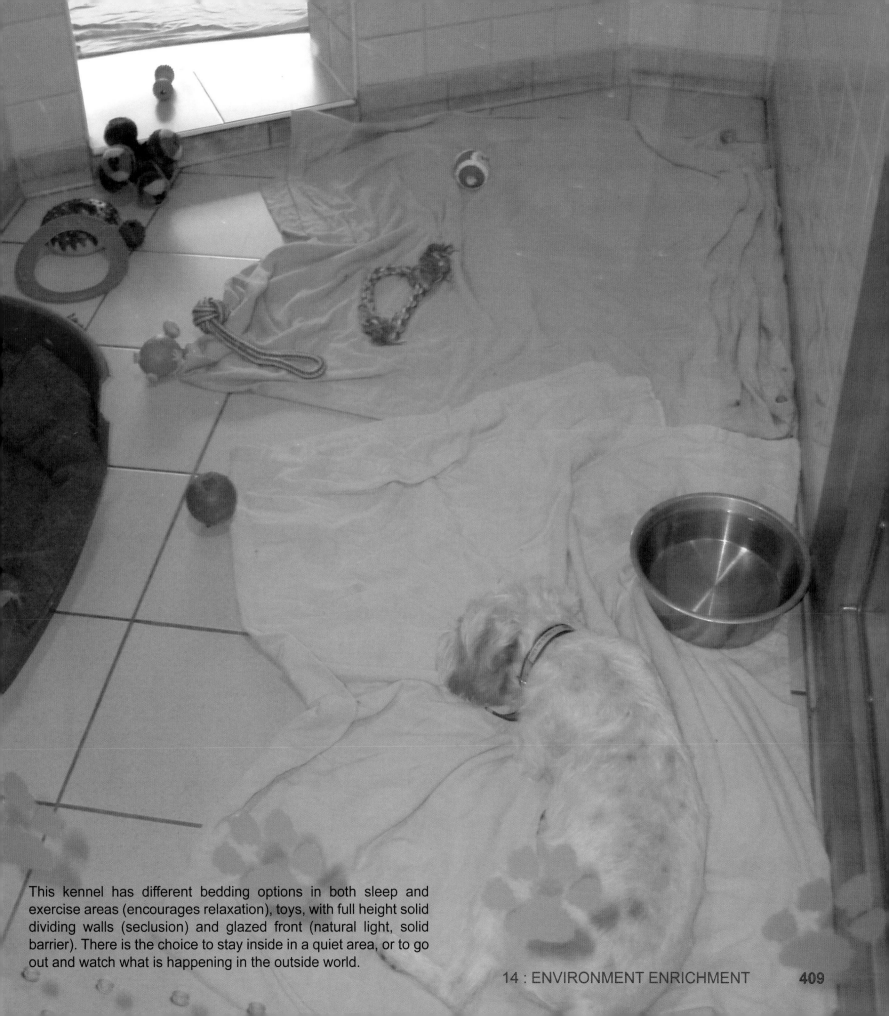

This kennel has different bedding options in both sleep and exercise areas (encourages relaxation), toys, with full height solid dividing walls (seclusion) and glazed front (natural light, solid barrier). There is the choice to stay inside in a quiet area, or to go out and watch what is happening in the outside world.

PROVIDE DIFFERENT LEVELS AND VANTAGE POINTS

Whichever benching or platforms are installed, they should be easy to clean and non-absorbent, have adequate width to fit bedding on and have a **lightly textured surface to prevent dogs slipping when jumping on and off**.

Ideas for levels and vantage points:

- Benches

- Platforms

- Canvas/fabric hammocks

- Walkways and ramps

- Plastic/disposable dog/child play centres

- Lower options for puppies and elderly/arthritic dogs

- Novelty or themed furniture

- For larger areas, a series of platforms can be used for vantage points, playing and also for grooming

- Human seats or chairs

- Child/canine/equestrian items may be used indoors or outdoors for an element of fun and shelter (such as plastic play equipment, jumps, play-houses, seats and tables)

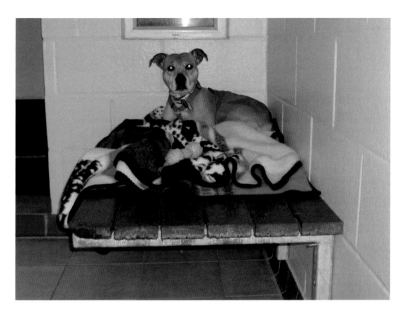

PROVIDE CHOICES AND INTEREST

Think laterally and use your imagination to create choices and interest that will provide a fun, exciting and stimulating environment for dogs both in the kennels and in exercise areas and paddocks. **Flat and empty areas are boring!**

Ideas for offering choice:

- Dogs are more likely to settle and get comfortable when offered a choice of bedding options such as blankets, beds, rubber matting and washable rugs - rather than just a cold concrete floor

- Different textures are exciting to explore, such as water, grass, sand, toys, tyres, tunnels, platforms

- Provide sunbathing spots and shady places, so dogs can choose areas that will make them more comfortable

- Create areas that allow and entice humans to spend quality time with the dogs in comfort (a chair or bench will do) rather than crouching or sitting on the floor

ENCOURAGING DOGS TO USE ALL THEIR SENSES

Use ingenuity to provide novel ways to encourage dogs to think and become more active by using all their senses.

Sight:

- Landscaping, planting, water and housing to attract wildlife

- Television and webcams (dog DVDs with birds and bugs to watch, wildlife documentaries)

- Things on strings to play with when supervised (can be toys that are attached to the cage or ceiling)

- Blow bubbles that float in the air – either the simple childhood toys with a plastic wand and bottle of bubble mixture (washing up liquid is a cheap alternative) or battery/electric powered toys that send out a stream of bubbles. You can even buy bacon-scented bubbles!

Sound:

- Classical music (do not leave it on all the time or it just becomes background 'noise' and loses its therapeutic quality). 'New Age' type music with natural sounds such as bird song, insects, water and gentle weather such as rain or the wind blowing softly (again, not all the time)

- Toys with a high-pitched squeak to mimic prey

- Use clicker-training to interact with dogs and get them thinking about how to earn treats, etc

- Talk to dogs in a soft voice and **always use the dog's name**, ask him/her to come to you

Smell:

- Items made of natural fabric that smell of owners and home retain comforting scent for a few days while settling

- Use dog-appeasing pheromones to comfort and soothe dogs. A spray can be used in the car, carrier or dog kennel, and a plug-in diffuser in the kennels. You will need to ensure that this is done at least 15 minutes before dog use

- Hiding titbits to 'sniff out'

- DO NOT use the household fragrance plug-in/spray fresheners (clean kennels will not smell). This is very strong to a dog's sensitive nose, and it will make visitors wonder what you are trying to cover up

Touch:

- Provide a variety of different materials for bedding such as vet bed, blankets, towels, fleece, cushions. Soft fleecy toys or teddies to curl up with. Somewhere comfortable for sunbathing (remember to provide areas of shade)

- Heated or thermal beds, microwaveable heated pads (safe for pets)

- Dog massage (there are quite a few books available on technique) and grooming (use different options such as hands, soft brushes, soft rubber groomers, combs)

- Soft spots such as ears, chin, cheeks, back (dogs may be less amenable to having some areas touched, such as paws, tummy and rear, and this should be noted in the dog's profile so carers are aware of preferences

KENNEL DESIGN: THE ESSENTIAL GUIDE TO CREATING YOUR PERFECT KENNELS

Taste:

Most owners feed their dog at regular times, and/or leave complete dry food available all day. This may be easy for owners, but it is certainly predictable for dogs.

In the wild, dogs would naturally spend many hours a day searching and hunting for food, using all their senses and focusing completely on the outdoor stimuli around them. A far cry from being confined and fed at the same time twice a day.

Ideas for food and nutrition:

- Treat-balls with interesting textures that dispense treats or complete dry dog food

- Hide tidbits to hunt, place food in several locations

- Warm food slightly as this may be more appealing

- Multiple feed-spots are ideal for more than one dog

- Try offering 'human' food if the dog hasn't eaten anything

- Dogs may not eat from steel bowls as they are very noisy. Try bowls with rubber bases, plastic or ceramic bowls instead

Ideas for water:

- Try flavouring water with a small amount of beef, fish or chicken stock

- Water Fountains (pet fountains or home use) especially for dogs that should be encouraged to drink more (kidney problems or diabetes)

- Provide large bowls of water for those dogs that love to 'play' with it!

SETTLING IN

Do you know how to help a dog settle in as soon as possible? Reading dog behaviour books and websites will help you start to build up your knowledge.

Ideas for how to help dogs settle in quickly:

- Clients can cause the dog stress inadvertently by being upset at leaving him/her – inform them
- Once you know the dog, could anything be done to settle the dog in more quickly next time? Make notes
- Provide somewhere for the dog to hide (e.g. a box, or leave the dog in its basket with the door open) to feel safe
- Spray corners of the carrier/kennel with dog appeasing pheromone (D.A.P) 15 minutes **before** placing the dog inside
- Play classical music quietly in the background
- Allow the dog to settle in the kennel, allowing him/her to decide whether it is time to make friends with you yet
- Increase your knowledge of dog behaviour (e.g. staring at dogs makes them uncomfortable and can frighten them)
- Use the dog's name at every opportunity
- Pay particular attention to being there for the first few meal times when settling the dog in
- Use treats and toys to help make friends with the dog
- Thoroughly understand how to recognise normal behaviour (eating, grooming, eliminating) and abnormal behaviour (pacing, circling, self-mutilation, excessive vocalisation, defensive aggression) and the signs of anxiety, fear, frustration, depression and stress
- Provide 'try-it' days and weekends and create special 'settling-in' programmes for different dog needs – dogs who have experience of kennels settle in faster

Dog Profile

A 'dog profile' will be extremely important to help you understand each dog's individual requirements, character, needs and normal environment at home. This information will not only be important for the dog's welfare, but the owners will be reassured that you will be caring for their pet in the best manner. Search the internet for 'dog profile' and you will find several examples that could be adapted for boarding or rescue kennels. A good example is www.animalsheltering.org just type 'dog profile' into the search box for the 'Canine Background Information Sheet/Form'.

If you take the time to look after a smaller number of dogs extremely well, and equally take the time to discuss their stay with the owner – a reputation as a caring and high quality kennels will be yours.

Clients will respect the professionalism of your care, be happy to leave their dog with you more often than they might otherwise, and recommend you to all their dog-owning friends.

Just think about how many of your friends also have dogs. Don't you discuss kennels, groomers, breeders, rescues, dog books and magazines, veterinary appointments, etc. with them? So will your customers, they are the best way of gaining new interest. Your best advertisement is your own product.

CASE STUDY:
MAKING A DIFFERENCE

Organisation: The Blue Cross Bromsgrove
Location: UK, West Midlands
Kennels Type: Semi-outdoor
Kennels Function: Rescue and rehoming
Number of Kennels: 40
Kennel Sleep Size: 2000 x 1500mm/ 6ft 6" x 5ft
Kennel Run Size: 2000 x 2400mm/ 6ft 6" x 8ft
Year Built: 2002

www.bluecross.org.uk

A RESCUE AND REHOMING KENNELS
PROVIDING SPACE, LIGHT, GOOD PUBLIC
ACCESS AND VIEWING TO ENCOURAGE
HIGHER ADOPTION LEVELS AND MUCH
IMPROVED DOG WELFARE

BLUE CROSS BROMSGROVE

As part of the charity's expansion programme, this former 8 acre commercial boarding kennel and cattery site was purchased in 1986.

Once the site was purchased and fully operational, the next stage was to carry out a modest level of upgrading and enhancement works to the kennels. These included such items as drainage, heating, and kennel-dividing panels.

In 1999 it was decided that the old kennel building had become no longer viable due to its design, structural issues, lack of suitable public access, etc.

THE DESIGN

The eventual design comprised 2 separate kennel buildings with an L-shaped configuration. Each building holds 20 kennels, these are sub-divided into two wings of 10 kennels each.

In addition to the kennels, the scheme also included the conversion of an existing steel-framed cattle building. This was to form the reception, staff welfare, meeting and educations rooms, etc.

PLANNING ISSUES

Although a great deal of thought and attention to detail had been given to the scheme, the local authority planning officer thought that the scheme was too large and recommended it for refusal.

After lengthy negotiations, a second smaller scheme was submitted. This provided the same number of kennels but the reception and ancillary areas were incorporated within the first kennel building. After a tense 8 week wait, the scheme was finally granted planning consent.

AIM OF THE DESIGN

The concept and aim of the design was to:

- Greatly improve facilities for dogs, staff and visitors

- Help reduce the amount of stress that dogs in charity kennels can be affected by (this is often a catch 22 situation with members of the public wishing to come and see the dogs to provide new homes, but this in turn creates a great deal of negative excitement for the dogs)

   The new buildings only have 10 kennels per wing. This allows a great deal of flexibility for the staff to 'zone' the building by grouping certain size/temperament of dogs in each section

- Provide the best operating systems for the foreseeable future

- Allow the dogs to be more relaxed, and offer the public a better chance to see how the dogs react to them (this could never be achieved in the old kennels)

- All-weather covered exercise runs

What are you most pleased with?

Manager Neil Edwards explains how he has found working with the building over the past the five years: *"The buildings have proven to be very effective at containing any disease outbreaks to individual areas; significantly reduced stress in the dogs and is a big hit with members of the public.*

What would you do differently?

"Try harder to have gained planning consent for the original scheme. After a short period of time we have already outgrown the office/staffroom space. Go for a higher specification for the wall coverings. The original paint system was not robust enough for constant daily washing. Recoating with a fibreglass-based system has proved to be an excellent finish."

The new kennels

The original old kennels

WHAT A DIFFERENCE!

MOVING THE DOGS IN

The first noticeable impression when the dogs were moved into the new kennels was that they were far more relaxed and far quieter.

As these were the same dogs being cared for by the same staff we can only put this down to the following reasons:

- The dogs now have the freedom to choose if they want to be either in the sleeping kennel or run

- All kennels have raised play platforms in both the sleep and run areas. These have proven to be a great success with dogs on look-out during the day

- A vision panel has been installed between some of the sleeping and exercise areas. This allows the dog to see out, even if it is in the sleeping area

- Large amounts of acoustic absorbing materials in both the sleeping and exercise areas to help reduce the noise levels

- Small numbers of dogs in any one area (we have only 10 kennels in one wing)

- Limited number of dog movements in front of other dogs due to the design

- A **mixture** of dividing panels between the kennels. Some are full height in blockwork, some have glass vision panels so that the dogs can see each other in adjoining kennels and some have opaque plastic barriers so that only the outline of the dog is seen

- The public do not have access into the sleeping areas, only the covered walkway in front of the exercise runs. This allows the dogs to have a quiet, private area

Solid rubber matting in the play area proved to be an excellent non-slip, warm and easy to clean finish

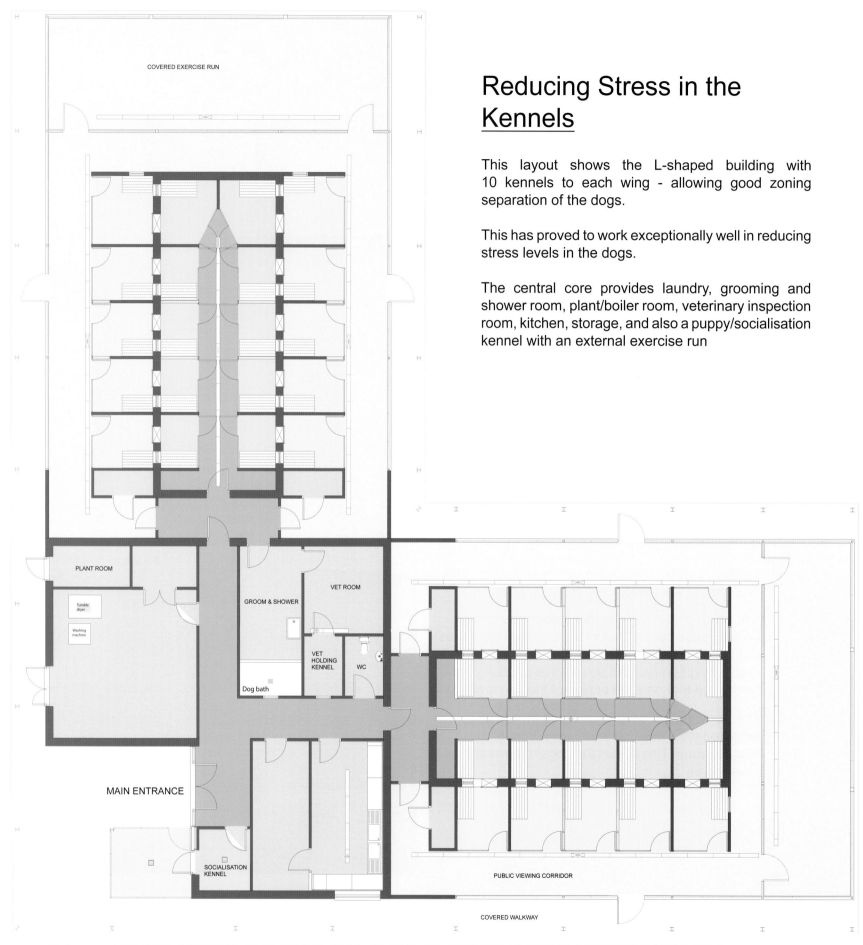

Reducing Stress in the Kennels

This layout shows the L-shaped building with 10 kennels to each wing - allowing good zoning separation of the dogs.

This has proved to work exceptionally well in reducing stress levels in the dogs.

The central core provides laundry, grooming and shower room, plant/boiler room, veterinary inspection room, kitchen, storage, and also a puppy/socialisation kennel with an external exercise run

COVERED EXERCISE RUN

PLANT ROOM

Tumble dryer

Washing machine

GROOM & SHOWER

VET ROOM

VET HOLDING KENNEL

WC

Dog bath

MAIN ENTRANCE

SOCIALISATION KENNEL

PUBLIC VIEWING CORRIDOR

COVERED WALKWAY

15 DRAINAGE, KITCHEN, CLEANING

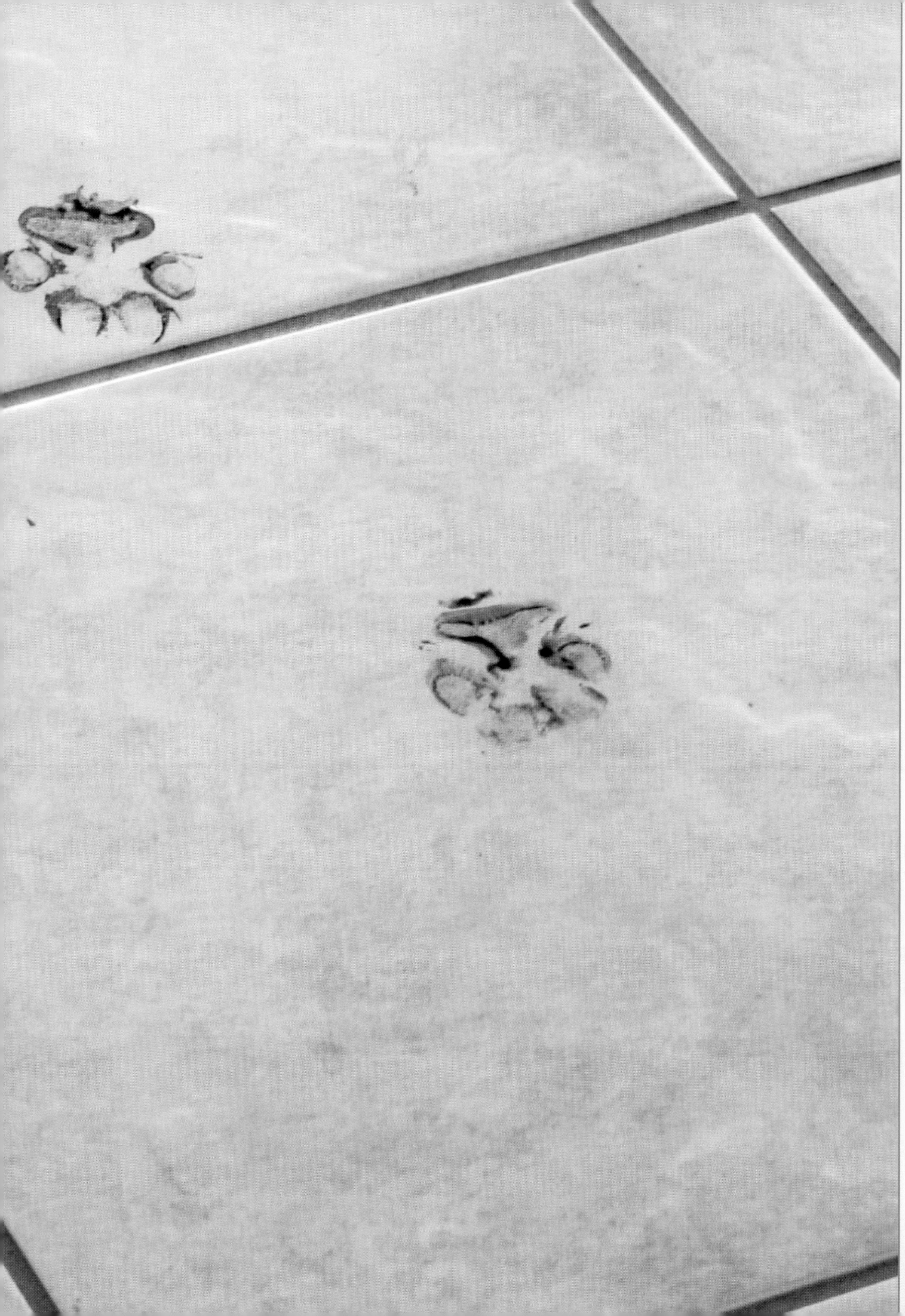

KENNELS DRAINAGE SYSTEMS

The scale of development, the design of kennels and the type of dogs that are going to be housed, company policy and the number of visitors the kennels receives will all help determine the type of drainage system to be installed.

All animal buildings should have efficient drainage systems if the cleaning policy is based on using hosepipes and large volumes of water. This should include both the internal sleeping area and the external exercise areas.

In the UK, USA and Canada all foul and surface water discharges are controlled by their Environment Agency (full details of the requirement are shown under site drainage and disposal systems).

Generally local authorities and the Environmental Agency will not allow any form of wash-down water to seep naturally into the ground; it must be channelled into an approved drainage collection system.

The type of system needs to be identified early in your design.

Equally important is the cleaning regime that will be used

As previously mentioned, many animal buildings are much too wet, simply because of the amount of water used in the cleaning process. This, combined with poor-quality porous materials, uncovered runs open to the elements, etc can all lead to long-term building and animal health issues.

The more common drainage systems used are:

- Preformed channels (trench drains)
- Ceramic dished channel
- Single outlet gullies
- Self-constructed/manufactured systems

Preformed Channels (Trench Drains)

The benefit of using a complete drainage system is that it will be easy-to-install, cost-effective and trouble-free.

The most commonly used material is polymer concrete. This is light in weight, and has a smooth internal surface (helping to prevent a build-up of sediment). It is available in pre-sloped sections, and is resistant to most acids and dilute alkalis. These channels are also available in plastic and stainless steel.

The main disadvantage of a trench drain with a grated cover, is that there is a potential risk for germs/bacteria to build up. However, with correct cleaning management and hygiene controls, this should not be a problem. There is a time factor involved in lifting and cleaning the gratings.

Note for pre-sloped channels:

if the floor is level, a pre-sloped channel system should be used. This will ensure that the water in the channel is self-draining and prevent foul, stagnant water settling in the channel, which would be an area for germs and bacteria to build up.

Below left: channel installed - the final wearing surface is still to be applied   Below right: close up view of channel

Ceramic Dished Channel

With a tiled floor, the obvious answer is to install a complementary channel tiled system. The major manufacturers all provide suitable systems with the necessary sections (i.e. stopends, corners, etc). The range of colours does tend to be limited.

The system, when correctly installed, is extremely durable, aesthetically pleasing and hygienic. The only problem found with these channel tiles is the shallowness of the dish; it is only 20mm deep. Where large volumes of water are used, this can swill over.

Note:

To achieve a constant fall, this system requires workmanship of a high standard.

The open nature of the channel has to be taken into consideration for areas such as hospitals when using trolleys, as it could present handling issues.

Below: ceramic dished channel with single outlet gulley (drain) with dog-safe metal grating

Single Outlet Gullies

These come in a range of sizes and are highly suitable for single rooms where the floor is laid in a four-way fall into the centre of the room. They are also useful for draining buckets of dirty water, rather than trying to lift into a high sink.

Self-constructed/Manufactured Systems

Many methods are used to provide adequate drainage, and most work extremely well. The two favoured methods used are half-round polyester-coated metal, or ceramic tiles used to form a square channel. Both systems will work extremely efficiently – when correctly installed.

NOTE:
As mentioned earlier, when choosing an open channel system it will be better to install twin channels (one on both sides of the corridor) as this will prevent the dilemma of trying to walk down the corridor and constantly crossing over a single channel in the middle of the corridor.

The important point to remember when installing any form of channel is to ensure it has an adequate slope so the water runs naturally into the drainage outlet.

CHANNEL GRATINGS

Gratings are used to cover linear/trench drainage channels to provide a safe, level surface. These gratings are lifted to allow access for cleaning the channel.

The more popular ranges of channel come with a variety of suitable gratings, from pedestrian weights right up to units suitable for airports. They are inherently safe, with secure, lockable gratings if required, and will handle a large volume of water without it splashing and swilling all over the floor (this system is often used by larger organisations).

Below:
The plastic 'heel guard' gratings shown below are the best all round for the kennel environment.

POTENTIAL DANGERS (BELOW)

Below left:
This photo shows a perforated stainless steel grating. Of all the grating systems shown, this one has the potential for injury to dogs. Due to the small size of the hole, the risk of dogs catching their claws is high. Once the claw is caught, the curve of the claw gets trapped, resulting in broken claws or even toes.

Below right:
Although this stainless grating looks smart, it would be uncomfortable for dogs to walk on the metal edges, and claws can also be caught, trapped and ripped.

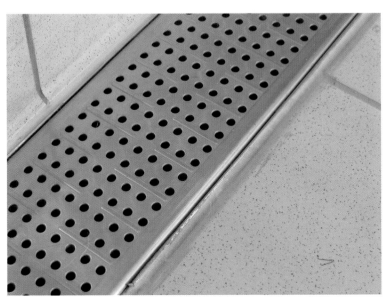

KITCHEN FACILITIES

The size and fitting-out of an animal kitchen can be as simple or as elaborate as you want it to be. It is highly dependent on your preference, the type of food used, image required, and the number of dogs housed.

A kitchen should have the following basic elements:

- **Food preparation sink _and_ cleaning sink** (twin bowls allow one each for clean and dirty work) to be kept totally separate to reduce the risk of infection and disease. Also two members of staff can work at the same time

- Adequate hot water

- Storage

- Staff hand-washing facility

It may also be desirable to consider including a dishwasher, which could be considered a luxury and extravagant; however, times and demands are changing, and time spent washing dishes is often considered to be wasted time.

FOOD PREPARATION, CLEANING AND SINK UNITS

In large welfare centres it has been common policy to install catering type stainless steel kitchen equipment. Although initially expensive, this has proved to be cost-effective in the longer term, easy to maintain and hygienic.

Furthermore, the cost of new equipment has plummeted in real terms and is now at a level where it can be purchased new for the same price as secondhand. This provides the added benefit of being able to purchase the correct size and specification for the particular application.

HOT WATER

A good supply of hot water is essential for all establishments.

Apart from washing dishes and general cleaning, some organisations have installed pressurised systems to enable hosepipes to be connected to the hot water system for daily washing down of the kennels.

The type of system used to provide the water will depend on the volume required and the mains utilities available.

The main hot water systems available are:

- Centralised boiler system

- Gas multi-point heaters

- Electric

Centralised Boiler System

This can be either gas, oil or solid fuel. However, solid fuel is not recommended because of the storage and manual handling problems

A boiler system for the kennels environment is exactly the same as installed in a domestic home; the only difference is that the size may be larger to provide a greater heat output and the volume of hot water required.

Clearly, it makes sense to combine and utilise the boiler for the kennels heating as well.

Boilers come in two system types:

- **Conventional system** – requires the installation of a hot water storage cylinder, a cold water storage tank and a feed/expansion tank for the central heating

- **Combi-system** – heats water directly from the cold mains, as required. Generally there is no hot water storage; consequently you will require an incoming cold water main with a reliable and constant pressure to enable these units to works efficiently. They have limitations for use on large-scale projects with multiple hot water points

Gas Multi-point Heaters

For large scale developments requiring large volumes of hot water, these units are extremely beneficial. They will provide unlimited amounts of hot water with fast recovery rates, and they can be linked to several outlets.

Electric

The cost of heating water by electricity is more than by gas or oil. It also has the disadvantage of taking longer to recover the required temperature.

The types of electric water heaters available are:

- **Pressure**
  This is probably the most suitable system for the kennel owner; it is basically a large hot water cylinder with storage capacities for 50 – 450 litres/13 – 118 gallons. The larger units normally have two heating elements, one in the bottom and the other at the top of the cylinder. The lower element will heat the entire contents of the cylinder and is often used on 'off-peak' electricity, while the top is used as a boost.
  This system will require the installation of a cold water storage tank at high level

- **Cistern**
  These operate on the same principle as the pressure cylinder, but they have their own built-in cold water storage tank. As the hot water is used, the cold water from the cistern replaces it. As a rule, they tend to be extremely limited in their use and capacities, normally with storage for around 25 – 135 litres/ 7 – 35 gallons

- **Open**
  These units are often installed over hand basins in toilets, staff rooms, etc. and are classified as 'point of use' heaters. They range in size from 6 – 136 litres/ 1.5 – 36 gallons, and normally have a single heating element. They can be either mains-supplied or connected to a storage cistern

- **Instantaneous heaters**
  These are designed for direct connection to the cold water mains. They operate on exactly the same principle as a domestic electric shower, i.e. a heating coil heats the water as it flows over it. They have limited benefit to the kennel owner. However, for buildings that receive only occasional use, they are an effective provider of hot water

Note for off-peak electricity (white meter):

If deciding to use electricity as your main source for central heating and water heating, consider installing an 'off-peak' meter. This will be supplied by your electricity company and operates between 11pm and 7am. The unit rate for this electricity is normally about a third of the daytime rate.

SUMMARY OF HOT WATER HEATING SYSTEMS

Fired boiler:

- Provides large bulk storage/volume; is cost-effective, one boiler can serve several buildings, and has quick heat recovery times. Professional installation is required

Electrical:

- Ideal for isolated rooms/buildings requiring only a small amount of water

- Extended recovery times

- High revenue costs

- Simple installation

Washing Facilities

Staff Hand-washing

With the ever-increasing legislation regarding health and safety, it is becoming more important to provide suitable staff washing facilities separate from those used for animal-related work.

Dishwasher

This might seem a luxury, but is not as extravagant as it sounds. A large kennels with 50 dogs will generate 100 dishes per day to wash. This will take a member of staff 1-2 hours to complete. **Remember this is a daily routine, which quickly becomes extremely boring and tedious.**

The installation of a dishwasher will release the staff member to carry out other duties and also give far more hygienic results due to the far higher temperatures of water used. **The greater temperatures involved will destroy most bacteria/ viruses and the inclusion of disinfectants will destroy any remaining**. These machines can be purchased secondhand through auctions, e.g. hotels, hospitals and catering equipment dealers. Before purchasing, ensure you have the necessary infrastructure to enable the equipment to be installed.

Kitchen Storage

The amount of storage space required in the kitchen is often overlooked, resulting in inadequate provision.

Ideally all sites require some form of central bulk storage facility; this combined with storage close to the centre of activity makes life far easier. The ideal place for your daily working storage is close to the kitchen.

Remember that to stock the store room, adequate and easy access is a major consideration

THE DIFFERENCE BETWEEN CLEANING AND DISINFECTION

The level and standard required will vary with each owner, the construction type and materials used and the function of the kennels. **However, whatever the type of facility you have, there will be times when a large part of the daily routine will involve a considerable amount of cleaning.** Obviously, for large scale developments, sanctuaries and charities with a continual turnover of dogs, this process becomes extremely important. The cleaning method and disinfection policy will depend on the function of the kennels (e.g.boarding/rescue, etc)

Daily Disinfection (Medical Model)

In the medical model, every wall, floor, item of bedding, etc is cleaned daily and the building flooded with water and disinfected. This model will be more important where there is a high turnover of dogs from unknown backgrounds and/or no environment enrichment is provided, as these dogs will already be stressed and have little resistance to pathogens. (Also see Admissions in the Chapter on Ancillary Buildings).

Where flood cleaning is the method used, it is critical that the floor has been installed with the correct falls, and that suitable drainage outlets have been allowed for.

Spot Cleaning (Ethological Model)

In the ethological model (scientific study of animal behaviour, especially as it occurs in a natural environment), the medical model is regarded as contributing to disease risk by increasing the level of stress in dogs (as all familiar scents are removed from the pen and replaced with scent the dog finds overwhelming, especially when there is no option to escape from it).

However, when spot cleaning, dogs can remain in their enriched kennels during cleaning. The walls can be spot cleaned with a clean cloth (change cloth between kennels) and bowls can be changed. **This method is only recommended for kennels where environmental enrichment is provided.** Many kennels use this cleaning policy. Instead of using hosepipes to clean the building, they simply use dampened cloths and mops, dustpan and brush. Clearly, this has many **advantages** such as cost, reducing the amount of water used, reducing the amount of stress in the dogs and therefore they will be less prone to disease or illness. There are also less environmental implications using this method.

The spot-cleaning method has also been known to REDUCE illness and disease, which is quite the opposite to what you might think. The reasoning behind this method is simple: where is the benefit in removing the bedding, etc, using strong-smelling chemicals (to which dogs are sensitive) simply to put the same healthy dog back into the kennel shortly afterwards? The dog has lost its own scent from the kennel and bedding (his/her safe and familiar area), and has to start all over again to place their scent back in the kennel. **Obviously, if the kennel is soiled it must be cleaned.** However, for the majority of dogs, (especially those vaccinated and with a known background, or for rescue environments with the luxury of a separate admissions building) a daily clean or tidy up is fine and total disinfection is unnecessary under everyday conditions.

One analogy is to compare it to the veterinary surgery. When an animal has been examined and is leaving, the staff will disinfect the table before the next animal is brought in. This is sensible and totally logical. A vet would never normally remove the animal from the table halfway through the examination, simply to disinfect the table and then place the same animal straight back on!

Try it for yourself, use the medical model in one area and the ethological model in another, and compare your disease rate and the stress of your dogs. We know that stress is such an important factor in many diseases affecting shelter dogs. We should reduce any and every source of stress to prevent disease and promote good welfare.

> Obviously, between dogs, or if the dog has been ill, then full and suitable cleaning and disinfection should be carried out.

It is interesting to watch staff who have managed old, outdated kennels with lots of gaps, nooks and crannies that were potential areas for the accumulation hair, urine, etc. to move over into brand new facilities. On the whole, they continue to use the same cleaning routine and regime as they have always done and no account is taken of the improved surfaces, finishes, sealed junctions, and easy-to-wipe wall surfaces.

Isolation

In isolation kennels it is essential to minimise the risk of disease as much as possible. Simple things such as having individual dustpan/brushes and cleaning cloths for each individual kennel, washing your hands between each kennel, etc. make a difference.

However, the biggest single route for disease transmission is either by direct contact (dog to dog), dog to food dish, or via staff. Clearly it is impractical to change your clothing between attending to each dog in the kennels.

How to Try the Spot Cleaning Method

SAME Dog daily routine: cleaning and tidying

- This will just be a question of 'tidying up' odd bits of dry food or dog hair (e.g. dustpan and brush) or 'freshening up' a kennel. Dogs have very sensitive noses and build up their own scents in a territory to settle themselves

- Cleaning up after any specific problems

- Cleaning corridors, especially if the public have access, or in wet weather

BETWEEN Dogs routine: disinfection

- **Mop and bucket**

- **Flooding with water (hosepipes or pressure washers)**
  This method is more usual in large kennels or shelters where correct drainage channels have been installed. The use of hosepipes in kennels is a quick way of cleaning. However, the kennel does need cleaning, not simply spraying with water.

- **Wet and dry vacuum cleaners**

- **Steam cleaning**

Cleaning Systems

There are many options available to help with the cleaning routine. With all disinfectants, ensure they are safe for use in the kennels environment. For pressurised washing/cleaning systems, good staff training and correct usage is essential.

Hosepipes

It is far easier to install points for hose connections around the building, rather than relying on one long length of pipe. These can be either permanently fixed, or simple snap-on connections that can be moved around the building.

Mop/Sponge and Bucket

For kennels that have good floor finishes (e.g. smooth, easy-to-wipe surfaces) a mop and bucket is still regarded as being the easiest and quickest method for daily cleaning of kennels where dogs are taken outside to toilet just like they would be at home. Obviously this depends on your kennel design and management systems.

Pressure Washer

The process of cleaning by the use of hot pressure washer is an extremely effective method. These systems can be either mobile or permanently fixed; the mobile system tends to be the more common option used. However, the majority of kennels simply do not lend themselves to this type of cleaning. The spray/steam generated can often do more damage than good.

Mobile System

These units normally have a working pressure of approximately 1500psi, this being adequate for most cleaning situations. The nozzle can be changed to suit the type of work required, from a fine spray to a jet of water; your requirement should be discussed with the sales representative. Most units are suitable for connection to a domestic 13-amp socket outlet and require only a domestic water supply. The majority of hot cleaners use diesel fuel to fire the built-in boiler, which heats the water. A suitable machine will have a working life of around 15 years. If using a mobile hot pressure washer, purchase additional lengths of lance hose. This will allow the machine to be left outside while the building is being cleaned. The noise, fumes and manual handling problems associated with these large, heavy machines can be a major problem.

Wet and Dry Vacuum Cleaners

These inexpensive cleaners have many uses for the kennel owner. The machines (which are also used for cleaning carpets and have a spray facility) can also be used to apply disinfectants and also to vacuum up any excess water, etc. Because they produce a fine mist spray (compared with a pressure washer) this makes them much more controllable, reduces the amount of water, and also clears it on completion.

Another option is the battery-operated hand vacuum cleaner. These lightweight, inexpensive machines are ideal for general day-to-day cleaning of the dog kennel, particularly if the only mess to be removed is a small amount of spilled or crushed dry food and dog hair.

Fixed System

The principle for fixed systems is exactly the same as that used on mobile systems; on the whole fixed systems tend to be larger and require three-phase electrical supplies. The advantage of this system over the mobile unit is that it is permanent, utilising fixed pipework in the building. All that is required is for the staff to connect a short length of hose into one of the outlets provided, ensure the machine is switched on, and start to clean. This system is particularly suited to large buildings or multi-storey complexes.

Disinfection Systems

Disinfection is either physical or chemical; most kennels will use chemical means, this being the most convenient.

Physical methods involve the use of heat and sunlight, while chemical use involves liquids, gases and steam. Whatever method used, it must be capable of destroying the virus/bacteria; it is no good using a sweet-smelling compound that masks any odour, but does not act upon any bacterium/virus.

Chemical Systems

Chemical disinfectants act in one of three ways:

- Oxidising agents, or as reducing agents

- Corrosives or coagulants, acting upon bacteria

- Bacterial poisons

Most chemical disinfectants are supplied in concentrated forms and require diluting with clean water before they can be used. It is accepted that warm water (not hot) is more beneficial during the mixing stage, as it increases the efficiency of the disinfectant. Once the solution has been applied, it requires a 'contact time' to ensure that the bacteria/virus has been killed; this is normally between 10-30 minutes; after this time it can be washed/rinsed away with clean water.

Notes:

- For any disinfectant to work efficiently and correctly to destroy the bacteria, the building will need to be cleaned beforehand to remove faecal matter, bedding, etc.

- Ensure disinfectant is mixed to the correct strength as recommended by the manufacturer – too strong a mixture will NOT improve the efficiency of the product

- Do not use or mix disinfectants from different manufacturers – this can result in both compounds working against each other

- Ensure all your staff know the correct dilution rates and how to mix them correctly. The reasons for this are twofold: first, extra strong mixtures are generally no more effective than the recommend strength, and second, it is a waste of money

- There are many disinfectants available to the kennel owner and these are constantly changing. Government/ environmental agencies may issue a list of approved disinfectants. However, these tend to have an agricultural predisposition and many will not be suitable for the kennels environment. It would be wise to contact your veterinary surgeon, licensing officer, or local animal welfare charity to see what they advise and use themselves

Physical Disinfection Systems

- Sunlight
  Sunlight is a natural killer of viruses and bacteria

- Steam cleaning
  Heat from the steam naturally kills off bugs and viruses.

MAIN UTILITY AND SERVICE SUPPLIES

These hidden supplies are the lifeblood of any building, whether it be kennels, a domestic house or a high-rise block of flats; a modern building cannot function without them. Whichever system is installed, it needs to be effective, trouble-free and readily available.

All kennels will require the following:

- Heating

- Electricity for lighting

- Clean drinking water

HEATING

As previously discussed, the type of heating has to be decided early in the project. Often the choice will be limited, (usually because the utility company does not have a mains supply in your area), and this will dictate the fuel used.

The main fuels are:

- Mains Gas

- Bulk Bottled Gas (LPG)

- Oil

- Solid Fuel

- Electricity

Mains Gas

This is the most convenient and cost-effective method for the provision of heating and hot water available. Where possible have a mains supply brought to the site. The problem for an isolated, rural centre is that the mains supply might be several miles away, and the cost of providing a service for a single property would be prohibitive. It is worth checking with the supply companies to establish their plans for your particular location, and obtain a quotation for the necessary works.

Bulk Bottled Gas (LPG)

For most rural locations without the luxury of mains supplies, this is one option available.
Once installed, the boilers require only minor adjustment to enable them to run on liquid petroleum gas (LPG). This system differs from a mains supply in that there will be a tank (or tanks) installed on your land; these tanks remain the property of the supply company, and a quarterly rental is paid for each tank. Although this system works extremely efficiently, on the whole this type of gas is more expensive than mains supplied and at the time of writing more expensive than oil.

The size of tank required will depend on the usage, the size of the boilers and the number of boilers on the site. An average tank capable of running a large boiler will measure 2m x 1m/6ft x 3ft, the delivery driver will need reasonable access to fill it, and it must be sited at least 3m/10ft away from your boundary, and at least 6m/20ft away from a residential building.

Oil

You will need to install a suitable tank; the minimum capacity should be 1,000 litres/165 gallons.

The larger tanks are suitable for large commercial boilers with high outputs (BTU), a central storage system serving several boilers, or a site with potential access problems, particularly during the winter months. Unlike gas, which is distributed under pressure, most oil systems work on gravity (i.e. the tank has to be at the same height as the boiler) which might require the tank to be raised on blocks.

Oil comes in two grades for domestic use – 28 second (kerosene) and 35 second (gas oil).

When ordering oil or replacement/additional boilers, this must be borne in mind and compatible units installed.
A boiler designed and set to run on one grade will not run on any other grade without some modification to the burner. Kerosene is the cleaner of the two fuels, and therefore is slightly more expensive. Tanks for commercial operations will need to have a bunded or double-wall system built around it to prevent leakage into the ground.

Solid Fuel

This is another option available. However, it does have many disadvantages, such as the storage of fuels and the considerable time and effort required to top-up the boiler (even with a modern hopper feed system), is a major consideration.
It involves considerable manual handling, compared with the alternatives available; it has little to offer a large, busy kennels complex, which would not generally have the dedicated staff to look after such systems.

Electricity

A site can be powered entirely by electricity; it will be relatively cheap to install, but the running costs will be extremely high. It has **several other disadvantages**; it is not as flexible as gas or oil when dealing with large volumes of hot water; it is extremely limited when considering commercial laundry equipment; it does not have the flexibility of many of the other systems available; and is more likely to be affected by adverse weather or interruptions to the supply.

For a large all-electric site, the incoming supply will probably be three-phase; usually on a commercial tariff and billed monthly or quarterly. The choice of whether electricity is to be used for heating is highly dependent on the construction and design of kennels, and whether heating individual kennels or much larger spaces.

On the whole, it is not recommended that a large site be powered entirely by electricity. The nature of animal work means it is common to find the majority of electrical appliances, lighting, etc will be switched on during the working day, especially during the winter months. If the heating is by electricity, this has a tremendous draw on the available supply. Therefore, the incoming supply needs to be adequate to provide all your power requirements, whatever the situation.

Note:

When electricity loading-supply calculations are made for most domestic situations, there is an element of 'diversity' allowed within the calculation. This means an assumption is made that all the electrical loading WILL NOT be required at the same time. However, in a large, busy kennels it is often the case that **all of the electrical loading WILL be required at the same time**, and this high demand should be discussed with the engineer.

WATER SUPPLY

All kennel buildings will require a water supply. The supply size and capacity will depend largely on the scale of the development. Clearly a large site with many staff all requiring water at the same time could result in a lack of supply when required; this can be very irritating for staff and become a considerable waste of time in the long term.

Historically, all hose outlets and showers were connected directly to the main local authority service supply. This is known as a direct-feed. However, with increased concerns about possible contamination, or back-siphonage into the main supply - there has been a change of policy. This has affected animal-related establishments such as kennels, catteries, stables and veterinary surgeries. The main areas of concern are hosepipes, showers and laundry equipment. In fact, any item that is connected to the main supply, which could result in back-siphonage into the main supply.

In order to comply with the increased legislation, the kennel owner has several options:

- Install separate break-tanks into each building with type AA air gap, connected or linked to a main booster pump

- Install one large day tank for the entire site with booster pump/s

- Don't have items of equipment that are connected directly to the main cold water feed

The decision on whether to use smaller individual tanks or one large tank is a matter of choice and depends on several factors. These are the flow rate and size of the incoming main, the size and layout of the site, the number of staff working at the same time, the length of the pipe runs, the amount of washing that has to be done and use of washing machines, all have to be taken into account.

The single, large day tank has the advantage for sites that have poor incoming flow rates. Depending on the factors mentioned above, it is possible to provide one tank for the entire site that has all of the required storage capacity without having to install a new water main. In some areas, it is simply not possible to bring in an adequately sized main.

A day tank should be of sufficient capacity to enable all of the staff to work at the same time. The tanks should have sufficient capacity to enable the buildings to be fully washed down, laundry, etc., and to have approximately 20% spare capacity in the storage tank following the cleaning process.

The pumps will need to be sized to suit the requirement. Typically, a booster pump will operate at a pressure of 3-5 bar.

Right: large day tank with booster pump to serve the entire site of 40 kennels.

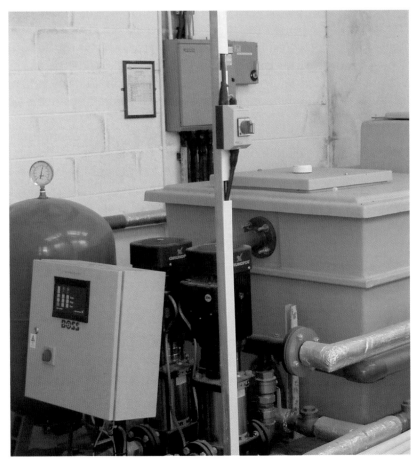

Water Usage

As a general guide, the amount of water larger centres use on a daily basis (e.g. 40 dog kennels and 30 cat units + laundry, etc is approximately 4,000 litres/880 gallons per day. This is based on a traditional kennels which use hosepipes for daily cleaning.

A typical UK mains supply coming from one of the water companies will be in three parts:

- Water company service main

- A service pipe that is the property of the Water Company.
  The pipe runs from the service main to the boundary of your property, where it is terminated by a stopcock.
  The size of the incoming service pipe will be determined by the amount of water that will be used; for a larger site either a 32mm/1¼" or a 50mm/2" service pipe would be suitable; the larger the pipe the higher the standing charge

- The supply pipe from the stopcock into the property, which is the responsibility of the consumer

Private water supply

Many isolated sites do not have the luxury of a utility company supply. For these properties, it is not uncommon to find the property being supplied from a bore well or aquifer (underground bed or layer yielding ground water for wells and springs, etc).

Whichever system is chosen, it must be capable of supplying all your requirements, all year round. It is pointless having a private supply that is incapable of providing water all year, the problems with private supplies being generally more pronounced during the summer months. If your supply is from a private source it must be tested to ensure it is safe to drink.

Water Meter

Within the next few years all commercial companies will have water meters; some areas have already started a compulsory programme of installing them. Meters, where fitted, are read on a quarterly basis by the water company; the water used is charged for as measured by the meter. With a large development at its starting point, it would be worth considering water-saving measures such as the installation of tanks to hold and recycle rainwater, etc.

17 ENVIRONMENTAL LEGISLATION

ENVIRONMENTAL LEGISLATION

All businesses have been affected by increased environmental legislation in recent years. This has been particularly noticeable for owners of animal-related businesses, including kennels, stables and veterinary surgeries.

It must be stressed that the scale of the development has the greatest effect on the level of environmental legislation to be complied with, and therefore the possible cost implications. The larger the project, the more closely the legislative bodies will examine it and state the corresponding requirements.

FOUL WATER DISPOSAL

The legal requirements for the discharge of sewage are covered by building regulations and the environmental protection agencies. The safe and efficient disposal of foul and surface water is taken as a 'right' in developed countries, and should be considered of major importance to the health and welfare of staff/visitors and animals on the site.

Any poorly-constructed system will not only affect your site, but could have far-reaching consequences with pollution to water supplies/courses and contamination to other land, resulting in prosecution. In the UK for example, the standard response from the Environment Agency to any planning application for the construction of any form of animal establishment (primarily kennels, catteries and stables) where mains drainage is not available, is to install a sealed cesspool.

The UK Environment Agency produces a useful guideline PPG4 that can be downloaded from its website: www.environmentagency.gov.uk and would also be a useful tool for other countries.

A kennel owner has several choices available for the proper disposal of foul/waste water.

The main systems are:

- Sewer (public and private)
- Pumped sewage system
- Cesspool
- Septic or settlement tank
- Biological filter or treatment plant
- Filtration mound
- Reed bed

Sewer

A sewer can be either private or public.

Most sewers built on private land since 1937 are private, but not all. The local authority should be able to give advice and guidance on this, as they are required to keep detailed maps. A private sewer is the responsibility of the owners of the buildings that it serves, and all costs are shared unless there has been a legal agreement drawn up, or it is documented in the deeds of the property.

Public sewers are generally sewers constructed before 1937, and can be of any size and can run across private land, although most run under the public road system.

All public sewers are maintained by the local authority, which acts as agents for the water authority. The local authority may insist that any site or property within 30m/98ft of a public sewer has its foul water drainage system connected to that sewer.

The problems experienced by sites located in rural areas and not served by a municipal sewage system can be a major source of worry, expense and difficulty to the property owner.

It is recommended to connect into the main sewerage system. In the long term this is far cheaper, with less problems likely to occur, and is generally a far cleaner solution.

In fact, the Environment Agencies prefer and have encouraged certain trade and commercial operations to discharge into sewers rather than watercourses, the reasoning being that the municipal treatment plants are more sophisticated and far more able to monitor and balance the overall quality of the effluent.

Sewerage undertakers control all trade waste disposed of into a sewer and are normally a subsidiary of the water companies.

Any form of trade discharge has to have the consent of the sewerage undertaker, who has the right to control:

- The nature of the effluent

- The maximum daily volume allowed

- The maximum rate of flow

- The sewer into which the effluent is discharged

Experience shows that there should not be any difficulties in obtaining permission to discharge into a main sewer.

The good news is that on the whole, the amount and type of discharge produced by even the largest kennels is still relatively small and non-toxic, being primarily clean wash-down, and is of little concern to the sewage companies.

Pumped Sewage System

Ideally, all drainage systems should work by gravity, with the effluent running into the sewer. Often, particularly in rural areas, a public sewer might be available, but some distance away, or at a higher level than your site necessitating the need to pump the effluent under pressure, uphill through small bore pipes.

For most situations, the installation of a packaged pumping station is the most cost-effective. These come in a range of sizes, grades of pump and are highly suitable for most applications. The pumps are generally submersible, electrically operated, and require little maintenance.

Helpful Hints:

- Make a full investigation of suppliers of package systems; these can vary tremendously in price

- Explain fully what the pumps will have to cope with (i.e. the type/amount of solid material)

- Most package systems require a three-phase electricity supply; single-phase pumps are available but are not as robust and capable of dealing with the larger solids. The use of an electrical converter will allow the use of a three-phase pump on a single-phase electricity supply. This is a cost-effective solution for a site that does not have a three-phase supply

- Install hair/grease traps to prevent dog hairs, etc. from entering/blocking up the pumps.

- Try to site the package system close to an access point, as it will require cleaning out periodically.

- Most systems have twin pumps – this is normally referred to as 'duty and stand-by'

Sewage Treatment and Disposal - Selecting the Best Option

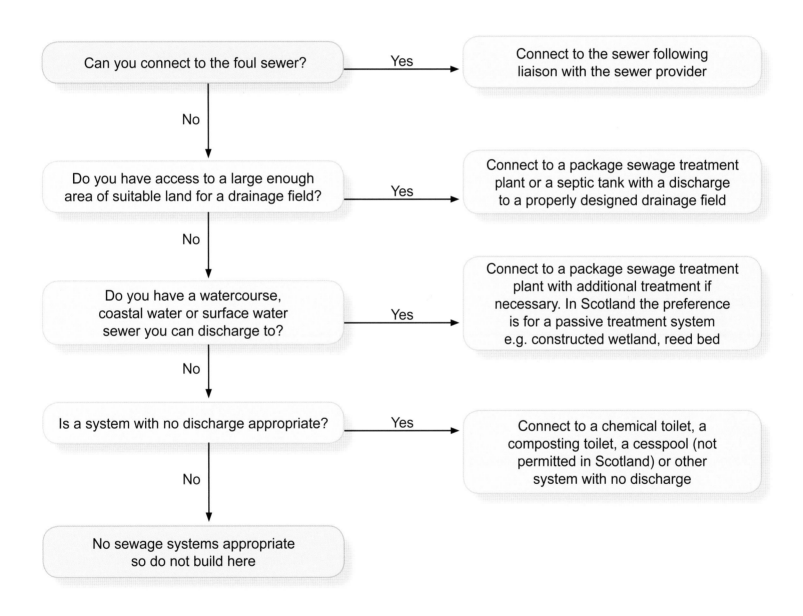

Source: UK Environment Agency PPG4

Cesspool

A cesspool is an underground, watertight storage reservoir used for both domestic and commercial purposes.

The size of the tank should be a minimum of 18,000 litres (18m³)/ 4,800 gallons for two users, and increased by 6,800 litres (6.8m³)/ 1,800 gallons for each additional user, but not more than 45,000 litres/12,000 gallons. Before installing such a tank, carefully establish the volume of liquids entering it, and the costs of pumping it out.

As already mentioned, a medium-sized centre with 30 – 40 kennels and 30 cat units, laundry, etc. will use on average approximately 4,000 litres/880 gallons per day, seven days a week. With the considerable costs to pump out and remove, this quickly becomes an expensive method of disposal.

Clearly kennels of 20 – 30 units will not use anything like this volume of water. However it is something that needs consideration. Your cleaning policy must also be taken into consideration.

Every country will have its own regulations on how far away from any dwelling, spring, well or stream used for drinking water it should be placed. (For example building regulations in the UK state that cesspools should be sited at least 15m/50ft away from a dwelling and 18m/60ft away from any spring, well or stream used for drinking water).

The use of cesspools is restricted to areas that do not have mains drainage, and where the subsoil conditions do not allow the use of septic tanks. The reasons for this are lack of permeability such as clay or dense rock, or being close to areas containing springs, wells and other drinking water supplies.

A modern cesspool is usually constructed of glass reinforced plastic (GRP), although brick, concrete and even steel systems are also used.

Cesspools need to be emptied frequently, usually every 4-6 weeks.

Helpful Hints:

- Ensure that there is good access for the tanker, within approximately 25m/82ft of the tank, account should also taken of the depth of the tank

- Ensure that no storm water enters the system, as this would quickly overload the tank and is expensive to have taken away

- Careful management needs to be maintained to ensure that excessive water is not used

Septic/Settlement Tank

If mains sewerage systems are not available, and for financial reasons it is not viable to install a cesspool, then several options remain, the cheapest and simplest being a septic tank or settlement tank. However, in some areas there is a wastewater disposal system called 'Large Capacity Cesspools.' These are similar to septic tanks, but do not provide any form of water treatment; they are simply shallow, bottomless concrete cylinders where wastewater enters and is allowed to slowly filter into the ground. However, these systems are slowly being restricted in their use, due to possible contamination fears of the surrounding land and drinking water supplies. Septic tanks differ from cesspools by having an outlet, which allows the effluent to soak away naturally by the use of surface, subsoil drainage pipes or to flow directly into a stream or river. Some of the latest building regulations and environment agencies suggest that septic tanks should be used only in conjunction with additional filtration systems, such as drainage mounds or reed beds. For obvious reasons, the use of surface irrigation is not ideal as it sterilises available land and, more importantly, can be a health hazard. The cleaner and preferred method is to lay a series of underground pipes, which are either open-jointed, porous or perforated, and which can be laid to either a herringbone or grid system. The consent of the environmental agency is required for all direct discharges from a septic tank (whether into a subsoil system, stream or river).

For a septic tank to function, particularly where a large volume of effluent is produced, it requires suitable porous subsoil such as sand, gravel or chalk. The extent of the subsoil drainage system will depend on the porosity of the land and therefore, before installing such a system, a site investigation or porosity test should be carried out. A ground engineer or reputable builder will be able to carry out this investigation work for you. Ideally this should be a person who knows the local ground conditions. One consideration to be borne in mind if installing a septic tank, is how to provide adequate soakaway for the final discharge. For larger centres or ground conditions that have poor porosity, the total length of the underground pipe system could be over 50m/165ft in length. A septic tank system should be airtight to ensure that anaerobic action takes place. Such a tank does not purify the effluent, but merely breaks down the solids by means of anaerobic bacteria, decomposing the organic matter into methane and carbon dioxide. The heavy sludge then falls to the bottom of the tank whilst the scum floats and settles on the top. A well-balanced tank will have a thick layer of scum on its surface; this will help exclude air and ensure that the system operates to its full efficiency.

One problem with using septic tanks for large-scale kennels developments is the 'loading' factor. Most kennels wash and clean in a relatively short period, but if the wash-down water is allowed to run directly into the tank it could overload it. To prevent this, a common practice is to install an in-line holding tank above the septic tank, which will allow the load to be balanced over a longer period of time. This loading factor is one reason why environment agencies are reluctant to give their consent to septic tanks for animal-related operations. This is also a problem for many older kennels and catteries. Although they can operate at present, any application to upgrade or expand the business will involve the environment agency and will often result in having to upgrade the entire system for the site. This can be expensive. Septic tanks come in a range of construction materials, and older systems used for domestic properties are often brick or concrete. Most modern tanks are glass-reinforced plastic (GRP). All systems work on the same design principle to a lesser or greater degree.

The operation of a modern GRP system is:

- Sewage enters the main chamber of the tank; this is the sludge holding and decomposition section

- From the sludge holding chamber, the effluent rises into smaller chambers where sedimentation of finer solids occurs, thus allowing large sediment to return to the lower chamber

- From this final chamber, the clarified effluent is discharged into the sub-soil drainage system, stream/river or has further treatment

- The solids will need to be removed by suction tanker. This is carried out approximately every 6 – 12 months. A small portion of the solids is left in the bottom of the tank to enable the active bacteria to multiply

Biological Filter or Treatment Plant

Biological filters are normally installed where the environmental agency requires higher discharge consent levels. Most modern biofilters are complete packaged systems, normally manufactured from GRP or polyethylene.

The systems used for animal accommodation are:

Activated sludge

These systems work on the principle of continuously moving or agitating the effluent, either by air or mechanical means. Effluent enters a primary settlement tank, where settlement of the solids takes place, from where the displaced liquid enters the main activation tank. During this aeration stage, the bacteria or activated sludge multiplies to remove most of the organic pollutants. After the agitation period, the effluent is allowed to settle for a further period, the activated sludge settles at the bottom of the tank and the clarified water is discharged into the drainage system.

Trickling filters

After the effluent has entered and settled in the primary tank, the liquid enters the main filter unit. The filtration unit makes use of irregular shaped pieces of plastic over which the effluent is allowed to trickle via a rotating system or a shaped disc with holes. Biological treatment takes place in the filter tank by the process of bacteriological oxidation, and the oxidising bacteria collect on the plastic media, and form a jelly-like substance called 'biomass'. A stage of final settlement is allowed to take place before the effluent is discharged in the watercourse or sub-soil drainage system. The method and means of air entering the system will depend on the manufacturer's specification; with some systems air is forced through the top, while with others air is blown in from the bottom of the filtration tank. See photo opposite top.

Rotating Biological Filters (RBCs)

These filters operate on a system of rotating discs housed within a packaged unit. They rely upon a colony of micro-organisms becoming established between the discs, which rotate partly submerged through the waste water. The colony is exposed to the air and to the organic material of the effluent. The design of the system to be installed must take into consideration the consent granted for the level of discharge, the volume of effluent and the number of people/animals on your site. The installation might be a combination of two systems (e.g. trickling filter and an activated sludge).
Where current systems are already in place but are not performing to the required discharge consent, then there is a need to install a secondary system.

The two main secondary/tertiary systems are:

- Filtration or drainage mound

- Reed bed

Filtration or Drainage Mound

A filtration mound is an extremely efficient way of polishing the final effluent. It is basically a large biological treatment plant and the size and extent of the pipework system will depend on the final level of treatment required to satisfy the environmental agency. The mound is normally installed below ground, with a network of perforated pipes being allowed to discharge the treated effluent, usually on a timed and batched process, through a series of layered sands and aggregates. A cut-off drain is installed and all of the polished effluent runs into this and is finally discharged into the watercourse or sub-soil drainage system. This system has given excellent results, e.g. one installation reduced the ammonia from 15 mg/L to 3 mg/L. Minimal maintenance is required and the ground above it can be used for lightweight operations (e.g. garden use). See photo opposite below.

Construction of a filtration mound. In order to improve the quality of the effluent, this filtration mound was linked to a sewage treatment plant. This photo shows the distribution pipes being laid out on layers of sand and gravel. This system has worked exceptionally well, with superb quality of final effluent. The field can still be used for dog exercising and even lightweight vehicles.

Reed Bed

The use of reed beds is becoming increasingly popular as a method of providing secondary treatment to septic tanks and treatment plants. This system has the benefit of being low maintenance, aesthetic in appearance, is economic and provides extremely high levels of purification.

Like filtration mounds, they require additional land, the size being dictated by the volume of effluent, numbers of people/animals and the consent standard granted. The system works by the reeds' ability to pass oxygen, absorbed by the leaf system, down to their roots. The polluted water passes around the roots and becomes purified by the high concentrations of micro-organisms living there.

There are two main designs of reed bed systems, horizontal flow and vertical flow.

Helpful Hints:

■ **Relevant information**
   Ensure that all the relevant information is given to the prospective suppliers, i.e. volume of water used, type and quantity of disinfectant, number of staff/animals on site. The manufacturer or consultant must take full design responsibility for this system, and this must be in writing

■ **Design**
   Check to see if the system is capable of dealing with dog faeces if applicable; some systems are not suitable

■ **Plan ahead**
   Take into account possible future expansion of the premises and an increase in the number of staff and animals. Perhaps it will be more cost-effective to look at a slightly larger plant

■ **Laundry**
   What laundry arrangements have been made? A large commercial machine will use a significant volume of water and detergents

■ **Disinfectants**
   All biofilters are highly sensitive to disinfectants, soaps, etc. and the micro-organisms can easily be destroyed by the use of too much disinfectant. The wrong type of disinfectant can also be detrimental

■ **Expansion**
   Allow for possible extensions or secondary treatment to your existing system. The legislation regarding waste is constantly changing and is generally becoming more restrictive. Plan accordingly, and allow for obtaining consent for a higher level of discharge in a few years' time

■ **Monitoring**
   Monitor the site and be flexible. If there has been a busy period with more visitors than normal, then the current sludge emptying cycle might not be sufficient, and may need to be increased

What to do if the system fails to achieve its discharge consent

The points given below show suggested actions to be taken should the filtration system fail to achieve the standard required for the appropriate consent:

- **Ensure the system is sized correctly, and is capable of handling the volume of water and waste for the size of the site, number of staff, visitors and dogs - to reach the authority discharge consent standard**

- **Contact the supplier/manufacturer for advice**

- **Ensure that the plant is regularly serviced**

- **Check to see if the circulation fans and pumps are working.**
  Most modern systems have some method to force air into the system

- **Has the plant been regularly desludged?**
  Is the frequency sufficient to ensure that the holding tank is not overflowing into the secondary chamber?

- **Has there been an overdose of chemicals?**
  Most treatment plants will take three/four weeks to re-establish themselves. This is the most common reason for poor performance of septic tanks and sewage treatment plants

- **Do you need to balance the hydraulic loading?**

- **Does the plant need the inclusion of additives**?
  This will help the micro-organisms build up to a sufficient level

- **Temperature**
  Most plants will have a reduction in efficiency during the winter particularly if a severe, and/or prolonged one. At any temperature below 10°C/50°F, the metabolism of the bacteria will decrease rapidly

- **Is the filter media becoming waterlogged or clogged?**
  If so, this will require flushing through with fresh water

- **Has the site grown?**
  Is this to the extent that the plant is not capable of reaching the original consent standard?

- **Maintenance**
  Once the system has been installed, remember that like all mechanical items need to be maintained and monitored

It is worth having samples of effluent analysed regularly by an accredited company/laboratory to establish if the system is working correctly. This also ensures that there is time to correct any problems found before they become major and the environmental agency becomes involved.

A copy of the analysis should be sent to the agency, even if the system has failed. This proactive approach will demonstrate your commitment to correcting the problem and, in the worst case, could prevent you from being prosecuted.

Groundwater Regulations

All consents for commercial discharges are the responsibility of the Environmental Agency (EA) in the UK, Scottish Environment Protection Agency (SEPA) in Scotland and the Environment Protection Agency in America (EPA). These official bodies set the standards for individual sites.

This standard is an individual one for each particular site and takes into account location, type of discharge point (i.e. stream/river or subsoil drainage) the volume of effluent, and the nature of the business, location of underground rivers, wells and aquifers.

The area of concern for any official department is the potential pollution to the receiving ground or river.

Once consent has been granted, the system will have to comply with set limits. It is normal for the Environment Agency to monitor effluent on a regular basis; this is usually 2–4 times per year. If the plant fails to reach the set standard, the problem must not be ignored; it will not resolve itself and must be corrected.

If the system has failed, then remedial action must be taken.

The UK Groundwater Regulations 1999 (UK discharge consents) help control the discharges of potentially dangerous substances; these are broken down into two categories:

- List I – Substances most toxic that must be prevented from entering groundwater. These include pesticides, sheep dip, solvents, hydrocarbons, etc

- List II – Substances less dangerous, but if disposed of in large amounts could be harmful. These include heavy metals, ammonia (which is present in sewage effluent)

Clearly the concern for most kennels, particularly the larger developments, is the use of disinfectants, and the potential effects it could have on a treatment plant and ground conditions.

Many of the modern disinfectants such as Trigene, Vircon, Virokill contain List II substances. However, as the daily amount used by most kennels is extremely small, say 0.5 litre/1 pint per day of concentrated disinfectant (of which only a small percentage is active ingredient). For practical purposes, the concentrations of List I and II substances are extremely small, and do not pose a risk either short or long-term, if used correctly.

The use of disinfectants needs to be carefully monitored and managed to ensure this doesn't become an issue for the kennel owner.

On this basis it is unlikely that an authorisation is required under the Groundwater Regulations 1999. However, a Discharge Consent is likely to be required.

Faeces Disposal

The categories fall into five groups for the varying levels of contamination, these groups are as follows:

- A

  1 – soiled surgical dressings, swabs and all other contaminated waste from treatment areas.

  2 – waste materials, where the Control of Substances Hazardous to Health Regulations (e.g. UK COSHH) assessment indicates a risk to staff handling them, for example from infectious disease cases.

  3 – all human tissue, including blood (whether infected or not), animal carcasses and tissues from veterinary centres, hospitals or laboratories and all related swabs and dressings.

- **B** - discarded syringe needles, cartridges, broken glass and other contaminated disposable sharp instruments or items.

- **C** - microbiological cultures and potentially infected waste from pathology, clinical or research departments.

- **D** - certain pharmaceutical and chemical waste.

- **E** - used disposable bedpan liners, urine containers and incontinence pads.

Disposal of animal faeces might seem a simple problem to overcome, but from experience it can be expensive, time consuming and very difficult to resolve.

Some companies classify all animal waste, including dog faeces, as clinical and put it in a Group A. However, some others put the faeces in Group E.

Group E waste is not defined as clinical where the risk assessment shows that there is no infection risk and so can go to a licensed land fill site.

The disposal options available are:

- Main sewer

- Biological treatment plant/septic tank

- Landfill

- Incineration

- Composting

- Sluice

  We will look at these in detail next.

Main Sewer

This is the preferred option, being the most convenient, hygienic and probably causing the least environmental damage. Most authorities categorise faecal matter under group E, which is suitable for disposal to sewers, particularly for small amounts. As already discussed, any discharges to the sewer require the approval of the sewerage authority; they will set the limits and conditions for the discharge.

Due to the relatively small amounts involved, these conditions are generally not too onerous.

Biological Plant or Septic Tank

The method of disposal of faecal matter into your treatment plant will depend on several factors, such as whether the plant can handle the type of organic load, and the final discharge point.

Will the Environmental Agency allow faecal matter to be disposed of in your area to a watercourse or subsoil drainage system? If so, this option is very similar to disposal via the main sewer, being convenient, hygienic and cost-effective.

Landfill

This option normally requires the services of a registered waste carrier. However before entering into an expensive contract, check with the local authority to establish the policy in force for the collection of animal waste. The collection of animal waste is still somewhat of a 'grey' area. Some local authorities would take this as normal commercial waste, while others would class it as clinical waste.

If the local authority or a registered carrier will take away the solid waste as normal commercial waste, this is the cheapest and most convenient option available to the kennel owner.

UK Tip:

The new Hazardous Waste Regulations 2005, are likely to impact upon the kennel and cattery owner at some stage, and may result in solid waste (special waste) being re-classified as hazardous waste. For areas where solid waste was previously classified as normal commercial waste, this may no longer be an option, and it may be re-classified as clinical waste and the cost and legal implications need to be considered. In July 2005 legislation came into force – The Hazardous Waste (England and Wales) Regulations 2005.

From July 16th 2004, the co-disposal of hazardous waste with non-hazardous waste at the same landfill was banned. As of 16th July 2005 the Waste Acceptance Criteria (WAC) came into force. This means that producers of hazardous waste will have to make sure that waste to landfill meets the WAC. It is therefore essential that businesses describe exactly what their waste contains, this will determine what can be done to minimise it, and ensure that it is correctly disposed of.

In essence this has meant that landfill sites that could in the past accept solid/special waste may no longer be able to accept the new Hazardous Waste. The easiest way forward is to use a specialist disposal company, clearly define the type of waste being disposed of and use the company's knowledge and expertise to avoid any legal problems.

Incineration

This is generally the most expensive option available to the kennel owner. The cost will depend on the frequency of collection, the distances involved for collection to the incinerator, and also on the availability of the specialist company.

It is not uncommon to find older kennels in rural areas that still use sawdust-shavings as bedding and using an open, smouldering fire to burn soiled waste. However, open burning is an offence (e.g. as under the UK Environment Protection Act 1990). **It is time consuming, does not create a good business impression, and is likely to upset your neighbours.**

Composting

Composting has been around for a long while, and is used extensively in Scandinavia for the disposal of domestic waste from isolated properties and communities. All animal waste will decompose naturally if left in the open air, but the process is slow. The other main obstacle to be overcome is the physical element of handling faecal matter. People often have little interest where all of our waste goes once it has left our property, so it is difficult to come to terms with the prospect of looking at alternative systems that are just not as convenient.

Decomposition of animal waste requires mixing it with some form of carbonaceous material such as straw, chipbark or newspaper to provide voids through which air can be blown. The amount of air is adjusted to provide the desired temperature for the waste. The optimum temperature is 55°C/131°F for decomposition, and the control of pathogenic bacteria; the end product is suitable for use as a fertiliser on the land.

If considering this option, then advice should be taken from the local environment agency office.

Sluice

Most solid dog waste is still taken away as dry waste. Where it is possible to flush it into the drain or treatment plant, consider a suitable sluice system.

If installing a sluice, the following should be taken into consideration:

- If the drainage system is suitable for faecal matter, some form of receptacle will be required for it to be tipped or flushed into. If there is no suitable manhole that has a hinged or liftable lid, a sluice is required; these are either ceramic or stainless steel. The basic principle is exactly the same as a domestic toilet, although most systems use larger diameter pipework

- If planning to install such a unit in or near the kitchen, it is better aesthetically and more hygienic to provide a dedicated room; this can also be used to store disinfectants, buckets, etc. In addition, a water supply/hosepipe to enable the utensils to be cleaned must be installed.

An alternative to the standard type of sluice is to install one of the proprietary macerator systems on the market. These consist of a sluice combined with an electric macerator pump; they normally operate from a 13amp socket and are plumbed into the drainage system. However, it would be worth checking with the manufacturers of the pump to ensure it is suitable and can cope with dog waste.

The easiest and cleanest method is to use a sluice system

Surface Water Disposal

The aim is to help minimise the volume of rainwater entering public and foul sewer systems. This can overload the capacity of the sewer, and lead to flooding. Depending on the locality, storm water drainage systems may be permitted when combined with the foul sewage system. This is not ideal, as it could also exacerbate the potential flooding issues with foul drainage. Certainly for a new, large development it is highly unlikely that the local authority would allow a combined system.

Modest Developments

For a modest development, the standard soak-away system (either a brick/rubble-filled or concrete ring system) will be adequate to dispose of surface water, providing the ground conditions are free-draining and will allow the water to disperse. Some ground conditions, such as clay, do not allow this natural seepage.

Larger Developments

For larger developments, it is likely that the local authority and environment agency will want to see a more substantial and engineered method to cope with large volumes of surface water. This is part of the longer-term aims to reduce flooding, by storing the water in underground tanks or large tubes, then releasing it at a controlled rate back into the ground to reduce flooding. This is known as Sustainable Urban Drainage Systems (SUDS).

The SUDS systems are roughly classified into four categories:

1. **Landscaping**
   The inclusion of ponds, construction of wetlands, permeable pavings

2. **Water Recycling**
   Surface water or 'grey-water' is collected in underground tanks and used for non-potable purposes such as washing the kennels, toilet flushing, etc

3. **Improve Soakaway Systems**
   The use of cellular plastic units has gained popularity in recent years. These units can be cut and shaped to fit any area. These units are lightweight and have void ratio of approximately 95% as compared with the traditional brick soakaway, which has a typical ratio of around 30%.
   The advantage of these units is their ease of handling compared with the concrete ring structures

4. **Attenuation**
   These are simply tanks or large diameter tubes that store water during a rainfall event, and then through a flow device release it slowly back into the ground at a controlled rate.

   It is becoming more common for local authorities to insist on attenuation in areas at risk of flooding to prevent sudden storm water surges flooding the underground sewer network.

WATER SUPPLY REGULATIONS

Some water providers are carrying out surveys to establish the type of water fittings, water supplies and cleaning regimes that kennels, catteries and stables use. Their concerns are about possible contamination of the main water supply by backflow or back-siphonage. Even with double-check valves, most supply companies will not accept these as an adequate safeguard to prevent contamination where animal buildings are involved and will require non-mechanical means to prevent any possible contamination.

UK Legislation

The UK water authorities have five fluid categories. The main elements of the five categories are:

- **Category 1:**
  Wholesome water supplied by the water undertaker and suitable for drinking

- **Category 2:**
  Water as in Category 1 except that it has a slight taste, odour, appearance or temperature
  Typical example:
  a.   Water that has been softened by salt regeneration
  b.   Category 1 and 2 water mixed via combination taps

- **Category 3:**
  Fluids presenting a slight health hazard and not suitable for drinking or other domestic purposes
  Typical example:
  a.   Clothes and dishwashing machines
  b.   Hand held garden hoses with flow-controlled spray

- **Category 4:**
  Fluids presenting a significant health hazard and not suitable for drinking or other domestic purposes
  Typical example:
  a.   Clothes or dishwashing machines other than for domestic use
  b.   Mini irrigation systems

- **Category 5:**
  Fluids presenting a significant health hazard due to the concentrations of pathogenic organisms
  Typical example:
  a.   Grey water re-cycling
  b.   Commercial dishwashing and clothes washing machines

The main distinction between category 4 and 5 is that the level of toxicity or concentrations of substances in category 4 fluids is such that a prolonged period of exposure is generally necessary, before serious harm to health occurs. To prevent any possible contamination, the water supply authorities require the kennel or cattery owner to install backflow contamination measures. Unfortunately, many businesses are unaware of this new legislation as most water providers are classifying kennels, catteries and stables as Fluid 5 Category for contamination. In essence, this means that backflow prevention measures have to be installed to the main cold water supply tank. The systems required for Category 5 fluids are either Type AA or Type AB. Generally with an 'A' gap tank there will be a requirement to install a booster pump in order to meet the minimum pressure required; this is usually a minimum 3 bar. The pump/s will need to be connected.

Inspectors normally visit premises to establish whether the site complies with current legislation. If the premises do not comply, a notice may be issued in which the modification works have to be completed within a stated time (e.g. within 28 days). If the works are not completed, there are legal and financial implications.

USA Legislation

It is interesting to see that many of the concerns regarding backflow or back-siphonage are very similar to the UK as listed previously. Therefore, before commencing any installation, it would be wise to check with the local water supply company to establish the local rules and regulations for your county or state.

Laundry

Unfortunately, for many owners, water regulations could affect the washing machines installed in your kennels.
Many domestic or older commercial washing machines only have a Category 3 fluid rating. Most local water authorities may insist that all washing machines used in a commercial operation, no matter what size or capacity, have a Category 5 Fluid Rating. This is applicable to all non-domestic businesses, and operations such as kennels and veterinary surgeries, etc.

Hosepipes and Dog Showers

Here again, similar issues and concerns about possible backflow relate to the use of hosepipes and showers in animal accommodation. This applies to any tap that can be fitted with a hosepipe.

The easiest and quickest way to overcome any potential legal issues is to install a storage tank with a suitable capacity for the day, this is then linked to a booster pump. The pump should have a minimum of 3 bar. However, for large organisations that might have several members of staff cleaning at the same time, the bar rating might have to be increased.

MAKING IT YOURS

EVERY KENNELS
IS UNIQUE AND
HAS ITS OWN
IMAGE AND
CHARACTERISTICS

MAKING IT YOURS

Now for the fun bit!

One of the biggest factors for making a business/organisation your own, is putting your own name or stamp on it. This can be dictated by a house name, location name (village, town, city, county), a theme you like, or you may decide to keep the original name if purchasing an existing business.

What you are providing in terms of services, location, construction, size, landscaping, accessories, logo and staff all present an 'image' to your clients. This will register in your personal communications on the telephone and face-to-face, in your brochures, website and any advertising and marketing.

Kennels proud of their buildings and image can easily promote this by using photographs on all kennels-related information sites. Remember, with a professional, well-designed website showing lots of clear, large photos will attract customers from further afield, especially if you are providing a building and service that is personal, professional, and one that educates and champions the use of behaviour knowledge for a dog-friendly environment.

The power of photographs cannot be underestimated - we know that clear photos of good kennels on websites mean that such kennels will make up the dog owners' minds about the kennel they wish to use and generate bookings even before visiting. We have found this on our www.boardingkennels.org website - the kennels providing photographs are also the ones who generate the most interest.

Think about what else you can do to provide the right 'feel' to your kennels and give your clients even more reason to talk about the services you are offering.

Outside

Initial impact:

- Logo, stationery and marketing materials such as brochures

- Website

- Welcoming signage and notices (opening times, logo, phone number, website)

- Landscaping – well kept and interesting

- Buildings clean and pathways swept

- Hanging baskets, well-stocked flower beds and pretty gardens to show off your kennels

- Well placed touches of humour and items with immediate impact

Incorporating images of dogs:

- Topiary

- Sculptures and statues

- Hanging basket brackets

- Wind chimes

- Weather vanes

- Murals and trompe l'oeil

Inside

- Professional record-keeping system

- Dog profiles

- Notes attached to the kennel for each dog

- Comfortable area to discuss dogs with their owners, take bookings or details

- When obtaining a business phone number, ask the operator to find you an 'easy-to-remember' number

- Once you have decided on your business name, purchase your web name. It would be wise to purchase both the country domain (.co.uk/.us/.ca/.au/.nz/.fr/.ie, etc) as well as the dot com (.com) address, as customers may not remember which one you use

- Boards or signs with helpful information or dog facts (especially for rescue centres)

Other Services You Can Offer

At some point you may be tempted to expand your business and construct more kennels. However, it would be worth stopping to think before you do so and ask yourself if you really do want to go to all that expense and effort. If you need to increase profit, you can make as much money from selling a few items to your existing clients as you can from boarding their dog for a weekend.

Many welfare organisations now sell retail items such as collars, harnesses, food and toys to increase their funding to care for more dogs.

This would be a viable alternative in terms of maximising your profit per client and providing a good quality service, rather than going to the expense of adding more kennels, taking up more land and going through the planning/zoning permission stage, or increasing noise concerns.

There is also the possibility that increasing kennel numbers may result in your losing the personal and friendly touch, or having to employ more staff.

Ideas of other services to offer:

- Collection and delivery
- Microchipping
- Grooming, nail clipping
- Pet transport and relocation
- Web cameras
- Veterinary services
- Massage
- Hydrotherapy
- Alternative therapies such as acupuncture
- Bach flower remedies
- Clicker training
- Behaviour
- Display arts and crafts from local artisans
- Retail sales on site or on the internet

Retail Sales/Store

For larger businesses, or those that have decided to opt for diversity of service rather than adding more kennels, a store could be useful to maximise profits from existing customers. This can be useful for both boarding and rescue as a way to increase sales, and can be done on a small basis (e.g. food and treats) or even to extend or grow into a larger business selling toys, bedding, bowls, beds, gifts, etc.

Ideas for products to sell:

- Food – tinned and dry food, treats

- Bedding, cushions, throws

- Collars, harnesses

- Toys

- Water fountains

- Gifts, photo frames, mugs, calendars, books, etc.

- DAP dog appeasing pheromone

Keep up-to-date with what is happening in the pet market. This is easy to do online, or at dog shows or trade fairs. This will help you find out what the latest trends are, so you can stock your shop accordingly. One of the biggest areas of change in the pet market food industry is that more people are spending money on convenience products such as single-serve pouch and gourmet pet foods and products such as age or lifestyle-targeted pet foods (e.g. indoor, mature, dog breed, dental, diet, activity levels, etc).

Another option is to use affiliate programmes to sell items from other online pet stores, and gain commission by placing links on your website to dog-related products, and gaining 2%-15% commission whenever a sale is made. This would allow you to 'sell' items on your website, without having the cost of paying for stock. This may be especially useful for you if you are just starting up and have no budget for store products as yet, but would like to provide more interest on your website.

BOOKINGS AND SOFTWARE

WORK SMARTER, NOT HARDER

As you may already know, or are certainly about to find out, the amount of paperwork that even a small business generates is quite surprising. It is in your best interests to spend as much time with the dogs in your care and their owners as possible, and the less time you spend on paperwork, the easier this is to do, and is obviously much better for you too. **It is a good idea to think about how you will handle the bookings and run your business at this early stage**. In fact, we would recommend that you download a free trial of a booking software program very early on. Not only will this help you familiarise yourself with how you want your business to run (so you can include this in your kennel design), but it can also help you 'picture' in your mind what it will be like to manage the business.

A revamped hotel computer program is not the answer. You are not just dealing with allocating 'rooms' but the need to record a great deal of information about dogs, owners and requirements

---

The sort of information you will need to record is varied. This can include everything from photographs, behavioural issues, likes and dislikes to important health, medication and veterinary requirements. Owner home/away details, emergency contacts and the dogs' usual vets will need to be documented to provide a personal and professional service.

PAPER, ROCK, SCISSORS

The advantage of a computer program over paper records or a diary are considerable. When you produce a new brochure or leaflet, change things on your website, or want to rekindle your existing customers' interest - you should be able to do it at the touch of a button, not have to trawl through umpteen record cards stapled together. Further advantages of a computerised system are the **impression this gives to your customers**, you can make your licensing officer's life easier, and you can find anything immediately as all the information is to hand. You should be able to search for any part of the customers' or dogs' details, which could be handy when someone doesn't leave their telephone number, but expects you to know exactly who Henry belongs to!

IT MUST BE EASY TO USE

Of course, your bookings and management software should be extremely easy to use and intuitive. This alone is a good reason to start trying out software early - after all, you will be using it every single day for as long as you are running your kennels. If you have some experience with computers this will probably already be obvious, but it is essential if you have not used computers in business before. **Your software should look attractive, be easy to use** and preferably provide easy-view charts or graphs to show you what you need to know quickly. It should be fully integrated with your operating system (e.g. Windows) and have a 'Help' or 'Tutorial' section to help get you started. However, with a good system, you should be given pointers on screen that are intuitive and allow you to start using it straight away.

TAILOR-MADE TO YOUR KENNELS

While you are at the stage of thinking about designing your kennels, try out a bookings program on **the sort of services that you want to set up** (e.g. boarding/rescue, grooming, microchipping, food or toy sales, medication, etc) and you can use this to help you visualise your whole service, and set up your fees and contacts.

This is where you will find out how customisable the software is - can you categorise kennels (puppy, senior, diabetic, nervous, isolated or active dogs) or give your kennels names, colours or fun themes rather than just numbers? Can you select breeds, categories, customers' purchases, colour schemes, special needs areas? Can it work out discounts for multiple dogs? You might decide to start selling a special new line of dog collars, books, or china with specific dog breeds on and want to select relevant clients to inform them. **Think about how you will use your booking system, and remember that flexibility for now and the future is important.** You will probably want to be able to use it both in the kennels reception and in your home (as most of our customers do). During the evening, availability can be checked and bookings taken/modified via your home computer in response to calls for bookings from clients.

You may want to expand the business in the future. The way to do this is to have your system fully network-able and as your business grows you can add more computers if required. Perhaps you will take on a groomer, receptionist or office/shop staff, trainee, rescue/fostering work?

WHAT TO CONSIDER

The following will provide a good idea of the kind of items you will need your booking system to be able to handle:

Bookings and Diary/Schedule:
- Capable of handling an unlimited number of customers, dogs and bookings and highlight 'no-show' customers
- Link family dogs to the same owner
- Booking confirmation letters, contracts and history
- Booking arrivals and departures
- Occupancy for the month ahead
- Handle all your contacts via an address book
- Control your workload with a diarised task schedule

Health:
- Dog details for the kennels or vet
- Vet, insurance and vaccination details including warnings for expired inoculations
- Daily reports (e.g. feed and medication schedules, exercise/welfare schedules, collection/delivery
- Dietary or medical requirements

Finance and Accounts:
- Customer invoices, outstanding debts
- Reports to assist with sales tax returns
- Forecasts by detail/summary or by period
- Payments between certain dates
- Payments by type (e.g.cash, cheque)
- Handle dual sales taxes such as VAT, HST, GST, PST

Ease of Use:
- Easy view of dog/owner details and photos to re-familiarise yourself
- Easy 'point and click' assignment of dogs to kennels and easily manage dogs that require isolation
- Easy view of categorised runs and availability
- Easily produce a 'stand-by' list - e.g. take details for bookings turned away, and this list is searched when you cancel another booking, notifying you of matches, helping you maximise your occupancy and turnover
- Easily export data to other applications

Marketing:
- Customer lists (select specific customers for mailings, special offers, Christmas cards, announcements)
- Include your logo and contact details
- Design your own letters, contracts, cards, invoices to cut down on stationery costs

PETADMIN

PetAdmin is the software management package designed to meet the requirements of any business where animals require boarding and associated services.

Our customers are worldwide (from the UK, Eire, Spain, South Africa, Australia and the USA), successfully using PetAdmin to save themselves costs, time and effort, and to enhance the image of their business to customers.

Download a trial copy of PetAdmin from our website or contact us to be sent a trial CD to try out at home:

www.petadmin.com

John Nyari
PetAdmin
Tel: +44 (0)1245 362211
www.petadmin.com

Woodhouse Technology
Woodhouse,
Woodhouse Lane, Little
Waltham, Chelmsford,
Essex, CM3 3PW, UK

YOUR WEBSITE

In the course of researching this book, we used the internet to source interesting kennel buildings, welfare improvement ideas and photos from around the world. Finding a good website of quality was rare.

So, to help us while we were working on this book and to look purely from the pet owner's point of view, we asked a pet-owning friend involved with breed rescues to try and track down interesting and noteworthy websites from existing kennels on the internet. After the first day of research, Sue came back to us quite disappointed and downhearted. Even though we had forewarned her that it would be time-consuming, she was still shocked (her words) at what she had seen.

Estimating that something like 1 in a 100 websites had anything of high quality or good ideas to show, she also confirmed that in direct contrast to this, over 90% had used the word 'luxury' to describe their kennels, no matter what the quality of building.
However, when she did come across a website of note, she was relieved and delighted – these kennels really stood out and encouraged her to spend more time there.

Discouraging findings of our tester were:

- **Small or off-putting photos** of dirty, old-fashioned buildings that seemed to be made of chicken wire and flaking paint.

- **Poor impression** – poor quality gives the impression that it must be very easy to get a licence.

- **'Cheap and tacky' looking websites**: some with only a home page, flashing gimmicky cartoons of dogs, plinky-plonk music played loudly and with no 'on-screen' way to turn it off, no detailed photographs and in many cases no photographs at all. Off-putting text such as 'pets are here at your own risk' compared with others who were more reassuring by mentioning they provided insurance

- **Inappropriate photos or images** of dogs that were obviously either frightened or bored. She found that no photos at all, or flashing cartoons only, made her feel highly suspicious of the organisation

- **Lack of welfare implies lack of interest**. No photographs or mention of toys, treats or walks offered was found. Many had bare kennels with no toys or alternative bedding (to provide a choice of places to rest)

Good ideas found by our tester were:

- **Web cams** - where you can log in and see what your dog is doing

- **Virtual tours** (clear, large or close-up photos, movies)

- Printable, online **brochure**

- **Fees** shown clearly

- Kennels where thought was given to **dog welfare** and amusement stood out a mile

A good photograph speaks a thousand words.

There are some very basic rules to creating a **good** website.

A website is the 'clicks and mortar' representation of a business – and it is available to everyone. If a poor quality kennel has nothing to shout about, then you wouldn't expect to see big photos and lots of descriptive text – but a good quality kennel should have a website that reflects this by providing plenty of photographs (preferably ones that can be enlarged for a better view) and lots of descriptive text to give a feeling for the kennels and care available.

Appeal to your audience and provide lots of photos

Your kennels and website **must** appeal to your clients, visitors or 'audience'… in this case of course – dog owners.

So, ask yourself, what do dog owners love about their dogs? This will give you an understanding of what will appeal to them. Aim for a website that is well designed, attractive, understated, interesting, full of photographs and with obvious links such as contact, tour, about your kennels, fees, terms and conditions, special needs catered for and descriptions that help visitors understand quickly what your business has to offer.

Make it easy to use

Have a simple, easy-to-navigate layout with the logo in the top left corner and the navigation links/buttons in the same place on every page (either at the side or at the top). Have anything of importance highlighted. Visitors should 'get' your site without having to think about it – people 'scan' web pages, they don't read them. Purchase the .com web name (domain name) as well as the country-based one. That way, if clients cannot remember which version you use, it won't matter as you can automatically direct one to the other. Once you've captured your visitors' imagination, they will relax and look at your website properly.

Visitors are always in a hurry and will want to be able to find out whether your business is worth further investigation quickly, so:

- **Use soft or appealing colours**

- **Make links stand out** (use larger text or buttons) so they're easy to find

- Have **navigation** links/buttons to obvious things like fees, tour, terms, contact, photos, questions

- **Include photos of your kennels**, not just pictures of your pets, and avoid cartoons and flashing images

- **Keep the layout as simple as possible** – busy pages put people off

- **Keep the pages short to medium**. Keep away from 'miles-and-miles-and-miles-of-text-all-on-a-single-page-with-no-photographs'

- **Text should be in short paragraphs and have titles** to help people 'scan' to find what they want

- Ask friends to test drive the website for you, they will come up with suggestions and ways to improve it

- **Provide an online brochure** by providing a PDF document from your existing marketing material (anyone, anywhere can read a PDF using the free Adobe Reader). You can then place this on your website, or send it by email (recording clients' email addresses is a fast way to send out updates).

    You can even convert your documents online for free by going to www.adobe.com

Aim to make your website and kennels of such high quality that everyone who visits will want to refer their friends to you.

YOU ARE ALWAYS WELCOME TO VISIT US FOR MORE INSPIRATION @ WWW.KENNELDESIGN.COM

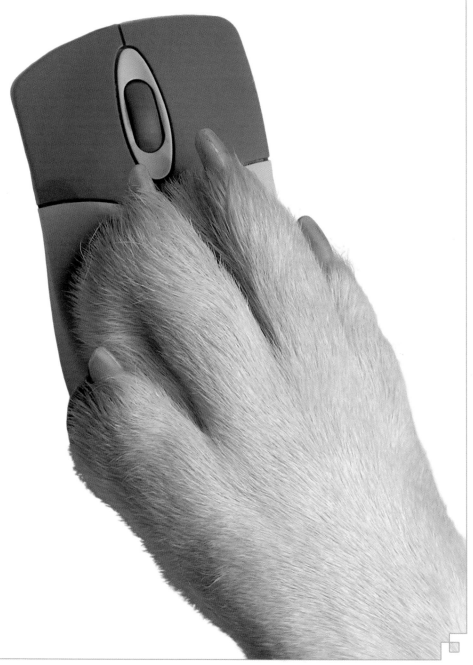